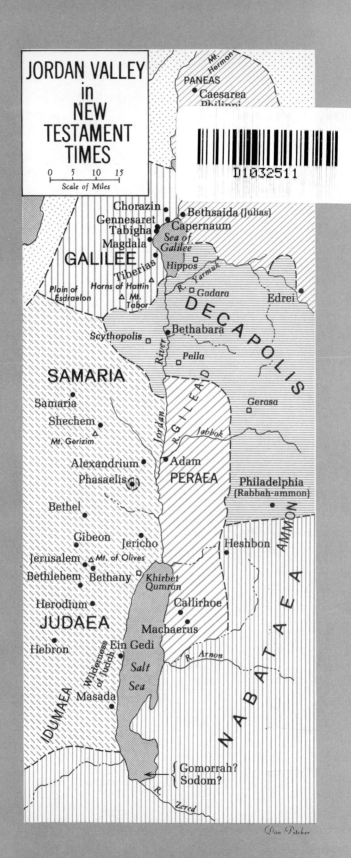

JORDAN VALLEY
in
NEW
TESTAMENT
TIMES

0 5 10 15
Scale of Miles

Mt. Hermon

PANEAS
• Caesarea
Philippi

Chorazin
• Bethsaida (Julias)
Gennesaret •
Tabigha • Capernaum
Magdala • Sea of Galilee
GALILEE
Hippos ☐
Tiberias
Horns of Hattin R. Yarmuk
Plain of Esdraelon △ Mt. Tabor ☐ Gadara Edrei •

DECAPOLIS

Scythopolis • Bethabara
Pella ☐

SAMARIA
Samaria •
Shechem • Gerasa ☐
Mt. Gerizim △ Jabbok

Alexandrium • Adam •
Phasaelis ◉ PERAEA
Philadelphia
(Rabbah-ammon)
Bethel •
AMMON
Gibeon • Jericho •
Jerusalem • △ Mt. of Olives Heshbon •
Bethlehem • Bethany ☐ Khirbet
Qumran
Herodium • Callirhoe •
JUDAEA Machaerus •
Hebron • Ein Gedi •
Wilderness Salt R. Arnon
of Judah Sea
IDUMAEA Masada •

NABATAEA

Gomorrah?
Sodom?
R. Zered

Don Pitcher

ROLL JORDAN ROLL

Books by Robert St. John

Roll Jordan Roll

The Man Who Played God

They Came from Everywhere

Israel: Life World Library

The Boss

Builder of Israel

Ben-Gurion

Foreign Correspondent

Through Malan's Africa

This Was My World

Tongue of the Prophets

Shalom Means Peace

The Silent People Speak

It's Always Tomorrow

From the Land of Silent People

ROBERT ST. JOHN

ROLL JORDAN ROLL

THE LIFE STORY OF A RIVER
AND ITS PEOPLE

1965
DOUBLEDAY & COMPANY, INC.
GARDEN CITY, NEW YORK

ROLL JORDAN ROLL

1

A river is water at its sparkling best. It is nature at its loveliest. It is beauty in motion. A river is the most human of all inanimate things, and so the life story of any river is a biography, as much as if it were an account of a man. Every river has a personality of its own. This is not true of oceans. Although a certain spot on a certain seacoast may have a unique character, the ocean in its entirety has no particular id or ego. But every river speaks with a personified voice and has a variety of nuances for different occasions. A river can laugh and sing, whisper or roar, depending on how it feels. No one can really fall in love with an ocean. Falling in love with an ocean would be as unsatisfactory as falling in love with some tremendous generality. A sea is too large for loving. Lakes endear themselves to some people, yet how many poems and songs have all the lakes in the world ever inspired? Mountains are more intimate and become more closely identified with human joys and sorrows, yet a love affair with a mountain is certain to be a one-sided experience. Rivers are more personal and more responsive. Rivers can be sullen or soothing, grave or gay, boisterous or benign, angry or happily in tune with human spirits. A river can inspire love because of its friendliness, or hate because of its destructiveness; fear of its torrents, or trust in its faithfulness; awe of its power, or scorn for its perversity.

Rivers have infinite variety. They can move as subtly as a summer fog enveloping the evening, or be as noisy and obvious as a thunderstorm. In many ages and in many places rivers have been worshiped. The ancient Chinese were accustomed to sacrifice a black horse to appease the river gods before crossing the Yangtze.

A river bank is the best place there is to profess a great love, recite a good poem, renew an old friendship, play with children, or cleanse the mind of hate and nonsense.

Most rivers have their birth in some quiet mountain fastness and after a long maturity flow to eternity in a great ocean. (". . . even the weariest river winds somewhere safe to sea.") Thus there is a happy correlation between the birth-to-death course of a river and the life cycle of man.

Rivers never sleep; always and forever they are in restless motion. That is part of their allure.

Nearly all rivers are highways that facilitate and encourage travel from here to there, from there to yonder. Most rivers bring men closer together. Mountains and oceans are barriers, dividing mankind. So too are large lakes. But rivers are joiners, linkers; they give the possibility of coordination, cooperation, consolidation.

Those are the generalities about rivers. The Jordan is a river, yet it violates most of the rules. It contradicts almost all the clichés. It defies categorization. This is a river unique, conforming to nothing, not even to the laws of conduct that it established itself, for itself, a few miles back.

The Jordan has many distinctions. It flows through the deepest crack or rift in the earth's surface; a colossal ditch created millions of years ago by a "geological spasm," as one archaeologist explains it, that also brought into existence the Valley of the Nile. There are waters elsewhere in the world that are also considered holy, but none that attracts pilgrims from such far corners of the world as the Jordan's. No other river, anywhere, has been so much spoken about by mankind. For the peoples of three great world religions, the Jordan Valley has had in times past—and today still has—profound significance. Miracles have been performed in Jordan's waters, on her banks, and in her Valley. George Adam Smith, a conservative, nineteenth century British professor, who wrote the first modern historical geography of the Holy Land, made an observation more than seventy years ago that has become a classic:

"There may be something on the surface of another planet to match the Jordan Valley; there is nothing on this."

In its flow from the Syrian mountainside to the south, the Jordan used to go through two lakes (one has recently been drained) and empty into a third. The full rich story of the Jordan cannot be told without narrating what happened not only on the river itself, but on and around the three lakes, in the Valley through which the river flows, in the hills that rise on either side of the Valley, and on the main tributaries, the feeders, the sources—the thin veins that are all a living part of the Jordan.

The Jordan flows through what has always been—and still is—a place of fierce individualism. This is one reason for such profound disagreement among writers, painters, poets, historians and scientists about the Jordan.

There are half a dozen contradictory explanations of where the river got its name, and what the word "Jordan" really means. How many sources does the Jordan have? Depending on which authority one consults, anywhere from three to thirty. Where, exactly, was this or that ancient Valley city? Even the archaeologists disagree.

In the Christian world the Jordan's chief importance is that therein Christ was baptized by John the Baptist, but where, exactly? The Latin church long ago decided on one spot. But the Greek Orthodox and Abyssinian Christians have two different locations that they are equally certain is the correct one.

For Jews the Jordan has been principally important because the ancient Israelites crossed over the river into the Promised Land. But where? Again, there is uncertainty and disagreement, just as there is over another academic question: When the river bed suddenly went dry, so that no Israelite's foot even got wet, was it because of a miracle performed by God, or an act of nature, possibly an earthquake that dammed up the river temporarily?

Is the water of the Jordan muddy or clear? Does it move quickly or slowly? What is its color? Down through the ages, men writing in many languages have disagreed. They have conflictingly called it a stream fierce and sullen in its isolation; a beautiful river of sweet water; a river fickle in its turbulence; the River of Wrath, the great Holy River, the Fateful River, the Great Divider. Men who have actually seen the river have variously described the flow as lazy, turbid, swirling, turgid, raging, impetuous, flashing. They have written of Jordan's grumbling rapids and of how the river frequently seems bored, unable to decide just where it wants to go. It has been called wandering, meandering, a capricious, noisy brook, a sluggish stream, a furious torrent, an angry river, a slimy green snake, a river leaping noisily over the rocks, a turbid little stream racing underneath a double line of weeping willows; a confused, disorderly, disturbed river. Its water has been described as clear, limpid, blue, muddy, slimy, green, turquoise, colorless.

Between Lake Tiberias and the Dead Sea the Jordan travels one hundred and fifty miles to cover a distance of sixty-five miles, as a bird would fly it. Here, the river has been likened to a twisting, writhing, green snake; to a gigantic human intestine; to a rope of green silk tossed down carelessly onto a carpet of sand; and once it was even called, in print, the crookedest river wot is. It has been said to wiggle, to squirm, to tumble, to rage, to burrow, to meander in unending sinuosities. It winds tortuously. It zigzags crazily. It squirms like a snake fighting for its life. It is impetuous, flashing, restless, wandering, angry, and grymboling. (Some writers have even felt the need to invent words to describe the Jordan.)

Few men or women have ever succeeded in remaining neutral in describing the river, or the narrow jungle that lines its banks, or Lake Tiberias (the Sea of Galilee) through which it flows, or the Dead Sea, into which it goes to its ultimate rest. Otherwise moderate and re-strained writers have either eulogized or castigated the Jordan in emotive, prejudicial and sometimes violent words: a refuge of lies; an emblem of violent and sudden change; a region of desolate, eroded hills; an unprofitable waste, a dreary and lonely wilderness, for which *eremos* is the most appropriate word. The wind blowing over the Jordan Valley has been called the breath of Jehovah's displeasure with His people. The sunlight that beats down on the river has been described as heightening every touch of ugliness and desolation. A British adventurer wrote that after seeing the river he could understand why Hebrew poets sang no praise of the Jordan.

Even the *Encyclopaedia Britannica* in its latest edition presents this example of emotive reaction to the Jordan: "On the whole it is an unpleasant, foul stream, running between poisonous banks . . ."

David Ben-Gurion, first Prime Minister of modern Israel, who left his home in Poland at the age of eighteen to settle in the land of his young dreams, once said that the greatest disappointment in his life was his first sight of the Jordan. He had imagined that it was "a really great river, something like the Vistula, not far from which I was born."

W. M. Thomson, a nineteenth century American missionary, wrote: "I had an indescribable feeling of disappointment as I eagerly looked at the line of willows which marked the tortuous course of the river. Something like this must have been in the mind of Watts when he expected it to burst on his delighted eyes at every turn. Not until I actually reached the very brink did I see water enough to fill a thimble and when I was there it was hard to believe that what I saw was the whole of the Jordan . . . As boys we used to sing with enthusiasm, 'On Jordan's stormy banks I stand' and we supposed it was as large as the Ohio, at least, and as stormy as the Northwest Passage . . . I now begin to believe there is more fancy than fact in the costume and drapery of many of our hymns!"

And yet songs, hymns, poems and much purple prose have been written about the Jordan by men and women who were favorably or even ecstatically impressed. They have described the somber and silent flow of the fluvious water, sliding and curling out of the jungle; the roaring beauty of it; the nobility of this holy river; one of mankind's most beloved streams. They have spoken of the Jordan Valley as the sacred soil of God's predilection; the Valley of Jahweh and the prophets; a place honored and hallowed by events of the noblest significance and religious memory.

These characterizations, many of them seemingly contradictory, have a certain amount of validity, every one of them. It all depends on when and where the river was observed: in what century; at what spot; in what season of the year; at its source or as it emptied into the sea; as it flowed through the swamps of Huleh years ago, or now, as it passes on its man-directed way across land that has been drained and is a swamp no more. It depends on whether it is seen at flood tide or when the heat of the burning summer sun has reduced it to a mere trickle. It is virtually impossible to tell a falsehood about the Jordan. Almost anything is true about it, or was, somewhere, somehow, at some time or in some place.

It depends not only on the mood of the river, but on the observer himself. How much subtropical heat was he able to stand? What effect did below-sea-level air pressure have on his heart, his lungs, and his objectivity? A man infused with extreme religious fervor sees the Jordan with different eyes than an atheist.

Is the Jordan Valley bleak, forlorn, and sparsely settled? A man who knows of all the significant historical events that have had this place as their setting can half-close his eyes and repopulate the Valley with a host of actors and actresses: long-bearded prophets; the giant King Og; Israelites crossing the river with their tablets of stone; original Christians witnessing a historic baptism; later-day Christians, going to their death by drowning, in their eagerness to submerge themselves in the holy water; Turkish soldiers fighting to save a tumbling empire; modern Israelis, establishing themselves once again on at least part of the river bank. To a man with imagination and memory, the Jordan is no ordinary stream, however narrow it may be, however slow the current, however shallow the water bed.

Nor is the Jordan a comfortable, placid river on which lovers can go paddling in a canoe, having romantic dreams of a peaceful life in a tranquil world. The Jordan is a violent river, heavy with thousands of years of fierce history. One generation after another, one civilization after another, has strewn the Valley with ruins. Every bump on the horizon is now suspected of being a tell. In Hebrew the word *tel* simply means "a hill," as in Tel Aviv, "Hill of Spring." But to an archaeologist a tell is a hill formed by the ruins of some ancient community, now covered with a protective blanket of sand. When archaeologists dig into a tell hereabouts they sometimes unearth the remnants of as many as twenty-one different periods of civilization piled one on top of the other: ancient history in neatly arranged layers.

No single spot in the world has been eyewitness to so much history as the Jordan Valley. The evidence is everywhere, for those willing to look. Almost anywhere a tourist goes, if he scuffs up the earth with the toe of his shoe, it is possible he will bring to light a Roman coin, a fragment of a Greek column, or a stone from a pagan temple. The ruins in the Jordan Valley tell the story of at least fifty thousand years of man, perhaps even a hundred thousand. Each dig brings to light new mysteries, and sometimes solves an old one or two.

The Jordan is unique in the world; without parallel or peer, anywhere. As it enters the Dead Sea it is almost thirteen hundred feet below sea level: as low as man can get on this planet, unless he descends in a submarine or goes down in a mine. On a small-scale map the Jordan appears to flow north to south, but it actually twists and turns so madly that there is not a single direction of the compass in which it does not flow, at least for a certain short distance. Yet there is one direction in which it never seriously turns—toward the Mediterranean, the natural outlet of most of the rivers of Southern Europe and the littoral countries of the Middle East. Historians and geographers have theorized that the past, present and future of this part of the world—perhaps the entire chronicle of mankind—would be different had the Jordan early in its course turned to the west and entered the Mediterranean.

The Jordan is unlike most rivers in that it has never served as a highway, bringing men closer together. Instead it has often been regarded as a barrier to be crossed, not a waterway to be followed. Throughout most of its history it has exerted a separatist influence, dividing a nomadic population from more advanced people. Crossing the Jordan has nearly always been regarded as a historic event worth recording. At no time has the river been regularly navigated by any form of water vehicle, except for crude ferry boats that were—and in several places still are—pulled back and forth across the river at certain points by ropes. It is only in relatively modern times that the Jordan has been spanned by many bridges, and today no one uses what bridges there are, unless both banks of the river at that point are in the same country. Although a child can wade across the Jordan at certain spots in the heat of the summer when the sun, acting as a magnet, has wheedled almost all the water out of the river, there are times of the year when even the bravest swimmer would risk his life if he tried to reach the far shore.

For Jews whose ancestors were required to wait so many years before being permitted to cross over into the Promised Land, the Jordan became the Great Divider; the divider between exile and the land on which a majority—but not all—the twelve tribes would make their home. (The German-Jewish historian Graetz called the Jordan "not only a natural but a spiritual line of demarcation.")

In Christian thinking it continued as an emblem of separation, but after the baptism of Christ it became, also, a symbol of the start of a new spiritual life. Passing over the Jordan became, in religious song and fable, a happy experience—the entrance into heaven.

The Jordan and the Styx have little in common. The river of separation in Greek and Roman mythology was a dark and dreary stream, flowing with "poisonous" water. (The Encyclopaedia Britannica writer may have been confusing the two rivers.) Dead souls had to be ferried across the Styx by Charon, the boatman. On the other side lay not heaven but the throne of Pluto, waiting there to pass judgment. Those whom he deemed worthy of reward were sent to far distant Elysian fields, whereas the doomed remained on the other side of the Styx, in the dismal valley of Tartarus. Crossing the Jordan came to mean the start of one's eternal reward, but crossing the Styx meant the grave possibility of consignment to the place of eternal damnation.

The Jordan is unique in that it has seen the flowering of most of the great civilizations of history. It has witnessed man at his ugliest, and man reaching for the stars with an eagerness born of great spiritual hunger. It has seen brutality and terror, pomp and splendor, poetry and beauty.

It has been the cockpit of unending conflicts since the start of time. Here the hatreds and the madness of man have often exploded into violence beyond modern conception—until the days of the Nazis. The history of the Jordan is a chronicle of conflict and war, of civilizations enduring only as a result of perpetual strife. For centuries men of many degrees of pigmentation, many races, many religions, and from many distant places fought each other in this Valley. Most of the great empires of the past, at one or another juncture in their history, met their rivals here and contended with them for supremacy. What tumultuous drama has been enacted on this stage! One of the most symbolic tragedies of human history—the destruction of Sodom and Gomorrah—took place on the shores of the sea into which the Jordan ultimately flows. The Valley has been likened to a hub around which revolves the slow-moving wheel of time, the axle often greased with blood.

Much of the Jordan story is a tale of murder, suicide, carnage, and other forms of violent death, as is most history that goes back so far, and as is, also, the Old Testament. Here humans by the thousands were sacrificed on pagan altars. Here kings sat day after endless day watching the slaughter they had ordered of sometimes tens of thousands of helpless enemy soldiers who had been taken prisoner. Here at one time a lady could ask her lover to have a certain man's head served up to her on a silver platter, and the wish would probably be graciously granted. Human decapitation was common. When they talked of the Jordan running with blood instead of water, it was not a figure of speech. Life was cheap, and it was normal to kill to obtain what you wanted, whether you were a king or a peasant. And so it is that red is the color in which many chapters of the Jordan's biography must be written.

But gentle people have also roamed this Valley: monks and hermits, saints and men of peace. Here the humble and modest Essenes lived in retirement from the getting and spending, the cruelty and the killing of their day, practicing their own unique brand of pacifism, austerity and frugality close by a river that so often, at that precise period in history, was witnessing death and destruction. Here Hillel the Elder, long before the birth of Christ, put the Jewish religious ethic into a minimum of words when he said: "What is harmful to thee, do not unto thy fellow man." Here a carpenter's son preached his doctrine of kindness, gentleness, and consideration of other people. From the beginning of time the Valley has been a breeding place of new ideas, a cradle of new systems of thought, a testing ground for new patterns of social organization, an incubator of new languages. In this Valley the word "vengeance" was often used, but here, also, the idea of turning the other cheek to an aggressor was at least preached, even if never widely practiced, by either nations or individuals. Here prostitution was elevated, for a time, to a fine art, but here, also, some of the early Israelites followed a way of life so austere and based on such self-discipline that they were likened to the Spartans. Here, in this meeting place of divergent cultures, ideas have often clashed as violently as armies.

This Valley has been called man's spiritual cradle. Long ages ago the object of all religious adoration here was the moon, symbol of beauty and nocturnal mystery. Then Helios, the sun. (It is only lately that scientists have discovered that the sun has greater power, if it could only be tapped, than all the nuclear bombs now stockpiled by twentieth century giants, yet evidence dug up in the Jordan Valley indicates that ancient man knew instinctively about this power, and therefore worshiped it.) Serpents were once venerated here, and also the golden calf. There was one long age during which human sacrifices were eagerly made, because this was thought to be the desire of the gods. (One pagan sect believed that the gods especially liked tender young children.) And then an era in which animals were slaughtered on the holy altar in order to win the favor of the gods—or of God. In the Valley pagans engaged in exotic revels and orgiastic fertility rites, described by some historians as "lascivious," yet designed to teach the deities exactly how creation and multiplication could be accomplished, if the deities would only watch and listen. Temples were built here to Pan and his nymphs, and to Baal the All-Powerful. Statues were carved of emperors, who were revered almost as gods. Then, thanks to the Jews, monotheism was born here. Then Christianity. Here converts were sought for the Muslim idea of individual resignation to the divine disposal. Here much of the sacred literature of the Jews was written and many of the events of the Christian gospels took place. In more recent years, in this same Valley, dialectical materialism has become, at least for a few people, almost a new religion.

Despite heat and desert (an excess of both) and altitude (a lack of it) and all the other handicaps that nature has imposed on this area, it was once one of the most cosmopolitan places on the surface of the earth. Here, in what has become during recent centuries a wasteland, great and important cities flourished in the Greco-Roman period, and even before. Here there were towns that were centers of culture and learning. The ground is still strewn with traces of the Valley's former grandeur: the arm of a Roman gentleman carved twice life size, a marble leaf from the capital of a Corinthian column, cold stone evidence that here noble architecture once stood and splendid civilizations flowered. Here it is not uncommon to stumble onto a native hut constructed entirely from the masonry of antiquity. Here one often has a feeling of time going backward. In ancient days there were great temples here, and amphitheaters built to last not years but millennia and to seat as many as six thousand people, and luxurious baths for ladies and gentlemen of leisure, of whom there were many, for at that time the populace labored diligently to create joys and delights for the few.

Here were royal palaces in which kings lived as well if not better than anywhere else, and great monasteries in which pious scholars contemplated the eternal verities, and impregnable Crusader forts in which armored knights, fresh from battle, regaled each other with stories of inexcusable slaughter committed in the name of what they believed was a glorious cause.

Here the poetry and art of the noble Greeks were seen in their burgeoning, and the legal and administrative genius of the Romans was brilliantly demonstrated. Here at least some of the basic aspects of nineteenth and twentieth century democracy were not only evolved but put to the test in actual practice. Here one culture after another came to flower.

Archaeologists believe that at least a million and a half people once lived in the Jordan Valley—an area that in more recent times has stood almost empty, a desolate waste, inhabited for hundreds of years by only a thin sprinkling of nomad tribesmen. A million and a half people! It is certain that they were not scattered across the landscape in tents. No one doubts the evidence that many of them lived in urban centers that were showpieces of that epoch's most advanced culture. Some of these rich cities have vanished so completely that not a trace of them has yet been found. Their names appear in no geography books and are marked on no maps, not even as "ancient site," because their exact locations are in doubt. But their names are known and something of what happened to give them fame such a long time ago. As the archaeologists dig and theorize, they have become convinced that some of these olden cities in the Valley and in its contiguous hills were in existence thousands of years before Abraham came this way. There are reasons to believe that on the shores of Lake Tiberias alone there were once nine important cities. Then there were the five Cities of the Plain, and the many Cities of the Hills, and the Decapolis, a league of ten model cities (later increased to eighteen), some of them not far distant from the Jordan, each one considered a noble example of Greco-Roman material, intellectual and artistic progress.

Then there was Shittim, on one of the tributaries of the Jordan, where the Israelites, before crossing over into the Promised Land, had an almost catastrophic lapse into whoredom and idolatry.

And Caesarea Philippi, far to the north, on one of the Jordan's sources, where shrines were built by successive generations to Baal, to

Pan, to one of the Caesars, and finally to Muslin al-Khidr, the Islamic counterpart of St. George of dragon fame.

And Gadara, the only city in the world whose renown rests on how two thousand pigs one day happened to be drowned.

And Heshon, mentioned thirty-eight times in the Old Testament, because, in rather rapid succession and generally at a great cost in blood, it passed hands: from the Moabites, to the Amorites, to the Israelites, to the Tribe Reuben, to the Tribe Gad, to the Levites, back to the Moabites, and then to the Israelites again.

And Succoth, the Pittsburgh of ancient Jordan River days, center of an industrial area where metal objects were made for use in the Jerusalem Temple.

And Hazor, the city which commanded the Jordan crossing and was burned to the ground on Joshua's orders because it stood in the way of the dream's realization.

And Beth-Shan, an Early Bronze Age city at the junction of the Jordan and Jezreel valleys, where Saul's beheaded body was impaled on the city wall, to be feasted upon, so they thought, by vultures.

And Adam, or Adamah, marking the spot to which the Jordan's waters backed up, to enable the Israelites to make their dry crossing.

And Gilgal, which became the Israelites' base of operations after they had crossed the river.

And Gerasa, or Jerash, one of the cities of the Decapolis, its streets lined with great stone columns, theaters, shops, pagan temples, baths, and other evidence that the raising of corn, the city's chief source of revenue, was not without profit.

And then the six Cities of Refuge, three on each side of the Jordan, thus designated in an attempt to prevent family blood feuds, for if a man protested that he had committed a murder unintentionally, without wilfulness, or "unawares," he could demand asylum in any one of these Cities of Refuge.

And Ein Gedi, where David once hid in a cave from the wrath of Saul, and Solomon found inspiration for a love poem.

And Masada, where, after the Second Temple had been destroyed and Jerusalem resacked, a few hundred men and their families held out on a great plateau for several years against a Roman army of more than ten thousand, and when they could resist no longer, killed themselves to the last man—two women and five children lived to tell the story—in one of history's most heroic mass suicides.

And Jericho, which the archaeologists think may be the oldest city in the world, already an ancient place when Abraham first came this way.

And Sodom, Gomorrah and the many other cities of the Dead Sea area, of which not a trace remains, not even the broken handle of a ceramic jar, or a rusted coin.

And Chorazin, condemned to a greater punishment than was being reserved for Tyre and Sidon.

And Bethsaida, which in Roman times became so large a city that it was honored by having its name changed to Julias, after the daughter of Augustus Caesar.

These are but a few of the towns and cities that lined the river, encircled Lake Tiberias and the Dead Sea, or stood on the hills or in the wadis leading down to the Jordan. Some, today, are being repopulated. Some still lie in stark but magnificent ruin.

At Gerasa, now part of the Kingdom of Jordan, the total, permanent, 1965 population of the city, once such a glorious and thriving place, consisted of the man selling old Roman coins to tourists, and the cook, waiter, and dishwasher in a tourist restaurant.

At Masada during a few months of each recent year there have been almost as many men and women digging into the ancient ruins as ever lived on that forbidding mountain top, except, perhaps, when Herod the Great was in residence at his Masada palace.

Most of the Jordan's ancient cities are still buried under sand, a scrub growth of vegetation, and forgottenness. Yet the Jordan remembers.

In few other places in the world have so many different races played major and minor roles in such a long, continuous drama. Across or through the Jordan, up and down and over the Valley, often mixing their blood with the sanctified water, came Chaldeans, who stormed into the Valley as invaders and left as conquerors; Nabataeans, who developed in the desert not far from the Jordan a system of irrigation now, almost two thousand years later, being revived and copied; Druses, practicing mystic religious rites that still defy complete explanation; Phoenicians, who came to the Valley from Sidon and Tyre; Greeks, who brought to the Valley the ideal of a free and cultivated life, respect for learning, and appreciation of beauty; Romans, who left the deepest stamp of all foreign people; Bedouin tribesmen, who for a thousand years or more pitched their black goatskin tents among the ruins of past empires, and pastured their flocks where pagan gods and goddesses once held court; Circassians, a strong, stolid, and stubborn race from the Caucasus, who were used by the Turks to dispossess the Bedouins; Samaritans, remembered for more than nineteen hundred years because of a single kind act of "a certain Samaritan"; Hittites, Hivites and Horites, not to be confused; Canaanites, who believed they were all descendants of the eleven sons of Canaan, grandson of Noah; Philistines, who lost Palestine, but bequeathed a name to the place; Abyssinians, who found sanctuary from religious persecution in or near the Valley; Egyptians, who built temples and erected statues here, in the brief days of their dominance; Crusaders, who constructed massive forts on heights overlooking the Jordan in an effort to conquer and hold the Land of the Book; Maronites from the North, who took over a village in which, so folklore said, Queen Esther lay buried; Arameans, ancestors of modern Syrians; Mongols, who came as invaders and remained for a time as farmers; Nusairiyehs, once described as "the most ignorant and debased race in the world, their religion more infamous than their external morals"; Scythians, White Russians and Turkomans from the East; restless nomads, crossing back and forth over the river, often to avoid punishment for crimes they had committed on the other side of the Jordan; Byzantines, who converted many of Jordan's synagogues and pagan temples into gold-encrusted Christian churches; Amorites and Moabites, whose warriors often passed over the Jordan, sometimes in frenzied flight, sometimes in hot pursuit.

Then, also, there were Mameluke sultans and Pharaohs from the South, Persians and Ayyubids, Ghassandes and Amalekites, Arabs and Israelites, Nestorian Christians, Kurds, Melchites, and black men from the Sudan.

Each of these peoples in a different way left its imprint on the land of the Jordan.

Many rivers have been the victims of old wives' tales and romantic nonsense. Generations of modern voyagers have experienced deep disappointment over the discovery that the water of the Danube is not as blue as Johann Strauss the Younger had led them to believe. Neither the Mississippi nor the Volga, the Ganges nor the Tiber is anything like the myth of it. But the Jordan and its Valley, and the Dead Sea into which it flows, have been especially misrepresented.

In the Middle Ages, when travel was difficult and fraught with some danger, especially in places like the Middle East, a few reckless men explored or dropped in on the Jordan and then made reports to their bishops, their publishers or their public, which are interesting today particularly because of the vast amount of misinformation they contain. Perhaps the heat had affected their minds, or they may have known that risk of being contradicted and exposed was slight, that it might be another hundred years before anyone else would follow in their footsteps. Whatever the cause or the excuse, they launched at least a hundred lusty myths that have not easily been put to death. But the propagation of misinformation about the Jordan did not begin with them.

Roman historians were especially guilty of circulating lurid and untrue stories. Many fabrications about the Jordan also found their way into the Talmud, that collection of oral laws and philosophical comment on Jewish manners, customs, belief and teachings, which is almost as important to religious Jews as the Torah itself. One of the learned Talmudic authorities launched the fantasy that the water of the Jordan is milky white, and so its course can be followed on its way through Lake Tiberias, and again as it flows into the Dead Sea. The most amazing piece of misinformation about the Jordan in the Talmud is that this milky water, after leaving the Dead Sea, flows somehow into the Mediterranean.

Again in the early years of the twelfth century, an authentic, first-hand, on-the-spot report from an impeccable source, a clergyman named Saewulf of Worcester, England, once more described the Jordan water as such a thick milky-white color that it could be traced for a long distance as it flowed *through* (sic!) the Dead Sea.

In 1232 a German Dominican from Strasbourg (or Magdeburg) named Borcard (or Burchard) went to the Holy Land and spent ten years there, during which time he wrote extensively if not accurately. He reported that the Jordan Valley was a place of utter desolation, without a saving touch of green anywhere: ". . . it bears neither grass nor any herb throughout its entire length."

Similar stupidities found their way into a book written a century later by a Venetian, Marino Sanuto, bearing the provocative title: *Secrets for True Crusaders to Help Them Recover the Holy Land*. What prospective Crusaders were told about the Jordan and its Valley made romantic reading, but contained far too little factual information to warrant the use of the word "secrets."

The myth that the Jordan water flows through Lake Tiberias without mingling in any way with the water of the lake itself was seriously reported to the Royal Asiatic Society of London by an erudite speaker in the early 1800s.

The explorers, adventurers, scientists and pseudoscientists of the nineteenth century who wrote about the Jordan Valley—with or without ever having been there—spread the myth that the Valley could not now be populated, and never had been populated, because of (a) intolerable heat, (b) diseases, some of them so rare that there still were no names for them, and, of course, no idea about causes or cures, (c) wild beasts, and (d) savage men. The Valley, they theorized, has always been an arid, barren desert, a place of desolation, unpopulated and unpopulatable. Since then archaeologists have uncovered close to a hundred important ancient sites (as well as some of lesser importance), many dating back thousands of years, and have found more and more evidence to confirm their estimate that the Jordan Valley population at one time reached a million and a half.

It was not until 1905 that a contributor to an American periodical, *The Biblical World,* attempted to shatter some of the myths by writing: "Until recently people viewed this great rift in the earth's surface as a place of ill omen. They have seen threatening and danger where none existed and have transformed a fair corner of God's earth into a brooding terror." Since then many people have seen, photographed, lectured on, and written about the Jordan, and have reported truthfully.

But a myth dies a slow and lingering death.

Almost every important river in the world has inspired at least one song: "Where the River Shannon Flows," "The Watch on the Rhine," "Song of the Volga Boatmen," "Flow Gently, Sweet Afton," "Missouri Waltz," "On the Banks of the Wabash Far Away," "The Blue Danube," "Swanee River," "Beautiful Ohio," "Ol' Man River." But no river has inspired the number of songs the Jordan has. More significant, the Jordan has found its way into dozens, perhaps hundreds, of spirituals and folk songs, generally as a symbol of death and resurrection; an end of this life of toil and tribulation, and a happy entrance into heaven. This was a favorite theme with overworked slaves whose solace in their dark hours was the thought of a rest and a reward—in the beyond—because they knew they would never get it in the present. American Negroes identified themselves with the "Hebrew chillun" and adopted certain biblical characters, notably David and Moses, as their own special heroes. And the Jordan became their favorite river, a symbol of deliverance and freedom. On the other side of that river the work-weary Negroes expected to be issued, forthwith, white robes, golden crowns, harps, and tickets entitling them to eternal leisure, free food, and the right to sing and be happy forevermore. No wonder that the Jordan was, for them, a river to dream about! The ecstasy inspired by the mere thought of crossing over the Jordan was best expressed in "Swing Low, Sweet Chariot":

> I looked over Jordan and what did I see,
> Coming for to carry me home?
> A band of angels coming after me,
> Coming for to carry me home.

"One More River" is essentially a ballad about Noah and his ark, yet the chorus is entirely concerned with the Jordan.

"Roll, Jordan, Roll," was the first spiritual to appear in sheet music. It was published in Philadelphia in 1862, arranged and adapted by C. Everest, whose heirs thirty years later copyrighted the words and tune. The chorus:

> Roll, Jordan, roll; Roll, Jordan, roll.
> I want to go to heaven when I die
> To hear Jordan roll.

2

The story of the Jordan River begins on the slopes of Mount Hermon, a snow-capped eminence of much more importance to the Middle East than its 9232-foot altitude and twenty-mile length would indicate, for it is the great giver of water, revered by mankind since early ages, worshiped in pagan times, respected always; a solitary and impressive mountain that dominates the landscape and is visible as far as the Dead Sea, 120 miles away; a mountain that also at times has dominated the thinking of those dwelling under its shadow.

The Arabs call it *Djebel el Thelj*, the Mountain of Snow, or *Djebel esh-Sheikh*, the Mountain of the Sheikh, because to them its snow-capped summit resembles a venerable, white-haired old man. It is mentioned often in the Old Testament as Baal-Hermon. It was a sacred mountain for the pagans, connected with the ancient tradition of worship on the high places. The Canaanites believed that it was the seat of the Most High; that there dwelt the lord of the sun and the clouds. In Roman times the mountain itself was regarded as a god, and many temples were built on its slopes. Those who were both religious of mind and strong of body made frequent pilgrimages through the snow to the summit to offer sacrifices. The ancient Israelites sometimes called it Mount Sion (meaning "the highest" and not to be confused with Zion), and one of the psalmists became ecstatic over the dew of the Hermon. The Amorites called it Senir; the Assyrians, Saniron; the Phoenicians, Sirion, and they all revered it, impressed, even as modern men still are, by its grandeur and sense of eternity, its coolness and its fertility. In the New Testament it is thought by some to have been "the high mountain apart" and it was, perhaps, the inspiration for one apostle's vision of "the great white throne." Present-day Syrians call it the Great Hermon.

It stands astride the Lebanese-Syrian frontier, with its three peaks in Syria and some of its foothills in Lebanon, but the people of many countries consider it *their* mountain. When the air is not full of particles of fine sand, obscuring vision, the summit of the Hermon may be seen by Israelis in such far-off places as Tiberias, Haifa and Jaffa; by King Hussein's subjects in the northern towns of Transjordan, and by Syrians in distant Damascus. They all look up at the snowy crown, some in awe, some in fear, but most with great thanksgiving for the moisture the Hermon sends down to irrigate their fields. In more superstitious times men living at the base of the mountain practiced a rite known as the *Yerid*. With great ceremony once a year they would fill numerous vessels with water from wells, or from the distant sea, and carry them, with singing and jubilation, to the summit, where they would pour the water through an immense stone funnel into the very heart of the Hermon. This, they believed, gave delight to the mountain and inspired it to accelerate the flow of its underground streams, so that the fields below would be well watered during the ensuing year. (The remains of one of these stone funnels, nearly twenty feet high, may still be seen on the summit of Mount Hermon's second tallest peak, *Qsar Antar*.)

An old Jewish legend tells how, when God delivered the tablets of the law to Moses on Mount Sinai, all the other mountains of the Holy Land appeared before Him in a body and complained that He had been guilty of favoritism. Why Sinai? God was especially impressed when a small hill called Hermon burst into tears. To console it He decreed that henceforth it would be the tallest mountain in the land, that it would wear a crown of snow, and that it would become the envy of all the other mountains. The tears Hermon had shed, says the legend, became one of the sources of the Jordan. (Mount Hermon was once in the northernmost part of the land of the Israelites and therefore *was* the tallest peak in the land, as the fable relates.)

It is odd that a holy river should have its birth in a pagan cave, and yet—

The slopes of the Hermon are covered with dense groves of stately oaks, broad-boughed sycamores, and trembling poplars. A solemn stillness reigns here, broken only by the singing of birds. Even the light that filters through the trees seems quiet and gentle. There is a deep, haunting sense of aloneness, of remoteness from the world of men. The tranquility is profound. It is no wonder that nature worship was practiced on these slopes. Pagans said prayers to their gods under these trees, believing them to be inhabited by nymphs and dryads, as well as by major deities, and so they buried their patriarchs at the base of the trees, secure in the belief that their gods and their deceased holy men would be able to wander happily together through the forest when no mortals were looking.

In this verdant place, almost at the base of Hermon, in what is now Syria, more than a thousand feet above sea level, one suddenly comes into an extensive clearing strewn with boulders, the ground between blanketed with moss and grass, and the whole scene made brilliant by the colors of oleander blossoms. There are small streams everywhere, gurgling, frolicking, racing with each other; sometimes joining, sometimes suddenly separating and going their individual ways, only to come together again, a little later, as if they were lovers playing a game, with everyone well aware that eventually they will become permanently joined. The silence is broken now by the melodiously monotonous music that water makes as it rushes over rocks, or falls and splashes.

Tracing the small streams upward, one comes to a limestone cliff almost a hundred feet high, streaked red and brown, the discoloration caused by iron seeping through the rock in solution. In the face of the cliff there is a deep cavern and the remains of an ancient temple carved out of the soft rock.

This spot of such great natural beauty has a tangled web of historical and religious associations, having been, in turn, of sacred significance to the Baalite, the Israelite, the Greek, the Roman, the Christian, and the Muslim.

Baal, god of the sun and master of fertility, and Ashtoreth, goddess of love (and, inconsistently, also of war) were once worshiped here by the Canaanites in sensuous rites characterized either by a joyous naturalness or by repulsive lasciviousness, depending upon the point of view. (One anti-pagan writer has called this "the high place of Canaanite abomination.")

Those niches in the face of the cliff were, of course, once filled with the statues of idols. They are empty now, but under the largest of them —a deep recess with an arched and beautifully fluted roof—these Greek words are still plainly legible:

PANI TE KAI NUMPHAS

What a perfect spot for Pan, son of Mercury, the Greek god of the meadows and the forests, protector of shepherds, hunters and fishermen! With little tax on the imagination, one can see the strange creature with curly hair, short horns, crinkled beard and feet of a goat frolicking happily on these slopes with his friends the nymphs, while playing on a musical instrument of his own invention, the syrinx, or pipes of Pan, fabricated out of all that was left of a metamorphosed victim of one of his amourettes. The half-goat Greek god could not have wished for a better habitation than this place of rugged cliffs, deep grottoes, serene groves and gushing fountains.

After the Greeks came the Romans, who built here a white marble temple at the order of Herod the Great to the memory of Augustus. Perhaps it was an earthquake that sent the temple tumbling into ruins, or it may have been intentionally destroyed by those who came later, but anyone who now wishes to see even a single stone of the memorial to Augustus must search in the heap of miscellaneous stones and rocks at the base of the cliff—the religious debris of many epochs— or study the stones that have been used to build some of the relatively modern habitations in nearby villages, for this spot has been used as a quarry by sixty or seventy generations of men to whom a stone is a stone is a stone.

To the left of Pan's temple and higher up there is a Muhammadan shrine to Sheikh Khudr (St. George), which the Islamites claim stands directly over the substructure of the temple to Augustus.

The water that helps to create the Jordan may once have burst from one of the caverns in the face of this cliff, but now it seems to percolate through the ruins, gushing forth in many places and creating innumerable rills that join together to become rivulets. Then the rivulets combine to create a rushing torrent that cascades to the south, finally becoming a six-mile-long river, the Banias.

The Banias is a misnomer. The Greeks called the town they built near here Paneas, in honor of the lusty Pan, but the sound of "p" does not exist in the Arabic language and is so difficult for an Arab to master that in present-day Egyptian schools teachers of English put a lighted candle a foot or so in front of a pupil and make him practice propelling the letter "p" from his lips until he can, in so doing, blow out the candle. And so Paneas became Banias, and the easternmost source of the Jordan became the Nahr (River) Banias.

While the Banias is the most dramatic source of the Jordan, the longest is the Nahr Hasbani, which somehow completely escaped the notice of ancient geographers and writers.

Some twenty miles to the north of Banias is an area known as the Land of the Underground Streams because of the considerable number of springs which the earth suddenly seems no longer able to contain, so they burst through the surface and almost at once become part of a full-born river, much as Aphrodite suddenly was born from the foam of the sea. Six such springs scattered over an area of five or six square miles in the southernmost part of Lebanon, near a village called Hasbaya, one of the main centers of the Druses, are called the source of the Hasbani, or Hisbani. The principal spring is not far from a main highway, yet it is seldom visited by anyone anymore, because it is close to the frontiers of both Syria and Israel and therefore in a military zone, which is out of bounds for tourists unless they have a special military pass. Here, as the water comes to the surface from dozens of small geysers, crystal clear and far too cold to swim in, it forms a pond that is encircled by the luxuriant green of trees, bushes, flowers and ferns. In happier days, when frontiers were not ringed with soldiers, and Lebanese sportsmen passed by here on their way to hunt and fish in what is now the northerly part of Israel, many would stop at this place for refreshment. There is still a rusted metal sign nailed to a tree at the edge of the pond advertising an effervescent soft drink called *Bubble Up*.

Those two words tell perfectly the story of how the Jordan originates. It bubbles up from the earth in many lovely places.

The third of the principal sources is in the northeast corner of Israel, five hundred feet above sea level, not far from where Lebanon, Syria and Israel all meet, and at the western end of an artificial hill, thirty or forty feet above the plain, called Tel Dan, or Tell el Qady in Arabic, which is believed to contain the remains of the biblical city of Dan, referred to nine times in the Bible in defining the boundaries of ancient Israel as being "from Dan even to Beersheba" or "from Beersheba even to Dan." (One reason the archaeologists connect the two is that the Hebrew word *dan* means "judging," while the Arabic *qady* means "God the judge.")

When the Phoenicians held this place it was called Laish or Leshem. Then it was conquered by the Tribe of Dan. Later a temple was built here to house one of King Jeroboam's golden calves. In the Greek epoch the name of the goddess Daphne became associated with this place, so Dan became Daphne.

Laish, called Dan, called Daphne was then destroyed by enemies from the north and its old names were temporarily forgotten.

This source is similar to those in Syria and Lebanon in that the water is both abundant and pure as it bubbles up from seven never-failing springs and forms a crystal pond at least a hundred yards across. As it comes from the earth the water has a constant temperature of 44.6 degrees Fahrenheit. Even after it has stood a long time in the pond under the glare of a summer sun it still seems ice cold to the touch.

This is a place of almost equatorial beauty, of wild glory. Modern Israelis who live here call it "Our Garden of Eden." Blue dragonflies and butterflies of exotic colors wing their way back and forth over the pond. Against the background-sound of running water, birds sing songs that sound happy and gay. The oleanders here are not only the usual reds, pinks and yellows but seem to have shadings and tints peculiar to this place alone. As the water gushes from the seven springs, it is under such great pressure that it causes the entire pond to effervesce, as if it were filled with champagne instead of water. The pond's edge is lined with wild mint, watercress and several plants indigenous only to this particular area.

As the water leaves the pond it tumbles over a slight precipice, the first real waterfall of the many between here and the Dead Sea. Then it goes racing off, like an eager, enthusiastic young man in search of adventure. This river, the Nahr Dan or el-Liddan, is the shortest of the Jordan's sources, yet it contributes the greatest annual amount of water, 258 million cubic meters, compared with 157 million by the Hasbani and 157 million by the Banias. (These figures were officially established by the Main Report in 1953.)

Some authorities list one other source of the Jordan as the Nahr Bareighit, the most westerly of the four. It has its rise in the meadowland at the foot of the Lebanese town of Merj 'Ayon, also called Marjayoun and known in the Bible simply as Ayon. But by June there is no trace to be found of it.

There are other minor sources. Exactly how many depends on when the count is made: in midsummer when even the Jordan itself has become small and puny, hardly a river at all, or when the winter rains come pelting down, or later when the snow on the Hermon melts and all the dried up wadis become alive and water flows in many directions, much of it finding its way into the Jordan through various tributaries. On Mount Hermon there is a lake which would seem to have no connection whatsoever with the Jordan, yet sometimes in the spring when it gets overly full and spills over, some of the water is said to reach, eventually, the Jordan. This, then, could also be called a source.

But none of these northern sources is faithful, reliable and regular in feeding the Jordan. Two-thirds of the water they contribute to the Jordan is delivered in the rainy one-third of the year. In the case of the Hasbani, the ratio between summer and winter flow is 1.4. In the case of the Banias, one quarter of the annual flow is delivered in several days—sometimes within a few hours.

The total annual flow of all the Jordan's water sources has been estimated at 1880 million cubic meters. Of this amount 1308 mcm comes from tributaries, wadis and floods farther south, with the Yarmuk River alone contributing 475 mcm of that amount, almost as much as all the headwaters combined. (These figures were correct until various diversionary developments were undertaken. Today the Jordan receives much less than 1880 mcm.)

In medieval times the exact geography of this part of the world was only vaguely known, and public information was subject to the whim and the fantasy of both writers and mapmakers. So it is that on a crude map made in the year 1300 and still preserved, only two sources of the Jordan are given, one called the Dan, which is shown commencing not far from Damascus, and the other the Jor. The Jor is a river of mystery, for there is no reference to it in either the Old or New Testament, and the word has no meaning in either Hebrew or Arabic. The ancient map shows the Jor following the general direction of the Hasbani. If the Jordan actually were formed by two such tributaries, the Jor and the Dan, the origin of its name would be beyond question. But the story seems to be a fabrication.

The word Jordan is a transcription into Greek of the Hebrew name of the river, *Ha' Yarden.* Some Hebrew scholars contend that Ha' Yarden means "the Descender," referring to the steep gradation of the river, while others argue that it designates "the river to which people went down." Still another theory is that Yarden comes from the two Hebrew words *yar,* river, and Dan, so that it means the River Dan. An argument against this theory is that the name Jordan or Ha' Yarden was applied to the river as far back as the time of Abraham, five full centuries before men of the Tribe of Dan came from the south, settled here, and changed the name of the town from Laish to Dan. The Arabs call the river *Esh-Sheria,* meaning "the watering place." Often the words *El Kebir* are added, making it "the great watering place."

Arguments about the Jordan's derivation continue, but an old legend has settled how the Hebrew word for judging, *dan,* and the Arabic word for judge, *qady,* came to be applied to the river's principal birthplace.

In ancient times there were three rivers flowing in various directions through the land of the Israelites, and a violent quarrel broke out among them as to which was the largest and most important. Unable to settle the question, they asked God to arbitrate. The Lord descended to earth and sat on a small hill near the three rivers, while He listened to their arguments. Finally He pronounced judgment in these words: "Rivers, ye are all three dear to me, so hearken unto my command. Unite, and then, together, ye will, indeed, be the greatest river." So they did, and thus the Jordan was formed, and the hill on which God had sat as He heard the case and pronounced judgment was henceforth called Tell Dan, the Hill of the Judging.

Just a few miles southwest of where the ancient city of Dan is believed to have stood, the cool, clear water of the Dan and the equally cool, clear water of the Banias flow together and then continue on, briefly, as a river without a name. After tumbling and cavorting together for about a mile, they suddenly meet the Hasbani, flowing down from the northwest. Here a marriage and a birth take place simultaneously: the marriage of the three principal sources, and the birth of the Jordan.

The natal place is Upper Galilee, in what is today the State of Israel, a country that at this point is a mere eight miles in width. It is less than three miles to Syria on the east, only about five miles to Lebanon on the west, and about four miles to Lebanon on the north. The elevation here is 220 feet above sea level. At birth the Jordan is sixty to eighty feet wide, depending on the season, and four to fifteen feet deep, depending upon whether it is a period of flood or drought. The infant river, its water clear and unpolluted, goes on its laughing way at first in a south-southwesterly direction, flowing effortlessly, rapidly, because in these few miles it descends 213 feet. Until modern man took a hand in modifying nature, it plunged recklessly into the tangled brakes and muddy marshes of Huleh, one of the Jordan's three lakes. But now there is no Lake Huleh. During the 1950s the river was channeled, the marshes were reclaimed, and all that is left to recall what this place was once like is a nature reserve: a small sample of the old Huleh. The reclaimed land is the most fertile in all of modern Israel.

Before it was drained, Lake Huleh was one of the most unhealthy spots in the entire Middle East. Modern man knew that the chief plagues were malaria and black water fever, but in earlier days the fact that Arab children died during a certain period of each year almost as fast as they were born was blamed on a belief that Allah was angry with the child, or it had had a sunstroke, or it had drunk some Huleh water, thought to be poisonous.

There was never agreement about how long Lake Huleh was—three miles? four miles? five miles?—because no two authorities were of a like mind as to just where it began and ended, or what was lake and what was just marsh. There was also disagreement for centuries over whether this was the Merom of the Bible, by the waters of which the decisive battle took place between Joshua and the Canaanite Confederacy. (Most authorities now say no.) It apparently *is* the body of water called Semochonitis by the Roman historian Josephus, who, with his customary flair for exaggeration, fixed its length at eight miles, about double the truth. (Undoubtedly the lake and its marshes did vary greatly from age to age.)

Lake Huleh could not have been pleasing to a self-respecting river like the Jordan, for the marshes impeded the happy flow, and there was much stagnant water here. An infant river was in danger of suffocation in this tangle of cane, reeds and bushes. In some places Lake Huleh seemed a solid mass of floating vegetation. It was therefore a delight for birds. The Jordan Valley has always been—and still is—on the direct route of birds migrating between Europe and Africa. Here they are assured, on their long flight, of a stretch of fresh water, with heavily wooded banks to provide food and shelter. And so the Jordan Valley was—and still is—one long, continuous aviary, and twice a year is alive and vibrant with the music the birds create, as if in thanksgiving. In the old days when the birds reached Lake Huleh they seemed to grow ecstatic and their songs became a mighty cacophony that caused the air to tremble. More than 450 species of birds were counted here. Once an estimated ten thousand storks were seen at one time feeding, while an equal number circled gracefully overhead. There were also partridges, crested grebes, herons, wild ducks, woodcock, rooks that lived in the canebrakes just to the north, and the strikingly noble white pelican. There were crows and rooks here "by the millions," so one traveler reported, making Huleh one of the most populous rookeries in the world. From here they would fly off on long pilgrimages, returning at night and reporting to each other on their adventures, cawing and screaming in what seemed to humans a state of near hysteria.

In one of his psalms of lament, David, telling of his troubles, calls himself a "pelican of the wilderness," the comparison being to the austere, somber bird that even in his time populated the Jordan Valley, and especially the Huleh region.

Before Lake Huleh was drained and before a semipermanent state of war in the Middle East made it impossible for anyone to cross national frontiers legally, hunters, not only from all over Palestine but also from Syria, Lebanon, Transjordan—even from Europe—came to Huleh, to the marsh, the plain and the surrounding mountains to hunt panther, leopards, wild boars, wolves, jackals, hyenas, the fleet gazelle, and even bears. Also to fish.

On hot days—and most days are hot in this area—water buffalo from nearby villages would lie almost entirely submerged in marshy pools, demonstrating their intellectual superiority over their cousins the cows, who would stand only knee-deep in the water, thus permitting the broiling sun to beat down on their backs.

Many of the Arabs who lived hereabouts before the drainage built their houses on poles, to escape the scorpions.

In the days of Huleh the Jordan's water was responsible for nourishing a peculiar variety of lily that grew here, although it was sometimes also found along the Valley and in the hills. It actually was probably a species of iris, but with inner petals of velvet softness that formed a canopy or bower. It was considered by some biblical students to be the flower Solomon had in mind when he sang: "I am the rose of Sharon, and the lily of the valleys," and the flower Christ meant when He said: "Consider the lilies of the field, how they grow; they toil not, neither do they spin: and yet I say unto you, that even Solomon in all his glory was not arrayed like one of these." The Huleh lily generally grew in a clump of thorns, as if to defy man to pick it.

Huleh was most celebrated for having given the world its finest writing paper. Here, before the drainage, there was the greatest solid mass of papyrus anywhere—many square miles of it. Some of the parchment the ancient Egyptians used was made from papyrus obtained here. The stalks grew to a height of sometimes twenty feet and were triangular instead of round, two or three inches thick at the base, tapering upward and ending in a tuft of large, bell-shaped flowers. The papyrus stalk is so graceful that ancient Egyptian artists often used it as a motif. The pith is utilized in the making of paper. The common name among the people of Huleh for the plant was *babeer,* and they used it in the construction of their homes, and for making mats. The Arabic is *berdi* and the Hebrew *gome,* which somehow became translated into "bulrushes" in the Bible, in the story of the hiding and finding of the infant Moses. (Oddly, the only other place in the Bible the word bulrushes is mentioned is in describing a certain ship said to have been built of "bulrushes.")

From a distance it appears that the Huleh plain is bounded on the north, the west, and the east by rather high mountains, and on the south by low volcanic hills, and that our young river is thus completely trapped. But the Jordan somehow managed to cut itself a deep channel through the obstruction to the south and now wanders off in that direction, peacefully at first, through quiet meadowlands, until it reaches the *Jisr Benat Ya'kob,* the Bridge of the Daughters of Jacob. Just beyond the bridge, near the remains of a Crusader fort, the Jordan suddenly seems to lose control of itself and goes plunging down in one of the most precipitous adventures any river anywhere ever had. During the next few miles it rages and roars, a turbulent, mad creature. The altitude at Huleh was seven feet above sea level. The altitude of the Lake of Tiberias is . . . No two authorities agree. The British Government, in the days when it was administering all of Palestine under a mandate from the League of Nations, officially fixed the level at 708 feet below sea level. But the Jewish Agency, which later became the Provisional Government of Israel, fixed it at 689 feet. Other figures go as low as 680. It is not a matter of politics, but depends on the time and the method of measurement. In Mandate days a measurement taken in December 1934 was twelve feet lower than a previous measurement made in March 1929. But the drop from where Lake Huleh used to be to where Lake Tiberias still is, at an average season of the year, is about seven hundred feet, and the Jordan makes the plunge in about ten miles—a drop of almost seventy feet per mile—which justifies the observation that at this point the Jordan is neither a river nor a valley, but a very steep, very narrow staircase; an almost continuous, ten-mile waterfall. Down, down, down it goes, in a series of sparkling cascades, giving the impression that it is having a delightful time. As it approaches Lake Tiberias it is almost a thousand feet lower than it was at its birth, such a short distance back, near the frontiers of Syria and Lebanon. In this wild drop it has gathered unto itself a conglomeration of mud, rocks, pebbles, twigs and all sorts of other debris, thus giving the water a far different coloration and character than it had at the start.

Few peoples and few places have as many names as this lake in which the waters of the Jordan now pause, after their wild adventure. It is mentioned only three times in the Old Testament, twice as the Sea of Chinnereth, and once as the Sea of Chinneroth. In the New Testament it is most often called the Sea of Galilee, although this is a misnomer, for the standard definition of a sea is a large body of water, either salty or brackish. The Sea of Galilee is not large, and its water is only slightly salty, and is not at all brackish. St. Luke refers to it as Lake Gennesaret, after a plain by that name on the northwest shore, while St. John calls it the Sea of Galilee and Lake Tiberias, both in the same sentence. The Roman historian Josephus wrote of it as Genezareth, while the Greek geographer Strabo called it Gadara, after a city southeast of the lake. The Talmud dropped the Old Testament name and called it Lake Tiberias, which is the meaning of the Arabic name, *Bachar Tabaria.* The Government of the State of Israel, in which the lake now wholly lies, officially calls it *Yam Kinneret,* yam being Hebrew for "sea." Chinneroth, Chinnereth and Kinneret are all derived from the Hebrew word *kinnor* which in biblical days meant harp, although in modern Hebrew it has come to mean violin. There are two versions why this lake was named after a harp. The more poetic is that the pleasant sound of its waves lapping the shore resembles the clear rich music of a harp. More prosaically, the lake is the shape of a harp, although others think it is pearlike. The Hebrew word for Tiberias is Teveriya, derived (some say) from *tov reiya,* meaning "beautiful view." Many spots in many parts of the world boast of a "beautiful view," but here, no matter where one stands, no matter in what direction one looks, there is beauty of a very special sort. Across the lake are the Mountains of Golan, impressive because of their ever-changing colors, serving as a majestic background to the lake.

On the northern horizon, noble Mount Hermon. When it gets so hot that the air seems to burn the lungs with each breath, it is some comfort to look up to the Hermon's crown of white and be reassured that somewhere—close enough to be seen with the naked eye—it is cool enough for snow to remain on the ground without melting. Closer, but in the same general direction, the Mount of the Beatitudes. And to the west, the Mountains of Galilee, and the peak called the Horns of Hittin, where one of the most vital battles of human history was fought.

During the day, when a light breeze ruffles the lake, the surface becomes almost too dazzling to contemplate: millions of diamonds, each one reflecting, from each one of its innumerable facets, the brilliance of the sunlight. But it is when the sun drops behind the mountains that Lake Tiberias becomes a place of such beauty that a man trembles in its contemplation. Sunset and twilight last only a short time in this part of the world. Perhaps as compensation nature creates an especially strong concentrate of beauty at that time. The Mountains of Golan turn breath-taking shades of pinks, yellow-browns, then violets and finally deep purple. At the same time the lake reflects the colors of the sky as well as the shadings of the mountains. Normally a brilliant turquoise, the water of Tiberias becomes dappled with colors not its own at all. If the twilight silence is unbroken by any of the harsh noises of civilization, as is often the case, the spectator finds himself, sometimes unwittingly, overwhelmed with semiphilosophical thoughts of what was, and what is, and what still could possibly be.

Josephus, describing the Tiberias region, wrote: "One may well call this place the ambition of nature." A later traveler in Galilee wrote: "Whether approached at sunrise, when the sun appears suddenly from behind the hills on the eastern shore, lighting the small fishing craft casting far out into the deep, or at solemn sunset, when the blue-green waters are ruffled with color and life as they play about the tumbled, stone quays of long-abandoned towns, its shores and waters preserve the atmosphere of peace and storm, success and doom." The nineteenth century explorer-observer George Adam Smith called Lake Tiberias "at once food, drink and air, a rest to the eye, coolness in the heat . . . an escape from the crowd, and a facility of travel very welcome in so exhausting a climate."

The lake is thirteen miles long. This is certain, even though Josephus, with his flair for exaggeration, says sixteen. The width can be anything anyone wants to call it, from three miles up to eight, depending upon what part of the harp—or pear—is measured. The circumference is thirty-two and a third miles. Some archaeologists claim the lake was much shorter and narrower in the time of Christ, for some ancient sites are now covered by water. In calm weather a good swimmer can cross the lake from the town of Tiberias to the opposite shore, a distance of eight miles, in a little under three hours. (The record is two hours, twenty-one minutes, thirty-nine seconds.) In biblical times the lake was known for its fish, and it is again, now: forty varieties of which at least fourteen are peculiar to this particular body of water. One species, the *chromis,* has a peculiar habit. After the young have been hatched, the male takes over the task of nursemaid and carries the infant fish—thousands of them!—in his mouth. The tails of the young, hanging out of his mouth, make him appear to have a wiggly beard, so children call him "the fish with the whiskers." Until he deems the young able to go off on their own, the male parent is unable to eat normally. In order to subsist at all, he must, therefore,

engage in occasional infanticide. Another Tiberias fish, the barbut or
clarias macracanthus, has the habit of emitting a noise that is something between a howl and a scream.

Although the Jordan is muddy looking as it enters the north end of
Tiberias, its water is thoroughly sweet, but in the lake, almost immediately, it makes its first contact with water that is not only slightly
saline, but contains a considerable percentage of chlorides and alka-
lines. This is because the lake is fed not only by the Jordan but also
by springs that are so heavy with minerals that they make the lake
water seventeen times as saline as the incoming Jordan water (340
milligrams of chlorine per liter, as against 20 mg).

On the edge of the lake there are hot springs that spurt forth water
with a temperature of 143 degrees Fahrenheit—almost hot enough to
cook an egg. The smell of this water is sulfurous, and the taste is nauseous, but for more than twenty centuries the lame, the halt, the withered,
and even the leprous have been coming here to soak themselves in this
unpleasant liquid on the theory that its chemicals have phenomenal
curative powers. These hot springs are evidence that there are smolder-
ing fires not far below the crust of the earth. More acute evidence is
the frequency of earthquakes. There has been a disastrous earthquake in this general area in almost every century, causing the death
of many thousands of persons and destroying the finest monuments
that man has ever erected here.

Once, so the archaeologists and historians say, half a million people
lived on the fringes of the lake. It was a favorite area of the Romans
and figured prominently in early Christian history. The cities and towns
around the lake—and there were many—boasted great amphitheaters,
impressive palaces, marble baths. The ports bustled with commercial
activity. Once there was a Jewish navy and a Roman navy of sorts out
on the lake. This we know, for a serious naval battle between Jews and
Romans was fought here. At a later period it became a spiritual and
intellectual center for the Jews who fled north after the destruction of
Jerusalem, and many magnificent synagogues were built here. Agriculture flourished. The lake was fringed with plantations, vineyards and
groves of stately trees. Josephus said: "All kinds of trees grow here,
both walnuts from the cold countries, and palms which like heat. Beside them sprout fig and olive trees which require a temperate climate.
Nature has concentrated her every effort here to gather together her
most contrasting fruits, as in a courteous dispute between the various
seasons of the year, each claims the region as her own." Fishermen

made a good living from the lake, and life was pleasant here, for many people.

Yet in the Middle Ages history suddenly turned its back on the entire Tiberias region and for centuries the Jordan flowed through a scene of desertion and desolation. It was only in modern times, when the return of the Jews began, that there was any place of human habitation on the edge of the lake—with one exception—that could even be called a town. That exception was the city of Tiberias, which remained down through the ages a community of some importance to Arabs, Crusaders, Turks, and Jews. It was several times destroyed and rebuilt.

The lake has a maximum depth of 130 feet and normally serves as a catch basin for four billion cubic meters of water, more or less, depending upon the season of the year in which the measurement is made.

Authorities—and visitors who are not authorities—disagree about storms on the Lake of Tiberias. Some say the Bible, as well as medieval painters, libeled the lake by giving the false impression that it is subject to violent tempests, whereas the truth, they say, is that although sudden and unexpected squalls frequently occur, they are generally localized, and storms dangerous to anything but the smallest of fishing boats are rare. Yet other writers have described with powerful verbs and terrifying adjectives storms they have witnessed that lasted as long as thirty hours without surcease, destroying sea walls, and filling the Tiberias fishermen with fright. One explanation of the storms peculiar to this region is that they result from an old law of high school physics: nature abhors a vacuum. All day long the hot sun beats down, but as soon as the heat slackens a little at sunset, a vacuum occurs all along the Jordan Valley and especially over Lake Tiberias. When the cooler air from the mountains rushes in to fill this void, it whips the lake into a fury, making tall palms and other trees sway like dancing dervishes.

It is, of course, only a myth that the clear sweet water of the Jordan can be distinguished with the naked eye from the other water of the lake as it flows through Tiberias. It could not even be distinguished with microscope or test tube, for it quickly becomes one of the ingredients in a cocktail.

It is pleasant to think that as the Jordan moves slowly from north to south on its inevitable journey, it is a little reluctant to leave this place of serenity, where nature appears to be so at peace with itself.

At the southern end of the lake the hills seem to open up to make way for the river's passage. This, technically, is the start of the Valley of the Jordan.

The river we are following is as full of contradictions as it will be of gyrations from now on. In many respects it is ancient. Notice, as it leaves the lake and starts flowing at first a little westerly and then south, how deep a bed it has cut for itself. It took thousands, tens of thousands of years to wash away so much earth and wear away so much stone. Yet at the same time the Jordan is young in spirit, as we shall soon see—seldom content to follow a charted course, forever wanting to go on adventures, to rush off in some new direction. At times its tempestuous misbehavior makes it resemble an incorrigible juvenile delinquent. But there are limits beyond which the Jordan cannot go, for it is a prisoner of a phenomenon of nature, The Rift, a deep geological fault. This great valley is called the Ghor, an Arabic word meaning simply "depression." Like so much else about the story of this river, the Ghor is unique in the world. Nowhere else is there anything quite like it. At the bottom of the Ghor there is a wilderness or jungle called the Zor, Arabic for "thicket." During most of the year the Jordan flows circumspectly through the middle of the Zor, month by month cutting an ever-deeper channel for itself—behaving itself, as it remains at home in its self-made declivity within a declivity. But when the rains come, and the snow on Hermon begins to melt a little, and nature goes wild with the frenzy of spring, the Jordan rises quickly until it overflows its banks and floods the entire Zor. Then it rises still higher, as if aspiring to reach the level of the lake or sea that some people believe once filled much of the Ghor. It is then that it becomes completely undisciplined, racing first this way, then that, carving new channels for itself and behaving with fierce impetuosity. The sides of the Ghor are often precipitous, and the cliffs, being of marl—little more than clay—undergo constant erosion. When they collapse the Jordan is often blocked and the river must seek a new channel. Until they do collapse, the eroding cliffs are grotesque in shape. Only a diseased mind could even imagine such distortions. They give a visitor from more conventional surroundings the eerie feeling that he is on another planet where nothing is familiar—that this is what the landscape of the moon must be like.

The Zor is called in the Bible *Ge'on hay-Yarden* ("Where the Jordan Flows Over") or "the Pride of the Jordan" or "the Jungle of the Jordan." It may not seem a jungle by African standards, yet in places it does conform to the dictionary definition of "a tangled mass of vegetation" and "an almost impenetrable thicket." It is the haunt of wild animals and the dwelling place of poisonous reptiles. Once the animal that is called the king of the jungle made his home beside the Jordan, for the Bible contains 154 references to lion, lioness, lions, or lion's. Jeremiah and Zechariah both spoke of lions in the Valley. In the twelfth century, Phocas the Pilgrim wrote of a "vast mass of reeds" in the Jordan Valley, in which "herds of lions are wont to dwell." The Crusaders took home stories of lions encountered in these regions, and in the fourteenth century a German explorer, Ludolph von Suchem, saw lions on the Jordan's banks. The alleged death of Joseph, son of Jacob, was blamed on a "wild beast" of some sort, when his brothers brought home to their father Joseph's bloodstained coat, although exactly what sort of wild beast, the brothers did not specify. It was common in biblical times to threaten to feed an enemy to "the wild beasts." The Jordan Valley provided the best possible lair for these animals, whatever they were. Although bears are often mentioned by biblical writers, they must have frequented the mountains bordering the Jordan rather than the hot jungle. But tigers were often seen along the river's edge, as well as leopards or panthers. Wolves sometimes came down to the Jordan from the mountains, and the hyena was so common it even gave its name to *Gei Zeboim,* the Valley of the Hyenas. Well known to the Jordan were also jackals, wild boar, otters, badgers, lynx, wildcats, polecats, gazelles, hares, many species of rats, nocturnal jumping rodents called jerboas, and a peculiar variety of bat called the wrinkled-lipped bat. There were also buffaloes and hippopotamuses, either of which may have been the animals the Bible calls "behemoths."

The Jordan jungle is paradise for one bird in particular, the gray shrike. This provident creature has a unique food conservation practice: if it catches a beetle or other insect when it is not particularly hungry, it impales its victim on a sharp spike, where it remains available for future use. The thorn bushes lining the Jordan are perfect for this purpose.

Blue and green kingfishers add exotic color to the Jordan scene, while the *bulbul* or Palestinian nightingale contributes the most distinctive sound: a faint twittering. Fifteen varieties of snakes, twelve different lizards and two tortoises live in the Valley. The viper—one variety wears a beard—is the most poisonous, while the cobra has always been the most feared by Arabs. They call it "the flying snake" and insist that it jumps sideways through the air when it makes an attack. There is one snake peculiar to the Valley that is stone-blind; a lizard that has been known to attain a length of four feet; another lizard that is detested by members of the Islamic faith because they think it bobs its head up and down in mockery of the way Muslims move their bodies during their worship of Allah; still another lizard with a set of suction caps for feet that can move upside down with amazing rapidity across a ceiling; a chameleon that not only changes color to harmonize with its surroundings, but also has the ability to turn its eyes independently of each other in whatever direction it pleases, and can catch a fly at a distance of six inches by suddenly sticking out its tongue and covering the victim with a sticky liquid that renders it as helpless to fly away as if it were entrapped on a piece of flypaper; an earthworm-like animal that retreats into its hole in the ground when attacked, backwards, head last, obviously preferring to see it happen, if it is about to be pounced upon and killed; and a newt or salamander that can replace a lost leg, tail, or even an eye in an incredibly short time.

There is evidence that crocodiles once infested the Jordan. In modern times, friends of a French pilgrim, an eminent physician from Paris, reported that he was swallowed alive by a crocodile as he tried to immerse himself in the water of the Jordan at the spot that had been pointed out to him as the place where Christ had been baptized. But no one has reported having a friend swallowed by a crocodile since then.

The Valley is—or has been in relatively recent times—plagued by mosquitoes, borers, scales, ticks, and fruit flies.

At many places the Jordan is overhung by willows with long, pendulous branches, feathery tamarisks, brilliantly flowered oleanders, and evergreen oaks. They bend low over the water, as if with affection. The oleander, some believe, is the tree referred to in the Bible as "the tree planted by the streams of water . . . whose leaf shall not wither." Here, also, are gnarled olive trees, the gum-producing mimosa, and the wild indigo.

One of the oddest shrubs in the Valley is the zuksum, sometimes called the Jericho plum, bearing fruit that resembles an undersized date and is said by the Koran to be the food on which infidels are required to subsist in the place of eternal punishment. There are wild olives in the Valley, the oil of which the Arabs consider extremely efficacious in the treatment of serious wounds. There are twenty words in the Bible for thorns, and most of the twenty are or once were to be found in the Valley. In spring when they are tender they are used for fodder, in the winter for fuel, and always for fences.

There is a brassicaceous herb called the thlaspi, sometimes mistakenly referred to as the Rose of Jericho, which for ages was sold by monks as an aid in childbirth, because the fibers expand to a phenomenal degree immediately upon coming in contact with any liquid.

In the spring the Zor, the Ghor, and even the brown desertlike hills in the distance explode into color. The many-hued wild flowers give the ground the look of a richly woven Persian carpet, and fill the air with a heady perfume.

Since early times the Jungle of the Jordan has provided a hiding place for men in flight, for whatever the reason. Only a few roads or even footpaths lead down into the Zor and across the Valley. Bridges are a rarity. There is no road along either bank, paralleling the river, although at one point there are roads several miles back from the river running parallel with it. (They are in the area now held by the Hashemite Kingdom of Jordan.) If a man wanted to lose himself in the Jungle of the Jordan he could do so easily, even today, and it would take a small army to find him.

Neither the Ghor nor the Zor has ever attracted farmers. Those who supported themselves exclusively by agriculture in the Valley have always done so at the point where rivulets and springs flow into the Jordan.

In this strange part of the world, where nothing seems quite normal by the usual standards, even the seasons of the year collide with each other. Down in the deep trough it will still be hot enough for suffering, when the Hermon's white crown begins to get its first winter freshening-up. In summer the heat in the Valley is what a Frenchman would call *épouvantable;* what an Englishman would call appalling; what an American might say was terrific. The high banks that line the river so much of the way keep out any air at all—or so it seems. The sun beats down hour after hour, all day long, unmercifully. There are no clouds to screen out any of the pitiless glare. Stepping out of the slight shade offered by a tree into the direct rays of the sun is like moving directly into the path of heat waves coming from a blast furnace. This was one matter about which the historian Josephus did not exaggerate. In one of his books he wrote of the Jordan's heat as "unbearable"; in another as "insalubrious." The heat beats on your eardrums; it makes you suddenly very dizzy; it dulls your senses. It parches both man and nature. It dehydrates anything containing any hydration. It heats the rocks until touching them is like touching the black iron top of an old-fashioned kitchen stove. The waves of heat that fill the Valley make the weirdly shaped white hills of the Ghor seem to wiggle and writhe. Temperatures in the 120s—in the shade, of course—are not uncommon in the Jordan Valley. At Tirat Y Tsevi a temperature of 130 degrees was once recorded.

In the heat of the day there is silence, broken only by the sound of the Jordan's rushing water and the constant zinging of millions of locusts. Otherwise nature is remarkably still. There is something almost eloquent about the silence. And yet if you listen with enough imagination—or if the heat has gone sufficiently to your head—you can hear the noise of Roman chariots, the shouting of soldiers, the tumult of ancient battles, the loud prayers of frenzied pilgrims, the thunder of history.

Many who have come this way have felt the loneliness of the Valley. They have complained that here there is none of the lyrical loveliness of other river banks. This is correct. The Jordan demands from those who would understand and appreciate her something quite different from what other rivers demand. In certain subtle ways there is something frightening about the Jordan. Here, deep in the Ghor, wandering through the jungle on a simmeringly hot summer day, we begin to come into contact with the spirit of this river. The farther we follow it, the more awesome it will become. Already it seems to be defying man to look, to contemplate, to face the realities. This is not a river beside which pleasant love poems have ever been written. Yet it is a river to make men think. It is certainly a river of challenge.

When the sun sets and at last one begins to feel that maybe the door of the blast furnace has been at least partially closed, a pink-pale violet haze begins to settle over the hills; then over the Ghor; then the Zor. Now the feeling of mystery and imponderability becomes accentuated. A cool wind rushes in from above, bringing with it particles of dust from the desert. The sky commences its kaleidoscopic performance, changing first from Madonna-blue to pastel shades, and then to deep, strong purples, and finally to a gray darkness that is no color at all. When the stars appear they quickly take on a brilliance that seems peculiar to this place alone. It all happens very quickly. Twilight is brief. Darkness follows swiftly, softly, silently, mystically. The silence is now overpowering. The feeling of remoteness, of otherworldliness is almost more than a normal person can bear. It grips the mind. It seems to clutch at the soul.

Day comes as quickly as night—with little hesitation. There is the first streak of light and then, suddenly, it is morning.

From Lake Tiberias to the Dead Sea is only 65 miles, on a straight line, but it is almost 150 miles the way the Jordan does it. What the Jordan does in those 150 miles is to meander. The word comes from the French *méandre,* based on a Greek word *maiandros,* which in turn derives from Maender, the name of a river in Phrygia, that ancient land in Asia Minor between the Black Sea and the Mediterranean celebrated as the native place of Midas, the king with the golden touch, and his son Gordius, who became famous by tying a knot no one else could undo. The Maender twists and turns in many convolutions. So also does a river in the Province of Alberta, Canada, the Meander River. But the Jordan outdoes them both in its meandering.

In recent times geographers who specialize in the study of the formation and behavior of rivers have decided to call their science fluviomorphology, and they call themselves fluviomorphologists, a word so new that it is still not in most dictionaries. Some fluviomorphologists have written books dealing exclusively with meandering, and one book has been written about the meandering characteristics of this particular river, the Jordan, as it travels the 150 miles between Lake Tiberias and the Dead Sea.

From the name of the ancient Phrygian river, the fluviomorphologists have created a long list of nouns, adjectives and verbs. They speak of the "meandering habit" of the Jordan, of "single meanders," "stretched meanders," "compound meanders," "box-shaped meanders," "meander limbs," "meander patterns," "meander amplitude," "free meandering," "Omega meanders," the "meander belt," "ambiguous meandering," the "meander ratio," the "meander trough."

With the understatement of true scientists, one of them says that the Jordan displays a meandering habit "which in some respects departs greatly from that accepted as normal." One of the Jordan's unconventionalities is that it begins its meandering almost the moment it leaves the lake, traveling first northwest, then due west, then southwest, before finally deciding to go in the direction it is supposed to be taking: south. All this happens within the first mile. Even rivers that have the habit of meandering are not supposed to do this. As one fluviomorphologist put it, the Jordan "appears to contradict the empirical rule of Hjulström that rivers at their exit from a lake do not meander and may resume meandering only one to three kilometers downstream." But the Jordan, as any fluviomorphologist soon finds out when he begins to study it, is no ordinary river and it conforms to no rules, not even to the rules about eccentricities like meandering.

The more detailed the map or chart, the more wild the meandering of the Jordan seems to be. Again and again the river turns back on itself and for a time flows due north instead of due south, in defiance not only of the rules of fluviomorphology, but even, it would seem to a layman, in violation of the law of gravity.

One of the dictionary definitions of meander is "to wander aimlessly, listlessly." The Jordan vigorously contradicts this definition by the manner in which it does its meandering. There is nothing either aimless or listless about its sinuosity. Its chief purpose seems to be to rebel with all its strength against its inevitable fate; to try to avoid in every way possible going to its doom in the Dead Sea. It makes the struggle in anything but a listless manner. Whether it is traveling east, west, north or south, it moves with tremendous determination.

The difference in altitude between Lake Tiberias and the Dead Sea is 590 feet; the distance 65 miles. The drop, therefore, is more than nine feet in every mile. A river descending this rapidly has no business meandering, according to all the rules about rivers. The pull of gravity, the speed of the flow, ought to keep it on a fairly straight course. But not the Jordan. The fact that it wiggles and squirms for 150 miles in order to go 65 proves that it is more often than not going in a direction quite different from that of its ultimate destination. For every mile that it goes south, it goes considerably more than another mile in some other direction, either east, west, or even north. By so doing it manages to slow down its own speed and to outwit, to a certain extent, the power of its ultimate master, gravity. While the drop would be slightly over nine feet per mile if the Jordan went in a straight line, it decreases to about four feet per mile because of the meandering. Yet the descent is still rapid enough to create innumerable whirlpools, rapids, and small cascades. One of the few men who ever tried to explore the Jordan by canoe reported "there are no less than twenty-seven rapids which entirely stopped navigation and many others that rendered it very difficult." A later adventurer wrote that he had counted more than a hundred rapids, of which he considered twenty-nine "serious or dangerous."

The width and depth of the river, and the extent of the Valley, are none of them ever constant. They all seem subject to some great whim. Between lake and sea the Valley varies from two to fourteen miles in width. As the river leaves Lake Tiberias it measures a hundred feet from water's edge to water's edge.

The river is at its fullest from December until May. It reaches its lowest level in September, at which time in many places a small boy could easily throw a stone from one bank to the other, and a nimble-footed man could walk across by stepping on the high and dry spots in the river bed. But as soon as the rains begin, the Jordan suddenly becomes dangerous again, for both man and beast.

Anywhere and everywhere it is possible to observe how the river shapes the shore, hollowing out a bay, building up a new bank with silt; sometimes lapping gently at the roots of the growing things that line the banks and drink its water. Then suddenly, as if in anger, it rips bushes and even sizable trees up by the roots and sends them flying. The shores of some rivers seem to guide and control the stream they contain, now advancing, now retreating a little, now bending the stream in a gentle curve, now speeding it straight on its way. But this river is the master of its shore. The Jordan shapes its own destiny. It rips, snorts, tears, churns, roars, or, suddenly calm, spreads itself out and becomes deceivingly placid. But for a few moments only. Then it is on its mad way again, remembering the fate against which it feels that it must do battle.

One result of all its meandering is that the Jordan often creates its own islands, and—where the river is the boundary between Israel and Jordan—sometimes increases the land area of one country or the other by building up land on one side, while eating it away on the other side.

If one could ride down the Jordan on a floating observation bus, and if the man with the megaphone or the microphone knew ancient, medieval and modern history, and if the vehicle went slowly enough . . .

"Ladies and gentlemen, on your left in the distance . . ."

"Now on your right . . ."

"Look quickly to the left . . ."

"Now over there . . ."

In every direction, close to the river, or off on the horizon, there are sacred caves, crumbling ruins, sites of glorious memory, proof of the destructive force of earthquakes, scenes of never-forgotten biblical stories, spots where twentieth century events have occurred.

Due to the exigencies of modern history, the Jordan plays three quite different roles as it flows from the lake to the sea. For the first six miles (as the bird flies) both sides of the river are Israeli territory. Here Jewish colonists refer to it as "our river." Then, for the next seventeen miles (in a straight line) the international boundary between Israel and the Hashemite Kingdom of Jordan, as fixed by the armistice agreement signed by those countries in 1949, is the center of the river, with the west bank Israeli territory and the east bank Jordanian. The Armistice Line, as it is called, divides the river itself into two equal parts. Practically, however, there is no need to determine exactly where the line runs, because the people of each country draw their water from the bank on their side, leaving the middle untouched, but in terms of international law, each country *owns* half the bed of the river. As a result of this semimilitary, semilegal situation, neither side can very well refer to this segment of the Jordan as "our river." On the rest of its course to the Dead Sea—forty-two miles if you measure it on a straight line and ignore the way the river meanders—both banks are Jordanian and the Arabs refer to it as "our river."

Between lake and sea there are, today, fourteen bridges, not counting a number of so-called "ferry bridges," which are nothing but flat-bottom boats pulled back and forth by ropes, just as in ancient times.

Five of the fourteen bridges are not now in use because they are in that area where the center of the river is the international boundary, and so one end of each bridge rests on Israeli soil and the other end on Jordanian soil. For seventeen years there has been no legalized movement of human beings or animals back and forth over these bridges. Soldiers guard all the frontiers, including this stretch where the frontier is the river, and so it would be almost certain suicide for anyone to attempt to cross any of these five bridges. Four are in the neighborhood of Naharayim, at the confluence of the Jordan and Yarmuk rivers, where a hydroelectric plant was built by Palestinian Jews in what was then Transjordan and now is the Hashemite Kingdom of Jordan. Two are for railroad trains, the other two for automobiles, horse-drawn vehicles, donkeys, goats, sheep, and even camels. One of the railroad bridges is in ruins because a Jordanian soldier in 1954 by accident set off some explosives that had been placed under the bridge for use in an "emergency." The fifth bridge that has been out of use since 1948 because it links two countries that are in a state of armed noncombativity is the Sheikh Hussein bridge, about one-third the way down from the lake to the sea, at a point where the Jordan for a short distance behaves in a most nontypical manner, making not a single plain or fancy meander in the course of one entire mile.

In the area where both sides of the Jordan are Israeli territory there are three substantial bridges, all close to where the river flows out from the lake. The inhabitants of Israeli agricultural settlements hereabouts also make use of ferry boats.

In the area in which both sides of the river are Jordanian territory, there are two major ferries and six bridges, all of them clustered at the lower end of the river, not far from where it flows into the sea. These are the bridges best known to tourists, for they carry automobile traffic from Jerusalem to the capital city of Amman, and from Jerusalem to such southern points as Petra, the rose-colored city carved out of solid rock, which is Jordan's principal tourist attraction, after Jerusalem. Not all these six bridges are available for civilians and animals; some are reserved exclusively for the military—the Jordanian military.

Between lake and sea there are sixty-five declivities in the landscape leading down to the Jordan, some on one side, some on the other. Only a very few can properly be called rivers. The rest are wadis that most of the year look like ordinary parched valleys, but when the rains finally come they fulfill their geographical function and become river beds, funneling enormous quantities of water into the Jordan. (The Arabs smile when one of the larger wadis, the Yabis, is sometimes mistakenly called a river, for *yabis* is the Arabic word for "dry," implying that it is not perennial and therefore is a wadi, not a river.)

On its way south from the lake to the sea, the first major tributary the Jordan meets is the Yarmuk (once called the Hieromax), a stream revered by all Islamites, for on the banks of the Yarmuk in A.D. 638 Mohammed's followers gave Byzantine forces a defeat that changed the political and religious history of the entire Middle East.

Overlooking the Yarmuk and Jordan valleys is Gadara, with its crumbling ruins of theaters, temples, aqueducts, and colonnaded streets to prove that here, in what is now such a forsaken place, a civilization of noble proportions once thrived.

Next, close to the river, an Arab village bearing a curious name, Tell Abu el-Kaml, the Hill of the Father of Lice, the derivation of which not even the present-day inhabitants themselves can explain.

Now, on the right, high on a commanding hill, the remains of a Crusader fortress sometimes called Beauvoir, sometimes Belvoir, and in Arabic called *Kaukab el-Hawa* (The Star of the Winds) because of its great height.

Then Bethabara, where John the Baptist labored. Then the Valley of Jezreel, where some historians contend the modern concept of human rights and the modern idea of democracy were first tried out. Still on the right, where the Valley of Jezreel meets the Valley of the Jordan, a place with many names: Beit-Shean, Beth-Shan, Beisan, Scythopolis, Tell el-Hosn. Findings of archaeologists prove that this was already an extremely ancient place when the Greeks made it one of the ten cities of their Decapolis; that it may have been a settled community as far back as four, five, or even six thousand years ago. The Valley of Beit-Shean in ancient times was called the "Gateway to Paradise." Its fertility is due to forty springs and a river sometimes called the Harod, sometimes the Jalud, the second of the four principal perennial streams flowing into the Jordan. Here two great battles were fought: Gideon's defeat of the Midianites and the Mamelukes' victory over the Seljuks.

Now, on the west side, Mount Gilboa, where Saul and the Philistines had their final clash, and on the east side, Pella, another city that was so favored by the Greeks that they made it a member of their League of Ten.

Everywhere, in whichever direction one turns the head, there is history, a legend, a story buried under rocks and sand. On the right is one of the spots where they say Elijah the Prophet was born, and directly across the river, far in the distance and high up, is Ajlun, center of a great industrial area in Solomon's time, for here iron was mined and copper was smelted. Over there, the remains of a once formidable Arabic castle. Farther south, Succoth, named after the Hebrew word for the "booths" that the Israelites built for themselves during their wanderings on the desert. Succoth has been the scene of some gory chapters of history, yet today, all over the world, the word Succoth (sometimes spelled Sukkoth or Sukkot) is used by Jews to designate their happiest religious holiday, when for eight days in the autumn, under specially constructed bowers of green, they celebrate the successful conclusion of the wandering in the desert and the passage of their Israelite ancestors over the Jordan into the Promised Land.

Two-thirds the way down from lake to sea, the Jordan welcomes its third major tributary, the Jabbok, which commences as a spring on the edge of Amman, the Jordanian capital, once called Philadelphia, city of brotherly love. At first the river bears the name Amman. Then, as it runs over a stony bed of gray-blue, it acquires the name Zarqa (sometimes spelled Zerka), the Arabic word for "blue." Before it joins the Jordan it has become known as the Jabbok. It was on the banks of the Jabbok that the Patriarch Jacob wrestled with God. The water of this tributary is so shallow most of the year that it is fordable at many points, yet when the rains come the Jabbok becomes an almost continuous series of sparkling cascades and tumbling waterfalls. Close to where the Jabbok flows into the Jordan are the remains of Adam, also called Adamah, or El Damite, or Tell ed-Damiyeh. When the Jordan suddenly became dry, to permit the Israelites to make their historic crossing, the waters backed up, so the Bible says, to this precise spot—to Adam.

Across the river, a great valley comes down from the northwest. Some spell it Far'ah; others Fari'ah, or Fara. Some call it a mere wadi, others say it merits being termed a river because it pours at least a trickle of water into the Jordan every day of the year, even in times of great drought.

On and on. Everywhere there are names from the Bible, from the history books, from the writings of Josephus, from the Talmud, from the Koran, from chronicles of the Middle Ages—even from the front pages of yesterday's newspapers.

Es Salt, Tyrus, Phasaelis, Shiloh, and Beth-Nimrah, sometimes called "the House of the Leopard," sometimes "the House of Pure Water."

This whole region is paradise for those who like to dig in the earth, looking for traces of ancient civilizations or for clues to the solution of age-old mysteries. Here, close by, are the Hills of Judah and the Hills of Benjamin, brown for so many centuries. On the southern horizon are the Mountains of Moab, rich in biblical lore. Soon the Dead Sea will be in sight.

Rapidly the Valley widens—to six miles—to eight—to ten—now to fourteen. This is what the old Canaanites called "the Round of the Jordan."

The sea is now only seven miles away. The fate of the Jordan cannot be much longer delayed. Its contortive meandering has considerably postponed the inevitable, yet very little time is now left for the enjoyment of its independence.

These last few miles through which the Jordan passes are saturated with history. Jerusalem is only twenty-six miles across the Hills of Judah to the southwest. Jericho, claiming to be the oldest inhabited community on earth, is just six miles away. The shallow place in the river in which Christ was baptized is here, close by. Elisha, Joshua, Cleopatra, Antony, and Herod the Great were all characters in historical dramas that had their setting not far from this bend in the river. Just a short distance to the southeast, Moses one day stood on the summit of Mount Nebo and was shown the great green oasis of Jericho, the Jordan with its lush jungle, the wide Ghor, and the rest of the Promised Land, stretching all the way to the Mediterranean.

On the other side of the river, almost the same distance away as Mount Nebo, lies Nabi Musa, where the Muslims claim that the Jewish Prophet who led his people out of the wilderness lies buried. Strangely —in view of the present-day politico-religious conflicts between these two Semitic peoples—Muslim Arabs each year assemble at Nabi Musa to pay their respects to Moses, whom they consider as much their own Prophet as they consider the Jordan their own river.

In the Bible the Garden of Eden was often referred to as "the Garden of God." That same expression was used in describing what Lot saw as he looked over this particular part of the Jordan Valley: "the plain of Jordan." In those days and for most of the centuries since, the Jericho oasis has been a brilliant green relief from the surrounding brown desolation. No wonder the Jordan, as it flows on its way, engages in a final frenzy of twisting, turning and writhing, trying desperately to flow in any direction except south to the sea.

After roaring angrily under a steel bridge that for years was named after the British general who liberated the Holy Land from the Turks, but now bears the name of Jordan's young king, the river passes Gilgal, which was the Israelites' headquarters after their crossing of the Jordan, and was the scene of so much later history. Then, as if finally reconciled, it surrenders and flows on a fairly straight line to the sea.

The Jordan started out as a river 102 miles north of here, as the bird flies. To cover that distance it traveled almost 190 miles by its own, unique method of meandering. It started out at the foot of Mount Hermon as a stream of sparkling clear water, cold to the touch, refreshing to drink, as pure as the snow on Hermon's crown. As it now pours into the sea it is almost the color of milk because of the great quantity of marl that it carries in solution—the dissolved hills of the Jordan Valley. To drink it might not be dangerous, but it would be no pleasure. In these 190 miles the Jordan has dropped more than fifteen hundred feet—more than a quarter of a mile. At times and in places it has been a raging torrent. At other times, in other places along the way, it has seemed to be too unimpressive to be worth a second look, or a second thought. And yet, despite all the water that has been taken from the Jordan along the way to irrigate fields and supply fish ponds in both Israel and the Kingdom of Jordan, it has (until various recent diversions took place) been pouring a billion and a quarter cubic meters of water per year into the Dead Sea, which figures out almost four million tons of water on an average day.

If a cork was tossed into the Jordan at its point of origin as a full-fledged river, just south of Dan in northern Galilee, and if the cork was not delayed in Lake Tiberias, and if it was permitted by man and nature to float freely through Lake Tiberias and then around all the meanders of the Lower Jordan, and if it was not held up by any frontier formalities as it left the soverign territory of Israel and entered the sovereign territory of the Hashemite Kingdom of Jordan, it would take just fifty-three hours for it to reach the Dead Sea, so short is the river, so swift its flow. (Few studies have been made of the velocity of the Jordan, which of course varies from season to season, place to place. In 1947 Goldschmidt, Cvi and Kornic measured the velocity at Allenby bridge at 1.37 to 1.69 meters per second, or about from 3.6 to 3.7 miles per hour, which is the basis for the fifty-three-hour estimate.)

In the United States alone there are more than a hundred rivers longer, wider, sustaining more people than the Jordan, yet without fame or importance, except to those who live on their banks or in their valleys.

There are nineteen rivers in the world more than two thousand miles long. Seven of them are well known, even by schoolboys. They are, in the order of their length: the Nile, 4145 miles; the Amazon, 3900; the Yangtze, 3400; the Congo, 2718; the Missouri, 2466; the Mississippi, 2348, and the Volga, 2290. But how many university graduates, any-where, could name the other twelve: the Ob-Irtysh, 3460; the Huang, 3000; the Amur, 2700; the Lena, 2680; the Mackenzie-Peace, 2635; the Niger and the Mekong, each 2600; the Paraná, 2500; the Murray-Darling, 2310; the Madeira, 2100; the Yenisey, 2080, and the Purus, 2000? (These spellings and distances are from the current issue of the World Almanac. Other sources give other spellings and other distances.)

The Jordan, even if we follow its meanderings, is less than 190 miles long, yet who (at least in the western world) has never heard of this relatively shallow, often narrow, in many ways unimportant river?

The body of water into which our river is now pouring is as unique as the Jordan itself. It has even more names. In the Old Testament it is most often called the Salt Sea, although biblical writers also refer to it as the Sea of the Plain, the East or Eastern Sea, the Sea of Arabah (derived from a Hebrew word meaning "desert plain," or "steppe," or "wilderness") or just the Sea.

It was early Greek and Roman writers—especially Pausanias, the Greek topographer, Galen, the Roman physiologist, and Trogus, the Roman historian—who connected it with extinction or destruction by calling it the Sea of Death. The historian Josephus used the name *Lacus Asphaltites* or the Lake of Asphalt. The Arabs have called it, at various times, *Bahr Za'rah,* after Zoar, a city that stood on the edge of the sea in ancient times, or *Bahr Lot,* the Sea of Lot, or *Bahr el-Miyet,* the Dead Sea, or, more picturesquely, the Stinking Sea, or the Sea of Overwhelming. At times it has also been called the Bitter Sea and the Prisoned Sea. Some Talmudic writers referred to it as the Sea of Sodom.

Those are some of the proper names that have been used to des-ignate the final resting place of the Jordan—proper names in the sense of being respectable, and also capital-letter proper names. As for the improper, common-noun, emotive-adjective names that the sea has been called, it would take many pages of print this size to begin to list them. Almost a hundred years ago a count was made of the num-ber of authors who, between A.D. 33 and A.D. 1878, wrote books containing descriptive matter about the Holy Land. The total was 3515. Not 3515 books, but books by 3515 authors. The introduction to the most reliable atlas on modern Israel estimates that since 1878 a quarter of a million additional books and articles have been written on this same subject. Most of these authors have had at least something to say about the Dead Sea, and many have tried to outdo their predecessors in finding ever stronger and more colorful words and phrases to describe the sea.

Those who wrote the various books of the Bible, although often caustic, even sometimes bitter in their language, never used emotive words about the Salt Sea. This may have been because the shores of the sea in biblical times were lined with cities of considerable size, so the biblical writers never thought of the area as either barren, forsaken, melancholy, repulsive, or lonely. Whenever the Salt Sea is mentioned in the Old Testament it is in a matter-of-fact, geographical manner. It was the classical writers who began referring to it disparagingly and emotively. Pliny wrote of the Jordan's reluctance to flow into the sea, which he called "a pestilential place."

In modern times preachers, religious writers, and composers of hymns and spirituals, whenever they have referred to the Jordan, have unanimously used it as a symbol of good, and with almost equal unanimity have made the Dead Sea a symbol of bad. There were some excuses, some justifications. The wicked sea had swallowed up the good river. Now, instead of having a strong personality of its own, the Jordan's individualism was lost in the "witches' brew of corruption." Sodom, Gomorrah, and the other Cities of the Plain that were destroyed by God because of their excessive wickedness had once stood on the shores of this sea; now they were somewhere below the surface, adding further contamination to the "poisonous water." For hundreds of years the shores of this "pestilential" lake had been bereft of cities, towns, villages—of any population at all—just as its waters now knew no life. And so, gradually, the Dead Sea became a symbol and an object lesson. Here was a body of water without an outlet. It *received*, from many sources, but it did no *giving*. Therefore, it was selfishness personified. And see what punishment God had inflicted upon it, for this sinfulness! It was an ugly place, to be scorned by righteous men forevermore.

Sometimes Lake Tiberias and the Dead Sea were compared, as in this passage from an article published in 1926: "The Sea of Galilee makes beauty of the Jordan's waters, for the Sea of Galilee has an outlet. It gets to give. It gathers in its riches that it may pour them out again to fertilize the Jordan Plain. But the Dead Sea, with the same water, makes a horror of it, for the Dead Sea has no outlet. It gets to keep."

Gradually the Dead Sea became the most maligned body of water in the world; one of the most denounced places on earth. Myths of all sorts sprang up. Some authors spiced their writings with pseudo-scientific facts about the Dead Sea, out of a simple desire to intrigue their readers. Others, perhaps unwittingly, passed on secondhand tales that grew more preposterous with each repetition. Many a moralist stretched a fact here and there, to make a religio-philosophical point.

Three Roman historians—Josephus, Pliny, and Tacitus the Younger —started the myth that no one had ever been drowned in the Dead Sea, the implication being that this was impossible.

Josephus also stated it as a fact that the Dead Sea would support the heaviest object anyone could throw onto its surface, and that the water did a complete change of color three times regularly each day.

Another chronicler of truth as he saw, or heard it, the Roman historian Gnaeus Pompeius Trogus, wrote that there never had been any boating of any kind on the Dead Sea and never could be, because "nothing lifeless can float on those waters."

The Roman geographer Pausanias was responsible for the myth that a dying creature sinks at once to the very bottom of the Dead Sea, and that the corpse remains there forever—apparently in a happy state of nondecomposition.

A learned Talmudic authority "confirmed" the Roman canard that no human being had ever been drowned in the Dead Sea.

Many an ancient writer stated as fact that no birds had ever flown over the Dead Sea; that if any were ever to try it they would drop like plummets to their death in the "poison" water. (The truth is that fish-eating birds do shun the Dead Sea, but only because they know it contains no food for them.)

The thirteenth century German Dominican, Borcard, compared the Dead Sea to "hell's chimney" and said it was "dark and always smoking." It was the smoke from this "chimney" that had killed off all living matter the entire length of the Valley, he wrote.

There were many myths about the Dead Sea in *Secrets for True Crusaders to Help Them Recover the Holy Land.*

In 1350 Ludolph von Suchem wrote *Description of the Holy Land and of the Way Thither,* in which he declared that the Dead Sea "has a most unbearable and evil stench, whereof, when the wind blows, it poisons all the country round about." If pebbles along the shore were picked up, he said, they would taint the hand with an intolerable odor that would persist for exactly three days, no matter how often and how vigorously the hand was scrubbed.

A British contemporary of that imaginative German, Sir John Mandeville, exhibited little respect for the intelligence of his readers, for, after following the Jordan its full length, he seriously reported that it was impossible for any living creature to die in the water of the Dead Sea, and also that a piece of iron, no matter what its weight or size, would float on the surface. Also, that a feather would sink immediately to the bottom.

Another myth, propagated by several nineteenth century writers, was that Dante visited the Dead Sea in his youth and there got inspiration for his dreadful conception of Inferno.

But most of the damage to the Dead Sea's reputation has been done by the use of innuendo, emotive language, bitter adjectives; by the painting of word-pictures so depressing that they frighten the timid and enchant those who delight in horror.

The Dead Sea has been the victim of such execrations as these: "a place of sterile bitterness," "the graveyard of all water," "a mighty sepulchre," "a nightmare of a world."

One British writer compared the surrounding mountains to the badly broken molar teeth of some repulsive-looking human. Another writer called them something out of a sculptor's nightmare; "emblems of sterility."

The most picturesque language used about the Dead Sea has come from the pens and mouths of Christian preachers. The Reverend William M. Thomson, for forty-five years a missionary in Syria and Lebanon, wrote a monumental work on the Holy Land, published in London in 1883, in which he described the Jordan's "disappearance forever" into the Dead Sea, "that melancholy bourne from which there is neither escape nor return." But then with true Christian faith and hope, he worked out a soul-satisfying explanation of the Jordan's fate. The water of the Jordan pours into the Dead Sea; the Dead Sea has no outlet; but constant evaporation takes place, and so, argued the Reverend Mr. Thomson, the Dead Sea "is but the Jordan's highway to heaven. Purified from every gross and earthly alloy, it is called back to the skies by the all-attracting sun, emblem of that other resurrection when Christ shall come in clouds and all the holy angels with Him." What the Jordan, thus cleaned and purified, leaves behind is all the marl, the salt, the noxious chemicals that it had carried down into the Dead Sea with it.

A modern-day Irishman, Sean O'Ceallaigh, with an Irish flair for picturesque language, wrote emotionally of a trip he took to the Dead Sea, which he said was like "going down to hell." He sprinkled his sparkling prose with references to death, sulfur, salt, Lot's wife, "a city without even ten just men," fire and brimstone, "the men of Sodom endeavoring to commit sin with God's angels," "a place that connotes everything evil," a place "blasted, forsaken, forever damned."

The Reverend Franklin E. Hoskins, a missionary in the Middle East for many years, wrote in 1905 about "the Dead Sea of human helplessness," a sea which, he said, "hides wrecks of monstrous iniquity." By contrast, this ecclesiastical authority considered the Jordan a "sacred stream," its "cooling, cleansing waters" a source of great refreshment to "the heated brow and the sinful heart."

Another missionary of the same era wrote of "an unnatural gloom that hangs over the sea and the whole plain below Jericho." He compared it to "a vast funeral pall that had been let down from heaven," a pall which, he said, hangs, always, "heavily over the bosom of this mysterious lake."

The Reverend George Croly, writing in London in 1855, described the Dead Sea as a "mighty sepulchre," a place of "hopeless aridity," of cliffs "utterly naked," of the "deep cauldron of sterility," of "burnt rocks," of "mountains that are the emblem of sterility," of "deathlike silence." This ecclesiastical gentleman was neither the first nor the last to use "sepulchre," "cauldron," and "sterility" about the Dead Sea. Those three words became the favorites of many preachers and writers in the late nineteenth and early twentieth centuries.

The Reverend R. Cody, a Presbyterian pastor from Amsterdam, New York, writing in the *Biblical World* in 1903 about his own explorations in the Dead Sea area, called it a "prisoned sea" and said it had an effect on a person "unlike that of any other spot on earth." He called it "an awful gulf," "a dreary wilderness," and said "the utter desolation is oppressive." He approached the Dead Sea by the road from Jericho, thus passing the Inn of the Good Samaritan, which he called "a wretched Turkish café serving only coffee." When the sea came within his sight he wrote: "As you approach the Dead Sea you seem pulled down, down by unseen forces. The mysterious mountains of Moab look like a small pyramid erected by the Creator to keep back the Arabian desert." The "utter loneliness of the place" seemed to obsess him. The body of water itself was, for him, "a rolling sea of desolation." He described how "the sun pours its rays into this vast cauldron. The air is stifling."

George Adam Smith once wrote: "In this awful hollow, this bit of
the infernal regions come up to the surface, this hell, with the sun
pouring into it, primitive man laid the scene of God's most terrible
judgment on human sin. The glare of Sodom and Gomorrah is flung
down the whole length of scriptural history."

Even so eminent and factual a scientist and archaeologist as Nelson
Glueck found it difficult in his younger days to contemplate the Dead
Sea without emotion. Writing in a magazine of geography and exploration a quarter of a century ago, he spoke of "the witches' brew
now known as the Dead Sea."

The most vitriolic combination of fact and fancy, of diatribe and
defamation, is in a book on the Holy Land by a nineteenth century
British clergyman who wrote: "So bitter is the Dead Sea that the Jordan and other rivers for thousands of years have poured in their contributions of sweet water, yet the sea continues as nauseous and deadly
as ever. Nothing lives in it. Neither fish nor reptiles nor even *animalcu-
lae* can abide its desperate malignity . . . It is a sulphurous sepulchre,
steaming up like a huge cauldron of smouldering bitumen and brimstone. Neither rain from heaven nor mountain torrents nor the Jordan's flood, nor all combined, can change its character of death. It is a
fit symbol of that sea of depravity and corruption which nothing human can heal. Science and art, education and philosophy, legislation
and superstition may pour their united contributions into it forever,
but they cannot mitigate its malignity."

A few of the castigators eventually added half-apologetic words of
faint praise. The Reverend Mr. Thomson conceded that the Dead Sea
landscape had certain aspects of "stern grandeur." The Reverend Mr.
Croly added to his comments the observation that the surface of the
sea served as "a vast mirror, reflecting every color and radiance of
the sky," and he said he had been impressed by "a sense of the monumental." The romantic Irishman, O'Ceallaigh, reported: "But I saw
beauty there. The waters sparkled. The blue mountains of Moab rose
up sheer above the eastern shore and stood proudly arrayed in purple
against the azure sky . . . even the gaunt hills of the Judean desert
had about them a strange, unearthly loveliness."

Pliny, who had gone so far as to call the Dead Sea a "pestilential
place," completely reversed himself later by calling it *amoenus*. This
Latin adjective has no exact English equivalent. It meant, in Pliny's
day, lovely, delightful, pleasant and charming, and was about the highest praise that it was possible to pay to anything inanimate.

The Encyclopaedia Britannica that had been so critical of the Jordan River, calling it an "unpleasant foul stream" running between "poisonous banks," came to the defense of the Dead Sea with this passage: "To think of this lake as sombre is quite an illusion; its intense coloring, its varied effects of lights, its scarped overhanging slopes broken by deep gorges produce a picture of wild and sublime beauty . . . The scenery is sublime and romantic, far beyond that of many of the world's winter resorts."

Dr. E. W. G. Masterman, an eminent Middle Eastern expert, lecturing before the Geographical Society of London in 1918, went so far in opposing the majority opinion about the Dead Sea as to declare, to the astonishment of many in his audience: "Perhaps the Dead Sea, with its lofty mountains, is the most beautiful thing in the land. The visitor looks for sterility and death, and he finds a lake of ever changing colors and varied movements, and plenty of life at many points, set in the midst of majestic mountain chains . . . I recall the brilliant moonlit nights when on the Dead Sea shores one watched the distant wavelets like rows of diamonds in the reflected moonbeams."

So much for the conflict of impressions and opinion. But even in the field of statistics there is little agreement about this death-place of the Jordan River.

The length of the Dead Sea is between forty-six and forty-nine miles, depending upon how much of the salt pan area at the southern end is included in the measurement. The sea's width varies from three to ten miles. It is generally agreed that the maximum depth is about 1310 feet and that this profundity occurs not far out from the eastern shore. This is approximately the same depth as that of the deepest spot in Lake Maggiore in Italy. The total area covered by water is about 405 square miles. Except for the Great Lakes there are few bodies of water in the United States nearly as large. For example, the Dead Sea has a much greater area than Lake Champlain. It is fourteen times the size of the largest lake in Great Britain, Loch Lomond. There is no lake in Central Europe as large. Many years ago a piece of statistical misinformation appeared in a Palestine guidebook: that the Dead Sea and Lake Geneva (Lac Léman) in Switzerland are identical in size. Frequently over the years this misstatement has been picked up and reprinted, until it has become—like many frequently mispronounced words—popularly accepted. Actually the Dead Sea is almost twice the size of the Swiss lake, which is the second largest lake in Central Europe—223 square miles against the Dead Sea's 405. It is also almost twice the size of Lake Balaton in Hungary, the largest lake in Central Europe.

When the Dead Sea is called "the lowest spot on the surface of the earth" the reference is to the altitude of the water level. This level varies slightly from season to season, and has changed considerably over the centuries. For this reason there is great disagreement among the authorities as to what the correct figure is. The most recent Israeli guidebook says −1300 feet. So does the Encyclopaedia Britannica and the Universal Jewish Encyclopedia. Official Jordanian Government publications give it as −1297. A guidebook approved and endorsed by the Israeli Government says −1292, as does the Encyclopedia Americana. The Information Please Almanac and Chambers Encyclopedia say −1290. Archaeologist Nelson Glueck, an authority on the area, has consistently used the figure −1286 in his writings. This is the figure which also appears in the World Almanac, the World Book Encyclopedia, the latest editions of Webster's Geographical Dictionary, and on all maps in the *National Geographic Magazine*. The New Bible Dictionary says −1280.

Despite these confusing discrepancies, all sources agree that when one is standing on the shores of the Dead Sea, no matter whether the water level is −1280, −1286, −1290, −1292, −1297, or −1300 feet, one is as low as it is possible to get on any piece of land on earth. (Death Valley, California, is a mere 282 feet below sea level.)

Next to being the lowest spot on earth, the Dead Sea is most noted for its peculiar chemical content. It is approximately four times as salty as the Atlantic, the Pacific, or the Mediterranean. The preacher who said the Jordan makes a constant contribution of sweet water to the Dead Sea, which the Dead Sea immediately contaminates, wrote more poetically than truthfully. The water of the Jordan that flows into the sea contains a considerable percentage of salt and other chemicals. As evaporation takes place, the residue is added to the high chemical content of the Dead Sea, which in this way becomes constantly more "contaminated"—to use the preacher's word—by the Jordan itself. Of course the Dead Sea also has its own chemical sources.

In a paper read to the Royal Geographical Society of London years ago, a noted chemist-explorer estimated that "one million tons of mixed chlorides of sodium and magnesium" are delivered into the Dead Sea per annum. He spent years seeking to determine the exact source of these chemicals and finally decided that "there is a huge saline spring in the bed of the Jordan just above the Allenby Bridge." But a majority of the chlorides, he said, came all the way from Lake Tiberias, the source being springs in the bed of the lake or on its shores, which greatly affect the original purity of the Jordan's water as it flows through the lake.

Ordinary sea water contains four to six percent solids. Dead Sea water contains twenty-four to twenty-six percent, of which about a tenth is common salt. A gallon of ordinary water weighs 8.33 pounds. A gallon of Dead Sea water weighs more than 12¼ pounds. This heaviness is due entirely to the chemical content. If one gallon of ordinary sea water is boiled away, approximately half a pound of solids will remain. But a gallon of Dead Sea water will yield three and a quarter pounds of solids. Nearly all these chemicals have a commercial value. The potassium is used in making high explosives and fertilizers, the bromine, magnesium, chlorine and sulfur for various other industrial purposes. The potash now stored up in the Dead Sea would meet world demands for the next two hundred and fifty years.

Despite this chemical content, the water of the Dead Sea is not in the least unattractive, whether seen in a glass or as part of the landscape. It appears from a distance to be slightly greenish-blue. There is some truth to the bon mot that the only water in the world bluer than the water of the Dead Sea is the water of the Red Sea. It has many exciting ways of reflecting sunlight, depending on the time of day and the season of the year. This is what led to the myth propagated by Josephus that the water actually changes color three times a day. In a glass the water looks quite drinkable, but any contact with it causes at least an unpleasant reaction, if not actual discomfort, or even suffering. To the taste it is far more bitter and unpleasant than ordinary sea water. It puckers the tongue and mouth, as would a strong solution of alum. Its smell? The word "nauseous" used by some writers may be too strong, but it is not exactly attractive. When Dead Sea water gets into the eyes they smart, as if washed with oil of camphor. On the skin the water produces a burning, prickling sensation. It stiffens the hair, as pomatum would. It is smooth and greasy to the touch. This is because of the vast quantity of bitumen, a natural derivative of crude petroleum, that the sea contains. There have been many technical and mythological explanations of where and how this material originated in the Dead Sea. The Arabs have always believed that it forms rather mysteriously on rocks in the depths of the sea and is shaken loose by earthquakes, which cause large chunks of it to rise to the surface.

After the great earthquake of 1834 large slabs of bitumen floated to the surface, one of which, when finally brought ashore, was found to weigh more than six thousand pounds. During the earthquake of 1837, which was so severe that it demolished both Safed and Tiberias, immense pieces of bitumen again appeared on the surface of the Dead Sea. One was of such a size that seventy Bedouin tribesmen were able to stand on it simultaneously.

Often the size of these floating blocks of bitumen is so great that they are mistaken for islands, leading to many myths about "the islands of the Dead Sea." Historian Trogus wrote that the surface of the sea was often so thickly strewn with bitumen that "winds could not ruffle it"—no doubt an exaggeration.

Josephus mentioned that boats were used on the sea for collecting the floating bitumen. This may or may not have been true. The fact that Tacitus also mentions it is not confirmation, for Tacitus had a reputation of plagiarizing freely from Josephus. (It had not been a great many years back that Historian Trogus had contended that boating on the Dead Sea was utterly impossible because nothing inanimate could float on the surface.)

In 1930 forty tons of bitumen floated to the surface and was collected by a British chemical company and hauled by camel-back to Jerusalem for export.

The Greek historian Diodorus Siculus reported that in his day— the first century B.C.—bitumen was salvaged from the Dead Sea by men on rafts, armed with bows and arrows to protect themselves against rival collectors.

From the various classical writers it appears that early winter was the best time to collect bitumen, because the Dead Sea at that season became unusually agitated and it was then that pieces of the valuable material were most likely to be shaken loose from their moorings and float to the surface.

Because bitumen is highly inflammable, there is a belief that the destruction of Sodom, Gomorrah, and the three other ill-fated Cities of the Plain occurred when lightning struck a large quantity of this oily material, causing a devastating conflagration that spread from city to city.

In the Bible bitumen is called slime or pitch. Bible scholars believe that Noah calked his ark, inside and out, with a preparation of bitumen from the Dead Sea. After the Deluge, descendants of Noah used it to bind together the bricks out of which they made the Tower of Babel. In the ruins of ancient Babylon there is evidence of its use as mortar. Later, the Egyptians employed it in embalming their dead. The Book of Exodus tells how the mother of Moses daubed the ark of bulrushes, before she hid it by the edge of a river, with "slime and pitch."

When cold, Dead Sea bitumen is as brittle as glass, but in the heat of the sun it starts to melt. Galen, the Roman medical authority, said the best bitumen of his day—widely used in the compounding of certain medicines—was that from the Dead Sea.

It was bitumen that gave the Dead Sea the name Josephus and other Roman historians preferred for it: *Lacus Asphaltites*.

An American missionary who explored the Dead Sea in 1903 wrote this vivid account of what happened during a storm:

"Oil flowed freely from our oars in filmy sheets. We saw pieces of sulphur as large as a man's fist and lumps of bitumen as big as a man's head . . . The thunder was terrible. Black clouds seemed to rest on the sea. Sheets of lightning were extinguished in the water. I expected to see what Abraham of old witnessed when 'the smoke of the country went up as the smoke of a furnace.' Breakers and waves made a deafening noise, each breaker as it struck the side of the boat sounding like a wild beast crashing through the jungle."

Another phenomenon of this strange body of water is a broad belt of whitish foam occasionally observed down the entire length of the lake. One explanation is that it is caused by gases rising from a fault or fissure in the sea's bed. In this foamy strip the water bubbles like champagne and is in constant motion, as if it were a stream running through the center of the sea. This has led to the theory that it is the water of the Jordan flowing along independently and refusing to mix with the water of the Dead Sea, an explanation not held in very high scientific favor. Some observers have also reported a white streak stretching across the sky in the same general direction, which is seen only on nights when the belt of foam is present in the sea.

The density of the Dead Sea water enables a person to float without effort, although there is a tendency for the head to sink lower than the rest of the body, and for the feet to come out of the water. It is not an entirely pleasant experience, for there is also the necessity of trying to keep the stinging water out of the eyes, off the lips, and out of the mouth. Tourists generally take their shoes and stockings off and wet their feet in the Jordan River, and when they get to the Dead Sea go for a swim, but when the novelty wears off, after a few minutes, so does the pleasure. Clever photographers have occasionally posed four people floating in the Dead Sea, sitting up, around four sides of a card table, playing bridge or having lunch. But it is not as easy as it looks.

In addition to the Jordan, there are three other rivers worthy of being called rivers that empty into the Dead Sea, all on the eastern side. The most noteworthy is the Zerka or Zarqa Ma'in, known in biblical times as the Nahaliel. The water it pours into the sea is almost hot enough to boil eggs, because of famous warm springs not far from the mouth. At the extreme southern end of the sea is the Hasa, a mountain torrent known in the Bible as the Zered, the banks of which the ancient Israelites used for a brief time as a camping ground. About halfway between these two rivers is the Mujib, known in the Bible as the Arnon, which delineated the southern boundary of Palestine in the days of Christ, a perfect frontier because the sheer cliffs lining its banks form a barrier almost impossible for any army to cross. The cliffs are so high that the sun seldom reaches into the valley. The chasm or canyon is at places thirty-five hundred feet deep and has such an echo that if a small stone rolls down into the river it sounds like a thunderous landslide.

These rivers and the Jordan together pour into the Dead Sea every day millions of tons of water. Because the Dead Sea has no outlet, this impounding ought to raise the level of the sea half an inch per day, or twelve feet in a year. But evaporation keeps the level almost constant. The sun pulls up out of the sea more than a billion gallons of water per day, just about what the rivers pour in. The solids, of course, are all left behind. The sun also draws up two to five inches of water that falls into the Dead Sea each year in the form of rain.

The presence of so much moisture in the air may have something to do with creating the pale purple haze that gives a special character to a landscape that is otherwise mostly a solid, monotonous, ocher-gray color.

It takes a hot sun to boil away a billion gallons of water a day. The sun *is* hot. It keeps the temperature at 110 degrees Fahrenheit during most of each summer day. It is a temperature that many people cannot stand. From May to December the entire Jordan Valley and Dead Sea are tolerable only for those willing to take a great deal of punishment from nature, in return for the solitude, the stern grandeur, and the sense of utter remoteness from the getting and the spending of modern life. It is so hot here in midsummer that one of the clefts in the hills is called the Valley of Fire.

The smells of the Dead Sea bother sensitive noses. There is not only the stench caused by the presence of a great quantity of sulfur in the water, which is somewhat the odor of rotten eggs—only more so—but there are also the dead fish. They come via the Jordan all the way from Lake Tiberias. Those that survive the hundred and fifty miles of cascades and meanders die almost instantly upon contact with the chemical-ridden water of the Dead Sea. The Arnon has an even greater piscatorial population as it empties into the sea, and its fish meet a similar fate. The corpses are washed ashore and as they decompose and putrefy under the rays of the broiling sun, they make a noxious contribution to the combination of odors.

The belief, long held, that nothing in the animal or vegetable kingdom can live in the Dead Sea has often been denied. Amateur scientists frequently come forward with "proof" that is not always entirely convincing. A declaration signed jointly by a dozen tourists hung for years before World War I on a wall of a Jericho hotel, attesting to the fact that they had all seen fish swimming in the Dead Sea. But the spot mentioned in the document was a cove, into which springs poured a constant supply of fresh water that diluted the Dead Sea in this particular spot enough to permit a limited amount of piscatorial life. As early as 1891 microbes were discovered in Dead Sea water. Later some seaweed was found. It is an undebatable scientific fact that certain diatoms (microscopic unicellular marine or fresh water algae) and some pathogenic bacteria (vegetable microorganisms that cause disease) can survive in Dead Sea water. The absence of other life—normal marine animal and vegetable life—is not due, as generally supposed, to the high salt content, but to the presence of so much magnesium bromide.

In addition to being valuable for industrial purposes, the Dead Sea chemicals have been known, since ancient times, to have considerable medicinal worth. Under Jewish religious law all work was forbidden on the Sabbath, yet drawing water from the Dead Sea was approved, if the water was to be used in the concocting of medicines, and therefore in the saving of lives. At the height of the Roman Empire, the wealthy sent all the way from Rome for containers of Dead Sea water for medicinal use. In recent years both Dead Sea water and clay from along the shores have been found to be rich in hormones. The possibility of the Dead Sea area becoming a health resort comparable to some of the great European spas is therefore not beyond contemplation.

There are many questions about the Jordan Valley and the Dead Sea that historians and archaeologists have thus far been unable to answer. The principal mystery has always been, and still is: Where were Sodom, Gomorrah, and the other Cities of the Plain that were destroyed with fire and brimstone? The "plain" was for long believed to be the Valley of the Jordan where it broadens out, just before meeting the Dead Sea. But in recent years preference has been given by the guessers to the low-lying land at the southern end, now covered by shallow water. At various times over the centuries explorers have returned from the Dead Sea with tales of having seen great stone pillars and other "fragments of buildings" below the surface of the sea, in one place or another, sometimes at the north end, sometimes at the south. Always those who made the reports were positive they had discovered the remains of the lost cities. Yet no tangible evidence has yet been brought to the surface and so the mystery persists: Where are Sodom, Gomorrah and their ill-fated companion cities? The excitement caused by the rich archaeological findings at Hazor, Megiddo, Caesarea, Masada and in the Bar Kosiba caves will probably pale by comparison with the public reaction there will be if and when some ambitious and lucky archaeologist some day comes upon the burial place of history's most sinful cities.

On Lake Tiberias the winds are erratic and unpredictable. Here they follow a pattern. Dawn is always ushered in by a gentle eastern or northeastern breeze. Later it veers to the southwest. Toward sunset it is normal to have a north or northwest breeze. By midnight all movement of the air suddenly stops. The fact that there are breezes does not mean there is relief from the heat. The air serves only as a vehicle for the transportation of heat from a different direction. It brings no coolness with it.

There is a great democracy about the weather here. Everyone gets treated alike. The Dead Sea heat, the below-sea-level depression, the manner in which the sun cracks the lips and blisters the skin, the dehydrating of the body, the way the mind sometimes seems to become affected—it happens to nearly everyone alike. There is no way to buy exemption, unless you wish to live in an air-conditioned automobile while visiting the Dead Sea.

This place is a perfect lesson in the law of compensation. If you can bear the heat, if you can ignore the lack of all the twentieth century's niceties, there is a reward in the gradual discovery that here there is beauty of a strange, indefinable sort. It is not the comfortable beauty of the Bernese Oberland in Switzerland, or of the pleasant villages of rural England, or of the well-tended hills of northern New England. Here, first, there is a feeling of frightful and frightening loneliness and utter desolation. Then gradually the awesome grandeur begins to make itself felt. Not everyone who finds beauty and tranquility in Vermont's Green Mountains will—or can—respond to this. Yet the reward is great for those who are able. This is a place of lofty heights and profound depths in more ways than one. On the east side of the Dead Sea the Mountains of Moab rise precipitously to a height of as much as 3000 feet, and the floor of the sea goes down to a depth of 1310 feet below the water level. The mind and the emotions go to the same sort of extremes.

In both Jordan and Israel there are good highways to the Dead Sea, black-top roads built, in both countries, with American financial and technical assistance. Air-conditioned tourist cars regularly travel these roads. Some day someone with experience in the winter resort business will build a great air-conditioned hotel at the Jordanian or Israeli end of the sea with a fresh water swimming pool in which tourists will be able to wash off the salt and the grease of the Dead Sea. But the peculiar spirit of this place is not to be savored in such a manner. It is necessary to sweat and steam, to become dehydrated, to go a little out of the mind, in order to appreciate the peculiarities offered by this death-place of our river.

When the heat and the ocher-gray monotony become too much, there is always Ein Gedi. The oasis called Ein Gedi (or En Gedy or Engeddi) was there in the time of Abraham. It was probably there in the time of Adam. It may have been there long before man came into existence. Now it is being made as available as possible to tourists. Soon air-conditioned buses and low-flying helicopters will spoil it. This is the price a small country pays for wanting foreign exchange. Ten dollars for the bus, sixty cents for postcards, and a few more coins for soft drinks, multiplied by a million, equals enough to bring in a great many new immigrants who may be leading a third-class life in some place where they no longer belong. Yet there ought to be a campaign to get people to read about Ein Gedi and promise never to try to go there.

Ein Gedi is in the Bible. This is where David went into hiding when King Saul got into one of his periodic moods of wrath. Ein Gedi is mentioned six times in the Old Testament, yet none of the six biblical writers even attempted to describe it. Solomon in his great song paid tribute to Ein Gedi, saying: "My beloved is unto me as a cluster of camphire in the vineyards of En-gedi." (Bible experts say Solomon did not really mean camphor but the henna plant, widely used in the Middle East in his day in the making of cosmetics. Henna still grows wild in Ein Gedi.) At one period in its long history perfume was made in Ein Gedi, because this was one of the few places in the land where the non-indigenous balsam tree flourished. The Seyal tree from which gum arabic is obtained grew here, too, as well as the thorny nabk, with its fruit resembling thorn apples, and the pistachio, a tree of considerable size, with large clusters of flowers, and the nightshade plant that produces the vegetable called eggplant. But the most unusual growing thing at Ein Gedi was the Dead Sea apple, or apple of Sodom, which ancient writers described as "externally fair of appearance, but dissolving into ashes and dust when plucked," thus making possible the simile: "He had seen the fruits of victory turn into apples of Sodom." (In Egypt the caustic juice of the plant was used as a depilatory, and in India for the treatment of skin diseases.)

Ein Gedi is halfway up the west shore of the Dead Sea, just two miles short of an invisible line marking the frontier between the Hashemite Kingdom of Jordan to the north and the State of Israel to the south. The caves used in A.D. 135 as hideouts by the followers of Bar Kosiba, leader of the last great revolt against the Romans, are just a few miles to the south. To the north, in Jordan, is Khirbet Qumran, where in a cave in 1947 the Dead Sea Scrolls were discovered.

The words Ein Gedi mean Fountain of the Kid. In ancient times there were many wild goats here, which inspired an American rabbi to write a book published in 1961 with the euphonious title *The Wild Goats of Ein Gedi*. A few of the same breed of wild goats, a type of ibex, still inhabit Ein Gedi.

This place of the wild goats has been called a freak of nature. Maybe so. But it is good that nature, often so cruel, can have a whim and make an Ein Gedi.

If you approach Ein Gedi directly from the west, which only the very young and the very adventurous should ever try to do, you must cross the Wilderness of Judaea, so wild a place that throughout history it has been a shelter for people in distress, and a refuge for runaways, rebels, criminals, and others who have had compelling reasons to hide from someone, or who were fleeing from the harassments of civilization. The Wilderness of Judaea is not kind to either man or beast. It is a wilderness in every sense, a place of wild crags and forbidding canyons. There are no towns or villages, no people, no water, no growing things, no mercy to the stranger. Men who have crossed the mountains of Persia and Lebanon, and who know all the hazards of the Alps, have called the pass that leads through the Wilderness to Ein Gedi the worst they have ever encountered. The Wilderness drops down to the level of the Dead Sea (not to sea level, which is something quite different) at a precipitous angle, sometimes at the rate of five hundred feet per mile, which is steep enough to satisfy most professional mountain climbers. Often it is necessary to go down the almost perpendicular face of a cliff. No wonder David chose this area for his hiding place, and that many men since him have done likewise.

Approaching Ein Gedi by road, from Beersheba, as the tourists do, one passes through a new Israeli town, Arad, the tenth to be built in the past four thousand years on this ancient site. En route to Ein Gedi one first sees the *kibbutz* or communal settlement that has taken to itself the ancient name. On all sides there is the grim Dead Sea desolation that depresses most people: the bare rocks, the eroded hills, miles and miles of changeless yellow-gray, unrelieved by any happy colors. Then, suddenly, the fields and orchards of the kibbutz, as green as if they were in the Jungle of the Jordan. It is a shock to come so suddenly onto something so different. But this is not yet the place of the wild goats. Ein Gedi itself must be approached on foot, which is as it should be. Once there was a city here with hundreds, perhaps thousands of inhabitants; now there are the fifty or so members of the kibbutz and at Ein Gedi itself two or three guides, and a man who sells postcards and something cold out of a bottle.

You head due west, with your back to the sea. The climb is steep in spots. You *hear* Ein Gedi before you see it. You hear, at first far in the distance, then closer and ever louder, the most exciting, happy sound that this part of the world offers: the music made by water in movement.

The singing water has created an oasis several hundred feet wide, with vegetation that is both lush and luxuriant. The overall color seems to be emerald green. The lowest and last pool formed by the water is called David's Fountain, in honor of the most celebrated temporary resident the region ever had. Without doubt he bathed here often during his period of hiding. The pool is only about a quarter of a city block wide. Many film actors in California have larger private swimming tanks. It is encircled with green vegetation: trees, bushes, wild flowers of exotic coloring, and some plants to be found nowhere else in the world. Vines that recall Equatorial Africa form a canopy overhead. Pan and his nymphs would have liked this rustic bower; there is something pagan about it. The pool is deep enough in the center for a little shallow-water swimming. The temperature of the water is a constant 81 degrees Fahrenheit, 36 degrees warmer than the water that gushed from the springs at Laish, at the source of the Jordan in Galilee, yet it feels cool and refreshing to the body, after the heat of everywhere else.

This one pool is not all. A well-trodden path winds up through the heart of the luxuriant gorge, never far from the sight or sound of the water as it cascades in a silver spray over moss-covered rocks, then pauses briefly in some natural basin, before moving on to spill its sparkling splendor over more stones and form more pools below. When one beauty spot palls, you climb a little higher and reach another pool that seems even greener, lusher, sweeter-smelling, closer to God.

The Ein Gedi source is nearly six hundred feet up, in a wild, luxuriant grove. It seems fitting that this pellucid water, which seems so happy as it tumbles over the rocks on its way down the mountainside, will soon be joining water from the Mountain of Snow and from Banias; water that had its origin in the Temple of Pan and in the Land of the Underground Springs; water from Laish called Dan. This is why Ein Gedi is a legitimate part of the Jordan story.

Here is a good place to end the geographical chapter of this biography of a river. It began with pure, clear, clean, fresh, unpolluted water gushing from the ground at the foot of Mount Hermon. It ends with pure, clear, clean, fresh, unpolluted water gushing from the ground on a mountainside, close to the spot where David hid from Saul and where Solomon found inspiration for one sentence in his *Song of Songs*.

3

It may seem odd to commence the chronological biography of the Jordan four and a half billion years ago, but that is where it really must begin, although the river's actual birth occurred much later.

Four and a half billion years ago—if one accepts the most recent hypothesis of American scientists—an adventurous star passed so close to the sun that something happened, exceptional even in the unpredictable world of the planets. Scientists do not yet agree on the exact nature of the event, but the theory now most widely held is that the passing star pulled out of the sun a long streamer of filament or hot gases, which formed beadlike lumps that eventually became planets. Thus our earth was born. Or, if you prefer, there is the older Nebular Hypothesis: as a mass of intensely heated gas spun in space and began condensing, the centrifugal force hurled out smaller masses of matter, which became the planets. In either case, as the earth began to cool, the surface became as smooth as that of a billiard ball, if viewed from far enough away. Yet if the billiard ball were to have been studied under a telescope, bumps and depressions would have been seen beginning to form on the smooth-looking surface. The world's most fascinating serial is the still-unfinished story of how those bumps and depressions— the mountains and the ocean beds—were created.

About thirty or forty million years ago an intensive movement of certain areas of the earth's surface, called the Alpidic Folding, resulted in the creation of some of the world's most important mountain chains —the Andes, the Himalayas, the Rockies, the Alps, and, closer to the scene of our present interest, the Anatolian mountains of Asia Minor.

In this period Mount Hermon and the hills of Palestine came into being.

As a direct result of this laborious period of mountain-making, two more or less parallel cracks appeared on the earth's surface, starting in the north of what is now Syria and extending to a point far below the Equator in Africa. Then, the earth's surface between these two cracks began to sink. The action was part of the birth-writhings of the earth; the cooling of gases; the equalizing of stresses and strains below the crust; the contraction of the exterior surface of the planet; local adjustments to crustal movements; reaction to the upheavals that had elevated the world's most impressive mountain chains.

The creation of what is known as the Great African Rift began, therefore, in the Pliocene Period, which dates back about fifteen million years. If the earth is considered to be an eighty-year-old man, the Rift began to be formed only three months ago. Geologically speaking, it is a very recent occurrence.

Exactly how long it took for the Rift to reach its present level no one knows. Even if mankind had then existed, it was not an event for which any prehistoric promoter could have sold tickets. The sinking did not occur in an hour or a day or even a month. It took millions of years, which is only a moment or two, the way geologists measure time.

The sinking went on throughout the Pleistocene Period, which dates from about 600,000 to 100,000 years ago. Just before or during the Pleistocene Period mankind appeared, but the rate of drop was so slow that no primitive man could possibly have been conscious of it. It is even possible that the sinking may still be continuing, unbeknown even to those who live on the land lying between the two cracks.

The formation of the Rift was accompanied by frequent earthquakes and the spewing forth of a great deal of hot lava through the cracks in the earth's surface. Areas covered with this Pliocene and Pleistocene lava can be found today on both sides of the Valley, especially in the Galilee mountains and on the east side of the Jordan, north of the Yarmuk River. This continues to be a weak area in the earth's crust, and even in modern times severe earthquakes have occurred in the Valley that have destroyed whole cities. Other by-products of the formation of the Rift are the numerous hot springs found in many parts of the Valley.

Fifteen million years ago, when the formation of the Rift began, the earth was not much different, in many ways, than it is today. The scenery of 15,000,000 B.C. would have been quite recognizable to modern man. There were palm trees, beeches and birches, ivy and holly, bees and butterflies, extensive forests, and valleys covered with grass. The mammals that roamed the world then included some that at least resembled twentieth century horses, deer and elephants. There was one odd animal that was a cross between a giraffe and a camel. However, nothing even remotely resembling man had yet put in an appearance.

Some scientific writers object to the word "rift" or "gulch." They say that "trough" is more accurate; that "sag" is, technically, the best. But it has gone down in history and literature and even in much scientific writing as the Rift, or the Great Rift, or the Great Syro-African Rift.

It begins at Alexandretta in Syria, where it created the Valley of the Orontes, then, moving southward, formed the great depression between the Lebanon and Anti-Lebanon Mountains, then the Valley of the Jordan, the Dead Sea declivity, and the trough called the Aravah that runs from the Dead Sea south to the Gulf of Aqaba. The fault then goes through the Red Sea, traverses Kenya, Tanzania and Malawi, and finally ends at the Zambesi River. This vast trough reaches its lowest land depth on the shores of the Dead Sea, almost thirteen hundred feet below sea level. The floor of the trough at this point—the bottom of the Dead Sea—is almost half a mile below the level of oceans. In the Red Sea the floor drops another two thousand feet or more.

Exactly what happened in the Great Rift during the millions of years since the sinking first began is, like everything else about the Jordan, a matter of disagreement. Some authorities believe that at one time— many millions of years ago—it was filled with an immense body of salt water; that it was an arm of the Red Sea or the Mediterranean. Others scorn this theory, insisting that a diagonal ridge of limestone between the Dead Sea and the Gulf of Aqaba—a ridge that now rises 720 feet above sea level—prevented the waters of the Red Sea from flowing any farther northward; that the lakes of the great declivity were always endoreic.

Still others contend that the ridge was created later, and that it was this upthrust of land which converted part of the Great Rift from an arm of the ocean into a land-locked lake. (Most authorities consider this very unlikely.) But there is no argument over the fact that down through the centuries, the millennia, the millions of years, dramatic changes have occurred in the Valley, geologically as well as historically. It is relatively certain, also, that during the last million years the only water that flowed into the Rift came from the sky, from the drainage of the mountains, and from springs.

In the Pleistocene Period, when Europe and North America were having their ice ages, this area was being subjected to great rains, which created in the Valley an immense body of water called by geologists the Lisan Lake, about twelve miles wide by more than a hundred miles long, extending from the Tiberias region at least to the tongue of land that now extends from the east shore out into the Dead Sea near the south end. (One authority contends that it extended eighteen miles south of the present southern extremity of the Dead Sea.) If this lake still existed in its original size, it would rank as one of the larger lakes of the world.

There were many fluctuations in the size of Lisan Lake during the various pluvial and interpluvial periods. Some sources say its water level was at one time higher than the present level of the Mediterranean; others that it was always below sea level. But starting about a hundred thousand years ago the lake began to dry up, leaving two or three terraces which had been the shorelines of the lake at various times, and which can be seen today, high above the river level.

The simplest theory about the creation of the Jordan River is that as the waters subsided, the great lake, like an amoeba, procreated by the process of division: the one large lake became two smaller lakes, Tiberias and the Dead Sea, with the Jordan River connecting them. One exponent of this theory, Isaac Schattner of the Hebrew University department of geography, explains it in technical language thus:

"On the Rift Valley floor, laid bare by the recession of the lake, a central drainage channel (the Jordan River) began to establish itself, hierarchizing all the affluents of the former lakes, and the water courses developed on the Rift Valley floor."

Another theory is that the Jordan River is older than Lake Tiberias, which was formed later when the area to the south was subjected to a lifting that interrupted the flow of the river enough to form the lake.

And so how old is the Jordan? Certainly less than one hundred thousand years. Perhaps only twenty thousand. Maybe even as young as ten thousand. It is one of nature's very recent creations, in the eyes of geologists who think in terms of millions of years. And yet if one looks at it with the eyes of a historian and considers what it has seen in its brief life-span, it is a very, very old river.

In the days of its youth no one would have said of the Jordan that it was "an unpleasant, foul stream." Compared to the Jordan of today it was a mighty torrent, deep, dangerous and destructive. The water that came tumbling down from the mountains in the north tore its way through the Valley and slashed a channel for itself in the clay bed, wearing, eating away, sweeping aside anything and everything in its path, and often changing its circuitous course as it sought out spots of least resistance. It brought down from the mountains immense quantities of alluvium, which partly filled up the north ends of Lake Tiberias and the Dead Sea. It also delivered into the Dead Sea soluble salt from the rocks over which it flowed and chemicals it picked up from hot springs along its course, making the Dead Sea more and more saline in the course of thousands of years, as the Dead Sea water kept evaporating and the salts remained. (This theory is more generally accepted than the idea that the Dead Sea's minerals are oceanic, left over from the days when it was connected with the Red Sea or the Mediterranean.)

In modern times the Jordan often overflows and inundates the whole of the Zor, which accounts for the rich vegetation that lines its banks. The "badlands" appearance of the Ghor, with its strange, conical hills, more often resembling something out of a nightmare than anything in nature, is the result of the action of the rain and the wind, and the erosion of mountain streams that for thousands of years have eaten at the soft stone of the hills, changing their contour in a most weird manner.

For those who prefer fables to fact, there are many about the Jordan's creation. One explains the quantity of rocks:

When God made the world He gave one of His angels a sack full of stones, to be scattered evenly over the surface of the earth, but as the angel was flying over the Jordan Valley the sack burst open and all the stones fell on that one area alone. (The same story is told in Switzerland, Vermont and many other rocky or mountainous parts of the world, always with a local application, but it originated in the Jordan Valley centuries ago.)

The Jordan's youth was not dull. Something was always happening. Somewhere a volcano would unexpectedly erupt. Often there were earthquakes. Now and then, by some twist of geographical fancy, a new river would be formed and would try desperately to make liaison with the Jordan so it could join in the exciting trip to the south. Mountain sides would collapse, the debris blocking the river momentarily until a new channel could be found. New animals would develop. Old animals would change their shape, form, size, character. Not suddenly, of course, but gradually, over thousands of years.

In the Jordan's early days mammoth beasts roamed the Valley: elephants, hippopotamuses, rhinoceroses, and cave oxen. Some of their bones and teeth have been found lately in the Jordan area. From an ancient bed of the river, near the Bridge of the Daughters of Jacob, archaeologists in 1935–36 dug up an elephant's tusk six feet long and tools belonging to Paleolithic men who lived perhaps half a million years ago and who were making much greater developments than their contemporary European cousins.

One of the most provocative archaeological finds ever made in the Valley was the discovery in 1925 in a cave in Wadi Amud, near the western shore of Lake Tiberias of four skulls believed to be between fifty thousand and one hundred thousand years old. This primitive man was nicknamed Paleoanthropus Palestinensis. This link between Neanderthal man and Homo Sapiens apparently developed gradually, over many hundreds of thousands of years. Not only was there self-development—from beast, to manlike beast, to beastlike man, to man— but also it is believed that Paleoanthropus Palestinensis, over a long period of time, may have driven from the Valley some beastlike men more primitive than himself.

One of the questions archaeologists and geologists like to ask themselves is where Paleoanthropus Palestinensis came from. Did he, like the mammoth beasts of the jungle, arrive over an intercontinental land bridge, of which the Jordan Valley was an integral part? Some scientists think so. Evidence that has passed certain carbon tests indicates that he came, along with the beasts, from Africa and Asia, and then went on to Europe.

If, after coming here, Paleoanthropus Palestinensis drove the more primitive Neanderthal creatures out of the Jordan Valley, where did they go? A possible answer is suggested in the finding of seven Neanderthal skeletons in the Zegros Mountains, north of Baghdad, all estimated to be between fifty thousand and seventy-five thousand years old.

Some geologists and archaeologists speak of Paleoanthropus Palestinensis as "the first real man"; others call him "one of the oldest real humans." He was a hairy creature, with a receding forehead, huge eyes, protruding cheeks, small but very wide nose, almost no chin but a heavy jaw, and extremely strong teeth. He was heavily built. The calves of his legs were larger than his thighs. It is doubtful that he was able to walk in a perfectly perpendicular position. His brain was equal in size to that of modern man, which, of course, is not the same as saying that he had the intelligence of modern man. His brain was, however, well developed in matters of sight, touch, and control over the physical functions of the body, although the part of the brain dealing with pure thought and with speech was small. Paleoanthropus Palestinensis was right-handed. This is known because the left side of the brain, which serves the right side of the body, was larger than the other side. It took this Valley creature only a short time (geologically speaking) to become acquainted with the advantages and benefits of fire. He knew enough to take shelter when the elements were in a bad mood. He found ideal shelter in caves, but had to compete for them with animals. To drive the animals out of the caves and keep them out, he needed weapons, so, as his intellectual development down through the ages continued, he fashioned crude killing devices out of flint, basalt and bone. Thus, here in the Jordan Valley, military science may have been born as Paleoanthropus Palestinensis (or his lineal descendants) armed themselves against the beasts.

In addition to the flesh of the animals he killed with his crude weapons, he ate berries, fruit, bugs, watercress, fungi, the eggs of birds, grubs, insects and snails, as well as the flesh of fish he caught in the river with his bare hands.

Being a primitive man, he kept close to his water supply, which meant he never wandered far from the Jordan, its tributaries, or Lake Tiberias. On the banks of the Jordan he learned to dry and cure skins, and use them as protection against the weather, or to lie on them when the ground was damp.

Paleoanthropus Palestinensis slept in a reclining position, but never sat; instead he squatted. His favorite squatting place was just inside the entrance to his cave. He always stayed close to the opening, apparently fearing the dangers that might be lurking in the remote interior.

Gradually he learned to hunt big game in the jungle of the Jordan: elephants, rhinoceroses, hippopotamuses. To bag these goliaths he constructed traps, for it was impossible to kill such immense creatures with the small, crude weapons he had.

And so it began, the contest along the banks of the Jordan between man and beast—a curtain-raiser to what would gradually develop, as man developed, into the contest between human and human.

When and where did man learn to make the earth work for him? The experts are not yet in agreement. Some say not until the Neolithic Period (seventy-five hundred to four thousand years ago). Others say in the Mesolithic Period (between 12,000 and 7500 B.C.). Many have held, and some still hold, that the first agriculturalists in the Jordan Valley were the Natufians. They were direct descendants of Paleoanthropus Palestinensis, but were more like twentieth century men in appearance, having finer shaped heads and more delicate features. They were slim and short, averaging not much more than five feet in height. At first they obtained their food by hunting in the jungle on either side of the river, and by fishing, just as their ancestors had done. But then, somehow, they made one of the most revolutionary discoveries in the entire history of man: that a seed poked into the ground will grow, and that what it produces will sustain the body of man. And so—if the Natufian theory is correct—here in the Valley and in the hills beyond the science of agriculture may have been born.

Year by year, generation after generation, they kept improving the farming tools they had devised. They dug up the earth with flint plows and used stone sickles with bone handles to reap their grain, which they ground into flour in stone bowls with stone pestles. They built substantial houses on stone foundations and made good use of many varieties of domesticated animals. The Agricultural Revolution had begun. How vital this was in human history becomes apparent when one considers that today, two-thirds of the way through the twentieth century, there are nomads and even some village people living along the banks of the Jordan, who, almost untouched as yet by either the Industrial Revolution or the Nuclear Age, live not much differently than their Natufian ancestors did, tens of thousands of years ago. The last contribution of civilization to influence the pattern of their existence was the Natufians' development of an agricultural way of life.

These early Valley people improved their weapons, fashioned jewelry for their women, and used reeds to make baskets. Their desire for self-expression was so great that they became self-taught sculptors, and so, here in the Valley, the plastic arts may have had their birth.

The primitive life was over. A well-regulated sedentary society was being developed. For better or for worse—with all its advantages and all its drawbacks—civilization had been born, or was in the process of being born, on the banks of this new-old river. Such modern painters and sculptors as Picasso and Henry Moore owe much to those first Natufian artists who, with no precedent to guide them, taught themselves to paint and to sculpt. The roots of Frank Lloyd Wright and Le Corbusier are in the architecture of the Natufians who designed the first buildings in the world that were in any way comparable to the houses of modern man. Henry Wallace's hybrid corn is the natural outgrowth of what the Natufians so long ago learned about seed culture. In approximately 8000 B.C. in the Valley of the Jordan, or at least within sight of the Valley, the human explosion was set off. Man was now on his way.

Unless and until archaeologists find good evidence to the contrary, Jericho is generally accepted as being the oldest still-inhabited city in the world. Nelson Glueck has suggested that the story of civilization might well start with the words:

"And in the beginning there was Jericho."

Most archaeologists agree that history really begins in this place; that history is at home here. Some claim that here are "the earliest traces yet to be found of man as a civilized being."

Jericho is just six miles as the bird flies due west from the Jordan, on a height looking down into the Valley. It is seven miles on a straight line northwest from the Dead Sea and ten miles by road from the spot where the river flows into the great salt lake. Behind Jericho, rising abruptly, are the Mountains of Judaea. Jericho is favored by nature, being irrigated by water from one of the Jordan's minor tributaries, the Wadi Oelt, and it has another never-failing source in the fountain Ain es Sultan ("Source of the King").

Some trace the word Jericho back to a root meaning, "the fragrant place," but the more accepted version is that it comes from *Yare'ah* ("moon").

The story of Jericho commences, as far as we now know, in about the year 5000 B.C. Or perhaps 7000 B.C. Maybe as early as 8000 B.C. In those days Jericho may have been to the Valley what Rome became, a few millennia later, to the Roman Empire, or what Cairo eventually became to Egypt, or what Paris is today to France. However, there is a strong belief that the entire Valley in those days was already heavily populated; that Jericho may have had sister cities; that there were other towns of almost equal importance in other parts of the Valley; that while Jericho may have been the fountainhead of this new civilization, it was not an isolated city surrounded by barrenness. This belief continues to spur archaeologists in their hunt for those lost places.

At one time it was thought that the abundant springs of Jericho inspired primitive man with his first agricultural ideas and that here the earth was cultivated for the first time. Subsequent discoveries, however, have confirmed that at least one thousand, perhaps even two thousand, years earlier the Natufians down in the Valley had not only already learned about planting and harvesting but had developed a well-founded agricultural economy.

The early men of Jericho took the empiric knowledge of the Natufians and built on it, just as future generations again and again would build a new Jericho on top of the old Jericho. Rapidly they developed skills and craftsmanship of a high order. For example, they made flints called microliths, so delicately carved that they resemble thin razor blades. (What use they put them to is still one of the minor Jericho mysteries.)

With the architectural ability of the Natufians, plus their own rapidly developing knowledge of the basic principles of engineering, they built houses as tall as seven stories, which, even today in many rural Middle Eastern towns, would seem like mansions. Some of these houses had the luxury of interior staircases. The walls were painted red and then polished until they resembled the surface of a piece of fine mahogany furniture.

The Jerichoans, as well as other settlers in the Valley, at first worshiped the moon, which is one version of how the city obtained its name. They worshiped her for her rhythm, her power, and her beauty. They made sacrifices to her when troubles beset them and thank-offerings when nature seemed to bless them. This soon led to fertility rites, primitive but logical to people who were impressed by the phases of the moon, the recurring periods of fertility and sterility, and the rhythm of the seasons, all so well ordered and logical.

As the Jericho sculptors developed more talent and imagination, they modeled clay replicas of their domesticated animals, which were placed on altars as subtle hints to the moon-god to make their animals increase in number. Not so subtle was their use of phallic symbols when they prayed for an increase in their own fertility. From moon-worship the Jerichoans went on to ancestor-worship. As evidence, they left behind one of the most curious forms of sculpture man has ever devised. The skull of some venerable ancestor was used as a base. Then the sculptor molded the face just as the elders of the community said it had been in life, making the nose, the ears, the mouth, and even the eyelids as realistic as possible. Finally the eyeballs. Each eyeball was made of two small shells fitted together so that the slit between them gave the effect of an eye half closed in death. Then the sculptor would call in an artist and the plaster would be tinted to resemble the color of human flesh. If the deceased had had a mustache or beard, it would be painted on. The venerable ancestor now took on the rank of a household god and would be addressed frequently and fervidly in thanksgiving or supplication.

If the advancement of a race can be measured by its degree of civic and political organization, the people of Jericho were well on the road to maturity, for they left evidence that their city was well governed and their civic affairs well managed, even by twentieth century standards.

The Jordan could now be proud. Its Valley and its hills had begun to fulfill their destiny. They were already becoming what they would continue to be for the next six to eight thousand years, with only occasional slight interruptions: a breeding place of ideas.

One of the many mysteries of the Valley that still remains to be solved dates back to about this time, between 5500 and 4000 B.C., the Dolmen Riddle. A dolmen is a prehistoric monument, believed to have been a tomb. It was made of large flat stones called megaliths. The word "dolmen" is Celtic, derived from words meaning "rock table." Megalith comes from two Greek words meaning "great stone." The original dolmens—those in the Jordan Valley—date back more than five thousand years. The slabs of stone are often seven feet long, five feet wide and as thick as two feet. Each one weighs tons. One of these flat stones was first placed on the ground, as a floor, then three or four others were set up on end around it. Finally, one more immense stone was placed on top, as a roof. After the body of the deceased had been interred inside this crude tomb, the opening would be sealed up, and the entire dolmen covered with earth or sand. The mystery is: Who were the men who built thousands of these dolmens up and down the Valley, and even in some of the surrounding hills? They vanished without leaving a clue—except the crude tombs of their dead. Archaeologists admit almost complete ignorance of them. How did they quarry so many stones, all exactly the right length and width? How did they transport them from the quarries? How did they put them in place? They surely understood the principle of leverage, but how did they get the immense stone that was to serve as the roof so carefully and perfectly in place?

By 5000 B.C. an agricultural civilization had spread from the Valley of the Jordan itself up some of the river's chief tributaries, especially the Yarmuk, where a way of life developed that has been called the Yarmuk Culture: a settled community of people working the land; fertility rites; stone carvings; some pottery; polished cutting tools; domestication of animals.

Until now mankind had been in the various stages of the Stone Age: the Paleolithic, down to 12,000 B.C.; the Mesolithic, from 12,-000 to 7500 B.C.; the Neolithic, from 7500 to 4000 B.C. Now came the Chalcolithic or Copper Stone Age. In the Valley the next thousand years saw the development of more and more towns and villages, the erection of round as well as rectangular houses, the introduction of copper, and great progress in the use of ivory and stone by artists and artisans.

In the mounds at Tileilat-Ghassul, across the Jordan, northeast of the Dead Sea, archaeologists have found the remains of Chalcolithic farmhouses, in which one corner of the main room had a stone floor and was used as a kitchen. There were storage places for water, the courtyard was surrounded by sturdy barns, and the walls of the buildings were decorated with mural paintings that showed considerable artistic development. Small clay houses served for the burial of the dead.

The development of agriculture had one tragic by-product. In times of famine nomads would steal the produce of their farmer-cousins, who now made the discovery that the weapons they had fashioned for killing beasts of the jungle could be used against their fellow men, for the protection of their property. In the ruins of ancient Jericho evidence has been found that man may have been battling man as early as the Mesolithic Period. From now on the story of the Jordan would be at least partly written in blood. Men of the Valley, who heretofore had been fighting only nature and beasts, now began to fashion weapons primarily for use against each other. The exact date at which armies were first created and began engaging in what could be called war in the modern sense is uncertain. It is only history books that keep track of such matters, and as yet there were no books of any sort; writing had not even been thought of; nowhere in the world were there people who even had an alphabet. But already man was killing his own kind and defending himself against those who wished to kill him.

During the Copper Stone Age more and more Valley men, displaying a preference for a settled agricultural life rather than a nomadic existence, sought out the most fertile locations in the Jordan area. For this reason, as early as 4000 B.C., many settled in the well-watered, subtropical spot where the Valley of the Jezreel comes sweeping down from the northwest to join the Valley of the Jordan at a place that has since come to be called Beit-Shean, or Beth-Shan, or, in Arabic, Beisan, names that some scholars have translated as "the Temple of the Serpent God." The theory that snakes actually were worshiped by the early dwellers of this important Valley city is at least partially confirmed by the discovery of pottery entwined with serpents having human breasts, under which the sculptors placed bowls to catch the milk. The fertility of the Valley of Beth-Shan was so great, thanks to forty springs, that it came to be called "the Gateway to Paradise."

In many places far from the Jordan, the Early Bronze Age, from 3150 to 2200 B.C., was a period of spectacular development. In Egypt people who had at first worshiped wind and water, air and moisture, earth and sky, and who considered the baboon, the cat, the crocodile and the jackal as sacred animals, began talking to each other, and to future generations, on papyrus and in stone, in picture-writing called hieroglyphics. In the lower part of Mesopotamia, now Iraq, men with clean-shaven heads as well as clean-shaven faces, invented a system of writing called cuneiform ("wedge-shaped"). They scratched symbols to represent objects, with a wedge-shaped stylus, on tablets of soft clay, which later were dried in the sun or baked. It was at first only a modification of picture-writing, but it was the start of the conveyance of thought by some method other than gesturing and speaking.

This was an era in which man began communicating not only by writing but also by traveling. Isolation ended, as great roads were built over which people could move from country to country. The oldest of these international highways was called the Way of the Sea. It connected Egypt with the lands bordering on the Euphrates and the Tigris. One branch of the road traversed the Valley, crossing the Jordan a few miles south of Lake Tiberias. The other branch went to Damascus by way of Dan, thus avoiding the necessity of a Jordan crossing. Along this route, which for thousands of years would be of great value, both strategically and commercially, important cities sprang up, several of them in the Jordan area. Beth-Shan was one of the Valley cities that prospered because of the trade caravans that now came streaming by over the Way of the Sea. A second important international route, the Way of the Kings, also connecting Cairo and Babylon, ran parallel to the Jordan, but at some distance east of the river. During this era the men of the Valley established their first real contact with the people of Egypt, Mesopotamia, Anatolia, and even the island of Cyprus. In this manner they learned much from the outside world, and passed on, in exchange, all that they had discovered themselves about the mysterious world in which they lived. Travel was still ponderously slow, but isolation had ended.

Early in this Early Bronze Age the migrations that began over the international highways led to the arrival in the Valley of Semitic people who came to be called Canaanites. They had originated in the Arabian desert, and worked their way farther and farther north until they finally occupied all of what today includes Israel, Syria, Lebanon and Jordan. With the appearance of these foreigners, the argument now began over whose land this really was. Was it the exclusive property of the direct descendants of the Natufians? Or was it the sacred domain of only those who could prove direct descendancy from Paleoanthropus Palestinensis? The argument would go on for thousands of years and considerable blood would be shed, without any definitive settlement ever being reached. The Canaanites resembled the Egyptians in many ways.

They had learned something of Egyptian art and craftsmanship, but they wrote in cuneiform, as the Babylonians did.

The first extensive fortifications in the Valley were built in the Stone Copper Age. Man, having learned to kill, now had to worry about being killed, and so he was forced to build walls around his cities. The first city (as far as anyone now knows) that was really fortified was Jericho. At first the protection there consisted merely of stone facings put up against mounds of debris. Later perpendicular walls were built, and still later a fosse or moat was dug in front of the wall. Multiple walls came later. Now many places besides Jericho began fortifying themselves. The walls built around some of the Valley towns in this time measured as much as twenty-six feet thick. From now on, until man learned to fly over cities and rain destruction from the air onto people huddled inside their walls—for the next four thousand years or more— man would have to use his time and his ingenuity to convert all his major dwelling places into fortresses.

In this age, a short distance to the north of Lake Tiberias and just on the edge of the Valley, on a rectangular plateau, the foundations were laid for what would become one of the most important cities of the next many centuries, Hazor. About the same time, at the south end of the lake near where the Jordan flows out of Tiberias, Valley men built a city that came to be called Beth Yerah, "House of the Moon." Its grain silos were the largest that have been discovered anywhere in the Middle East, and the wall around the city was twenty-five feet thick. There is archaeological proof that the people who at first dwelt in Beth Yerah paid strict religious obeisance to the moon in gratitude for the fertility of their soil and the abundance of grain that often filled their silos, as immense as they were, to overflowing.

4

Abraham had the honor of being the first man with a name to cross the River Jordan. For thousands of years before his time, human beings had been living on the banks of the strange stream; many cities had been built near its shores; there had already been several migrations of importance up and down the Valley, or from one side of the river to the other. But history had been vague until now; the name of no individual had figured in the Jordan story until the arrival of Abraham.

Not everything is known, definitely, about Abraham that a biographer or even a historian would like to know, and there are those who pleasure themselves in casting doubt even on what is recorded. Some advance the claim that it is all a myth; that Abraham is the personification of a group of people; that there never existed such an individual. But here is the story, be it all fact, or all fable, or part of each:

About four thousand years ago (the exact date is uncertain) in the city of Ur, capital of the Chaldees at the mouth of the mighty Euphrates River, in what is now Iraq, a son, Abram, was born to Terah, a Babylonian or Chaldean chieftain of wealth who worshiped idols and whose name had some connection with the moon-god. Abram had a distinguished line of ancestors, being descended from Shem, the oldest son of Noah, who was one of the eight persons to survive the flood in his father's ark and who, two years later, at the age of one hundred, begat a child, and lived another five hundred years, which was in the family tradition, for his grandfather had been one hundred and eighty-two years old when Noah was born, and Noah, in turn, conceived his first child at the age of five hundred.

The father, Terah, for a reason nowhere explained, took his son Abram, and Abram's wife, Sarai, and Lot, the offspring of another of his sons, now deceased, and emigrated many miles up the Euphrates River to the city of Haran, an important commercial center surmounted by a temple to the moon-god Zin, in what is now Turkey. There Terah died at the age of two hundred and five. While the father was still alive Abram rejected the polytheistic religion in which he had been reared and smashed the idols that were so sacred to his elders. When he was seventy-five he was commanded by God to "Get thee out of thy country, and from thy kindred, and from thy father's house, unto a land I will shew thee." Obediently Abram packed up and set out, accompanied by his nephew, Lot, and his wife, Sarai. They took with them the family servants, their sizable flocks and herds, and tents in which to live along the way.

It took the writer of the Book of Genesis just sixteen words to get the emigrants from Haran to the Land of Canaan, about five hundred miles southwest. There the Lord appeared to Abram, saying: "Unto thy seed I give this land." The only description of the route is that they went "unto the place of Sichem, unto the plain of Moreh." The Plain of Moreh and the town of Sichem (also called Shechem in the Bible) are thirty-one miles north of Jerusalem, now in the Hashemite Kingdom of Jordan. Biblical scholars can only guess at the route they took from Haran down to Sichem. Some of the theoretical maps show the line of their itinerary going through Damascus and crossing the Jordan just a few miles north of the Sea of Chinnereth (as Lake Tiberias is most often called in the Old Testament). Others show the crossing between Chinnereth and the Salt Sea, the Old Testament name for the Dead Sea. The pity is that the writer of this biblical passage either had no words to spare for narrating the details of the trip, or perhaps was lacking information as to how they passed over the river—whether on a crude bridge, or by raft, or, if it was summertime, when the river was low, perhaps by wading. As this was the first important crossing in history, it would have been interesting to know.

What was this land like that Abram saw when he crossed over the Jordan? It was already an ancient place, for man had lived here already for thousands of years. There were sizable cities, more of them on the east side of the river because on that side there were more abundant sources of water. In whatever direction Abram looked he saw thriving and populous villages. There was already considerable uniformity about the houses, most of them built of stone.

Despite the advancement man had made already, in so many diverse ways, there was one practice in the time of the Patriarchs that by modern standards seems exceptionally primitive: child-sacrifice. It was Neolithic man who began the custom of killing his own kind in order to appease gods who he was sure were literally bloodthirsty whenever they visited adversities upon him. In those earlier days adults and children alike were slaughtered to win favor with the deities. In Abram's time, men in the Valley no longer killed adults, but it was still a custom to sacrifice the first-born child to assure the continued fertility of the mother, the fruitfulness of the fields, and the multiplication of the domesticated animals.

From Sichem and the Plain of Moreh, Abram and his company continued due south until they came to a mountain ridge from which they could see, to the west, the comparatively new town of Bethel, and to the east, in the immediate foreground, the town of Hai, and in the distance, across less than twenty miles of yellow-brown sand, the lush green of the Jordan Valley. On this ridge Abram erected an altar, but then he moved on, still traveling south, for the land was in the grip of a great drought. They went across the Negev to Egypt, where they prospered, thanks to a ruse. Abram's wife apparently was a woman of rare beauty. When several young Egyptian princes beheld her, soon after her arrival in the Egyptian capital, they promptly informed the Pharaoh, who was so impressed that he decided to add her to his harem. Abram in his astuteness had foreseen such a possibility. Before they even reached Egypt, he had said to Sarai: "Behold now, I know that thou art a fair woman to look upon: Therefore it shall come to pass, when the Egyptians shall see thee, that they shall say, This is his wife: and they will kill me, but they will save thee alive. Say, I pray thee, thou art my sister: that it may be well with me for thy sake; and my soul shall live because of thee."

Abram's lie was only half a lie, for Sarai, in addition to being his wife, actually was a half sister, being the daughter of Abram's father, although not of his mother.

The Pharaoh was so pleased with Sarai that he gave Abram a considerable number of sheep, oxen, asses, male and female servants, and even camels. To punish the Pharaoh, God inflicted a series of plagues on Egypt. Somehow the Egyptian ruler discovered the reason for these punishments and in order to obtain relief from them banished Abram and his entire company, but permitted them to take all the wealth they had accumulated in the form of herds, flocks, tents, and gold and silver. It must have been a formidable caravan that headed back north. Among the female servants was an Egyptian girl, Hagar, whom Sarai would one day give to Abram as a concubine. The entire story of Abram's trek from Haran to Canaan, then to Egypt, his experiences in the land of the Pharaohs, and his return to Canaan is told in twenty-two short sentences in Genesis. The account gives not even a rough estimate of how many animals they took back with them to Canaan, but the number must have been great, for soon after their arrival in the plain to the north of Jerusalem, violent argument broke out between the herdsmen of Lot's cattle and the herdsmen of Abram's cattle, because there was not enough pasturage in the region for all the animals.

Abram, obviously a man of gentle character, said to his nephew: "Let there be no strife, I pray thee, between me and thee, and between my herdsmen and thy herdsmen, for we are brethren.

"Is not the whole land before thee? Separate thyself, I pray thee, from me; if thou wilt take the left hand, then I will go to the right; or if thou depart to the right hand, then I will go to the left."

It was a gracious offer, the older and stronger giving the younger and weaker the chance to choose.

The two men apparently were standing on a great height, for the storyteller continues:

"And Lot lifted up his eyes and beheld all the plain of Jordan."

This is the first specific reference in the Bible to the Jordan or its Valley, for the crossing of the river on the way down from Haran is not described.

". . . and beheld all the plain of Jordan." The presumption is that they were somewhere in the vicinity of Bethel; probably on the ridge between Bethel and Hai where Abram had built the altar.

As Lot considered which way to go in search of pasturage for his cattle, he turned his face away from the Judaean hills toward the Jordan and its broad Valley, which he observed to be fertile, luxuriant, and "well watered everywhere . . . even as the garden of the Lord." On each side of the river lay a lush jungle, of considerable depth, and then back of the jungle a verdant plain. The "garden of the Lord" extended to the north as far as the eye could perceive, and to the south until it reached the Salt Sea. To the far north were the peaks of Galilee, and the lofty, snowy summit of Mount Hermon, and a dot of blue, which would be the Sea of Chinnereth. As Lot looked again to the south he could see, so close it almost seemed possible that a man could throw a stone down into it, a much larger body of water, the color of an emerald, with a setting of much darker green. Opulent cities lined the shore of this inland sea. It was a splendid panorama.

If Lot turned the other way, to the west, he could see the hills of Judaea, and in the far, far distance the Mediterranean, called the Great Sea. There might be good pasturage somewhere off to the west, but to the east, in the direction of the Jordan, there seemed to be everything that man could desire, and so . . .

"Then Lot chose him all the plain of Jordan; and Lot journeyed east: and they separated themselves the one from the other."

That might have been the end of the story, with both living happily ever after, for the Valley was indeed fertile and the rest of Canaan was extensive, with plenty of pasturage for the herds of Abram. Yet this was only the start of a tale involving considerable death and destruction, most of it taking place in the Jordan area.

In telling how Lot chose the Jordan Valley as his own personal domain, the biblical writer almost at once introduced the two most infamous names in the Old Testament, Sodom and Gomorrah. It is implied several times in the account of how Abram and Lot divided the land between them that these two cities were at the north end of the Salt Sea, perhaps even on the banks of the Jordan. "And Lot lifted up his eyes and beheld all the plain of Jordan that it was well watered everywhere, before the Lord destroyed Sodom and Gomorrah." Several verses later, after Lot has made his decision, the narrator says: "Abram dwelled in the land of Canaan and Lot dwelled in the Cities of the Plain and pitched his tent toward Sodom." The clear implication is that the Cities of the Plain, as they have always been called —Sodom, Gomorrah, Admah, Zeboiim, and Bela or Zoar—were within Lot's immediate vision and therefore must have been at the north end of the sea.

Wherever Sodom and the other Cities of the Plain were located, they were already condemned, for the narrative at this point says that "the men of Sodom were wicked and sinners before the Lord exceedingly."

After Lot left, God appeared before Abram and said:

"Lift up thine eyes and look from the place where thou art, northward, and southward, and eastward, and westward: for all the land which thou seest, to thee I give it, and to thy seed for ever. I will make thy seed as the dust of the earth: so that if a man can number the dust of the earth, then shall thy seed also be numbered. Arise, walk through the land in the length of it and in the breadth of it; for I will give it unto thee."

Abram thereupon moved his tent to the plains of Mamre, on the edge of Hebron, twenty miles south-southwest of Jerusalem and only about seventeen miles due west from the Salt Sea. Hebron was the highest place in the entire region; later, when Palestine became a geographical entity, it was the highest town in all Palestine. To reach Hebron from Ein Gedi or any other spot on the Salt Sea meant hours of torturous travel through the Wilderness of Judaea. (After the Armistice Agreements of 1949 between the Arab countries and Israel, Hebron became part of the Kingdom of Jordan.)

The exact date of the migration of Abram, Lot and Sarai from Haran to Canaan, then to Egypt, and back to Canaan is uncertain. In geological periods dates are understood to be plus or minus a few thousand or even in some cases a few million years. Beginning with the Christian Era, dates may be off no more than a year or two. But in the time of the Patriarchs, the discrepancies can be hundreds of years. There is even disagreement over what centuries to include in the Middle Bronze Age, the historical-archaeological period during which the Patriarchs lived. Some authorities fix the Middle Bronze Age as 2200 B.C. down to 1500 B.C. Others make the dates earlier or later. The birth of Abram is variously figured to have been about 2000 B.C., or about 1800 B.C., or by one authority even as late as 1400 B.C. (The Carbon-14 method of computing the age of organic matter is reliable only for matter more than five thousand years old. It is therefore of little value in determining biblical chronology.)

Abram, Lot and Sarai were not the only voyagers during their time. Throughout the Middle Bronze Age people were on the move all over the Middle East. Amorites, who dwelt in the hill country on both sides of the Jordan; Horites, who had once been cliff dwellers; Hittites from the north, and many smaller groups of people were in constant migration, seeking more favorable dwelling places. This was also the age in which kings developed the science of military conquest. Some of the migrants, bent on simple resettlement, and others interested in bloody adventures, streamed through the Jordan Valley, or used the international highways to the east of the Jordan, or those near the Mediterranean coast.

In those days Egypt was at the height of her imperial power. King Menes, founder of the First Dynasty, had united the separate kingdoms of Upper Egypt and Lower Egypt, creating an Egyptian nation, with its capital first at Memphis, later at Thebes. A national government had been founded, and writing was being practiced by more and more people. By applying their newly acquired knowledge of mathematics and by requiring all able-bodied men to give several months of labor a year, the Egyptians had built twenty major pyramids, one of them (at Gizeh) containing more than two million blocks of stone, each weighing an average of two and a half tons. But the Age of the Pyramids was soon succeeded by a period of political and social chaos, during which rival families for a hundred and fifty years competed for power. This was a time in Egypt of civil war and a great decline in trade, but it resulted in a revolution in principles and values, with justice for the first time becoming more important than property. Now, in Egypt, those who could prove that they had led lives of virtue might be declared gods and live forever in a place of eternal reward. By this time the Egyptians had perfected ways of preserving or mummifying the human body, the method involving the use of bitumen, that natural petroleum material so plentiful in the Dead Sea area. Because there were no closed frontiers in those days, a constant migration took place between the Jordan Valley and Egypt. Abstract ideas as well as practical knowledge flowed back and forth, but the secret of mummifying was never learned by men of the Valley, although in 1964 a skeleton coated with black asphalt was found during the excavating of Sa'id-Iyeh in the Jordan Valley, indicating, the archaeologists said, a crude Jordanian attempt in the Middle Bronze Age to make a mummy in the Egyptian manner.

Another indication of the contact between the river people and the Egyptians is in Execration Texts dating back to this time that have been found in the ruins of several Valley cities. Execration Texts were a Pharaonic attempt at political witchcraft; a primitive form of psychological warfare. The names of Egypt's enemies, potential enemies, or imagined enemies were inscribed on ceramic bowls or vases, along with an execration or curse expressing utter abhorrence, loathing, and detestation of the person or the place. Any individual thus named or the inhabitants of any cities listed in an Execration Text were considered untouchables. Later the Egyptians improved their system of execrations by carving the words on small statues of men with their hands and feet bound together, the figurines representing enemy soldiers who had been taken prisoner. The Egyptians believed that if such a figurine or bowl was smashed, the malediction would become effective. It is possible that merely carving on the bowls or figurines a list of the cities that had been marked down for destruction in the event of hostilities may have been enough to keep the rulers of such places if not friendly, at least subservient and in awe of the power of the Pharaoh. Execration Texts have always been a delight to archaeologists, for after the pieces of the bowl or figurine have been patched together, they provide a wealth of precise historical information.

In the time of Abram there was a great difference between the people in the Valley and those dwelling in the hills and mountains only a short distance from the Jordan. It was like the difference between relatively primitive people in the remote mountain areas of such regions as the Balkans or southern Italy, and the inhabitants of modern Rome, Milan or Vienna. Through the Valley ran roads that led eventually to Thebes, Damascus, Babylon and the other centers of civilization, so foreigners came and went. In the Valley a relatively high materialistic and cultural level had already been reached, while in the hills and mountains life was simple and advancement was slow.

In these times the fortifications of Valley cities underwent a revolution. Now perfectly vertical stone walls were built, strengthened at frequent intervals by towers from which invaders could be either speared or scalded. The gates of the cities were always shut and barred at night.

The Cities of the Plain must have been rich and tempting in those days, for the first time the word "war" is used in the Bible is in a passage telling the story of four kings from Mesopotamia (the ancient name for parts of modern Syria and Iraq) who came down from the northeast to attack the Cities of the Plain. No details of this military operation are given. There is no estimate of the size of the invading armies; nothing about the sort of weapons they had; no explanation of how long the battle lasted. We are not told whether the invaders came down the east side of the Jordan, or crossed the river somewhere up north, in what is now Galilee, and came down the west side. All must be conjecture, except that we are given the names of the four invading kings, what part of Mesopotamia three of them were from, and we are told they "made war" on the kings of the five Plain Cities, and won. For the next twelve years the kings of Sodom, Gomorrah, Admah, Zeboiim and Bela were required to serve Chedorlaomer, who apparently was the leader of the invading coalition. But finally, in the thirteenth year, the kings of the Plain Cities and their subjects rebelled against their absentee rulers, and either killed or expelled the officials Chedorlaomer had put over them. This act of defiance was used as a pretext for the first major military operation in history—at least in this part of the world. Considerable time must have been spent in preparing for the invasion, since it was not until "the fourteenth year" that the four kings, led by Chedorlaomer, came sweeping down from the northeast again. This time they followed the Way of the Kings, the highway far to the east of the Jordan. It was a punitive expedition that left every village along the line of march in ruins. Archaeologist Glueck, who has dug up tangible evidence of the destruction, calls it "an orgy of annihilation"—strong words to come from a scientist. The countryside was converted into a wasteland, which for centuries thereafter continued to resemble an abandoned graveyard strewn with shattered monuments. The biblical account lists only a few of the many cities, towns and villages that were pillaged, and only a few of the tribes that were wiped out or led off into captivity: the Rephaim, the Zuzim, the Emim, the Horites, the Amalekites, and the Amorites. The writers of Genesis used the word "smote" for what the invaders did to all these people. Archaeological evidence leads to the assumption that "smote" meant virtual obliteration. There are indications that the invaders may have penetrated as far south as the Gulf of Aqaba on the Red Sea, before turning north again. Everywhere they went they conquered, pillaged, looted. They achieved impressive military victories over any people foolish enough to try to resist them. It was a conquest such as that part of the world had never seen before, yet it set a pattern for the future. It would not be the last "orgy of annihilation." Finally the victorious forces approached the Plain Cities from the south and the kings of Sodom, Gomorrah, Admah, Zeboiim and Bela went out with their armies to meet them. The battle took place in the Vale of Siddim. This valley has never been positively located, but it is thought to have been a fertile region just to the south of the Dead Sea. The Bible says it was "full of slime pits," which is the biblical way of describing beds of bitumen or asphalt. These black, sticky deposits played a strange part in the dénouement. The battle apparently went badly from the start, for the defending forces. The attackers were flush with their months of victories along the way. They had raided and ravaged with fury, living well off their booty. Now they were goaded by their leaders into inflicting upon these five rebellious cities a defeat that would not be forgotten. The defenders were already losing the battle when the kings of Sodom and Gomorrah decided to flee. As they did, they apparently slipped and fell into one of the beds of bitumen. The accident was not fatal—at least not for the king of Sodom, because he appears in a later chapter of the story —but humiliation must have been added to defeat. After the people of the Plain Cities who had not been taken prisoner had fled to the mountains, the invaders plundered all five cities, looting everything of value, especially food supplies. As they left for home they took with them an impressive quantity of booty and a number of captives, including women. Lot, nephew of Abram, was their prize prisoner. By now he must have become a wealthy man, for the narrative specifically mentions that all of his possessions were seized.

One man escaped from the catastrophe of Sodom and made his way to Mamre, where he informed Lot's uncle of what had happened.

Abram had three hundred and eighteen "trained servants, born in his own house." Some biblical authorities think that "servants" is an improper translation; that these men constituted a private army. Judging by their performance, they at least must have been extremely well trained in the use of the military weapons of the day. Abram armed them and they set out at once in pursuit of the Mesopotamians, who were moving northward through the Jordan Valley. Abram was accompanied by three Amorite brothers, Mamre, Eshcol and Aner, who are described as his friends and allies. Whether they also had small private armies is not clear.

The chase was long, the distance great. The fleeing invaders had a good head start, for Abram's informer, the man from Sodom, had had to make his way through the Judaean Wilderness to Mamre, near Hebron, and now the pursuers had to go east to the Salt Sea and then north through the Valley until they caught up with the men from Mesopotamia. A forced march was necessary. It was impossible for them to accept the hospitality that the Valley people must have tried to press upon them. Theirs was an errand of both rescue and revenge; there could be no tarrying.

Finally they caught up with the Mesopotamians at Dan, close to one of the sources of the Jordan.

The historian Josephus—probably out of his vivid imagination—supplies some details that are absent in the biblical account; he says Abram did not follow the Valley, but headed diagonally northeast, traveling with his men by way of Bethlehem, Salem, the plains of Sychar and the Esdraelon; that on the fourth day, from the heights of Napthali, Abram saw the armies he had been stalking, "carousing in careless security around the fountain of el Dan." Paraphrasing Josephus, a nineteenth century religious historian tells how a force of a mere 318 men pitted themselves against the armies of the four kings:

"Having made the necessary disposition for the attack, Abram waited for the veil of darkness; then, like an avalanche from the mountains, he rushes down upon the sleeping host. The panic is immediate and universal, the confusion inextricable, the rout wild and ruinous."

Lot, however, was not rescued that night. The Mesopotamians who had survived the surprise attack fled, with their booty and their prisoners, first to Damascus, and then beyond. After a chase of another fifty miles or more, the final battle took place at Nobah, to the northeast of Damascus.

"Slaughter"—defined by the dictionary as "the violent, ruthless or wanton destruction of life; carnage"—is used often by biblical writers, apparently with justification, in narrating the history of the Jordan Valley and the rest of the Promised Land, but the first time the word appears anywhere in the Bible is in the account of what Abram's men did at Nobah: "the slaughter of Chedorlaomer, and of the kings that were with him." It is uncertain whether this word is meant to describe merely the fate of the four kings, or of their followers as well, although Josephus' account would indicate that the slaughter was general.

There is no description of the return of Abram, Lot and the other liberated prisoners, but it must have been a triumphal journey. It ended at Salem, a city which scholars think stood on the spot where Jerusalem now is. To reach Salem they must have crossed the Jordan. It is possible they went from Damascus back to Dan and then followed the Valley for most of its length. They were met near Salem in the Valley of Shaveh by two kings, the king of Sodom, who had come north to welcome them, and Melchizedek, the king of Salem, who set out food and drink for them, and gave them God's blessing. In his speech of thanks and congratulations, he said: "Blessed be Abram of the most high God, possessor of heaven and earth."

An interesting colloquy then took place between the king of Sodom and Abram. The king remarked to the hero of the day: "Give me the persons, and take the goods to thyself."

Abram replied: "I have lift up mine hand unto the Lord, the most high God, the possessor of heaven and earth, that I will not take from a thread even to a shoelatchet, and that I will not take any thing that is thine, lest thou shouldest say, I have made Abram rich: save only that which the young men have eaten, and the portion of the men which went with me, Aner, Eshcol, and Mamre; let them take their portion."

Presumably they then all went their separate ways. Abram and those of his three hundred and eighteen followers who had escaped death in the fighting went back home to Mamre. The others returned to Sodom.

The next chapter of Abram's story has no direct connection with the Jordan: his wife Sarai, embarrassed over her failure to bear him a child, suggested that he take as a concubine her Egyptian servant Hagar, which he did, and Hagar bore him a child, Ishmael, when he was eighty-six years old.

When Abram was ninety-nine, God appeared and made a covenant with him, which included the promise that he should have all of Canaan as an "everlasting possession" for himself and his people; that his name should henceforth be Abraham, meaning "father of many nations"; that Sarai should henceforth be called Sarah, meaning "princess"; and that despite her advanced age she should bear him a child.

One day Abraham, sitting in the entrance of his tent, saw three strangers approaching. Sensing that they were representatives of the Lord, he rushed to meet them, showed them a place to rest under a tree, gave them water to wash their feet, had Sarah bake cakes for them out of the finest flour, and served them with butter and milk, and with the meat of a freshly slaughtered calf. During the course of their visit, the Lord, speaking to Abraham through the mouths of the strangers, said:

"Because the cry of Sodom and Gomorrah is great, and because their sin is very grievous; I will go down now, and see whether they have done altogether according to the cry of it, which is come unto me; and if not, I will know."

The three strangers then departed in the direction of the Jordan and the Cities of the Plain. Abraham, greatly distressed by the implication of what might be done to Sodom, where his nephew Lot and Lot's family dwelt, then conducted an amazing conversation with the Lord, during which he bargained for the lives of the people of Sodom, saying:

"Wilt thou also destroy the righteous with the wicked? Peradventure there be fifty righteous within the city: wilt thou also destroy and not spare the place for the fifty righteous that are therein? . . . And the Lord said, If I find in Sodom fifty righteous within the city, then I will spare all the place for their sakes.

"And Abraham answered and said . . . Peradventure there shall lack five of the fifty righteous: wilt thou destroy all the city for lack of five? And he said, If I find there forty and five I will not destroy it.

"And he spake unto him yet again, and said, Peradventure there shall be forty found there. And he said, I will not do it for forty's sake.

"And he said unto him, Oh let not the Lord be angry, and I will speak: Peradventure there shall be thirty found there. And he said, I will not do it, if I find thirty there.

"And he said, Behold now, I have taken upon me to speak unto the Lord: Peradventure there shall be twenty found there. And he said, I will not destroy it for twenty's sake.

"And he said, Oh let not the Lord be angry, and I will speak yet but this once: Peradventure ten shall be found there. And he said, I will not destroy it for ten's sake."

Abraham apparently was convinced that he had saved Sodom, for surely there were at least ten righteous people in the city.

The biblical account continues with two angels arriving at Sodom, in the guise of weary voyagers. Lot, sitting at the city gate, saw them and offered them hospitality, just as his uncle had done with the strangers who had visited him. Lot suggested that they wash their feet, spend the night in his home, and then go on their way in the morning. He prepared an elaborate dinner for them, but before they had a chance to retire for the night, a large crowd of men of all ages from every quarter of the city, having heard that Lot had two strange young men as guests, encircled his house and demanded that Lot make the pair available to them. To protect his guests, Lot offered the lustful mob his two daughters, declaring that they were virgins, and saying, " . . . let me, I pray you, bring them out unto you, and do ye to them as is good in your eyes: only unto these men do nothing; for therefore came they under the shadow of my roof."

The men of the mob rejected the offer and were behaving menacingly when the two angels pulled Lot into the house and then caused the men who were threatening to break down the door to be afflicted with blindness. That ended the threat, but the visitors then turned to Lot and declared that God had sent them to destroy Sodom; that Lot should quickly gather together his daughters, his sons, his sons-in-law, and anyone else he particularly cared for, and flee from the city. When Lot discussed the matter with his sons-in-law they expressed disbelief and refused to leave, so the next morning, Lot, his wife, and his two daughters, guided by the angels, fled from Sodom without the two young husbands. As the angels were taking their leave of Lot they said: "Escape for thy life; look not behind thee, neither stay thou in all the plain; escape to the mountain, lest thou be consumed."

But Lot tried to bargain with them, declaring that if he went to the mountains, surely some evil would overtake him and he would die. Therefore, he asked, would it not be all right for him to stay in the Jordan Plain if he went to a certain small city he knew.

"Behold now, this city is near to flee unto, and it is a little one: Oh, let me escape thither, (is it not a little one?) and my soul shall live."

The Lord replied through the mouths of the two angels that He would accept the compromise and would not destroy this particular small city.

"Haste thee, escape thither; for I cannot do any thing till thou be come thither."

Thereafter, according to the Bible, the name of the little city, which had heretofore been called Bela, was known as Zoar, a Hebrew word suggesting smallness.

By the time Lot and his family reached Zoar it was already sunrise. It apparently had taken them most of the night to get there.

The biblical chronicler tells the story of the destruction of Sodom and Gomorrah and the other Cities of the Plain with great economy of language; in a mere forty-one words:

"Then the Lord rained upon Sodom and upon Gomorrah brimstone and fire from the Lord out of heaven; and he overthrew those cities, and all the plain, and all the inhabitants of the cities, and that which grew upon the ground."

The strange death of Mrs. Lot is narrated in even fewer words:

"But his wife looked back from behind him, and she became a pillar of salt."

(At the south end of the sea there are today many columns or cliffs of salt, which, from a distance, resemble human figures.)

Meanwhile, many miles away, in the hills of Canaan, Abraham arose early that day and as he looked in the direction of the Plain of Jordan saw the smoke from the fires that were consuming the cities of wickedness.

Lot, now a widower, dwelt for a time in Zoar but then, fearing that this city might also be destroyed, went with his two daughters into the mountains and lived with them in a cave, from which they apparently were able to look down onto the ruins of the destroyed cities. One of the strangest episodes in the Bible follows:

One day the elder of Lot's two daughters said to her sister:

"Our father is old, and there is not a man in the earth to come in unto us after the manner of all the earth: come, let us make our father drink wine, and we will lie with him, that we may preserve seed of our father."

The daughters, looking down at the ruins, may actually have believed that their father was the last male alive, although they should have been aware that Zoar was still undestroyed and presumably still inhabited.

"And they made their father drink wine that night: and the firstborn went in, and lay with her father; and he perceived not when she lay down, nor when she arose.

"And it came to pass on the morrow, that the firstborn said unto the younger, Behold, I lay yesternight with my father: let us make him drink wine this night also; and go thou in, and lie with him, that we may preserve seed of our father.

"And they made their father drink wine that night also: and the younger arose, and lay with him; and he perceived not when she lay down, nor when she arose.

"Thus were both the daughters of Lot with child by their father."

Archaeological investigations in recent years have disclosed that about 2000 B.C. there was a great catastrophe of some sort that emptied the Jordan Valley and the Salt Sea area for hundreds of years. The general supposition is that it was an earthquake, which destroyed cities, towns and villages, killing off a large part of the population, and causing whatever survivors there were to flee from that region. The earthquake is believed to have been accompanied by the release of gaseous deposits which exploded and set off tremendous fires that swept through the Cities of the Plain. The presence there of so much inflammable material—bitumen—is thought to have aggravated the catastrophe, for it fed the fires that swept through the doomed cities. Those who attempt to reconcile biblical narration and scientific discovery advance the idea that the earthquake—if it was an earthquake that caused the destruction—was God's instrument for inflicting punishment on the Cities of the Plain.

Biblically, the Cities of the Plain—and Sodom in particular—became a symbol of brazen sin. One biblical author after another pointed to the destruction as a warning that when God obtained proof of man's vileness, He acted in wrath, yet with mercy. Amos, Isaiah, Jeremiah, Ezekiel and Zephaniah all dwelt on the fate of the wicked cities. There are forty-eight references to Sodom, in eight books of the Old Testament and six books of the New Testament. There are twenty-four references to Gomorrah.

Centuries later Moses used the destruction of Sodom, Gomorrah, Admah and Zeboiim as an example of the anger and wrath of the Lord, describing the whole area as a place of "brimstone, and salt, and burning, that it is not sown, nor beareth, nor any grass groweth therein."

The catastrophe in the Salt Sea area apparently had a disastrous effect on the Jordan Valley, for historians have noted that from about 2000 B.C. until about 1400 B.C. the entire area was in a state of decline. The total population greatly decreased, cities shrank in size, and some smaller places vanished entirely.

The year after the Cities of the Plain were destroyed Sarah gave birth to a child whom they named Isaac, from the Hebrew word for "one laughs," because Abraham, when he was first informed that he would conceive a child at the age of ninety-nine "fell upon his face and laughed," and his wife, who was ninety-one when she bore the child, also found the situation so amusing that she said: "God hath made me to laugh, so that all that hear will laugh with me."

Although Abraham made his home until his death in the Beersheba area, Sarah died (at the age of one hundred and twenty-seven) in or near Hebron, and there Abraham had her buried, within sight of the Jordan Valley.

The most severe test of Abraham's life came when he was commanded by a divine message to take Isaac into the land of Moriah and there, on a certain mountain top, build an altar and sacrifice his beloved son as a burnt offering. The spot selected by God is shown on no map and experts have never agreed on exactly where it was. The only clue is that it took Abraham, Isaac, two companions, and an ass loaded with wood for the sacrificial fire three days to reach the place. Some historians theorize that it was one of the hills on which Jerusalem was later built; others say the mountain must have been Gerizim, which overshadows the modern city of Nablus, two miles northwest of ancient Shechem. In either case the incident took place on a mountain from which the Jordan Valley could be seen. Few stories in the Bible are told with such fine restraint yet so vividly as the account of how Abraham tried to obey the command to kill his own son.

"And Abraham said unto his young men, Abide ye here with the ass; and I and the lad will go yonder and worship, and come again to you." (The word "lad" is the only clue to Isaac's age at the time.)

"And Abraham took the wood of the burnt offering, and laid it upon Isaac his son; and he took the fire in his hand, and a knife; and they went both of them together.

"And Isaac spake unto Abraham his father, and said, My father: and he said, Here am I, my son. And he said, Behold the fire and the wood: but where is the lamb for a burnt offering?

"And Abraham said, My son, God will provide himself a lamb for a burnt offering: so they went both of them together.

"And they came to the place which God had told him of; and Abraham built an altar there, and laid the wood in order, and bound Isaac his son, and laid him on the altar upon the wood.

"And Abraham stretched forth his hand, and took the knife to slay his son.

"And the angel of the Lord called unto him out of heaven, and said, Abraham, Abraham: and he said, Here am I.

"And he said, Lay not thine hand upon the lad, neither do thou any thing unto him: for now I know that thou fearest God, seeing thou hast not withheld thy son, thine only son from me.

"And Abraham lifted up his eyes, and looked, and behold behind him a ram caught in a thicket by his horns: and Abraham went and took the ram, and offered him up for a burnt offering in the stead of his son."

The Jordan comes into the patriarchal story again when Abraham, some years later, sent his eldest servant across the river and up to Haran, the city of his brother, Nahor, in Mesopotamia, to find a wife for Isaac, out of his insistence that his son marry one of his own kindred, rather than a Canaanite, in order to found a race which, he had been promised, would soon become as numerous as the stars in the heavens or the grains of sand on the seashore. The servant crossed the river twice, once on the way up to Haran at the head of a caravan of ten camels, and again some days later, when he returned to Canaan with Rebekah, the daughter of one of Abraham's nephews, riding on the lead camel, followed by "her damsels" on the other camels. Rebekah had been chosen because she had passed a strange test the servant had devised, in his eagerness to find a perfect wife for Isaac. He stationed himself outside the city walls of Haran near a well just at the evening hour when the women were coming to draw water, determined to select the first girl who, when he asked her for a drink from her pitcher, not only gave him water but volunteered to draw water for his camels, too. The exact route the servant took up to Haran and back is not specified, but it is possible that he traveled the length of the Jordan Valley both going and coming.

Abraham is described as now being "old, and well stricken in age," for he was long past a hundred, but he took himself another wife, Keturah, and by her conceived six more sons. The children he had by Keturah and various other concubines he sent "eastward, unto the east country," and so they crossed over the Jordan and in many cases founded new families or tribes, such as the Midianites, founded by one of the six sons of Abraham by Keturah.

Because there is such uncertainty about Abraham's dates, it is a matter of speculation how old he was when the Hyksos invasion and occupation of Egypt took place. Strangely enough, the word Hyksos appears nowhere in the Bible, although it describes a group that dominated Middle Eastern history for more than a hundred and fifty years and brought about a revolution in the manner of waging war.

Hyksos is an Egyptian word, sometimes translated "rulers of foreign lands"; sometimes more simply, "foreign kings"; sometimes more pejoratively, "robber shepherds." But none of these translations helps to identify them. It is certain they were Asiatics and many historians have assumed they were a Semitic group, although a number of Hyksos scarabs bearing non-Semitic names have been found.

In this period—early in the Second Millennium—there were adventurers and soldiers of fortune by the thousands roaming the Middle East. When they could, they sold their services to kings and princes who were in need of military manpower, or, failing such employment, they often banded together and raided defenseless towns. It is possible that the Hyksos force included some men of this stamp, gathered together from many regions and with a wide variety of backgrounds. What is known for certain is that sometime about 1720 B.C. a well-organized army from the northeast swept down through Canaan en route for Egypt. At some point the invaders crossed the Jordan, probably in the far north. The main body of troops then headed for the Mediterranean and invaded Egypt by way of the coastal highway, but there is evidence that at least some of the invasion force went down through the Valley. These foreigners brought with them a superior military technique as well as a superior culture. Not only did the soldiers wear suits of heavy armor and carry weapons the like of which had not been seen in the Valley before, but many of them rode in chariots driven by horses. By now throughout most of the inhabited world, the waging of war was part of the accepted way of life, but the Hyksos army revolutionized the science of killing as dramatically and as definitely as the airplane and the atom bomb would, thousands of years hence. This was the start of mechanized warfare. From now on at least part of most armies would ride instead of walk into battle. The chariots invented by the Hyksos would undergo continual improvement until they would finally become mechanical monsters called tanks.

Memphis fell quickly to the invaders and before long all of Egypt for the first time in her history was under foreign rule. The occupation lasted for a full century and a half. The powerful Hyksos empire eventually extended from the Euphrates in Mesopotamia all the way to the upper reaches of the Nile, including the entirety of Syria and Palestine.

The Valley especially felt the Hyksos influence. This was an era of widespread prosperity, with a constant flow of wealth in various forms back and forth between Africa and Asia, much of it being transported through the Valley or at least across the Jordan. During this period luxury goods began to appear in the Valley, imported from Egypt.

The Hyksos were the first to provide burial grounds outside the confines of a town, thus separating the dead from the living and perhaps supplying the inspiration for the "clean and unclean" laws the Israelites would adopt, much later.

As fast as they conquered an important city, the Hyksos would secure it against loss by building an enlarged fortification, always rectangular, always massive, and always of beaten earth, known to archaeologists and historians by the French term, *terre pisée*. One of the largest of such new-style fortifications was at the northern end of the Valley, protecting the city of Hazor. Another was at Shechem.

When the Egyptians finally grew strong enough to repossess their own land from the foreigners, they drove the Hyksos back across Sinai and then farther and farther north, through Canaan. The Valley was the scene of some of the battles. One lasted for three years.

Many Hyksos refugees who had lost their homes in their enforced flight from Egypt settled permanently in the Valley, adding another element to what was already a considerable mélange.

While the Hyksos were still dominant in the Middle East, Rebekah, wife of Isaac, after twenty years of barrenness, gave birth to twins. The first to be delivered was called Esau. His brother was born clutching Esau's heel, and so was named Jacob, from the Hebrew word for "he clutches." Almost a quarter of the Book of Genesis is devoted to the story of the twins, who were to be the seed of the nation to which God had promised the land. Much of the action took place in or near the Valley.

Esau, the elder, whose hands, arms and body were covered with hair almost as thick as an animal's, became a cunning hunter and, accordingly, the favorite of his father, because Isaac had a great liking for venison meat. Jacob was "a plain man, dwelling in tents," but he became his mother's favorite. The conflict between the brothers began when Esau, coming home one day from the fields, weak from hunger, and seeing his younger brother stirring a pot of red lentil soup, asked him to share the food with him. Jacob refused, unless Esau would agree to trade all his rights as the elder son for some of the soup. Esau, in agreeing, replied, "Behold, I am at the point to die: and what profit shall this birthright do to me?"

The first-born son in those days normally inherited twice as much of the paternal estate as all the other children together. As well as this legacy, the heir acquired a special social and religious position in the community as the prospective head of a family, which was symbolized by his receiving the blessing of the father. To obtain this blessing, Jacob, with his mother's assistance, played a trick on his almost blind father. Isaac, wanting to taste his favorite dish before he died, called his son Esau and asked him to go hunting and bring back some "savory meat." As soon as Esau departed, Rebekah, the mother, having overheard, told her favorite son Jacob to bring her, quickly, two young goats. After she had cooked them in the manner that she knew would please her husband, she covered Jacob's hands and neck with the skins of the goats, so he would appear as hairy to the touch as Esau, and gave him the "savory dish" to take to Isaac. When Jacob announced that he was Esau and that he had brought the meat his father had ordered, Isaac, suspicious, insisted on feeling his son's hands. When he found them hairy, he said in perplexity, "The voice is Jacob's voice, but the hands are the hands of Esau." But then, at Jacob's request, he gave him his blessing, saying:

"Therefore God give thee of the dew of heaven, and the fatness of the earth, and plenty of corn and wine:

"Let people serve thee, and nations bow down to thee: be lord over thy brethren, and let thy mother's sons bow down to thee: cursed be every one that curseth thee, and blessed be he that blesseth thee."

Thus Jacob became the inheritor of not only God's promise to Abraham and Isaac, but also all the rich land of Canaan, whereas Esau would receive the much less fertile region that some day would come to be known as Edom, a rugged, mountainous land in the great depression lying between the Salt Sea and the Red Sea.

When Esau finally returned with venison meat and learned of the trick, he swore eternal hatred of his younger brother, declaring that he would kill him the moment an opportunity presented itself. His words were repeated to the mother, who persuaded her husband that Jacob should be sent to her own home city of Haran in Mesopotamia to seek a wife.

With Isaac's blessing, Jacob set out from Beersheba, covering some sixty miles the first day, probably by fast camel. He spent that night on a ridge in the hill country, on the edge of the Jordan Valley, close to where his grandfather Abraham had built the altar to God. As he slept he had a vision of a ladder stretching between the earth and heaven, with angels traveling back and forth in a constant two-way procession.

Then, from above, he heard the voice of the Lord confirming to him the promise given to Abraham, and assuring him of divine protection. In the morning Jacob commemorated the dream by taking a stone he had used as a pillow and setting it up as a pillar, then pouring oil over it.

The biblical story jumps from Bethel to Haran, Jacob apparently having had no other noteworthy adventures as he crossed over the Jordan and continued on to the northeast.

The Jordan area appears again in the story twenty years later. During all that time in Haran, Jacob had worked for an uncle, Laban, his mother's brother, had married two of Laban's daughters and had conceived by them and their women servants eleven sons and at least one daughter. When the uncle broke an agreement whereby Jacob was to have received all the animals impure in color, Jacob took his two wives, his many children, and the animals he claimed as his own, and set out for Canaan. He went down the east side of the Jordan, through an area known as Gilead, which had often served as a refuge for fugitives. One of the wives, Rachel, brought along the teraphim, or household gods of her father. The law in that day provided that the possession of such idols by a woman's husband assured him the right to inherit the father-in-law's property. It may have been Laban's distress over the disappearance of the household idols, or the loss of his animals, or his desire to see his daughters and grandchildren again, but whatever it was that motivated him, when he returned home from days of sheep-shearing and was informed of the flight, he set out in fast pursuit. In seven days he covered four hundred miles and caught up with the fugitives on a mountain in Gilead that has never been located definitely by biblical scholars, but is thought to have been some distance north of the Jabbok River, one of the Jordan's chief tributaries, flowing in from the east between Lake Tiberias and the Dead Sea.

Confronting Jacob, the father-in-law told him that if he, Jacob, had only given him the chance, he would have sent him on his way "with mirth, and with songs, with tabret, and with harp." The older man also complained that he had not been given a chance to kiss his daughters and grandchildren good-bye. But most especially, he seemed to be worrying about his idols.

Jacob, not knowing of Rachel's theft, invited his father-in-law to search all their tents. This Laban promptly did, but Rachel had hidden the idols in the saddle of the camel she had been riding and thus outwitted her father. Finally Laban and his son-in-law made a pact, with the father-in-law dictating the terms: his daughters were not to be ill-treated; Jacob was not to take another wife, and a demarcation line was to be drawn over which neither would ever cross. A pillar was erected to commemorate the covenant, and God was called upon to punish whichever party might break the agreement. Then a sacrifice was made, and both men sat down to a hearty meal as a sign of their goodwill toward each other.

After this meeting, Laban returned to his home on the Euphrates, while Jacob took his wives, his children, his camels, and his other animals and headed south, still on the east side of the Jordan. After a short time they were met by an escort of angels, but despite this symbol of divine support, Jacob was possessed of a great fear. Even after all these twenty years, his brother's vow still rang in his ears, troubled his sleep, tormented his soul. The nearer he came to the River Jabbok the more nervous he became. The voice of his conscience kept repeating the accusation that he had robbed his brother and had played his own father false. And Esau had sworn vengeance. Could Esau forgive? Had time cooled his brother's wrath? In his anxiety to find out what the prospects were for a reconciliation, he sent scouts ahead to the mountains of Seir, where Esau dwelt. Instead of bringing back a favorable report, the messengers returned with the news that Esau, having already subdued the powerful Horites who had formerly held Seir, had now gathered together a force of four hundred men and was heading northward.

Terrified, Jacob divided his people, his flocks, his herds, and his camels into two equal groups. Now, no matter which group Esau and his men attacked, the other group would have a chance of escape and survival. Then Jacob said a prayer in which he reminded God of God's promise to him. Admitting his fear of Esau's vengeance, he asked for divine protection. In this prayer Jacob said to God: "I am not worthy of the least of all the mercies, and of all the truth, which thou hast shewed unto thy servant; for with my staff I passed over this Jordan; and now I am become two bands."

This is the third biblical reference to the Jordan but the first specific mention of the river by name.

(The Bible never uses an article with Jordan or the word "river." It is always "this Jordan," or "across Jordan.")

Then, apparently to make triply sure that he and his family would escape the wrath of Esau, Jacob sent his brother a gift in the form of two hundred female goats, twenty male goats, two hundred ewes, twenty rams, thirty milch camels with their calves, forty cows, ten bulls, twenty female asses, ten foals.

That night, still nervous, Jacob took his two wives, two women servants, and children down to the edge of the Jabbok and sent them
across, while he remained behind, on the north bank of the river. There
during the night he became a participant in the strangest wrestling
match in history. The Bible tells the story most succinctly:

"And Jacob was left alone; and there wrestled a man with him until
the breaking of the day.

"And when he saw that he prevailed not against him, he touched
the hollow of his thigh; and the hollow of Jacob's thigh was out of joint,
as he wrestled with him.

"And he said, Let me go, for the day breaketh. And he said, I will
not let thee go, except thou bless me.

"And he said unto him, What is thy name? And he said, Jacob.

"And he said, Thy name shall be called no more Jacob, but Israel:
for as a prince hast thou power with God and with men, and hast prevailed.

"And Jacob asked him, and said, Tell me, I pray thee, thy name.
And he said, Wherefore is it that thou dost ask after my name? And he
blessed him there.

"And Jacob called the name of the place Peniel: for I have seen God
face to face, and my life is preserved."

Peniel (or Penuel) appears on all historical and biblical maps, on
the north side of the Jabbok River, less than eight miles as the bird flies
due east of the Jordan. Up to this point the Jabbok has been flowing
down from the hills of Gilead through a deep and narrow canyon, but
here, as it rushes to blend its waters with the Jordan, its valley widens
considerably.

At this spot a nation was given a name. "Israel" is Hebrew for "God
strives." It became first a synonym for Jacob and as such is used
throughout the Bible. Then Jacob's immediate descendants were called
"the children of Israel" and eventually their land became "the land of
Israel," and then, thousands of years later, the modern nation that was
established on the soil of the ancient land became simply Israel.

In commemoration of Jacob's wrestling experience, the Bible says
that "therefore the children of Israel eat not of the sinew which shrank,
which is upon the hollow of the thigh, unto this day: because he touched
the hollow of Jacob's thigh in the sinew that shrank."

Esau and Jacob finally met, at a spot not far from Jabbok, after
twenty years of separation. They embraced and kissed, and Esau accepted the gifts his younger brother pressed upon him. The peace
meeting ended with Esau going back to his own home on the slopes of a

mountain in Edom, south of the Dead Sea, while Jacob and his family headed due west, stopping just short of the spot where the Jabbok flows into the Jordan. In this wide and fertile section of the Valley he discovered perfect pasturage for his animals, good earth for plowing, and plenty of water, so here he "built him an house" and made booths or sheds for his cattle, and named the place Succoth.

In this pleasant spot Jacob apparently intended to remain permanently, for instead of merely pitching his tents, as was the custom with wandering herdsmen who had to move their cattle from place to place in search of good pasturage, Jacob built a permanent dwelling place for his family. But before long he was on the move again. Why he left Succoth—one of the most verdant spots in the entire Jordan Valley— is a minor historical mystery. Perhaps it was because of a deep-rooted desire to cross over the Jordan and get back onto the land of God's promise. Here is the first subtle indication of the Jordan's role as a divider between there and here; between outside and inside; between the Diaspora (place of dispersion) and home.

So Jacob crossed over the Jordan again and went to a town near Shechem, on the west side of the river. There is evidence that twenty years earlier, on his way north, he had crossed the Jordan at a bend in the river called Adam (now called Damiyeh in Arabic) which, before many more centuries, would be the scene of a historically and religiously important event. Here the ground on either side of the river was low and flat, and except when the Hermon's melting snow made a torrent out of the Jordan, it was possible to ford the river without great danger. Having discovered twenty years earlier what an ideal spot this was for a crossing, Jacob must have intentionally sought it out again, because now he had not only himself to get to the other side, but a caravan that included two wives, innumerable servants, children of a wide range of ages, and all his livestock. There is no record of how many animals he took with him from his father-in-law's herds and flocks, but the sheep, goats, cattle and camels he gave to Esau as a peace offering numbered five hundred and fifty, which must have been only a fraction of his total possessions, and so he undoubtedly had the problem of getting at least several thousand animals, as well as the humans, across the Jordan.

There was cause for celebrating when he arrived safely with his full company on the other side of the river. Now finally he had his feet once again on the soil of Canaan that his grandfather Abraham and his father Isaac loved so deeply. This was the land God meant when he said twenty years earlier, on the hilltop at Bethel, "I am the Lord God of Abraham thy father, and the God of Isaac: the land whereon thou liest, to thee will I give it, and to thy seed."

After crossing the Jordan, Jacob led his large family in a northwesterly direction up the Wadi al Fari'ah, and then into the hills to the place where his grandfather had pitched his tents on his arrival in the Jordan area. This loveliest of all the vales of Canaan must have had the same effect on Jacob as it had had on Abraham, for he decided to remain there and for a hundred pieces of money bought a parcel of land, and dug a well, and was happy. But then a domestic tragedy filled him with such loathing for the place that he was forced to move on.

Jacob's daughter, Dinah, young and fair to look upon, was seduced one day by a prince of the region, Shechem, son of Hamor the Hivite. (In Hebrew *hamor* means "donkey.") During a conference Hamor and his son pleaded with Jacob for the right to legitimize the affair by marriage. Dinah's brothers replied that the Hivite prince could not possibly marry their sister because he was uncircumcised. If, however, he and every male in his kingdom were to become circumcised, not only could the young prince have Dinah for wife, but the sons of Jacob would also agree to intermarry with the Hivites. Hamor and his son were pleased and quickly persuaded their male followers to undergo circumcision. On the third day after the mass operation, when the male Hivites were still in pain and somewhat incapacitated, two of Jacob's sons took great swords and murdered all of them.They included among their victims both Prince Shechem and his father. Then they plundered the Hivite city, seized all the sheep, oxen, and asses of the dead men, and made prisoners of their wives and children.

Jacob's rebuff to his sons contained a classic phrase: "Ye have troubled me to make me stink among the inhabitants of the land, among the Canaanites and the Perizzites."

Because of this tragedy they all now moved on to Bethel, where Abraham long ago had built an altar, but before they left Shechem, Jacob insisted that Rachel bury under an oak tree the household idols she had stolen from her father, and that all the other women take off their earrings and bury them also in the same place.

Rachel died in giving birth to her husband's twelfth son at Bethel. From there Jacob went on to Mamre, the city overlooking the Jordan from which Abraham had watched the destruction of Sodom and in which Isaac was now living. The last time Jacob had seen his father, more than twenty years ago, the old man was almost blind and was expecting death momentarily. Now he was one hundred and eighty years old and had really reached the end of his days. When he did finally die, Esau and Jacob together buried him.

One of the best-remembered stories of the Bible is the account of how Joseph, Jacob's eleventh son and a somewhat spoiled child, was sold into Egyptian slavery by his jealous brothers and after an unjust imprisonment rose to the highest offices of state and then, by wise planning, saved Egypt during a famine. Apparently none of the episodes of the Joseph story took place in the Jordan Valley. The pit into which the brothers threw Joseph, before they sold him to the Midianite caravan, was at Dothan, more than thirty miles southwest of the Sea of Chinnereth and about eighteen miles due west from the Jordan River. However, there is a region just north of the lake that still abounds in strange legends about Jacob and his family. The stories have been passed down for thousands of years and in recent times have been kept alive by the Arabs. As late as 1880 there was in the Valley near the north end of the lake a hostel called the Khan Jubb Yusuf (the Inn of the Pit of Joseph). For a small fee the innkeeper would show his guests the well in which, he said, Joseph had been thrown, and not far away a mountainside strewn with large slabs of stone that once had been white, like all the other stones of the area, but had been turned coal black, so legend has it, by the tears Jacob shed on them while he was searching here for his lost son.

The most important bridge north of the Sea of Chinnereth is the Jisr Benat Ya'kob, the Bridge of the Daughters of Jacob. Why "daughters," plural? The question is often asked. Many verses in the Bible are given over to a detailed account of the number of children born to Jacob, partly because his twelve sons were to become the chieftains of the twelve tribes that would found Israel, and partly because of Jacob's complex marital situation. Yet there is mention of the birth of only one daughter, Dinah. However, when Jacob was mourning over what he believed to be the death of his son Joseph, the Bible relates that "all his sons and all his daughters rose up to comfort him." One explanation is that in those days daughters were considered of so little importance that they were seldom mentioned. (The Midrash contains a fable that each of Jacob's twelve sons had a twin sister, that each son married his twin sister, and that each begat children by his sister-wife.)

Tourists in the Valley are often given quite a different explanation of why it is called the Bridge of the Daughters of Jacob: tolls on the bridge at one time were collected by nuns from the nearby convent of St. James, so the bridge was called the bridge of the nuns of St. James. In Arabic, James is Tacub, but in time Tacub became Ya'kob and nuns became daughters, and a myth grew up that there was some connection between this bridge and the daughters of the patriarch Jacob. There are many groves of oak trees and sacred shrines in this same area dedicated to the perhaps mythical daughers of the patriarch. In Safed, not far removed from the Valley, there was once a Muhammadan shrine called the Mukan Benat Ya'kob, "the Sacred Place of the Daughters of Jacob." In one corner of the mosque a green curtain hung over the entrance to a cave. This was represented as being the tomb of "the seven daughters of Jacob." Visitors were told that the young women were still, after thirty-five hundred years or more, as beautiful in death as they had been in life; that they could be seen, however, "only by true believers"; that they were "quick to take offense and devoured anyone who came too near to their place of rest."

There is also a local tradition that Jacob, on his way back from Haran, crossed the Jordan at a ford in the river about a quarter of a mile south of where the Bridge of the Daughters of Jacob was later built. This, incidentally, is the only point in its entire course where the Jordan for a few yards flows along at exactly sea level.

Jacob was in Egypt when he died. There, upon Joseph's order, his body was embalmed. Fable has it that the embalming process took forty days, followed by seventy days of public mourning throughout Egypt. Then the mummy was transported to Canaan, to be buried, as Jacob had requested, in a cave in the field his grandfather Abraham had purchased from Ephron the Hittite, on a ridge near Mamre, looking down onto the Jordan and the Salt Sea.

It must have been an impressive funeral procession, for with Joseph and the eleven other sons went "all the servants of the Pharaoh, the elders of the house, and all the elders of the land of Egypt." Also, all the womenfolk. They left behind only the small children and the animals. In the procession were both horsemen and chariots, "and it was a very great company."

The best route from Egypt to Canaan was up the coast. This is the road Jacob and his sons undoubtedly took when they went south, and it would have been the logical road for the sons to have followed as they took the mummy from Egypt to Mamre. However, the biblical account says the procession went first to "Atad, which is beyond Jordan." No map, ancient or modern, shows Atad. Biblical dictionaries, atlases, and geographies list it as "Atad, Transjordan; exact location unknown."

One more biblical mystery is why this considerable number of people—men and women alike, Egyptians as well as Israelites—made so long a trek to the east to get to Mamre: through the Wilderness of Shir and the Wilderness of Zin, then up through the east side of the Salt Sea, through Edom and Moab and the land of the Amorites, then over the Jordan and back south again to Mamre. Some Talmudic scholars have surmised that this great detour was made to avoid the Philistines, who were established by this time along the coast and who might have seized the mummy, or at least have refused passage to the procession.

"And they came to the threshing-floor of Atad, which is beyond Jordan, and there they mourned with a great and very sore lamentation."

It was common practice to use the immense level floors of threshing places for both weddings and funerals.

While the word Atad gives no clue as to where the place was—because Atad means simply "camel's horn"—the reference to a threshing floor indicates that it was in the Jordan Valley, close to the river, for grain was always threshed near to where it was grown, which would have been in the Valley and not up in the hills.

The journey from Egypt across the Wilderness and up the east side of the Salt Sea was almost a rehearsal for the trip Moses and his followers would make along the same route so many generations later, but with so much more difficulty.

After spending seven days weeping over the mummy at Atad, the funeral party apparently crossed the river and then turned south to the Hebron district. Where was the crossing made? And how? We are given no details; unfortunately, because this was the first ceremonial crossing of the river in its entire history. It is possible the crossing was at about the same place where Joshua would lead the survivors of the exodus over the river so many generations later. On that later occasion the river would be crossed safely thanks to a miracle, or a timely act of nature. But how was it done this time? No one knows.

Another quite different interpretation of the biblical text suggests that it was not the Jordan at all that was crossed, but the River Zior, which formed the frontier between Egypt and Canaan; that Atad was not beyond the Jordan, but was in Canaan just beyond the River Zior. If this version is accepted, the funeral procession actually did go up the coastal road. This would clarify the biblical passage that says:

"And when the inhabitants of the land, the Canaanites, saw the mourning in the floor of Atad, they said, This is a grievous mourning to the Egyptians: wherefore the name of it was called Abel-mizraim."

The year of Jacob's death is fixed by some biblical reckoners at 1689 B.C. About a hundred years later, in Egypt, the infant Moses was hidden by his mother in reeds by the side of a river, was found by a daughter of the Pharaoh, grew up in court society, and in his maturity was charged by God with leading the Hebrew slaves—tribal descendants of Abraham, Isaac and Jacob—out of the country of their bondage to the land of promise, where they might become a nation. The Jordan and its Valley enter the epic of the Exodus for the first time when Moses, after leading his people over a dry path that suddenly appeared in the Red Sea and then across the Sinai Desert, was commanded by God to send twelve spies, one from each of the Tribes of Israel, up into Canaan. Their instructions were:

"See the land, what it is; and the people that dwelleth therein, whether they be strong or weak, few or many;

"And what the land is that they dwell in, whether it be good or bad; and what cities they be that they dwell in, whether in tents, or in strong holds;

"And what the land is, whether it be fat or lean, whether there be wood therein, or not. And be ye of good courage, and bring of the fruit of the land."

The spies spent forty days in the Promised Land (forty is one of the favorite figures in the Bible), part of the time wandering through the Valley of the Jordan. On the instructions of Moses they brought back samples of the fruit, including figs, pomegranates, and a single cluster of grapes. (The tourist bureau of the present State of Israel uses as an advertising emblem a painting of this single bunch of grapes, being borne, as described in Numbers 13:23, on a pole by two men, the grapes almost touching the ground.)

"We came unto the land whither thou sentest us," the spies reported, "and surely it floweth with milk and honey; and this is the fruit of it."

But then they made their military report:

"Nevertheless the people be strong that dwell in the land, and the cities are walled, and very great . . .

"The Amalekites dwell in the land of the south: and the Hittites, and the Jebusites, and the Amorites, dwell in the mountains: and the Canaanites dwell by the sea, and by the coast of Jordan."

At this point Caleb, one of the twelve spies, silenced the speaker and suggested that the Israelites ought to set out immediately to possess the land across the Jordan. He was convinced, he said, that "we are well able to overcome it." But a spokesman for the other spies answered him, saying:

"We be not able to go up against the people; for they are stronger than we."

Then the spokesman plunged his listeners into despond by mentioning a subject that apparently had long been a cause for concern, if not actual trepidation: giants.

"The land, through which we have gone to search it, is a land that eateth up the inhabitants thereof; and all the people that we saw in it are men of a great stature.

"And there we saw the giants, the sons of Anak, which come of the giants: and we were in our own sight as grasshoppers, and so we were in their sight."

This was not the first biblical mention of giants. Nor the last. In the Old Testament alone there are twenty references to "a giant" or "giants," starting with the statement in the Book of Genesis:

"There were giants in the earth in those days . . ." those days being the time of Noah.

Many of the giants were reported to have been in the Jordan area. Tales of their size and strength reached the ears of the harassed and footsore Israelites long before they came within sight of the Promised Land.

In the time of Abraham, when the four kings came down from the northeast to do battle with the five kings of Sodom and the other Cities of the Plain, they were reported to have conquered on their way the Rephaim, the Zuzim and the Emim, all of them described as races of "giants." The Rephaim, whose name was based on the Hebrew word for "ghosts of the dead," lived east of the Salt Sea. The Emim lived in Moab, and the Zuzim somewhere east of the Jordan, their principal city being Ham. Another race of giants, living in Ammon, were known euphoniously as the Zamzummim. Then there were the Anakim who dwelt in the Judaean hills near Hebron, to the west of the Salt Sea. These were the giants mentioned by the spies of Moses, who were so immense that they made the men from the Twelve Tribes seem like unto grasshoppers.

Between the time the spies made their report and the Israelites began sweeping northward up the west side of the Jordan to attack and conquer the lands that had been promised to them, their chief worry seems to have been whether they would be strong enough to subdue these various races of giants. There is evidence that Moses himself shared this fear of giants. In his long exhortation to his followers, after they had been wandering for almost forty years in the desert, he said:

"Our brethren (the spies) have discouraged our heart, saying, The people is greater and taller than we; the cities are great and walled up to heaven; and moreover we have seen the sons of the Anakims there.

"Then I said unto you, Dread not, neither be afraid of them."

A moment later Moses was telling them about other giants, the Emim, whom he called "a people great, and many, and tall, as the Anakims . . ."

As Moses tried to prepare his followers for what they would encounter across the Jordan, he said:

"Thou art to pass over Jordan this day, to go in to possess nations greater and mightier than thyself, cities great and fenced up to heaven,

"A people great and tall, the children of the Anakims, whom thou knowest, and of whom thou has heard say, Who can stand before the children of Anak!"

Still obsessed by their fear of the giants, the Israelites, after so many years of wandering and spiritual preparation, were led by Moses north toward the Promised Land, but many impedimenta still lay between them and their goal. First were the Edomites, who inhabited a large area at the south end of the Salt Sea. Moses sent a messenger to ask politely for free passage across their country. The road he wished to take through Edom was called the King's Highway, a well-established trade route over which flowed a constant stream of caravans that not only paid heavy tolls for use of the road, but also were charged something more than bargain prices for food and water. Moses pleaded for the right of passage, but the Edomites refused, out of fear that if a whole race were to be given the right of entry, it might result in their own eventual subjugation. When the request was refused, Moses led his people in a long, circuitous route around Edom, thus avoiding conflict.

Now they approached the land of distant kin. It had been five centuries or more since Lot had stood with Abraham on a height across the Jordan looking in this direction, as he tried to decide what territory to choose for himself and his family. Now the descendants of the sons he had fathered by incest with his two daughters, the Moabites and the Ammonites, were in possession of this entire area. They were people with a common background, yet strikingly different. The Moabites were peaceful and inoffensive, each family residing in a fixed place, cultivating its own land and grazing its flocks on its own pasturage. They were sun worshipers and sought to please their god by sacrificing humans, especially small children. Their land, Moab, is mentioned one hundred and fifty-eight times in the Old Testament. It was an extensive territory, covering three thousand square miles, and boasting of half a dozen important cities, but part of Moab had recently been seized by a fierce tribe from across the Jordan, the Amorites, who had driven the

Moabites to the south, into the area known as the Field of Moab, below the Arnon River.

Moses led his people in a wide circle around Moab and as they approached the land held by the Amorites he sent messengers to the king, Sihon, asking for the right of passage. No harm would be done to the Amorite vineyards; there would be no trespassing on Amorite land; foot would not be set upon any Amorite field; no water would be taken from any Amorite well. Moses even promised to see to it that no one in his entire band strayed off the principal highway.

King Sihon not only refused the request, but came out to meet the Israelites with a sizable army. The battle and the outcome are described with a paucity of words unusual even for the Bible:

"And Israel smote him with the edge of the sword, and possessed his land from Arnon unto Jabbok."

It apparently was a short yet decisive war. One by one the cities, the towns, and even the villages of the Amorites were occupied, until the whole of the country between the Arnon and the Jabbok was in possession of the Israelites, thus giving them control of more than half the eastern shoreline of the Salt Sea and a third of the eastern bank of the Lower Jordan. As a result of this victory, when the time came for them to cross over the river into Canaan, they would have a wide choice of fords.

But Moses seemed in no hurry to cross over the Jordan. Instead, apparently convinced that they should leave no enemies in their rear to harass them, he headed north through the hills of Gilead to the fertile land of Bashan, which had the Sea of Chinnereth and the Upper Jordan as its westerly boundary and extended all the way past Dan to the slopes of Mount Hermon and even to the outskirts of Damascus. This extensive area contained sixty fortified places, sometimes called "the Giant Cities of Bashan," all of them "fenced with high walls, gates and bars." Edrei, on a high, isolated bluff, was one of the kingdom's two capital cities. (Edrei is now known by its Arabic name, Deraia, and is in Syria.) This was the land of the giants. When the invading Israelites arrived there, they could tell from the size of the houses, the height of the doors, and the length of the sarcophagi, that the tales they had heard about the stature of the inhabitants of Bashan were true, just as modern-day archaeologists have confirmed the substance of the stories by what they have dug up in the ruins of the ancient Bashan cities.

The ruler of Bashan was Og, one of the most picaresque and picturesque characters anywhere in the pages of the Bible. He is mentioned twenty-two times in the Old Testament. Sometimes he is called merely

"Og, King of Bashan," but Moses himself, retelling in the Book of Deuteronomy what happened, describes Bashan as "the land of the giants" and tells how Og's iron bedstead measured nine cubits in length and four in width. (In those days all measurements related to parts of the human body, a cubit being the length of a man's forearm from elbow to fingertip, or about a foot and a half, so the bed of Og was approximately thirteen and a half feet long, by about six feet wide.) The bed was so impressive that it was later put on display by the Ammonites in their capital city.

The Bible itself gives no more details about Og, but centuries later the Midrash, a collection of apocryphal fables and rabbinical commentaries on the Bible, added a wealth of imaginary detail. One fable says that Og lived at the time of the flood, but escaped death by drowning because he was so tall that the waters came up only to his ankles. Another says he escaped by taking a few giant strides and thus reached Canaan, which had been spared the flood. A third says he begged Noah to save him from the engulfing waters and Noah agreed on one condition: that Og would spend the rest of his life serving Noah's descendants. Og accepted the condition, but he was unable to get through the door of the ark, so he rode astride the roof, with his feet dragging in the water. Noah fed him by handing food out to him through a window in the ark. One explanation of why Noah helped to save Og was that it was in order to demonstrate to future generations the power of God, who could at will both create and destroy such monsters as Og.

The fables also give Og a role in the saving of Lot, after his capture at Sodom by the armies of Chedorlaomer and the other four kings from the north. The Bible says that Abraham was informed of Lot's capture by "one who had escaped." This unnamed hero was actually Og, so the legend goes. One version is that Og was in love with Abraham's wife, Sarah, and urged Abraham to go to the rescue of Lot only in the hope that Abraham would be killed, thus making it possible for Og to marry Sarah. At that time Abraham was still childless and for this Og derided him. When Isaac was born, Og was invited to the banquet celebrating the event. The other guests asked the giant what he had to say, now that a son had finally been born to Abraham. Og replied that Isaac was not really a son; that he, Og, could easily crush the child with one finger. As punishment for having made that remark, God ordained that Og would live long enough to see Abraham's descendants multiply until they numbered a hundred thousand and that then Og would be killed in battle by one of them.

The Bible narrates that as the Israelites approached the capital of

Bashan, Og went out against them, "he and all his people, to battle at Edrei."

There is an indication that Moses still was a victim of the giant psychosis, in the passage in which God quiets his fears just before the start of the battle:

"And the Lord said unto Moses, Fear him not: for I have delivered him into thy hand, and all his people, and his land; and thou shalt do to him as thou didst unto Sihon king of the Amorites, which dwelt at Heshbon."

With this reassurance, Moses and his followers went into battle against Og.

"So they smote him, and his sons, and all his people, until there was none left him alive: and they possessed his land."

There are no biblical details as to how the giant king met his death, but the Midrash abounds in explanatory legends. One tells how Og, during the battle of Edrei, sat astride the city wall watching the conflict, with his legs that were more than sixty feet long just touching the ground.

Another story describes how, as Og and Moses were approaching each other on the battlefield, the giant king with one hand plucked a mountain from the landscape and hurled it at the leader of the Israelites, but Moses intercepted it and so no harm was done.

Another version of this story is that Og uprooted a mountain three miles long, hoping to use it to destroy the entire Israelite force, but while he was carrying it on his head a swarm of locusts so riddled it with holes that the mountain fell around his neck like a necklace. As he tried to throw it off, long teeth grew out from both sides of his head and kept the mountain permanently in place around his neck. Then Moses, who was fifteen feet tall, took a fifteen-foot axe and leaped fifteen feet into the air, in an effort to kill Og. He was able to reach up high enough merely to nick Og's ankle, but this felled the giant and Moses was then able to give him his coup de grâce with the axe.

Still another Midrash legend says that Og was so immense that after he died and his body lay rotting in the woods, a stag being pursued by a hunter ran into the hollow of one of Og's leg bones. The hunter continued in pursuit of the animal for three miles without catching up with it, and without reaching the end of the leg bone.

Another version says that the pursuer was a gravedigger and that he chased the deer through Og's thigh bone for three days.

With Bashan conquered, the Israelites now controlled the east side of the Jordan-Salt Sea area from the River Arnon, their frontier with

Lot's descendants, the Moabites, north along the upper half of the Salt Sea, then along the entire length of the Lower Jordan, the Sea of Chinnereth, and the Upper Jordan to its sources. They also controlled, even farther north, the land reaching to the slopes of Mount Hermon and the approaches to Damascus.

This immense tract was perfect for the pasturing of animals, for which reason it especially appealed to the Tribes of Reuben and Gad, both noted for the size and excellence of their flocks. When their leaders requested Moses to assign this land to them, he agreed on condition that their soldiers cross the Jordan with the other tribes and remain with them until the rest of the Promised Land had been subdued. Then they could recross the river and take up the life of herdsmen and shepherds. When the condition was accepted, the land was divided thus: Lot's descendants, the Moabites, would be permitted to retain the territory south of the River Arnon and would be given the cities north of the Arnon seized by the Israelites from the Amorites; the Tribe of Reuben, mostly tent dwellers, would take possession of the rural areas of the Amorite territory, from the Arnon north to a point just beyond where the Jordan flows into the Salt Sea; the Tribe of Gad would be allotted the land on the east side of the Jordan north from the Tribe of Reuben's territory to the point where the river flows out from the Sea of Chinnereth; the former Kingdom of Bashan would be assigned to the powerful half-tribe of Manasseh, the most militarily expert of the descendants of Jacob. Og's army had been quickly defeated, but to occupy all of Bashan would be a longer and more dangerous task, well suited to the talents of the fierce men of Manasseh.

The children of Israel now moved south again to the Plains of Moab, on the east bank of the Jordan just opposite Jericho. Moses had chosen a fertile and well-watered spot for his nomads to use as a resting place before making the crossing. The Plains of Moab were irrigated in those days by four streams that descended to river level through deep furrows in the nearby mountains. At one end of their great encampment, which covered an area eight by fifteen miles, was the town of Shittim ("the acacia trees"), sometimes also called Abel-Shittim ("the Field of Acacias"). Moses and his followers were now within clear sight of the Jordan and the Judaean hills across the river. Those who were fifty or sixty years old and therefore could remember the mighty Nile may not have been impressed, for even at floodtide the Jordan was narrow and shallow compared with the Egyptian river. But for the multitude, who had spent most of their remembering years in the desert, the Jordan was the first real river they had ever seen, and they were seeing it at the full harvest season, when the Valley was covered with a lush growth and rich crops; when the trees were thick with the blossoming promise of fruit; when the river ran fast and deep. And so they must have been greatly impressed by the Jordan and its Valley. More important, this was the river over which they would someday cross to reach the land of God's promise—their future home.

It was about this time that Balaam, son of Boer, appeared on the scene. He was a soothsayer who not only predicted the future but claimed to have the power to make his own predictions come true. He was hired by Balak, king of Moab, to rob the Israelites of their strength by putting a curse upon them, "for they are too mighty for me." One of the best-known stories in the Bible is the account of how God, because of his anger with Balaam, sent an angel to intercept him as he traveled on the back of an ass toward Moab, in response to the summons from Balak. Exactly where the dialogue between Balaam and his ass took place is not recorded, but it was somewhere between his home on the Euphrates and Moab, so it may well have been in the Valley of the Jordan.

While waiting for the command to cross the Jordan, the people of Israel greatly offended God by their promiscuity and their conversion to the pagan religion of the Moabites, who worshiped a local fertility god called Baal-peor. The Moab rites were marked by extreme lasciviousness and involved periodic child sacrificing.

Moses received an order from God to "Take all the heads of the people, and hang them up before the Lord against the sun, that the fierce anger of the Lord may be turned away from Israel." Moses' interpretation of this command was to order his judges to sentence to immediate execution every man who was currently engaged in—or ever had engaged in—worshiping the pagan god.

"And, behold, one of the children of Israel came and brought unto his brethren a Midianitish woman in the sight of Moses, and in the sight of all the congregation of the children of Israel, who were weeping before the door of the tabernacle of the congregation.

"And when Phinehas, the son of Eleazar, the son of Aaron the priest, saw it, he rose up from among the congregation, and took a javelin in his hand;

"And he went after the man of Israel into the tent, and thrust both of them through, the man of Israel, and the woman through her belly. So the plague was stayed from the children of Israel.

"And those that died in the plague were twenty and four thousand." Next, God commanded Moses to take a census of all his followers over the age of twenty who would be able to bear arms. The total came to 601,730. The Lord then commanded Moses to divide up the land across the Jordan by lot, according to the number of people in each tribe. Moses obeyed, assigning a precisely delineated area to each tribe.

Among those involved in the temptation of the Israelites had been the Midianites, descendants of Abraham's son by Keturah, whom Abraham had sent to the east, along with all his other progeny by concubines. There were now five Midianite princes, all of whom had joined with King Balak in hiring Balaam and who were accused of leading the people of Israel into idolatry and immorality. They had also been confederates of King Sihon the Amorite, before his defeat by the Israelites. For all these reasons, the Lord commanded Moses to take his revenge on the Midianites. Moses required each of the twelve tribes to supply a force of one thousand men. This army then made a mighty attack and "slew all the males. And they slew the kings of Midian." Then "the children of Israel took all the women of Midian captives, and their little ones, and took the spoil of all their cattle, and all their flocks, and all their goods.

"And they burnt all their cities wherein they dwelt, and all their goodly castles, with fire.

"And they took all the spoil, and all the prey, both of men and of beasts."

When the twelve thousand Israelite soldiers returned with their prisoners, "Moses was wroth with the officers . . . And Moses said unto them, Have ye saved all the women alive?

"Behold, these caused the children of Israel, through the counsel of Balaam, to commit trespass against the Lord . . .

"Now therefore kill every male among the little ones, and kill every woman that hath known man by lying with him.

"But all the women children, that have not known a man by lying with him, keep alive for yourselves."

The booty was listed as 675,000 sheep, 72,000 beeves (cattle), 61,-000 asses, and 32,000 women prisoners who "had not known man by lying with him."

In planning the division of Canaan among the tribes, Moses provided for the establishment of six cities of refuge, three on each side of the Jordan. In those days retribution was an important principle of jurisprudence, the duty of punishing a slayer resting upon the nearest male relative of the victim. But a distinction was made between a willful and an accidental slaying. It was essential that the willful murderer be put to death, but the man who had killed unintentionally was to be given asylum in one of the cities of refuge, the theory being that an un-intentional murderer is an instrument of God, and that God accord-ingly must see that he is protected. The basic purpose was probably to prevent an excess of family blood feuds.

While the Israelites were still on the east side of the Jordan, opposite Jericho, Moses celebrated his one hundred and twentieth birthday by delivering a long address to his people, which came to be incorporated in The Fifth Book of Moses, called Deuteronomy. It was the first day of the eleventh month of the fortieth year of the Israelites' seemingly aimless wanderings and seemingly purposeless encampments—years during which they had suffered from scarcity of food and lack of water, and had been plagued by many sorts of illnesses that had caused many thousands of deaths. In his talk Moses reviewed for them their forty unhappy years in the desert, as well as their recent military victories on the east bank of the Jordan. In a discourse of thousands of words he repeated God's promise, exhorting his followers to have no fear of the future, and announcing that when the day came to cross the Jordan into the Promised Land, they would not be led by him but by Joshua, for God had forbidden him to cross the river, in punishment for an act of blasphemy he had committed back in the Sinai Desert. Joshua, although about seventy years old, was a young man compared to Moses—half a century younger.

Soon after making this address, Moses received a message from God ordering him to climb Mount Nebo so he could "behold the land of Ca-naan, which I give unto the children of Israel for a possession . . . thou shalt see the land before thee; but thou shalt not go thither unto the land which I give to the children of Israel."

For centuries there was disagreement about which of the many mountains "in the land of Moab that is over against Jericho" was the one from which Moses saw the panorama of the Salt Sea, the Jordan and its Valley, and the land beyond. Christian tradition has settled on a mountain some nine miles east of the north end of the Salt Sea, whereas Muslims say it was Jebel Osha, a much higher peak from which they contend a view can be obtained that perfectly coincides with what the Bible says Moses saw:

"And the Lord shewed him all the land of Gilead, unto Dan,

"And all Naphtali, and the land of Ephraim, and Manasseh, and all the land of Judah, unto the utmost sea (the Mediterranean),

"And the south, and the plain of the valley of Jericho, the city of palm trees, unto Zoar."

The Bible does not give any more detailed description of what Moses saw, nor does it give his reactions, but those who, since biblical times, have been to the top of the mountain Moses is thought to have climbed have discovered that from such a height one sees a panorama across the river that is breathtakingly impressive.

By turning his head to the left Moses could have seen the flat top of Masada, a mountain in the Wilderness of Judaea, not far back from the western shore of the Salt Sea, which would some day become the site of a great fortress and a regal palace. Closer, he must have seen the rich greens of the oasis of Ein Gedi, rising from the edge of the sea to a considerable height, the playground of wild goats. To his extreme right, snow-capped Mount Hermon, standing supreme over all. In the immediate foreground the wide Valley, and through the Valley, twisting and squirming with the peculiar motion of a serpent, the Zor of the Jordan. At its mouth, where it emptied into the sea, the river would have been clearly definable, but off to the far right it was probably lost in a dim haze. Across the Jordan, the hills of Judah and Samaria; line after line of undulations. The color, even at this season of the year, would have been mostly brown. The landscape straight ahead, to the Great Sea on the horizon, was probably devoid of any sign of human or animal existence. It was cut by rugged ravines, deep wadis, and frowning battlements of bare rock. From his vantage point Moses could see all the way from Dan to Beersheba; Dan in the far north, in the shadow of the Hermon; Beersheba to the south, down across miles of formidable-looking desert. As he stared at this panorama, Moses must have wondered what it would look like in a hundred, a thousand years. This was the Land of the Great Promise. Soon his people would be crossing the river and traversing those hills in search of permanent abodes. After so many years. But another man would lead them.

"And the Lord said unto him, This is the land which I sware unto Abraham, unto Isaac, and unto Jacob, saying, I will give it unto thy seed: I have caused thee to see it with thine eyes, but thou shalt not go over thither.

"So Moses the servant of the Lord died there in the Land of Moab, according to the word of the Lord.

"And he buried him in a valley in the land of Moab . . . but no man knoweth of his sepulchre unto this day.

"And Moses was an hundred and twenty years old when he died: his eye was not dim, nor his natural force abated."

Biblical tradition has it that Adam, Cain and Abel, the first men on earth, were monotheists and that idolatry was born after the dispersal of mankind and the confusion of tongues, but that a small group— Abraham and his seed—kept monotheism alive. It is therefore wrong to say that monotheism was born in the Valley of the Jordan. Yet it was not until the time of Moses that it became the faith of an entire nation. It began during the forty years in the desert, but it developed, matured, flowered and reached a climax in the Valley, in the Wilderness, and in the hills overlooking the Jordan. This monotheism was based on belief in a single God, the righteous ruler of the universe, dispenser of justice, giver of the law; a God who derived his power from the fact that he was the creator of man and therefore required of man ethical responsibility and moral consciousness.

The God of Israel was not born, is both ageless and sexless, does not die, is not resurrected, and is the ruler of good and evil alike.

The monotheism that now began to develop in or within sight of the Valley had no faith in magic or in the miraculous power of any object, any act, any formula. It taught that just as there is divine freedom, so is there human freedom.

This was the great heritage left by Moses, a man of genius. He never crossed the Jordan, yet he is one of the principal characters in the Jordan story, for he led his people into the Valley, then pointed the way, and bequeathed leadership to one he had trained for so many years to succeed him.

After the death of Moses, Joshua received this command from the Lord:

"Moses my servant is dead; now therefore arise, go over this Jordan, thou, and all this people, unto the land which I do give to them, even to the children of Israel."

To his officers Joshua said:

"Pass through the host, and command the people, saying, Prepare you victuals; for within three days ye shall pass over this Jordan, to go in to possess the land, which the Lord your God giveth you to possess it."

The men of the two and a half tribes who had been given the land on the east side of the Jordan were told:

"Your wives, your little ones, and your cattle, shall remain in the land which Moses gave you on this side Jordan; but ye shall pass before your brethren armed, all the mighty men of valour, and help them."

After the land in Canaan was secured, they would be permitted to return to "this side Jordan toward the sunrising."

While the great multitude of men, women and children were preparing for the epochal trip across the river, Joshua sent two men to spy out the situation in Jericho. After crossing the Jordan and making their way to Jericho, they took lodging in the home of a harlot, Rahab. Their presence was reported to the King of Jericho who sent officers of the law to apprehend them, but Rahab hid them and told the officers they had gone back in the direction of the river; if they wished to catch the two Israelites they had better make haste. As soon as the officers had gone, Rahab said to the two spies:

"I know that the Lord hath given you the land, and that your terror is fallen upon us, and that all the inhabitants of the land faint because of you.

"For we have heard how the Lord dried up the water of the Red sea for you, when ye came out of Egypt; and what ye did unto the two kings of the Amorites, that were on the other side Jordan, Sihon and Og, whom ye utterly destroyed."

Then she said that if they would promise her that when the Israelites came to Jericho they would spare her father and mother, her brothers and sisters, and all other members of her family, she would help them escape.

The spies agreed and instructed her to gather together in her home all the people she wished to save and when the Israelites arrived she should hang from the window a piece of scarlet thread that they gave her. If she did as instructed, they said, they would guarantee that all those in the house would be spared.

In return for the piece of scarlet thread and their promise, Rahab let them down from a window onto the town wall, telling them to hide in the mountains for three days, before trying to make their way back across the river.

When the spies finally reached the Israelite camp on the other side of the Jordan there was rejoicing over their report that the people of Jericho were "faint because of you."

The exact date of the crossing of the Jordan by the hundreds of thousands of impatient Israelites is nowhere recorded. The King James Version of the Bible gives the year as 1451 B.C. The Bible Dictionary chronology says 1240 B.C. The discrepancy is more than two hundred years.

The Book of Joshua gives a somewhat detailed description of the actual crossing.

"And Joshua rose early in the morning; and they removed from Shittim, and came to Jordan, he and all the children of Israel, and lodged there before they passed over."

In the marching order, the priests bearing the ark of the covenant were told to go first. The ark was a rectangular box made of acacia wood, measuring four by two and a half by two and a half feet. It was covered with gold and was carried on poles that went through rings at the four lower corners. The ark served as a container for the two tablets of the Ten Commandments, for a pot of manna, for Aaron's rod (a symbol of God's guidance of His people), and for a copy of the written law. The crowd was to remain approximately one mile behind the priests and the ark.

The Bible does not identify the spot at which the crossing was made. The conditions necessary for a good ford or "passage of the Jordan" would have been shallow water, a firm river bed, and banks that could be easily negotiated. There are long stretches of the river that afford no possibility of a crossing because the water is too deep or the banks too steep. But there are at least three places in the Lower Jordan where the Israelites might have crossed: close to the spot where the river flows into the Salt Sea, at Makhada Hijla (makhada being Arabic for "ford" and Hijla being a place name); or just to the north of the present King Hussein (Allenby) bridge; or in the vicinity of the city of Adam (Damiya), twenty-five miles on a direct line north of the Dead Sea. Some authorities favor one, some favor another of the three possibilities.

In the summer the Jordan, as it approaches the Jericho area, is normally placid and not more than a few feet deep, but the Bible specifically mentions that this was "the time of harvest" and that the Jordan had overflowed its banks. It was just four days before the Feast of the Passover, so it was the last of March or early April. This is the time of year when winter rains and melting snow from the slopes of the Hermon fill the often-dry wadis with rushing streams, and transform the Jordan's feeder-rivers into wild torrents. At this season the Jordan itself becomes for a brief time a mighty river as it rushes down from the north, lashing out at anything that gets in its way; a mad thing, out of control. Three thousand years ago or more it was a larger stream than it is today, for then it drained a better-wooded country than now and must have been even wider than its present-day hundred feet or so. It may not have been deep, compared with American rivers, but its torrent at this time of the year must have been swift and dangerous. A nineteenth century traveler, well seasoned in dangerous undertakings, wrote this description of his crossing of the Jordan at about this same season and at about this same place:

"On both sides the space was thronged by fifty tall, wild-looking Bedouins, all stark naked, swimming and riding a number of bare-backed horses . . . Two naked men seized my horse, and a third snatched my gun from me. I felt as if set upon by naked savages. C. was ahead of me, and I watched him and his horse led into the water by a naked Bedouin, who had taken off the bridle, and held the steed by the halter, while another hung on to the tail, and a third kept on the lee side of the saddle. The stream, rushing with tremendous force, was about fifteen feet deep. Meanwhile, my saddle bags were carried off and placed on a man's head; and, having taken off my outer garments, I committed myself and horse to the torrent. The ford was very difficult and oblique, but the leader's horse was evidently experienced. An expert swimmer kept to leeward of my saddle, and held my leg close to my horse. Soon we had landed. Now the scene was of the wildest and strangest beauty. We agreed that such a spectacle was sufficient to repay all the trouble of crossing the Jordan."

But Joshua's problem was not as simple as that of the English adventurer. His task was to get across the mad stream hundreds of thousands of men, women and children, as well as all their possessions, their livestock, and their most cherished religious relics. Also, there was the embalmed body of Joseph, who had specifically requested before he died that his remains be carried to the land that had been promised to his father, his grandfather, and his great-grandfather, Abraham, Isaac and Jacob. Also, there was an enormous mass of household goods, cooking utensils, breakable vessels, tents, and other personal belongings.

The total number of people is nowhere mentioned, but the census of those capable of bearing arms—men over twenty—had shown 601,730. We can only guess at how many women and children there were, and how many sheep, camels, oxen, goats, cows and other animals, but there must have been many millions of two-legged and four-legged creatures.

If the Israelites had waited a few more weeks, the Jordan would have begun to subside and the hazards would have been fewer, but apparently there was no discussion of waiting any longer, once the command was given. They had been waiting for years—for decades—for a lifetime. They were in no mood to postpone the crossing. And so when Joshua announced that he had received God's order, they demonstrated their faith by preparing to move, apparently certain that Joshua would somehow get them across the river. The old people among them remembered how Moses had led them into the Red Sea and how that crossing had been made easy by a miracle. It is possible that the lack of fear on the part of the multitude, now, was due to the expectation of more divine intervention.

Joshua's instructions to the men carrying the ark were to walk into the water and then stop, while he addressed those assembled on the river bank in these words:

"Hereby ye shall know that the living God is among you, and that he will without fail drive out from before you the Canaanites, and the Hittites, and the Hivites, and the Perizzites, and the Girgashites, and the Amorites, and the Jebusites."

Then, explaining his faith in the possibility of a repetition of the Red Sea miracle, he said:

"And it shall come to pass, as soon as the soles of the feet of the priests that bear the ark of the Lord, the Lord of all the earth, shall rest in the waters of Jordan, that the waters of Jordan shall be cut off from the waters that come down from above; and they shall stand upon an heap."

It happened exactly as Joshua predicted. The moment the priests' feet touched the water, the river stopped flowing. Thus animals and humans alike were able to cross to the other side of the Jordan without even wetting their feet.

After all were safe on the west bank, Joshua assigned twelve men, one from each tribe, to return to the middle of the dry river bed and select twelve large stones, which he told them to put on their shoulders and carry to where they would be stopping for the night. Twelve other stones were set up to mark the spot where the priests were standing when the miracle occurred.

And now, just as dramatically as the Jordan had ceased to flow, it began flowing again.

"And it came to pass, when the priests that bare the ark of the covenant of the Lord were come up out of the midst of Jordan, and the soles of the priests' feet were lifted up unto the dry land, that the waters of Jordan returned unto their place, and flowed over all his banks, as they did before."

(It should be noted that in the Bible the Jordan is considered to be masculine.)

Just as an earthquake is given as one possible scientific explanation of the destruction of Sodom and the other Cities of the Plain, so an earthquake is advanced as one scientific explanation of the sudden drying up of the Jordan. Earthquakes were common in the Valley. It would not have been the first time that a slight tremor caused a landslide that temporarily blocked the onrush of the river, until it could cut a new channel. Or is it possible that a clay cliff on one bank of the river was undercut by the meandering of the Jordan until it toppled and temporarily blocked the onrush of the waters? On December 8, A.D. 1267, the Jordan dried up for sixteen hours because of a landslide in this exact same area, near Adam. In 1906 the river was again blocked for a few hours. In 1927 the Lower Jordan was dry for more than twenty-one hours, after a landslide.

Many more dramatic moments, many bloody chapters, many heroic incidents in the Israelite chronicle would occur in or close to the Jordan Valley, but nothing during the next three thousand years would equal this crossing of the river by a whole nation of nomads who had been wandering and waiting for almost half a century for the divine signal to settle down. Yet later Jewish writers left this event neglected and almost ignored. They referred eleven times in subsequent passages of the Bible to the Red Sea miracle. They mentioned the sin of Sodom and the destruction of that city in twenty-eight separate passages. But the sudden drying up of the Jordan, which enabled the Israelites to cross to the far side without incident or accident, is celebrated only once, when the Psalmist, in a burst of ecstasy, sang:

"When Israel went out of Egypt . . . the sea saw it and fled; Jordan was driven back."

After the crossing, the multitude made its way, at Joshua's command, to a village the exact site of which has never been determined. It is thought to have been about halfway from the Jordan to Jericho, three or four miles up from the river. It became Joshua's base of operations and there he ordered the twelve stones set up, explaining to his people:

"When your children shall ask their fathers in time to come, saying, What mean these stones?

"Then ye shall let your children know, saying, Israel came over this Jordan on dry land.

"For the Lord your God dried up the waters of Jordan from before you, until ye were passed over . . ."

The second divine command received by Joshua was:

"Make thee sharp knives, and circumcise again the children of Israel the second time."

Joshua obeyed and with sharp knives "circumcised the children of Israel at the hill of the foreskins."

Apparently none of those males who had been born during the forty years in the desert had until now been circumcised. After the mass circumcision, the place was given the name Gilgal, from the Hebrew word meaning "to roll," for the circumcision was supposed to serve as a sign of the deliverance of the Israelites from Egypt. ("This day have I rolled away the reproach of Egypt from off you," the Lord said to Joshua.)

The immediate effect of the miraculous crossing was that the enemies of the Chosen People were confounded, at least momentarily. Joshua reported:

"And it came to pass, when all the kings of the Amorites, which were on the side of Jordan westward, and all the kings of the Canaanites, which were by the sea, heard that the Lord had dried up the waters of Jordan from before the children of Israel, until we were passed over, that their heart melted, neither was there spirit in them anymore."

A few days later, still close to the Jordan, the Israelites celebrated the Passover holiday during which they gave thanks for their deliverance from the land of their enslavement by eating unleavened bread, sacrificing a lamb, and dedicating the first-born of each family to God. This particular Passover feast was one long remembered, for the Israelites from that day on no longer ate manna, as they had for so many years in the desert.

One day not long after the crossing Joshua went up to Jericho for some purpose and was met by a man with a drawn sword.

"Art thou for us, or for our adversaries?" Joshua demanded of him.

The stranger replied that he was "captain of the host of the Lord" and when Joshua fell on his face before the divine messenger, he was told:

"Loose thy shoe from off thy foot; for the place whereon thou standest is holy."

This is one of many biblical indications that not only the Jordan River but the entire Valley was considered sacred.

A short time after this incident Joshua, in compliance with divine instructions, sent seven priests with seven trumpets made from rams' horns marching for seven days around the city walls of Jericho. They were preceded by a body of well-armed men, and were followed by priests bearing the ark. Those in the procession were cautioned not to shout, not to make any noise, not to utter even one word until they were ordered to do so. On the seventh day, as the procession completed its seventh encirclement of the city, Joshua instructed them to shout, "for the Lord hath given you the city." So the priests blew their trumpets and the people made a great din with their shouting. Whereupon, the city wall "fell down flat."

The Israelites then entered Jericho and "utterly destroyed" all that was in the city, both male and female, young and old, as well as all the oxen, the sheep, and the asses.

Measured by twentieth century standards, such military behavior seems unjustifiably brutal, yet objective historians have frequently pointed out that rules of warfare have undergone many modifications down through the centuries, and that in those days it was normal procedure after capturing a city for the victor to put all the inhabitants to death, regardless of either age or sex.

On Joshua's order, the two men who had been sent to Jericho as spies went to the home of Rahab the harlot and rescued her, as well as her father, mother, brothers, and all her kin. Then every building in the city was burned to the ground. All that was taken was the silver, the gold, and certain vessels of iron and brass, which were "put into the treasury of the house of the Lord."

Joshua then declared a curse on any man who might attempt to rebuild the city.

The conquest of Canaan had begun. Proud, opulent and powerful Jericho, with its towers and battlements, now lay in ashes. The City of Palms, which may have been the oldest metropolitan center of civilized men, had been utterly destroyed. It would be many centuries before it would rise again. Biblical history and archaeological findings agree on this point, for modern men have found in the ruins of ancient Jericho evidence that the city was destroyed in the fifteenth century B.C. and was not rebuilt until the tenth century B.C., so Joshua's curse apparently remained effective for half a millennium!

The city of Ai lay due northwest from Jericho and about fifteen miles removed from the Jordan, in high hills looking down onto the luxuriant Valley. After Jericho, Ai was the next target of attack for Joshua's men. As usual, he sent spies ahead to assess the situation. They returned with a suggestion that two or three thousand men would be enough to take the city. When a force of this size was defeated, Joshua tore his clothing, put dust on his head, and cried in anguish:

"Alas, O Lord God, wherefore hast thou at all brought this people over Jordan, to deliver us into the hand of the Amorites, to destroy us? would to God we had been content, and dwelt on the other side Jordan!"

In reply he was told:

"Israel hath sinned, and they have also transgressed my covenant which I commanded them: for they have even taken of the accursed thing, and have also stolen, and dissembled also, and they have put it even among their own stuff."

Joshua was thereupon commanded to find the man who had turned thief during the destruction of Jericho and to see that he was "burnt with fire, he and all that he hath."

The culprit turned out to be a soldier named Achan, son of Carmi, son of Zabdi, son of Zerah, of the Tribe of Judah. In his confession he said:

"When I saw among the spoils a goodly Babylonish garment, and two hundred shekels of silver, and a wedge of gold of fifty shekels weight, then I coveted them, and took them; and, behold, they are hid in the earth in the midst of my tent, and the silver under it."

After the loot had been dug up, Achan, his sons, his daughters, his oxen, his asses, his sheep, his tent, and all his other possessions were gathered together and taken to a valley a few miles south of Jericho, and there Achan and the members of his family were stoned to death, and their bodies, along with their animals and other possessions, were burned to ashes. A great mound of stones was built to mark the spot, which was henceforth called the Valley of Achor.

God then informed Joshua that he was pleased and that now Ai would be taken as easily as Jericho had been. This time Joshua picked thirty thousand "men of mighty valour" and sent them from Gilgal to Ai, with instructions to lie in wait behind the city, while another force made a frontal attack. As soon as the defenders of Ai came out of their city to attack this second force, the thirty thousand men were to enter from the rear. Five thousand men were used for the feint. When the soldiers of Ai saw this smaller force approaching, they surged out of the city in attack, leaving not a single man to defend it. The five thousand fled, as if terrified. At this point the thirty thousand entered Ai from the rear and quickly set fire to the place. Then they attacked the soldiers of Ai who were thus caught in a pincers between the two Israelite forces and were slain to the last man. Then the Israelites went back to Ai and killed the women of the city.

"And so it was, that all that fell that day, both of men and women, were twelve thousand, even all the men of Ai. For Joshua drew not his hand back . . . until he had utterly destroyed all the inhabitants of Ai . . . And Joshua burnt Ai, and made it an heap for ever, even a desolation unto this day. And the king of Ai he hanged on a tree."

It was a momentous victory, for it opened the mountain land to the Israelites, who could now press on northward and southward. However, the story still centers close to the Jordan, for Gilgal remained the military and civilian headquarters for the Israelites, even after Ai was taken.

About fifteen miles west of the Jordan, overshadowing Shechem, where Abraham had built an altar and where Jacob had lived for a time, there are two high mountains, Ebal and Gerizim. Between them there is a natural amphitheater with amazing acoustical properties. From the other side of the Jordan, Moses had pointed to these two mountains and had issued instructions that after his people had crossed the river, half of them (members of the tribes of Simeon, Levi, Judah, Issachar, Joseph and Benjamin) were to go to the top of Gerizim, and the other half (those belonging to the tribes of Reuben, Gad, Asher, Zebulun, Dan and Naphtali) were to ascend Ebal. Those on Ebal were to shout curses upon anyone who violated the laws that Moses had handed down to his people. The priests would chant the curse and the multitude would shout back, "Amen."

"Cursed be he that lieth with his mother-in-law."

"Amen."

"Cursed be he that lieth with any manner of beast."

"Amen."

"Cursed be he that removeth his neighbor's landmark."

"Amen."

In like manner the Israelites on Gerizim were to shout blessings upon those who obeyed the laws of Moses.

Moses had chosen the mountains wisely, for Ebal, the place of the cursing, is a steep, rocky, bare peak without much to recommend it. It has rarely been ascended since biblical times. Gerizim, covered with verdure, has often been called "a smiling mountain," and shows on its face the reason it was chosen as the place of the blessing.

After the destruction of Ai, Joshua led his people from the Valley up to the twin peaks, where the Mosaic dialogue was carried out, exactly as ordered.

Returning from the mountains to Gilgal, Joshua and his lieutenants were one day astonished to receive a visit from a band of strange-looking men who came riding into the Israelite camp on small, skinny asses. Their clothes were old and ragged; their shoes worn and full of holes; their bread moldy and dry, and they carried it in sacks that were so old they barely held together. The visitors presented themselves as the ambassadors of a very far country. They had heard, they said, of the Israelites' long, forty-year march through the desert, and of the military victories over Sihon, king of Heshbon, and Og, the giant king of Bashan. Therefore their countrymen had sent them to seek a treaty of friendship with the Israelites. Their bread had still been hot when they started out, but the distance they had traveled was so great that it was now dry and moldy. Their wine bottles had been new; now they were broken. Their garments and shoes had been neat and presentable; now they appeared old and disreputable, the journey had been so long. Therefore, they pleaded, would Joshua and his Israelites, taking all these things into consideration, not "make ye a league with us?"

Joshua was taken in by the visitors and agreed that they ought to be treated as friends. The bedraggled men were happy when they heard this and left for their distant homes certain that they now had nothing to fear from the nomads who had so miraculously crossed both the Red Sea and the Jordan.

Three days later, Joshua somehow learned that he had been hoodwinked, for his visitors had not been from some far distant place at all, but from the city of Gibeon, only ten or twelve miles due west, over the hills, from Jericho, and from three towns adjacent to Gibeon. There was great discussion between Joshua, his lieutenants and the multitude as to what punishment should be meted out to the Gibeonites for perpetrating such a hoax. It was finally decided that the Israelites could not go back on their word, but that as punishment the Gibeonites would be compelled to become hewers of wood and drawers of water for the Israelites, "even unto this day." They continued to perform such services for many centuries.

After they had achieved several important military victories—one of them thanks to a providential hail storm, another as a result of Joshua's command to the sun to stand still—the Israelites turned their attention to the north. The strongest city in that area was Hazor, on the edge of the Jordan Valley, not far from the swamps of Huleh. The king, Jabin the Wise, the ablest man in the region, made a military alliance with all the other kings of the north, and formed a strong confederated army of well-trained soldiers under able leadership. Their first advantage was in numbers, for they were "much people, even as the sand that is upon the seashore in multitude." More important, they had many horses trained for battle, and innumerable chariots, armed with iron scythes that automatically cut down anyone approaching the chariot when it was in motion. Jabin's force assembled "at the waters of Merom." For centuries the "waters of Merom" were thought to have been identical with Lake Huleh. But more recently Merom has been placed almost ten miles west of the swamps, although still in the Jordan area. Biblical accounts give no details of the battle between the Israelites and the soldiers of the northern kings, but somehow, despite

all the handicaps under which they fought, the men who had come
from across the Jordan were victorious. At God's order they houghed
(or hamstrung) all the horses, burnt all the enemy chariots, and killed
the enemy soldiers until not one of them was left alive. Then Joshua
led his men from the battlefield to Hazor, where they "smote all the
souls that were therein with the edge of the sword, utterly destroying
them; there were not any left to breathe; and he burnt Hazor with fire."
King Jabin was among those killed. The Israelites went from Hazor to
the other cities in the league. In each place the king was killed, the
adult population was wiped out by the sword, the children were taken
prisoner, and the cattle and other wealth of each community were
taken as loot.

". . . neither left they any to breathe."

By the time this campaign in the north was over, Joshua's men had
defeated the armies of the two kings on the east side of the Jordan,
and the armies of thirty-one kings on the west side.

The time had now come to divide the conquered land. Originally
there had been twelve tribes, corresponding to the twelve sons of
Jacob, except that in place of Joseph were his two sons, Manasseh and
Ephraim, making thirteen. Because the tribes of Reuben and Gad,
and the half-tribe of Manasseh had been assigned land on the east side
of the Jordan, there remained ten and a half tribes to share the land
to the west of the river, except that Moses had decreed that the Tribe
of Levi, being confined to priestly functions, would need no land, but
would be given, instead, forty-eight cities in which to dwell, plus
some pasturage for their cattle. Joshua now had the task of dividing
the land on the west side of the river among the remaining nine and a
half tribes. The total territory to be divided actually extended much
farther than from Dan to Beersheba, for in the far north the land assigned to the Tribe of Asher went to the River Leontes, while at the
other extreme of Canaan, the Tribe of Simeon was given land extending
fifty, perhaps even a hundred miles south of Beersheba.

Seven of the twelve tribes had land bordering on the Jordan River:
the tribes of Reuben and Gad, and the half-tribe of Manasseh on the
east bank, and the tribes of Benjamin, Issacher, Ephraim, Naphtali
and the other half of the tribe of Manasseh on the west bank. The
land of the tribes of Simeon and Judah bordered on the Salt Sea.

After the military conquest of Canaan was concluded, Joshua permitted the soldiers who had been given land on the east side of the
river to return to their families, in accordance with his promise. As
they left Joshua said to them:

"Return with much riches unto your tents, and very much cattle, with silver, and with gold, and with brass, and with iron, and with very much raiment: divide the spoil of your enemies with your brethren."

By now the headquarters-city for all the tribes was Shiloh, about fifteen miles up in the hills from the river. The Ark of the Covenant had been taken there, and it was from this place that the two and a half tribes set out for home. If they went the shortest way they would have crossed the Jordan in the neighborhood of Adam. It is possible that they made the crossing at exactly the same ford they and their kinsmen had used for the east-west crossing so short a time ago. Somewhere on the banks of the Jordan they stopped long enough to build an altar. Biblical scholars and historians have long debated whether the altar was on the east or west bank. The historian Josephus (as usual in the minority) recorded that it was on the east bank, whereas other authorities said it must have been on the west bank if the purpose of the altar was to serve as a link between the two-and-a-half east bank families and the rest of the Israelites on the west bank. The Book of Joshua does not settle the matter, for one verse says the altar was built "over against the land of Canaan" and another verse merely says: ". . . when they came unto the borders of Jordan, that are in the land of Canaan," they built the altar "by Jordan."

When the tribes remaining on the west bank heard about the altar, they held a mass meeting at Shiloh. The consensus of the multitude was that they should make immediate war on their own kinsmen, even though they so recently had been fighting at their side against common enemies. But first a delegation headed by a priest and made up of one prince from each of the west bank tribes was sent to demand of the east bank tribes:

"What trespass is this that ye have committed against the God of Israel, to turn away this day from following the Lord, in that ye have builded you an altar, that ye might rebel this day against the Lord?"

Spokesmen for the east bank tribes replied that they had no intention of rebelling against the true god; the altar had been built because of their fear that the river might someday serve as a dividing force between the tribes on one side of the river and the tribes on the other side.

"In time to come your children might speak unto our children, saying, What have ye to do with the Lord God of Israel?

"For the Lord hath made Jordan a border between us and you, ye children of Reuben and children of Gad; ye have no part in the Lord: so shall your children make our children cease from fearing the Lord.

"Therefore we said, Let us now prepare to build us an altar, not for burnt offering, nor for sacrifice:

"But that it may be a witness between us, and you, and our generations after us . . . "

The delegation was pleased by the explanation and took it back to the tribes on the west side of the river, whose members decided not to do battle with their own kinsmen. Thus was averted a civil war between Israelites on the two sides of the river.

As Joshua was approaching death, he called the various tribes together at Shechem and reviewed Israelite history, from the time of Abraham down to the present moment. After the multitude had departed, Joshua died, aged one hundred and ten, and was buried on the Mount of Ephraim twenty or so miles west of the Jordan.

In the days of the judges, following the death of Joshua, Lot's descendants, the Moabites, caused fresh trouble for the Israelites. Having grown strong and ambitious, they swarmed across the Jordan, led by their king, Eglon the Mighty, supported by two sets of allies, the fierce Amalekites, descendants of Esau, and the Ammonites, descendants of Lot by the younger of his two incestuous daughters. At this time God was angry with the Israelites on the west side of the river for having integrated so completely with the Canaanites, the Hittites, the Amorites, the Perizzites, the Hivites, and the Jebusites, among whom they lived, and also because the Israelites had taken the daughters of these people as wives, and had given their own daughters to their new neighbors as brides, and had begun to worship the gods of these pagan people. The invaders pushed as far west of the Jordan as the ruins of Jericho. There King Eglon had his followers build him a great palace and for eighteen years he ruled over all the Israelites of the area. But at the end of this period God answered the prayers of the Israelites and sent them a deliverer in the person of Ehud, a left-handed young man of Benjamin, the tribe to which the Jericho area had been allotted. Ehud was chosen to deliver a gift to King Eglon, who, as everyone knew, was inordinately fat. Before he set out Ehud fastened to his right thigh, under his tunic, a sharp two-edged dagger, a cubit (a foot and a half) long. The Moabite king was sitting in his private summer pavilion when the young Israelite appeared. Ehud dismissed the servants who had come with him to carry the gift, then told the king he had a secret message for him. When the king dismissed his aides, Ehud said to him in a low voice:

"I have a message from God unto thee."

Ehud then "put forth his left hand, and took the dagger from his right thigh, and thrust it into the belly:

"And the haft (handle of the dagger) also went in after the blade; and the fat closed upon the blade, so that he could not draw the dagger out of his belly; and the dirt came out.

"Then Ehud went forth through the porch, and shut the doors of the parlour upon him, and locked them," and then, as speedily as possible, rushed back to the mountains, where his own people were waiting. After blowing a trumpet, as a signal for them to assemble, he shouted:

"Follow after me: for the Lord hath delivered your enemies the Moabites into your hand."

The Benjaminites, led by the left-handed rebel, rushed down to the Jordan, took possession of all possible fords over which the Moabites could cross the river, and waited. When the descendants of Lot, now leaderless, came streaming down to the river's edge in flight, the followers of Ehud "slew of Moab at that time about ten thousand men, all lusty, and all men of valour; and there escaped not a man."

A dozen miles or so south of the Sea of Chinnereth, a great green valley comes down from the northwest to merge itself with the Valley of the Jordan. This rich vale is called the Plain of Jezreel ("God sows") or the great Plain of Esdraelon, which continues on northwest until it reaches Carmel, the mountain behind Haifa. (Esdraelon is merely the Greek form of the word Jezreel.) The plain is a broad, fertile place between two lines of hills. Armies from across the Jordan often fought climactic battles on this stage, so well equipped with all the necessary exits and entrances. Even when there was no invasion, nomad tribesmen would come from across the river to prey or to pasture their animals.

The first of the historic Jezreel battles had a woman as its leading character. Deborah ("Bee") was a prophetess and the only woman magistrate and arbiter of disputes mentioned in the Bible. Israelites from various tribes who wished to have their disputes settled by Deborah would travel for days from all parts of the land to consult her. She would listen to their troubles as she sat under a palm tree in the high mountains fifteen or twenty miles northwest of Jericho, near Bethel. They brought her disputes too difficult for their local judges to settle, or disputes involving more than one tribe. She thus in some ways was a biblical version of the United States Supreme Court. It was because of her judicial and charismatic renown that she was one day consulted about a pressing military problem. The city of Hazor, north of the Sea of Chinnereth on the edge of the Jordan Valley, had been rebuilt and was now being ruled over by a king bearing the identical name of its former ruler, Jabin, who had been killed by Joshua. For twenty years this later-day Jabin had oppressed the Israelites, reducing them to vassalage. The commander-in-chief of all the combined Canaanite forces was Sisera, who was invincible, so Deborah was told, because he had a mechanized force of nine hundred "chariots of iron," while they, the Israelites, were forced by lack of both animals and machines to fight on foot.

Deborah sent for Barak ("Lightning"), whose home was in the Galilean hills at Kedesh-Naphtali, northwest of the swamps of Huleh, and told him that God had commanded him to recruit a force of ten thousand men and attack Sisera, whereupon the enemy would be delivered into his hands. Barak consented to lead a combined Israelite army on one condition: that Deborah accompany him onto the field of battle.

Deborah agreed, but only after warning the young officer that he would not have the satisfaction of conquering Sisera; that the credit would go to a woman.

The battle took place close by the River Kishon. The defeat of the Canaanites resulted from an act of God: a cloudburst. The river then overflowed its banks, the battleground was turned into a sea of mud, the nine hundred enemy chariots were swept away or rendered useless, and the entire Canaanite army was thrown into a frenzy of confusion. The Israelites, who were on higher land, then made their attack, putting the Canaanites to the sword until not a single man remained alive.

The fate of Sisera bore out the prophecy of Deborah. As he was fleeing from the battlefield in terror, the "invincible" Canaanite commander passed the tent of Yael, wife of Heber the Kenite, member of a Midianite tribe. The woman invited him in, saying:

"Turn in, my lord, turn in to me; fear not. And when he had turned in unto her into the tent, she covered him with a mantle.

"And he said unto her, Give me, I pray thee, a little water to drink; for I am thirsty. And she opened a bottle of milk, and gave him drink, and covered him.

"Again he said unto her, Stand in the door of the tent, and it shall be, when any man doth come and enquire of thee, and say, Is there any man here? that thou shalt say, No.

"Then Jael Heber's wife took a nail of the tent, and took an hammer in her hand, and went softly unto him, and smote the nail into his temples, and fastened it into the ground: for he was fast asleep and weary. So he died.

"And, behold, as Barak pursued Sisera, Jael came out to meet him, and said unto him, Come, and I will shew thee the man whom thou seekest. And when he came into her tent, behold, Sisera lay dead, and the nail was in his temples."

In the Song of Deborah and Barak, the murder is described even more vividly:

"She put her hand to the nail, and her right hand to the workmen's hammer; and with the hammer she smote Sisera, she smote off his head, when she had pierced and stricken through his temples.

"At her feet he bowed, he fell, he lay down: at her feet he bowed, he fell: where he bowed, there he fell down dead."

The song then turns sentimentally to Sisera's mother, who is sitting in a window wondering what has happened to her son, and through the lattice cries:

"Why is his chariot so long in coming? why tarry the wheels of his chariots? . . . Have they not sped? have they not divided the prey; to every man a damsel or two; to Sisera a prey of divers colours, a prey of divers colours of needlework, of divers colours of needlework on both sides, meet for the necks of them that take the spoil?"

The Song of Deborah and Barak ends:

"And the land had rest forty years."

In the year 1249 B.C. the Israelites living west of the Jordan were faced with a new crisis. The Midianites, Abraham's descendants by Keturah the concubine, had long occupied much of the land to the southeast of the Jordan, and often surged across the river at harvest time, to steal cattle and raid the threshing floors, taking by force of arms produce of the fields that others had produced by dint of extremely hard work. The two principal Midianite princes were Oreb the Raven and Zeeb the Wolf. They wore gay robes, and decorated themselves with bracelets, earrings and nose rings of beaten gold. Their men were noted for fortitude, bravery and (except during a war) exceeding politeness. About forty years after Barak's rout of the Canaanites, the Midianites crossed the Jordan at a ford just south of the Sea of Chinnereth and swarmed up through the Plain of Jezreel. The Tribe of Issachar, whose lands bordered the river, tried vainly to stop them. The Tribe of Manasseh was powerless to check their sweep to the south and the west. The Tribe of Ephraim was easily vanquished by the invaders. The Tribe of Dan was unable to halt them as they marched through Philistine, until they came to the City of Gaza. In all this time no single tribe or combination of tribes had been able to put up effective resistance. The total number of the invaders was said to be in excess of 135,000, being so numerous that the Israelites likened them to a plague of grasshoppers. They brought with them so many camels that the biblical account said "the camels were without number, as the sand of the sea side for multitude." The Midianites stole, killed, and consumed every sheep, every ox, every other animal they came upon. As they swept on, they left behind a scorched earth: Israelites without food; farmers without animals; desolation and destruction everywhere.

The Israelites were told that they were being made to suffer this punishment because they had done evil in the sight of the Lord by not obeying the divine commandments.

At this critical moment in the Jordan story, the heroic figure of Gideon, whose name means "The Hewer" or "The Smiter," appeared on the scene. He was of the clan of Abiezer, of the Tribe of Manasseh, which controlled most of the western bank of the Lower Jordan. His village was Ophranh, but no one has determined precisely where this place was. (At least three modern towns not far to the west of the Jordan claim to be ancient Ophranh.)

One day Gideon was engaging in a surreptitious occupation indicative of the times—secretly threshing wheat that he hoped to hide from the rapacious Midianites—when the angel of the Lord appeared, sat under a nearby oak tree, and flatteringly addressed Gideon as "thou mighty man of valour." Then the angel announced that God was appointing him commander-in-chief of an army that would save the Israelites from the invaders.

Gideon is one of the most likable of all biblical heroes: a simple young man, yet from a wealthy family, for he had many servants and his father had a private altar. With great modesty he questioned the validity of the "call." He asked why, if God was on the side of the Israelites, he had permitted them to fall on such bad times. God had performed great miracles in leading them out of Egypt and across the Red Sea and the Jordan; why had he now deserted them and why did he permit foreigners to sweep through the land of the Israelites? With humility and shrewd reasoning he asked why, even if it were true that God was now coming to the aid of the Israelites, God had chosen such a nonentity as he, Gideon, for leadership.

The answer he received was:

"Surely I will be with thee and thou shalt smite the Midianites as one man."

But the young skeptic was not convinced and once more risked the wrath of God by demanding proof. He received the sign he wanted in the form of a minor miracle. An angel commanded him to put the flesh of a kid and some unleavened bread on a rock and pour a pot of broth over them. Thereupon the angel touched the food with the end of a staff and fire rose out of the rock and consumed the meat and cakes. The angel then commanded Gideon to destroy the altar his father had built to the pagan god Baal, and to cut down a grove of trees beside the altar, and to use the wood to make a burnt sacrifice to the true god. Here was proof of how far paganism had reasserted itself—to such an extent that Gideon's father had built an altar to the ancient god of fertility. Gideon was terrified at what the reaction would be if he were to be caught, so he and ten servants waited until the black of night to carry out the three orders.

By now the main body of the invaders was gathered in the eastern part of the Plain of Jezreel, not far from the Jordan. Gideon called to arms the tribes of Manasseh, Asher, Zebulun and Naphtali, and thirty-two thousand men presented themselves, but even as they began to assemble, Gideon's doubts persisted, so he asked God for another sign.

"Behold, I will put a fleece of wool in the floor; and if the dew be on the fleece only, and it be dry upon all the earth beside, then shall I know that thou wilt save Israel by mine hand, as thou hast said."

The next morning he was able to wring a whole bowl full of water from the fleece, while the ground round about was dry. But still he was unconvinced, so he asked God not to "let thine anger be hot against me" but this time please would God permit the fleece to remain dry throughout the night, while the ground became covered with dew. The following morning it was exactly as he had asked—dry fleece, wet ground—so he began to prepare for battle, at last convinced.

Young Gideon soon demonstrated that he had certain qualities which have made generals in many ages victorious and famous: caution, courage, and quickness of movement once a decision was made. One powerful motivation was his memory of how his own brothers had been inhumanely butchered by the Midianites on Mount Tabor months earlier.

A strange conversation now took place between Gideon and God. The young commander was told that if he and his fellow Israelites won over the Midianites with a force of thirty-two thousand, they might decide that the victory was the result of their own prowess, so

Gideon was told to cut the size of his army by dismissing any soldiers who admitted any degree of fear. Twenty-two thousand of the thirty-two thousand took advantage of the chance to return to their homes. But God said ten thousand was still too many, so the number was further reduced in an odd manner.

The army was now in battle formation on the slopes of Gilboa, looking down on the vale in which the enemy soldiers were encamped. The only available water was in a well later called Ein Harod or the Well of Harod. It burst from the ground vociferously and was fed by two other springs, forming a stream with a deep bed and soft banks. After ordering his men to the edge of the stream Gideon gave them permission to drink. He had plans for a midnight march and a surprise attack. Such tactics could be spoiled by a few careless men, so he watched his ten thousand men closely as they drank. The vast majority—ninety-seven hundred—were obsessed by such a thirst that they threw themselves on the ground—on their hands and knees—and drank as dogs do, lapping up the water with their tongues, heedless of the dangerous fact that they were in full sight of the enemy on the plain below. These ninety-seven hundred men Gideon dismissed at once. But three hundred others merely crouched, when they came to the edge of the stream, drinking from cupped hands, while holding their weapons in their other hands, and keeping their faces to the enemy, ready for any surprise. Gideon decided that these men had the intelligence that would be needed to defeat an army of 135,000 enemy soldiers.

To fortify his courage Gideon made a surreptitious visit, accompanied by an orderly, to the Midianite camp. Cautiously the two men let themselves down from rock to rock until they stood among the tents of the enemy. There they held their breath as they listened to the conversation of two Midianite sentries. One was telling his companion how he had dreamed of a barley cake rolling down a hill and knocking over a Midianite tent. His companion interpreted the dream to mean that "the sword of Gideon" would triumph over Midian. This convinced Gideon that his name had already struck fear in the hearts of the enemy soldiers, who therefore might be easy prey to panic, so he decided on a bold move. Returning to the hilltop, he divided his army into three companies of one hundred men each, gave each man an empty earthenware pitcher, a torch, and a trumpet, and told them to follow him and do exactly what he did.

Mathematically, it was an impossible situation: a mere 300 Israelites against 135,000 Midianites—one Israelite against each 450 of the enemy! Rarely if ever before had an army faced such odds.

Stealthily they made their way down the pass between the hill of Moreh and the mountains of Gilboa, and approached the Midianite camp, their torches lighted but hidden in the pitchers, as people in many parts of the Middle East were in the habit of carrying their torches when the wind was high or the weather otherwise bad. It was the middle watch, the dead of night. The guard had just been changed. When they reached the edge of the camp of sleeping men, Gideon blew his trumpet, broke his pitcher, and shouted:

"The sword of the Lord and of Gideon!"

The stratagem was triumphantly successful. The sound of three hundred trumpets being blown in chorus shattered the stillness of the night. The sudden glare of the torches must have been equally terrifying to the rudely awakened Midianites, who thus obtained a greatly exaggerated idea about how many men were in the attacking party. The shouting of any battle cry by three hundred men under these circumstances would have been frightening, but the mention of Gideon's name bore out the Midianites' worst fears. Perhaps even more terrified than the Midianite soldiers were the Midianite camels that were as numerous "as the sands of the sea side." When camels become frightened they go on a rampage. This night the Midianite camels in their terror ran in wild circles through the encampment of tents, spreading confusion and death everywhere. Midianite soldiers, almost as bewildered as the camels, began slaying each other in their sleepy confusion. Soon close to 100,000 of the original 135,000 lay dead, killed by the handful of Israelites, slashed to death by swords wielded by their own companions, or trampled by the hysterical camels. Those who escaped death fled eastward toward the Jordan, hoping that once across the river they would be safe from the Israelite fury. Gideon had anticipated this and had asked the Ephraimites, who lived along the Jordan, to try to prevent a crossing by any of the fugitives. The Ephraimites, unbeknown to Gideon, were angry that they had not been invited to take part in the battle of the Jezreel Plain, but they cooperated to the extent of capturing two Midianite princes as they tried to ford the Jordan. Oreb the Raven was put to death on a rock, presumably about twelve miles south of the Sea of Chinnereth, just across the river, in Gilead. Zeeb the Wolf was executed on a winepress, in the same general area. The spot came to be known as the Winepress of Zeeb. Their severed heads were carried across the Jordan and ceremoniously presented to Gideon. Most of the other Midianites crossed the river at the fords of Succoth and then plunged into the mountains of Gilead, passing in flight the tower of Penuel, where Jacob had had his wrestling match with the angel of God.

Gideon and his men followed the fugitives, "faint, yet pursuing." After crossing the river and reaching Succoth, they asked the people of that place for food, explaining that they were in pursuit of the Midianites. When the princes of Succoth formally turned down the request, Gideon vowed that upon his return "I will tear your flesh from thee with the thorns of the wilderness and with briers." At Penuel the demand for food was repeated, and the refusal was also repeated. Gideon vowed upon his return to destroy the tower of Penuel.

The Israelites finally caught up with the Midianites far east of the Jordan, in the mountain heights beyond Amman. There they captured the two Midianite kings, Zebah and Zalmunna. On the way back the Gideonites kept their two promises. First they destroyed the tower of Penuel and killed the entire male population of the city. Then they thrashed the seventy-seven elders of Succoth with thorns and briars.

After thus avenging himself on those who had refused his men food, Gideon then dealt with his two royal captives. His conversation with them must have taken place somewhere close to the Jordan:

"Then he said unto Zebah and Zalmunna, What manner of men were they whom ye slew at Tabor? And they answered, As thou art, so were they; each one resembled the children of a king.

"And he said, They were my brethren, even the sons of my mother: as the Lord liveth, if ye had saved them alive, I would not slay you."

Then he instructed his eldest son, Jether, to slash off the heads of the two kings with his broadsword, but the boy was young and afraid, so the father himself did the executing.

When Gideon returned home, victorious, he was asked to establish a hereditary monarchy:

"Rule thou over us, both thou and thy son, and thy son's son, also; for thou hast delivered us from the hand of Midian."

However, as Cromwell was to do, so many centuries later in a similar situation, Gideon refused the offer. Instead of power, he asked for wealth, an indication to some of his biographers that his success had wrought mischief in his character, as was to happen also with Solomon. From each of his three hundred followers he demanded the golden earrings they had taken from the men they had killed. A garment was spread on the ground and one by one the three hundred paraded by, casting therein the Midianite jewelry, until the total weight came to seventeen hundred shekels (more than forty pounds). They also gave Gideon other loot: gold ornaments, collars, the purple raiment of the two kings, and the chains that had been around the necks of the thousands of camels.

Gideon's defeat of the Midianites was a major event in the history of the Israelites, for as a result they lived in peace almost half a century, years during which the people of the Jordan Valley prospered.

Gideon himself married many times, fathered seventy-one children, and died "in a good old age."

The tragic story of Abimelech, son of Gideon by a concubine of Shechem, was played out in the Samarian mountains just to the west of the Jordan. After the death of Gideon, Abimelech went to Shechem and persuaded the people of his mother's city to proclaim him king, and then with the assistance of his mother's relatives, committed sixty-nine murders, to avoid any family arguments over the throne, killing all his seventy brothers except the youngest, Jotham, who somehow escaped the blood purge.

When a revolt broke out in Shechem three years later, Abimelech cruelly suppressed it, burning to death a thousand men and women who had taken refuge in a wooden tower. From Shechem he and his soldiers went to Thebez, a town twelve miles west of the Jordan, as the bird flies. Abimelech himself was about to repeat the Shechem performance by personally setting fire to the tower of Thebez, when a woman threw a millstone at him. It struck him in the head and split his skull. Before he lost consciousness he "called hastily unto the young man his armorbearer, and said unto him, Draw thy sword, and slay me, that men say not of me, A woman slew him. And his young man thrust him through, and he died."

Slightly more than half a century later—about 1143 B.C.—the Jordan Valley was the scene of the slaughter of forty-two thousand Ephraimites. This mass murder was ordered by Jephthah, who is described in the Book of Judges as "a mighty man of valour," an immortal freebooter, as rough and wild as the mountains of Gilead in which he was born. Because Jephthah was the son of a common harlot, his life was made miserable by his more respectable brothers, so he finally fled from home to the land of Tob, a district east of the Jordan that has never been exactly located. When the Ammonites suddenly decided to make war on the Israelites, a delegation of Israelite elders came to Tob to invite the outcast to be their captain and lead them into battle.

"Did not ye hate me, and expel me from my father's house?" he asked them. "And why are ye come unto me now when we are in distress?"

However, Jephthah finally agreed to accept their offer on condition that after the war he should remain their leader.

At first he tried diplomacy. When the Ammonites argued that the Israelites by force of arms had taken land that did not belong to them, after their exodus from Egypt, Jephthah sent a message back that if Moses and his followers had been permitted to make a peaceful passage up the east side of the Salt Sea and the Jordan, there would have been no warfare and no seizure of territory. Besides, he argued, the Israelites had been living on the east side of the Jordan for three hundred years now; why had they waited three hundred years to complain? His arguments made no impression. When diplomacy failed, Jephthah decided to lead his men into battle, but first he made a vow to God:

"If thou shalt without fail deliver the children of Ammon into mine hands,

"Then it shall be, that whatsoever cometh forth of the doors of my house to meet me, when I return in peace from the children of Ammon, shall surely be the Lord's, and I will offer it up for a burnt offering."

The assumption is that Jephthah had in mind an animal, for he used the impersonal words "whatsoever" and "it."

The Israelites were outstandingly victorious, destroying twenty cities and laying waste great areas of vineyards, and committing "a very great slaughter," but when Jephthah returned home, "behold, his daughter came out to meet him with timbrels and with dances: and she was his only child; beside her he had neither son nor daughter.

"And it came to pass, when he saw her, that he rent his clothes, and said, Alas, my daughter! thou has brought me very low, and thou art one of them that trouble me: for I have opened my mouth unto the Lord, and I cannot go back.

"And she said unto him, My father, if thou hast opened thy mouth unto the Lord, do to me according to that which hath proceeded out of thy mouth . . .

"And she said unto her father, Let this thing be done for me: let me alone for two months, that I may go up and down upon the mountains, and bewail my virginity, I and my fellows.

"And he said, Go. And he sent her away for two months: and she went with her companions, and bewailed her virginity upon the mountains.

"And it came to pass at the end of two months, that she returned unto her father, who did with her according to his vow which he had vowed."

After her death on the sacrificial altar, "the daughters of Israel went yearly to lament the daughter of Jephthah the Gileadite four days in a year."

Across the Jordan, directly opposite the Gileadites, lived the men of Ephraim, who now quarreled with Jephthah, because he had not permitted them to share in the victory over the Ammonites. These were the same people who had complained that Gideon had not permitted them to share in the victory over the Midianites. Gideon had managed to pacify them, but they were not satisfied with the excuse Jephthah gave them, so the two tribes went to war. The battle was fought on the east side of the Jordan. When Jephthah's forces were victorious, those Ephraimites who had not been killed tried to escape to their own side of the Jordan, only to find that the fords were in control of Jephthah's men, who demanded of each soldier approaching the river:

"Art thou an Ephraimite?"

If the man said "Nay!" then "they said unto him, Say now Shibboleth (the Hebrew word for ear of corn or for stream), and he said Sibboleth: for he could not frame to pronounce it right. Then they took him and slew him at the passages of Jordan, and there fell at that time of the Ephraimites forty and two thousand."

(It was as difficult for the Ephraimites to pronounce the *sh* sound as it is for a modern-day Frenchman to pronounce the *h* in "the" or "Thursday.")

The slaughter of the Ephraimites is believed to have taken place either at Adam or near Succoth, at the same ford used by the Midianites when they were trying to flee from Gideon and his three hundred men.

The trick used to identify the Ephraimites gave the English language a new word: "shibboleth: a criterion, test, or watchword; a party cry or pet phrase."

It was in these times that a city on the headwaters of the Jordan called Laish or Leshem became Dan. It happened in this manner:

The Tribe of Dan, whose eponymous ancestor was born to Jacob by Rachel's maidservant, had been assigned land on the Mediterranean coast, including ancient Joppa (Jaffa) and the area now covered by the metropolis of Tel Aviv, but they had been driven back into the hills by their enemies the Amorites and were also being harassed by the Philistines, who had occupied most of the seacoast. In about 1406 B.C. the men of the Tribe of Dan took council and decided to move elsewhere, so they sent five men to "spy out the land." The exploratory journey took the spies across the Jordan and then up through the Valley. They circled around the Sea of Chinnereth and then continued north past the swamps of Huleh. Up there the Tribe of Naphtali occupied the land to the west of the Jordan, while the half-tribe of Manasseh had been given the land on the east side of the river. But north of the swamps there was a wedge-shaped territory occupied by the Phoenicians, whose capital city was Sidon, on the Mediterranean, and who were referred to in those times either as Sidonians or Zidonians. The spies found that this territory was well watered and rich. It contained one of the bubbling sources of the Jordan, the springs being called after a sizable city nearby, Laish or Leshem. The spies saw that the people of Laish "dwelt careless, after the manner of the Zidonians, quiet and secure; and there was no magistrate in the land that might put shame in anything." (The implication was that they had no government and no moral character, and were ripe for attack.) Also, a great chain of mountains lay between them and Sidon.

When the spies returned to their own tribe, they reported:

"Arise, that we may go up against them, for we have seen the land, and, behold, it is very good.

"When ye go, ye shall come unto people secure . . . a place where there is no want of any thing that is in the earth."

This report inspired six hundred Danites, well equipped with weapons of war, to set out on the long journey to the north. The spies suggested that they go by way of Mount Ephraim, for on their own exploratory trip they had come upon the home there of a wealthy man named Micah who had made a molten image and a graven image from silver, and had established a House of the Gods, complete with teraphim (lifelike figures used in idolatrous ceremonies) and an ephod (a robe in which pagan oracles are often dressed). Micah had employed a young Levite to serve as his priest and personal chaplain.

It was decided, therefore, to go by that route. When they reached Mount Ephraim, the six hundred soldiers stood by to render assistance if necessary, while the five spies entered Micah's House of the Gods and appropriated the graven and molten images, the teraphim, and the ephod. When the young Levite priest remonstrated with them, they told him:

"Hold thy peace, lay thine hand upon thy mouth, and go with us, and be to us a father and a priest: is it better for thee to be a priest unto the house of one man, or that thou be a priest unto a tribe and a family of Israel?"

Micah, accompanied by some of his neighbors, followed the six hundred soldiers down the road, protesting:

"Ye have taken away my gods which I made, and the priest, and ye are gone away: and what have I more."

The Danites replied:

"Let not thy voice be heard among us, lest angry fellows run upon thee, and thou lose thy life, with the lives of thy household."

Micah, seeing how greatly outnumbered he and his friends were, turned and went back into his own house.

"And they (the Danites) took the things which Micah had made, and the priest which he had, and came unto Laish, unto a people that were quiet and secure: and they smote them with the edge of the sword, and burnt the city with fire."

No help came from Sidon, because of the mountain chain. The six hundred were virtually unopposed in wiping out the original settlers and in establishing on the ruins of Laish a new city which they called Dan, and in which they set up the graven image and the molten image, and began worshiping Micah's gods, with the assistance of the kidnaped priest.

From now on Dan was often referred to as the northern limit of the Twelve Tribes. In the Bible there are seven references to "from Dan even to Beersheba" and two references to "from Beersheba even to Dan."

The Book of Ruth, which some biblical scholars think was written to counteract the stern attitude of Ezra and Nehemiah toward mixed marriages, and which many consider the most exquisite love idyll in the Bible, makes no mention of the route taken by Elimelech, his wife Naomi, and their sons Mahlon and Chilion, as they went from their native place, Bethlehem, to the foreign land of Moab, to escape a famine. They may have gone south from Bethlehem to the lower end of the Salt Sea, and then north to Moab. But it is more likely that they went north from Bethlehem and crossed the Jordan near where it enters the Salt Sea, and thence south to Moab.

In Moab the three men died. When Naomi decided to return to Bethlehem, Ruth, a Moabite, widow of one of the sons, declared to her mother-in-law:

"Intreat me not to leave thee, or to return from following after thee: for whither thou goest, I will go; and where thou lodgest, I will lodge: thy people shall be my people, and thy God my God:

"Where thou diest, will I die, and there will I be buried: the Lord do so to me, and more also, if ought but death part thee and me."

Exactly where were the two women when Ruth made this impassioned speech? The biblical account does not say. Nor are we told the route the two women took in going back to Bethlehem. They probably crossed the Jordan at the Jericho ford. However they went, the trip must have been long and excruciatingly hazardous for two grief-stricken women traveling alone. Not long after reaching the land of Naomi's people, Ruth married a man of Bethlehem named Boaz and by bearing him a son became the great-grandmother of Israel's King David.

Although the final chapter of a story about an unnamed member of the Tribe of Levi and his concubine is set in the Jordan Valley, the chain of events began in Bethlehem. The girl had returned to her father's house in that Judaean city and had been pursued by the Levite, who, after a five-day visit with her father, started back home with her. One night on the way, as they were passing through territory of the Tribe of Benjamin, which borders the Jordan just before the river enters the Salt Sea, they found rooms in the home of an elderly man in the town of Gibeah, in high mountains looking down on the Jordan Valley.

"Now as they were making their hearts merry, behold, the men of the city, certain sons of Belial (a synonym for "wicked men"), beset the house round about, and beat at the door, and spake to the master of the house, the old man, saying, Bring forth the man that came into thine house, that we may know him.

"And the man, the master of the house, went out unto them, and said unto them, Nay, my brethren, nay, I pray you, do not so wickedly; seeing that this man is come into mine house, do not this folly.

"Behold, here is my daughter a maiden, and his concubine; them I will bring out now, and humble ye them, and do with them what seemeth good unto you: but unto this man do not so vile a thing.

"But the men would not hearken to him: so the man took his concubine, and brought her forth unto them; and they knew her, and abused her all the night until the morning: and when the day began to spring, they let her go.

"Then came the woman in the dawning of the day, and fell down at the door of the man's house where her lord was, till it was light.

"And her lord rose up in the morning, and opened the doors of the house, and went out to go his way: and, behold, the woman his concubine was fallen down at the door of the house, and her hands were upon the threshold.

"And he said unto her, Up, and let us be going. But none answered. Then the man took her up upon an ass, and the man rose up, and gat him unto his place.

"And when he was come into his house, he took a knife, and laid hold on his concubine, and divided her, together with her bones, into twelve pieces, and sent her into all the coasts of Israel.

"And it was so, that all that saw it said, There was no such deed done nor seen from the day that the children of Israel came up out of the land of Egypt unto this day: consider of it, take advice, and speak your minds."

In response, four hundred thousand Israelite soldiers "from Dan even to Beer-sheba" assembled not far from the Jordan, in the town of Mizpeh, in the land of the Tribe of Benjamin, and when the Benjaminites refused to turn over to them the wicked men who had caused the trouble in Gibeah, they attacked that city.

In the first day's fighting, 22,000 Israelites were killed; on the second day, 18,000. On the third day, the Israelites killed 25,100 Benjaminites and set fire to many Benjaminite cities.

At Mizpeh an oath had been sworn by all present that no man of Israel would henceforth give his daughter to any Benjaminite as a wife. Now, having achieved victory over the Benjaminites, the other Israelites began to regret the desolation they had created and to bemoan the stark fact that the Tribe of Benjamin would soon die out, because of the scarcity of women, so many having been put to death in the three days. History does not record who it was who conceived an odd solution of this problem. It was based on the fact that no one had appeared at the Mizpeh assembly from the city of Jabesh-gilead, an Israelite town in the hill country just east of the Jordan River, roughly halfway between the Sea of Chinnereth and the Salt Sea. So, twelve thousand soldiers, each one personally selected for his bravery, were dispatched to Jabesh-gilead with instructions to kill with the edge of the sword all the men, women and children of the city, except girls who "had known no man by lying with any male." (The crossing of the river was probably made just opposite the Wadi al Yabis.) When the avenging soldiers returned, they brought back with them four hundred young virgins, after having killed all the rest of the inhabitants of Jabesh-gilead. The Benjaminites thanked them for this contribution of females, but protested that this number was not nearly sufficient to take the place of the Benjaminite girls and women who had been killed. In reply, the elders of the Israelites told them about a harvest festival held annually in Shiloh, in the hills of Ephraim, overlooking the Jordan Valley.

"Go and lie in wait in the vineyards; and see, and, behold, if the daughters of Shiloh come out to dance in dances, then come ye out of the vineyards, and catch you every man his wife of the daughters of Shiloh, and go to the land of Benjamin . . .

"And the children of Benjamin did so, and took them wives, according to their number, of them that danced, whom they caught: and they went and returned unto their inheritance, and repaired the cities, and dwelt in them . . .

"In those days there was no king in Israel: every man did that which was right in his own eyes."

Samuel, the last and greatest of the judges, ruled over the Israelites for many decades, during most of which time there was peace. By some of his contemporaries he was considered the greatest figure since Moses. When he grew old he shared his judicial responsibilities with two sons, Joel and Abiah, appointing them judges in the district of Beersheba. It was assumed that one of them would ultimately succeed him, but they were not of their father's stamp, for they "walked not in his ways, but turned aside after lucre, and took bribes, and perverted judgment." The elders of Israel debated the predicament in solemn meeting and then went to Samuel with a request:

"Behold, thou are old, and thy sons walk not in thy ways: now make us a king to judge us like all the nations."

Samuel delivered a long warning to them on the dangers and evils of a monarchy. But they refused to listen and kept shouting:

"Nay; but we will have a king over us."

The truth was that the Israelite nation had reached the low point of its history. The commonwealth established by the laws of Moses seemed to be failing. Moses himself had stressed the relationship between man and God, and had ordained that the state should be responsible to no monarch but only to Jehovah. Yet, foreseeing that his people might some day be tempted to copy the ways of the nations around them and choose a king, Moses set down strict requirements for any aspirant: he must himself be an Israelite; he must not encourage the importation or breeding of horses, lest his people try to copy those warlike races that used horses in battle; he must have only one wife; and he must not hoard gold or silver for himself.

But despite all the injunctions of Moses and the warnings of Samuel, the Israelites were now clamoring for a king. They wanted and needed a strong government. On the west side of the Jordan the Philistines had not only planted themselves in the hills of Benjamin, but had infiltrated into the Valley itself, down to the very river's edge. On the east side of the Jordan powerful tribes were arming for invasion. In all of Israel there was no blacksmith, and if the people wanted even farming tools repaired they must take them to the cities of the Philistines, who prevented the Israelites from becoming artisans, lest they make weapons for themselves. As a result, in case of war the Israelites had no means of defending themselves, except with ox goads and clubs.

Samuel the Judge finally acceded to their demands by selecting Saul, "a choice young man, and a goodly: and there was not among the children of Israel a goodlier person than he: from his shoulders and upward he was higher than any of the people."

Soon after being anointed by Samuel, Saul became an important character in the Jordan story. This chapter began when the Ammonite king, Nahash, moved his army up to Jabesh-gilead, the Valley city that had suffered such terrible reprisals for not having joined in the war against the Benjaminites. This time the men of Jabesh-gilead tried to make a peace pact, offering to serve the Ammonite leader in return for his promise not to destroy their city. Instead of accepting this abject surrender, King Nahash made the men of Jabesh-gilead a macabre offer: he would spare them and their dwelling places, their women, children and livestock, on condition "that I may thrust out all your right eyes." The elders of Jabesh-gilead replied by making a naïve request:

"Give us seven days' respite, that we may send messengers unto all the coasts of Israel: and then, if there be no man to save us, we will come out to thee."

The messengers went first to Saul, who was working in his fields. When he heard their news "his anger was kindled greatly" and "he took a yoke of oxen and hewed them in pieces, and sent them throughout all the coasts of Israel by the hands of messengers, saying, Whosoever cometh not forth after Saul and after Samuel, so shall it be done unto his oxen."

The threat worked. Almost immediately men from both sides of the Jordan began answering the summons. When Saul saw what the response of Israel was going to be, he sent a message to the elders of Jabesh-gilead:

"To morrow, by that time the sun be hot, ye shall have help."

It is unlikely that ever in military history—before or since—has such a sizable military force been assembled in so short a time. Three hundred and thirty thousand men—just short of a third of a million—started arriving in a matter of hours, after making a forced march from various parts of the country, and set off immediately on the rescue mission. Their point of rendezvous had been Bezek, about twenty miles from Jabesh-gilead—across the Jordan and then to the southwest, on the edge of a wadi. Saul had promised that they would arrive the next day, in the afternoon ("by that time the sun be hot"). There is no record of what season of the year it was, so historians can only guess at the width and depth of the Jordan, and how hazardous the crossing might have been, but the trip from the slight height on which Bezek was located, down through the Wadi el Khashneh, then across the river, and up the Wadi al Yabis to Jabesh-gilead was not easy, whatever the season.

"And it was so on the morrow, that Saul put the people in three companies; and they came into the midst of the host in the morning watch, and slew the Ammonites until the heat of the day: and it came to pass, that they which remained were scattered, so that two of them were not left together."

After this salvation of a city, Samuel called upon his people to assemble at Gilgal, the Valley town between Jericho and the river, which had served as the Israelites' base of operations after Joshua led them across the dried-up river bed. There they confirmed Saul as king "and all the men of Israel rejoiced greatly."

Saul had been ruling for just two years when the Philistines from the Mediterranean coast became such a menace that he sent out an order for the men of Israel to assemble at Gilgal prepared for battle. When the Philistines heard of this call to arms, they gathered their own forces at Michmash, in the mountains: thirty thousand chariots, six thousand horsemen, and so many foot soldiers that they were "as the sand which is on the sea shore in multitude." Many of the Israelites were so terrified that they "did hide themselves in caves, and in thickets, and in rocks, and in high places, and in pits." Others fled across the Jordan to Gilead. Saul was further handicapped by a lack of weapons for the soldiers who remained at his side. The hero on this occasion was Jonathan, Saul's eldest son, who made a surprise, psychological attack on the Philistines, accompanied by his armor-bearer and supported later by the few hundred men who had not fled or gone into hiding. In this manner the Philistines were dislodged and driven back west.

Some years later Samuel came to Saul with divine instructions: "Now go and smite Amalek, and utterly destroy all that they have, and spare them not; but slay both man and woman, infant and suckling, ox and sheep, camel and ass."

Saul took 210,000 soldiers and went to Sinai to carry out the instructions. After a quick victory, he returned to Gilgal. There he received a visit from Samuel, who, after hearing Saul's report that he had "performed the commandment of the Lord," asked:

"What meaneth then this bleating of the sheep in mine ears, and the lowing of the cattle which I hear?"

Saul confessed that his men had brought back the best of the Amalekites' sheep and oxen. His excuse was that they were to be sacrificed to God at Gilgal.

In the course of his rebuke of Saul, Samuel said:

". . . to obey is better than sacrifice, and to hearken than the fat of rams.

"For rebellion is as the sin of witchcraft, and stubbornness is as iniquity and idolatry."

Saul also confessed that he had spared the life of Agag, king of the Amalekites. The immense barbarian monarch had been taken prisoner, but instead of ordering him slain, Saul had brought him home to show him off as a trophy of war.

In his wrath Samuel turned on Saul and declared him unworthy to wear the crown of a great nation. When Saul begged for pardon, Samuel angrily told him:

"Thou hast rejected the word of the Lord, and the Lord hath rejected thee from being king over Israel."

The final scene is one of the most dramatic in the Bible. The impulsive Saul, in despair and disgrace, clutched at the skirt of Samuel's mantle and tore it, in his nervous excitement. Samuel immediately made a play on words, saying:

"The Lord hath rent the kingdom of Israel from thee this day . . ."

Then Samuel demanded that the barbarian king be brought into his presence.

"And Agag came unto him delicately."

Apparently the prisoner read his certain doom in the stern and inexorable features of Samuel, for he suddenly exclaimed:

"Surely the bitterness of death is past."

Then Samuel shouted to Agag:

"As thy sword hath made women childless, so shall thy mother be childless among women."

Then, as the humbled Saul crouched in fear, Samuel "hewed Agag in pieces"—a bloody conclusion to an unhappy chapter in the Jordan's history.

Despite Samuel's threat about the dethroning of Saul, the first king of the Israelites continued to function as the leader of his people. As reluctant as he had been to assume the throne, he now seemed just as reluctant to abdicate it. His pride was broken, and he seemed possessed of an evil spirit. He surrounded himself with regal pomp, put a golden crown on his head, compelled any who approached him to prostrate themselves, and even indulged in the royal luxury of polygamy. In order to soothe and drive out his periodic madness, he was advised to seek out some young man who was a cunning player on the harp. Thus David, youngest son of Jesse the Bethlehemite, became Saul's official armor-bearer, but in practice he was Saul's court musician and personal therapeutist.

"And it came to pass, when the evil spirit from God was upon Saul, that David took an harp, and played with his hand: so Saul was refreshed, and was well, and the evil spirit departed from him."

The story of David, youngest of eight brothers and great-grandson of Ruth the Moabite and Boaz the Bethlehemite, is one of the classics of literature. Some of its chapters were played out on the banks of the Jordan, or in the hills lining the Valley, or on the edge of the Salt Sea.

David was a strange young man, his character dominated by a combination of tenderness and courage, qualities he had learned as a boy shepherd. Like Joseph and Jephthah he suffered the jealousy of his brothers, perhaps because of the talents with which God had endowed him.

As for Saul, there was a Hamlet-like quality to his character. He had the dark and moody spirit of Shakespeare's hero. At times his melancholia approached deep madness. There have been other leaders, before Saul and since, who became moody creatures of caprice, their boundless jealousy, passion and turbulence often landing them in lunacy. As with many of these others, so with Saul: music seemed to be almost his only solace. It could temper his wild ambition, calm his ungovernable temper, dispel his dark and morbid moods.

At first Saul treated David as if he were a favorite son, bestowing honors and privileges upon him, and sending him off to lead troops against Israel's enemies. Then the trouble began. Its roots were jealousy.

Once, when David returned from directing a "slaughter of the Philistines," Saul overheard a crowd of Israelite women saying:

"Saul hath slain his thousands, and David his ten thousands."

The implication that David was ten times his superior sent him into a rage and helped to turn what had been a great friendship into hostile rivalry, which was encouraged by a group of men in Saul's court who saw a chance for personal advantage in adding whatever fuel they could to the fire of the king's new passion.

At first Saul punished the young hero by reducing him in military rank, denying him honors, and refusing to give him his eldest daughter for wife. Then he made three open and direct attempts to murder David. All three failed. Each time he tried to pin the young man to the wall by hurling a javelin at him. Each time David was too quick for him. When Saul's younger daughter fell in love with David and wanted to marry him, the father demanded that David go out and slay a hundred Philistines in battle, and prove it by returning with their foreskins, which Saul would accept in lieu of a dowry. Saul's ill-concealed hope was that the Philistines would do what he, Saul, had tried so obviously to do, and had failed so ignominiously in doing. David returned from the battlefield with the foreskins of two hundred slain Philistines.

Now Saul tried to enlist the help of his eldest son, Jonathan, and his servants, instructing them in how they were to do away with David. Not only did this attempt fail, but one of history's greatest friendships developed between David and Jonathan, despite conditions that would have destroyed any relationship less noble, less tender, less heroic. It began with mutual respect, and mounted, after David married Jonathan's sister, to amazing heights of self-denial and heroic devotion.

"The soul of Jonathan was knit with the soul of David, and Jonathan loved him as his own soul . . .

"And Jonathan stripped himself of the robe that was upon him, and gave it to David, and his garments, even to his sword, and to his bow, and to his girdle."

When David decided to flee the wrath of the mad king, Jonathan said to him:

"Whatsoever thy soul desireth, I will even do it for thee."

David's decision came after one more javelin attempt was made against him. He was helped in his flight by his wife, Michal. When her father, Saul, sent messengers to their home to try to prevent David from escaping, and to slay him the next morning, Michal assisted David in leaving the house through a back window. Then she put into David's bed a dummy she herself had made, using goat's hair to give it a realistic appearance. When the messengers discovered the hoax and reported it back to the king, Saul first was perplexed that a girl could love her husband more than her father, and then, in anger, demanded of Michal:

"Why hast thou deceived me so, and sent away mine enemy, that he is to escape?"

His daughter was evasive.

Saul's determination to kill his son-in-law led the young man to write many of his best psalms, among them Psalm 59 that begins:

"Deliver me from mine enemies, O my God: defend me from them that rise up against me.

"Deliver me from the workers of iniquity, and save me from bloody men.

"For, lo, they lie in wait for my soul: the mighty are gathered against me . . ."

From now on there was no peace for David; no safe resting place. He was hunted as if he were a partridge or a rabbit. No one would give him shelter for long, and his whereabouts was continuously being reported back to Saul.

At one point he joined a heterogeneous band of fugitives, men who had fled from society into the Wilderness because they had acquired debts they felt they would never be able to pay off, or were in some other personal distress, or were simply discontent with the ordered way of life in the city. They inhabited caves and depended for food on the generosity of village people or on raids into neighboring foreign countries. For a time David was the leader of four hundred such men.

The psalms David wrote at this period reveal the desperate character of his plight. In Psalm 142 he prayed:

"Attend unto my cry; for I am brought very low: deliver me from my persecutors; for they are stronger than I."

So he left Israel and went either across the Jordan or around the bottom of the Salt Sea to the land of his great-grandmother, Ruth the Moabite. There, for her sake, he was made welcome. He asked the king of Moab for sanctuary also for his father and mother. The request was granted and his parents came to live with him. They stayed for some time at Mizpeh, from which place David could see the whole panorama of the Salt Sea, and in the distance, to the right, the Jordan, and across the sea the impressive mountains of Judaea. While there he composed at least six psalms.

In Psalm 109 he cried out against his enemies:

"Let mine adversaries be clothed with shame, and let them cover themselves with their own confusion, as with a mantle."

In Psalm 35:

"Let not them that are mine enemies wrongfully rejoice over me: neither let them wink with the eye that hate me without cause."

In Psalm 52, in condemning a man who had informed against him, he wrote:

"Thy tongue deviseth mischiefs; like a sharp razor, working deceitfully."

No hint is given as to why David went back across the river to his native hills. It may have been that his love of home was stronger than his prudence. For a time he lived in the hills to the west of the Salt Sea; hills too savage to be called romantic, too sterile and desolate to be termed beautiful; an area properly known as the Wilderness. After roaming the Wilderness, at length he reached Ein Gedi and took refuge in one of the many caves in that paradise of bubbling springs, lush greenery, cool pools, and wild goats. The calming effect that the seclusion and comparative safety of Ein Gedi had on David's soul is seen in the psalms he wrote while there.

But the peace he found in Ein Gedi was not to last long. When Saul learned through an informant of David's new hiding place, he set off with three thousand men to deal with his former musician-therapeutist. But David also had his informants, and when he was warned that Saul was approaching the oasis, he remained hidden, until he was told that the physically exhausted king was resting in a nearby cave. One of David's own followers, pointing out that this was a heaven-sent opportunity for him to do away with the mad monarch, said:

"Behold the day of which the Lord said unto thee, Behold, I will deliver thine enemy into thine hand, that thou mayest do to him as it shall seem good unto thee."

Somehow David slipped past the soldiers guarding Saul, but instead of using his sword to kill the sleeping man, he used it as if it were a pair of scissors and cut off a piece of Saul's robe. When the king awoke and left the cave, unaware of what had happened, David went out after him, shouting:

"My lord the king!"

Saul, hearing, turned and saw his son-in-law "stooped with his face to the earth." In his hand he held the piece of the king's robe. With great emotion in his voice he addressed Saul, saying:

"Behold, this day thine eyes have seen how that the Lord had delivered thee to day into mine hand in the cave: and some bade me kill thee: but mine eye spared thee; and I said, I will not put forth mine hand against my lord; for he is the Lord's anointed.

"Moreover, my father, see, yea, see the skirt of thy robe in my hand: for in that I cut off the skirt of thy robe, and killed thee not, know thou and see that there is neither evil nor transgression in mine hand, and I have not sinned against thee; yet thou huntest my soul to take it . . .

"After whom is he king of Israel come out? After whom dost thou pursue? after a dead dog, after a flea . . ."

It was an effective speech. Saul was so amazed that he gasped: "Is this thy voice, my son David?"

Then with tears in his eyes, he said:

"Thou art more righteous than I: for thou hast rewarded me good, whereas I have rewarded thee evil.

"And thou hast shewed this day how that thou hast dealt well with me: forasmuch as when the Lord had delivered me into thine hand, thou killedst me not . . .

"And now, behold, I know well that thou shalt surely be king, and that the kingdom of Israel shall be established in thine hand.

"Swear now therefore unto me by the Lord, that thou wilt not cut off my seed after me, and that thou wilt not destroy my name out of my father's house."

David made the promise and they separated in peace. This experience led David to compose a more joyous psalm, number 57, in which he wrote:

"I will sing and give praise . . . I will praise thee, O Lord, among the people: I will sing unto thee among the nations.

"For thy mercy is great unto the heavens, and thy truth unto the clouds."

But about a year later, after the death of Samuel, Saul again led a band of hand-picked men—again exactly three thousand—to seek out and dispose of David, who now was hiding in the Wilderness of Ziph, above and to the west of Ein Gedi. This time David, informed by his spies where Saul and his men were encamped, went to the place at night, accompanied by one of his followers. They found Saul lying in a ditch, asleep, with his spear stuck in the ground close by him. David's companion begged, "Let me smite him, I pray thee, with the spear . . ." But David replied:

"Destroy him not: for who can stretch forth his hand against the Lord's anointed, and be guiltless?"

Instead, they stole the king's spear and his water bottle. After escaping from the camp they went to the top of a nearby hill and from there aroused the king and his men by their shouting. A strange dialogue ensued. First David chided the king's bodyguard for permitting anyone to steal the monarch's spear and water bottle. Then he addressed Saul himself, asking, once more, why the king kept pursuing him.

"What have I done? or what evil is in mine hand?"

Once more referring to himself as a flea, he said:

". . . for the king of Israel is come out to seek a flea, as when one doth hunt a partridge in the mountains."

Again Saul confessed that he had sinned, called himself "a fool" and promised to do David no further harm, adding:

"Blessed be thou, my son David; thou shalt do great things . . ."

So Saul returned home, but David, convinced that he would one day be killed by his father-in-law, decided to go and live among the enemies of his own people, the Philistines. The king of Gath, one of the five principal Philistine cities, made David ruler over Ziklag, a stronghold that had been captured from the Tribe of Simeon. During the year and some months that David dwelt among the Philistines, great numbers of his own people joined him, among them many who crossed the Jordan from the east side to cast their lot with his. The odd fact is recorded that some were adept at throwing stones or shooting a bow and arrow with either their left or right hands. Some were men "whose faces were like the faces of lions, and were swift as the roes upon the mountains." From the Tribe of Gad, which lay along the east bank of the Jordan, came eleven captains, each one at the head of at least a hundred men; in some cases at the head of a thousand men or more.

"These were they that went over Jordan in the first month, when it had overflown its banks; and they put to flight all of them of the valleys, both toward the east, and toward the west."

Several years later Saul led an army of Israelites against the Philistines. The battle was fought on the slopes of Mount Gilboa, not far from the Jordan. Early in the fighting Saul's three sons were killed. Later Saul himself was critically wounded by an arrow.

"Then said Saul unto his armour-bearer, Draw thy sword, and thrust me through therewith; lest these uncircumcised come and thrust me through, and abuse me. But this armour-bearer would not; for he was sore afraid. Therefore Saul took a sword, and fell upon it.

"And when the men of Israel that were on the other side of the Valley, and they that were on the other side Jordan saw that the men of Israel fled, and that Saul and his sons were dead, they forsook the cities, and fled; and the Philistines came and dwelt in them."

The morning after the battle, as the Philistines were stripping the dead of their valuables, they came upon the bodies of Saul and his three sons. They cut off Saul's head and stripped him of his armor, which they sent back to their own country as a souvenir. Then they fastened the decapitated body to the wall of Beth-Shan, the fortress city at the juncture of the Valley of Jezreel and the Jordan, which has already figured several times in the Jordan story.

When the people of Jabesh-gilead, who several years earlier had been saved from the Ammonites by Saul, heard of his death and the desecration of his body, they made their way quickly and in large numbers over the Jordan by night to Beth-Shan and found, impaled on the city wall, not only Saul's decapitated body but the mutilated corpses of his three sons. It took them until almost dawn to cross back over the river with the remains of the four men and reach home. There they burned the corpses and gave the bones an honorable burial under a certain tree, and for seven days the people of the city fasted and mourned, as a sign of the affection they had borne for the king who had once saved them.

When David learned of the death of the man who had forced him to live in hiding for so many years, he reacted in an unexpected manner.

"Then David took hold on his clothes and rent them; and likewise all the men that were with him;

"And they mourned and wept, and fasted until even, for Saul, and for Jonathan his son, and for the people of the Lord, and for the house of Israel; because they were fallen by the sword."

Then David composed a lamentation so powerful in its phraseology, so beautiful in its poetry, that parts of it have been committed to memory by countless millions in the past three thousand years:

"Tell it not in Gath, publish it not in the streets of Askelon; lest the daughters of the Philistines rejoice, lest the daughters of the uncircumcised triumph . . .

"Saul and Jonathan were lovely and pleasant in their lives, and in their death they were not divided: they were swifter than eagles, they were stronger than lions.

"Ye daughters of Israel, weep over Saul, who clothed you in scarlet, with other delights, who put on ornaments of gold upon your apparel.

"How are the mighty fallen in the midst of the battle! O Jonathan, thou wast slain in thine high places.

"I am distressed for thee, my brother Jonathan: very pleasant hast thou been unto me: thy love to me was wonderful, passing the love of women.

"How are the mighty fallen, and the weapons of war perished!"

At Hebron, David was anointed king of Judah. To the north, one of Saul's surviving sons, Ishbosheth, was made king of the other tribes, whose territory was now called Israel. Although those of the House of David and those of the House of Saul were all members of the Twelve

Tribes of Israel, with common ancestors, a common religion, and common interests, they began a civil war that lasted for years, with the pursued and the pursuers often chasing each other through the Valley, and sometimes back and forth across the river.

Again, as when David had been a fugitive from Saul, the tribes east of the Jordan went to his support. The Reubenites, the Gadites, and the men of the half-tribe of Manasseh sent to Hebron not only 20,100 men, but also "all manner of instruments of war." To avoid marching through Saul's territory, they prudently chose to wade the Jordan near the Jericho crossing. When they arrived in David's provisional capital they were welcomed with three days of feasting and drinking, "for there was joy in Israel."

Assassinations and political murders were common in these times. Ishbosheth's forces were in charge of Abner, a cousin of Saul. One day Ishbosheth accused Abner of intimacies with the concubine of the deceased Saul, the implication being that Abner sought to use this as a first step in trying to acquire the throne for himself. In his anger Abner decided to defect. Accompanied by twenty loyal friends, he paid a call on King David and offered his support. In gratitude David gave a banquet for him and treated him as a welcome friend. After Abner left for home, Joab, David's nephew and also his military commander, who had been away on a mission at the time, returned home, learned of Abner's visit and in his eagerness to eliminate a potential rival for the king's favor, pursued Abner and killed him. Soon thereafter, during the heat of the day when King Ishbosheth was resting, two of his own captains broke into his chamber and killed him, then decapitated him. During the ensuing night they transported the head to Hebron and presented it to David, saying:

"Behold the head of Ishbosheth, the son of Saul thine enemy . . . "

Instead of congratulating them and giving them the large reward they expected, he sternly castigated them, then announced that in punishment for their crime it would be necessary for him to "take you away from the earth." So he issued the necessary orders to his bodyguards, and—

" . . . they slew them, and cut off their hands and their feet, and hanged them over the pool of Hebron. But they took the head of Ishbosheth and buried it in the sepulchre of Abner in Hebron."

Soon thereafter David was made king of the tribes of Israel as well as of the Tribe of Judah, and immediately set out to conquer the enemies of all twelve tribes.

David must often have traversed the Valley and gone back and forth frequently over the river, for in those days it was customary for a king actually to lead his men into battle.

One of these across-the-Jordan military expeditions has remained forever cloaked in mystery: David's campaign against Moab. It was the land of his great-grandmother, the beautiful Ruth. It had once provided sanctuary for his ancestors, and recently he had been welcomed there himself, during his flight from Saul.

One speculation is that David's parents may somehow have been killed while they were refugees in Moab in the time of Saul, and that this attack was in revenge. At any rate, David "smote Moab" and destroyed two-thirds of the inhabitants with the sword, saving only one-third alive.

Measured by the standards of the day, the killing of only two-thirds of the population was not at all vindictive and cruel; most oriental princes of David's time would have pursued the currently accepted policy of putting *all* the vanquished to death. But there is still a mystery as to why David should have attacked Moab at all.

After this victory David remained on the far side of the Jordan long enough to wage war on Hadadezar, king of Zobah, a land to the north of Damascus. The wealth of the kingdom was indicated by the loot David's forces seized, including a thousand chariots. Enemy casualties numbered seven thousand dead cavalrymen and twenty thousand dead foot soldiers. Of the several thousand horses seized, all were hamstrung except a number sufficient to draw a hundred chariots. These were taken across the Jordan to be used in a triumphal home-coming parade. (It is interesting to note that David's army apparently was not as yet trained to operate either a cavalry unit or a chariot force. The words of Moses about "warlike races that use horses in battle" may also have been a factor.)

The area at the base of Mount Hermon, in which the Jordan has its beginnings, was the northernmost point to which the power of the Israelites had ever gone, although they had been promised territory far beyond. The city of Hamath, on the banks of the impetuous Orontes River, had been included in the Promised Land, as envisioned by both Abraham and Moses. The king of this area did not wait to be subjugated by David's forces. Instead, he sent his son to Jerusalem with valuable gifts of gold, silver and bronze. Thus David became the first real master of the entire Promised Land on both sides of the Jordan.

The river figures in a story that is often quoted to show the intensity of David's feeling about his deceased father-in-law, Saul, and Jonathan, Saul's son. During the period of peace that followed the defeat of the enemies of Israel and Judah, David asked:

"Is there yet any that is left of the House of Saul, that I may show him kindness for Jonathan's sake?"

The reply came from a servant in the House of Saul, Ziba, who said that Jonathan had had a son, Mephibosheth, who was "lame in both his feet," so David sent for him. He lived in Lo-debar, a city on the east side of the Jordan. After crossing the river and making his way to Jerusalem, he bowed low before David and was told by the king:

"Fear not: for I will surely shew thee kindness for Jonathan thy father's sake, and will restore thee all the land of Saul thy father; and thou shalt eat bread at my table continually."

So Saul's crippled grandson moved from Lo-debar across the Jordan to Jerusalem with his son, his many servants, and all his possessions, and for years "ate continually at the king's table," and David gave all of Saul's estates to Mephibosheth, with Ziba as their custodian.

But another attempt at kindness on David's part backfired. Death had come to Nahash, the king of the Ammonites, who in Saul's day had threatened to poke out the right eyes of all the men of Jabesh-gilead, but who had shown certain kindnesses to David, so David sent servants to Hanun, who had succeeded his father on the throne, to convey his condolences and good wishes. But certain Ammonite princes persuaded the new king that David had sent the servants to act as spies.

"Whereupon Hanun took David's servants, and shaved off the one half of their beards, and cut their garments in the middle, even to their buttocks, and sent them away."

When David heard the news, he ordered the servants who had been subjected to such humiliation to come back across the Jordan but to remain at Jericho until their beards grew out.

"And when the children of Ammon saw that they stank before David, the children of Ammon sent and hired the Syrians of Beth-rehob, and the Syrians of Zoba, twenty thousand footmen, and of king Maacah a thousand men, and of Ish-tob twelve thousand men."

David sent his military commander, Joab, with a host of mighty men across the Jordan to do battle with this combined Ammonite-Syrian force. The Syrians fled as far as Helam, a Transjordanian city. There Syrian reinforcements arrived from the north.

"And when it was told David, he gathered all Israel together, and passed over Jordan, and came to Helam. And the Syrians set themselves in array against David, and fought with him.

"And the Syrians fled before Israel; and David slew the men of seven hundred chariots of the Syrians, and forty thousand horsemen, and smote Shobach the captain of their host, who died there."

David then crossed back to his own side of the Jordan and for a time there was peace with the Syrians. This gave David a chance to deal with the Ammonites alone. He sent Joab to besiege Rabbah (or Rabbath), the capital of Ammon, about twenty-two miles east of the Jordan. Many things happened before the city fell. David had remained at home in Jerusalem, where, one evening, unable to sleep, he was pacing the roof of his palace on Mount Zion when he saw a beautiful young woman in a courtyard below, washing her hair. Inquiry brought the report that she was Bathsheba, wife of Uriah, one of the principal officers in David's army. He was not an Israelite, being descended from Hittites, the people from whom Abraham, so many generations ago, had bought the cave at Machpelah. Uriah was away with the army, engaged in the siege of Rabbah across the river.

"And David sent messengers, and took her; and she came in unto him, and he lay with her . . .

"And the woman conceived and sent and told David, and said, I am with child."

Eager to hide the parentage of the unborn child, David sent for Uriah and ordered a furlough for him, but nothing would induce the officer to sleep in his own house, not even the wine with which David finally plied him. In desperation David sent him back to Rabbah with a sealed letter for Joab, containing these instructions:

"Set ye Uriah in the forefront of the hottest battle, and retire ye from him, that he may be smitten and die."

Joab gave Uriah command of a force that was to make a hazardous attack on a strongly fortified sector of the city wall of Rabbah. Thus, as planned, Uriah was killed, by a well-aimed Ammonite arrow. After a month of formal mourning, David and Bathsheba were married and she bore him a son, but "the thing that David had done displeased the Lord," so the son fell ill and died.

"And David comforted Bathsheba his wife, and went in unto her, and lay with her; and she bare a son, and he called his name Solomon: and the Lord loved him."

By this time Joab sent word home that he had finally taken Rabbah, "the city of waters," which was the same city in which the iron bedstead of Og of Bashan had been put on permanent display after the death of the giant king. The siege must have lasted almost two years, to give time for the love affair with Bathsheba, the death of Uriah, the birth and death of the first child, then the conception and birth of Solomon. When victory was in sight, Joab, with great magnanimity, offered to delay the actual occupation of Rabbah until David could arrive on the scene. In his message to the king he said:

"Now therefore gather the rest of the people together, and encamp against the city, and take it: lest I take the city, and it be called after my name."

Thus David captured Rabbah and came into possession of King Hanun's crown of gold and precious jewels, weighing one talent (sixty-six pounds) which he set upon his own head.

"And he brought forth the people that were therein, and put them under saws, and under harrows of iron, and under axes of iron, and made them pass through the brick-kiln: and thus did he unto all the cities of the children of Ammon."

Then David and his army returned back across the Jordan to Jerusalem.

Part of the story of Absalom—an epic that reveals David's tenderness, caution, prudence and good judgment—took place in the Jordan Valley.

The favorite among David's many sons was his first-born, Amnon, whose mother was a Jezreelitess. The king's affection for the boy amounted almost to worship. In natural opposition were David's third son, Absalom ("Father of Peace"), and a daughter. Their mother was Maachah, daughter of Talmai, king of Geshur, a city across the Jordan and far to the northeast, in Syria. Absalom was an exceedingly handsome young man: ". . . in all Israel there was none so much praised as Absalom for his beauty; from the sole of his feet even to the crown of his head there was no blemish in him." It was the "crown of his head" that was his crowning glory—and his undoing. Whenever he had a haircut, which was perhaps only several times a year, the hair was weighed and a record kept. On one occasion the cuttings were found to weigh two hundred shekels (more than nine pounds).

Absalom's sister was extraordinarily beautiful, which was the direct cause of the tragedy. Because of her grace, she was named Tamar, meaning "Palm Tree," for the palm was considered the most graceful of all oriental trees. She was also well known by the entire royal family for her skill in making a special sort of cakes.

The family trouble began when young Amnon became deeply enamoured of his half sister, growing "morning by morning paler and paler, leaner and leaner," as a result of his desperate passion. Amnon had a cousin, Jonadab, typical of many a man in many a royal household who prided himself on knowing all the family secrets and on being clever enough to deal with any family situation. It was Jonadab who gave Amnon the dreadful idea. Acting upon his cousin's suggestion, Amnon played ill. When his father showed concern, he suggested that he might feel better if David would permit Tamar to come to his apartment and prepare her famous cakes in his presence. Unsuspecting his son's malicious design, the king sent Tamar to him. She was dutifully trying to please her half-brother in her best culinary manner when Amnon suggested that she come into his bed. She refused. But Amnon "being stronger than she, forced her, and lay with her." Then suddenly Amnon's passionate love turned to brutal hatred, and he drove the girl from his apartment. In a frenzy of grief and indignation, Tamar tore the sleeves from her royal robe—a gown of a design customarily worn by virgins—and with her arms now bare ran through the streets until she saw a pile of ashes. Grabbing a handful, she covered her head with them and then continued running, screaming and bewailing her fate, until Absalom saw her, took her into his own home, and learned from her what had happened.

King David was either emotionally unable or unwilling to act, and so, by oriental custom, it fell to Absalom to avenge the wrong to his sister. He waited a full two years before acting. Then one day he invited all of David's sons to a pastoral festival at his country home near Ephraim. When Amnon had drunk deeply of wine, Absalom instructed his servants to kill him. There was panic on the part of those who witnessed the murder. The other princes rushed to their mules and galloped back to Jerusalem, fearful that something desperate in Absalom's character had now opened up an immeasurable vista of vengeance.

The first report of the tragedy to reach David was grossly exaggerated, as is so often the case, even in modern times, with the first reports of disasters. David was told that all his sons had been killed in a terrible mass tragedy. The actual truth was dark and ugly enough for a man of David's sensitivity.

Absalom, fleeing from the parental wrath that he was sure would be even stronger than the grief, made his way from Jerusalem to Jericho, and then down to the Jordan and across to the far side, and up the east Valley until he reached Geshur, in Syria, where he sought asylum with his maternal grandfather, King Talmai. David mourned constantly, not so much for Amnon, now that his favorite son was dead, but for Absalom, who, he hoped, was still alive.

After three years David sent his commander-in-chief and nephew,

Joab, to bring Absalom back from the north country to Jerusalem. The errant son returned with Joab through the east Valley, across the Jordan near Jericho, and thence to Jerusalem, where he took up residence again in his own home. No punishment was meted out to him, but he was forbidden ever to see David. For two years father and son never met face to face. Then Absalom, in desperation, had his servants set fire to the barley fields of Joab. When Joab arrived to protest, Absalom demanded that he arrange an audience for him with his father, and "if there be any iniquity in me, let him kill me." Instead of killing him, David embraced him.

But not long after this Absalom conspired to overthrow his father. His first step was to set himself up in Hebron as a rival monarch. David was so distressed by reports of the support his son was winning among the people of Israel that he fled in fright from Jerusalem, declaring to his servants and staff:

". . . make speed to depart, lest he overtake us suddenly, and bring evil upon us, and smite the city with the edge of the sword."

No Israelite incident is narrated in as much detail in the Bible as David's flight from Jerusalem down into the Valley. He left the city accompanied by his entire court. The only members of his household who remained behind were ten women of his harem, who started out with him but were sent back to occupy the otherwise empty palace. The mules and asses were also left behind. Everyone went on foot. The long procession was led by a bodyguard of Philistines, followed by a great number of ordinary soldiers, then the high officers of the court, and finally King David himself in the midst of six hundred picked warriors, with their wives and children.

The procession went down into and across the deep ravine of the Kidron, now called the Wadi en-Nar, which is dry and sunbaked most of the year. This was a signal that David was truly determined on flight, and so a wail of grief arose from the whole procession and seemed to be echoed back by the very mountains themselves, as if "all the country wept with a loud voice." As the grief-stricken monarch and his court slowly and painfully made their way from village to village, town to town, there was a great stir among the people, for the tragedy was easily sensed. The king, who had intentionally gone barefooted, drew his cloak over his head and so the others did likewise. All were weeping. As the procession headed now for the Jordan, another burst of wild lament went up from those who were following David, for they suspected where he was going.

On the way down toward the river the procession was met by Ziba, the servant of Mephibosheth, grandson of Saul. He was driving a number of asses loaded with two hundred loaves of bread and one hundred bunches of raisins, besides other fruit and wine.

"What meanest thou by these?" David asked in surprise.

"The asses are for the king's household to ride on," Ziba explained, "and the bread and summer fruit for the young men to eat, and the wine, that such as be faint in the wilderness may drink."

Then Ziba falsely reported that his master, Mephibosheth, had deserted the king. David, in anger, decided that a fit punishment would be to give to Ziba all the property he had previously given to Mephibosheth. This was exactly the reward the servant had hoped for.

"I humbly beseech thee that I may find grace in thy sight, my lord, O King," Ziba said, as he turned back toward Jerusalem.

On the way down to the river the procession passed through the town of Bahurim. Here Shimei, who was of the House of Saul, came into the road and hurled both imprecations and rocks, first at David and then at those who accompanied him. Here was sad but tangible proof of the intensity of the conflict between the rival dynasties. The Benjaminite saw in David a "bloody man," who had betrayed the House of Saul.

The exiles were in a state of physical and emotional exhaustion by the time they reached the thickets of the Jordan and refreshed themselves while they awaited tidings from Jerusalem. The feelings that surged through the heart and soul of David that night as he prepared to sleep on the west bank of the Jordan are well expressed by him in Psalm 4, which ends:

"I will both lay me down in peace, and sleep: for thou, Lord, only makest me dwell in safety."

He recorded his feelings the next morning in Psalm 3:

"I laid me down and slept; I awakened; for the Lord sustained me.

"I will not be afraid of ten thousands of people, that have set themselves against me round about."

It must have been early the next morning when two messengers reached the edge of the Jordan with news that Absalom had arrived in Jerusalem from Hebron, but had decided to wait and mount a full-scale military operation against his father's forces rather than to take after him immediately. On hearing this news David arose quickly, "and all the people that were with him, and they passed over Jordan: by the morning light there lacked not one of them that was not gone over Jordan."

After fording the river they made their way to Mahanaim in Gilead, an ancient Transjordanian hideaway. There three potentates of the district came forward with offers of support. Of equal importance, they supplied David and his men with "beds, and basons, and earthen vessels, and wheat, and barley, and flour, and parched corn, and beans, and lentiles, and parched pulse,

"And honey, and butter, and sheep, and cheese of kine, for David, and for the people that were with him, to eat: for they said, The people is hungry, and weary, and thirsty, in the wilderness."

The fear that had possessed David now vanished. In this wilderness hideout his spirits revived, as he arranged his army into three divisions and began to plan how he would meet the forces of his own son in battle. He wished to take command of one division himself, but he was persuaded that his own life was worth that of ten thousand other men and that he should remain behind in the fortress of Mahanaim when the battle commenced.

Back in Jerusalem, Absalom, after he had been formally anointed king, put his army in charge of a cousin, then led the way across the Jordan in pursuit of his father.

The first battle of the family war was fought in a forest just south of the Wadi al Yabis and only a short distance east of the Valley of the Jordan. It is a measure of David's character and his feelings for Absalom that as the battle began he issued specific instructions to his commanders to make sure no harm came to the young revolutionary.

"Deal gently for my sake with the young man, even with Absalom."

In the first battle twenty thousand men were killed. The real tragedy of the day, however, began with a strange accident. Absalom, riding a mule, somehow got lost in a thicket—a geographical peculiarity on the west side of the Jordan but quite common on the east side. Suddenly he met a detachment of David's army. Wheeling his mule around, he tried to make off through the woods, but his long hair was caught by an overhanging branch of an immense oak tree. Apparently it was the season of the year when his hair had not been cut for a long time. The mule ran on, leaving Absalom suspended.

Joab, who was in charge of all three royal divisions, must have been near the scene of the strange accident, for a soldier rushed to him and announced:

"Behold, I saw Absalom hanged in an oak."

Joab berated the soldier saying:

" . . . why didst thou not smite him there to the ground? and I would have given thee ten shekels of silver, and a girdle."

The soldier replied:

"Though I should receive a thousand shekels of silver in mine hand, yet would I not put forth mine hand against the king's son: for in our hearing the king charged thee and Abishai and Ittai, saying, Beware that none touch the young man Absalom."

Impetuously Joab and ten attendants rushed off to the great oak tree. Absalom was still dangling, so they surrounded the tree, then Joab himself did what the others hesitated to do: he took three "darts" (probably pikes) and "thrust them through the heart of Absalom, while he was yet alive in the midst of the oak." Then with their swords the ten attendants finished the bloody job. Nearby there was a ditch or pit of vast dimensions into which the corpse was thrown, then it was covered with heavy stones.

David sat between the two gates of Mahanaim waiting for news of the battle. In a tower high above the gates a watchman scanned the horizon and reported down to the king everything he observed. Suddenly he shouted that he saw two messengers approaching rapidly, each apparently endeavoring to outstrip the other. The first to arrive was Ahimaaz, whose fleetness of foot was a legend on both sides of the Jordan. But he had been instructed by Joab to conceal the truth from David, and dutifully he did, merely giving a vague battle report. Then the second messenger (perhaps an Ethiopian slave or maybe one of the ten attendants) arrived and pantingly blurted out the truth.

David's spontaneous outburst of passionate grief is one more proof of the basic goodness of his character. His cry was one of the most simple yet tragic laments anywhere in history or literature:

"O my son Absalom, my son, my son Absalom! would God I had died for thee, O Absalom, my son, my son!"

Then David rushed up to the watchman's chamber over the gate and eight times repeated his lament. It has been the belief ever since, among at least some of the learned Jewish religious men, that at each cry one of the seven gates of hell opened, and that with the eighth, the lost spirit of Absalom was received into the place of eternal rest.

David returned home victorious but greatly saddened. How and where he crossed the Jordan this time we do know exactly, for the biblical account says that "Judah came to Gilgal, to go to meet the king, to conduct the king over Jordan." In the detailed account of this crossing, the biblical writers for the first time tell the precise means of getting over the river:

"And there went over a ferry boat to carry over the king's household."

This is the first and only time in the Bible that mention is made of ferry boats on the Jordan, although it is now thought that there were probably many of them, especially on the Lower Jordan. It has been suggested that David's men actually built a bridge of ferry boats over the river. This could have been done if it was midsummer, but in flood season no pontoon bridge could possibly have withstood the force of the current at this point.

On the banks of the river that day David received full proof of his own popularity. Never had such a company been assembled by the Jordan since Joshua led his followers across the dried-up river bed. Among the throng was Shimei, the Benjaminite who had cursed and stoned the king so short a time ago. Now he was present to greet David on bended knee and beg forgiveness, his petition strengthened by the presence of a band of a thousand of his stalwarts.

"For thy servant doth know that I have sinned: therefore, behold, I am come the first this day of all the house of Joseph to go down (to the river's edge) to meet my lord the king."

One of David's aides suggested that Shimei should be put to death, then and there, but David, in a spirit of happy forgiveness, said to his former reviler:

"Thou shalt not die."

Another emotional scene took place between David and the lame grandson of Saul. In the many months since David's flight from Jerusalem, Mephibosheth had "neither dressed his feet, nor trimmed his beard, nor washed his clothes," as outward signs of his loyalty. He must have been a repulsive sight, his long flowing hair matted with dirt, squalid in his squalor, but happy, now that the long period of mourning for his benefactor was over.

Ziba was also on the river bank; Ziba, who so short a time ago had supplied David with food and drink—and with a false report about the loyalty of his master. Now, desirous of retaining the king's good will, he had come to the Jordan with his fifteen sons and twenty servants, to pay his respects.

Barzillai ("Man of Iron"), one of those who had supplied David and his men with food when they first crossed the river, also came to take farewell of his friend. In gratitude for the kindness Barzillai had shown, David invited him to come and live in the royal palace.

Barzillai, with a smile, told the king that he was already eighty years old, too old to discern between good and evil, or to enjoy good food and drink, or to appreciate the music of singing men and women. He would go over the Jordan with David, but then would turn back and die in his own city and be buried by the graves of his father and mother.

But he suggested that his son, Chimham, accompany David, "and do to him what shall seem good unto thee."

David agreed. Then he, Barzillai, Chimham, and "all the people" went across the Jordan and on the far bank the king kissed and blessed his old friend, who then went back over the river to his home.

So "all the people of Judah . . . and also half the people of Israel" accompanied David as he made his triumphal way back through the Valley and up the hills to Jerusalem. Unfortunately, almost immediately a new civil war broke out. Those living in the north, in Israel, and those in the south, in Judah, began wrangling over David: did he belong to Israel or to Judah? The men of Israel complained that David had been "stolen" from them and had been escorted across the river by the men of Judah and demanded to know what right Judah had to him. The men of Judah replied "Because the king is near of kin to us . . . "

The men of Israel retorted:

"We have ten parts in the king, and we have also more right in David than ye: why then did ye despise us, that our advice should not be first had in bringing back our king?"

The feud terminated, for the time, when a Benjaminite named Sheba blew a trumpet and declared to the Israelites:

"We have no part in David, neither have we inheritance in the son of Jesse: every man to his tents, O Israel."

So the Israelites followed Sheba, while the men of Judah accompanied David from the banks of the Jordan to Jerusalem. The revolt that Sheba tried to stir up was brought to an end in a strange manner. David's men had just begun to besiege the city in which Sheba had taken refuge when a woman resident offered to kill and decapitate the rebel leader and throw his head over the city wall to David's men if they would call off the siege. David's commander agreed and a few minutes later Sheba's head was tossed over the city wall, and the fighting ended.

One more crossing of the Jordan occurred as an indirect result of David's attempt to put an end to a three-year famine that plagued the land between the years 1025 and 1022 B.C. When David was informed that the famine was divine punishment for Saul's slaying of so many Gibeonites in his effort to eliminate this remnant of foreigners who dwelt in a hill city in the heart of Israel, he asked the Gibeonites what he could do in atonement. Their reply was a demand that David deliver to them seven sons of the man who "devised against us." David picked two of Saul's sons born to him by the concubine Rizpah, and five sons of Michal, his own wife, who had been Saul's youngest daughter.

"And he delivered them into the hands of the Gibeonites, and they hanged them in the hill before the Lord: and they fell all seven together, and were put to death in the days of harvest, in the first days, in the beginning of barley harvest."

One of the strange yet charming features of David's character was his ambivalent attitude toward Saul, who in his dealings with his son-in-law had been both vindictive and murderously inclined, yet ambivalent himself. But to David he remained, always, his early benefactor and patron. Most important, he was "the Lord's anointed." Saul's death enhanced David's reverence for the man who had driven him from his home, outlawed him, and even robbed him of his wife. Now he decided to pay a last honor to his memory, so he went down to the Jordan, forded the river, traveled a long distance up the Valley to Jabesh-gilead and there personally supervised the exhumation of the remains of Saul and his son Jonathan, which were transported under David's supervision over the river for a third time, and were buried in the sepulcher of Saul's father at Kish.

The trip to retrieve the bodies was apparently the last time David crossed the river, but while he still lived there was a notable crossing by census takers, after God had instructed the king to "go number Israel and Judah." The task force was headed by Joab and included a number of captains. They crossed the Jordan and went down to the Reubenite city of Aroer, on the River Arnon, which marked the southernmost point occupied by any of the sons of Israel. Then they worked their way north until they came to the headwaters of the Jordan, in the area of Dan. Then south down the west side of the river all the way to Beersheba. At the end of nine months and twenty days they returned to Jerusalem with their report:

" . . . and there were in Israel eight hundred thousand valiant men that drew the sword; and the men in Judah were five hundred thousand men." This must have meant a total population, counting the young, the old, and females of all ages, of well over five million.

When David was "old and stricken in years" and was plagued by cold, no matter how many coverlets were placed over him, one of his servants suggested:

"Let there be sought for my lord the king a young virgin: and let her stand before the king, and let her cherish him, and let her lie in thy bosom, that my lord the king may get heat."

After a search through all Israel, a young woman named Abishag of the Tribe of Issachar was found dwelling in Shunem in the Valley of Esdraelon. She was sent to Jerusalem, probably by way of the Valley and Jericho, and was given the task suggested by the king's servant, but the scheme was unsuccessful.

"... the damsel was very fair, and cherished the king, and ministered to him: but the king knew her not."

On his deathbed David's magnanimity and sentimentality showed themselves, when, in giving last-minute instructions to his son Solomon, who was to succeed him, he asked that special kindness be shown to the sons of Barzillai, who lived across the river in Gilead, "for they came to me when I fled from Absalom thy brother."

Then he remembered another character in that chapter of his life, Shimei of Bahurim, the Benjaminite who had cursed and stoned him, but later had repented and had come to the banks of the Jordan to welcome him back across the river. David explained to Solomon that he had promised not to slay him, but had now decided that Shimei had actually been guilty of sowing dissension and should be punished, a suggestion Solomon carried out three years after he succeeded to the throne, when he suspected Shimei of conniving against him and ordered him killed.

In his last days, David the psalmist proved that his poetic fire had not yet been extinguished. Psalm 71, said to be one of the last he ever wrote, is considered by critics one of his finest. Without complaint, but merely as if he were putting something into the record, he wrote:

"Thou, which hast shewed me great and sore troubles ... Thou shalt increase my greatness, and comfort me on every side."

Then in Psalm 72, writing prophetically about his son Solomon, he said:

"He shall have dominion also from sea to sea, and from the river unto the ends of the earth."

The psalm concludes:

"The prayers of David the son of Jesse are ended."

In a warm and encouraging talk to his son Solomon, David said:

"Be strong and of good courage, and do it: fear not, nor be dismayed: for the Lord God, even my God, will be with thee; he will not fail thee, nor forsake thee ...."

They are words that have strengthened the hearts and quickened the determination of many Jews and Christians alike, since then.

And so, in his seventieth year, David died and Solomon mounted the throne.

During the forty years of Solomon's rule, the people of the Valley knew both peace and plenty. Because he had inherited an immense empire, his main task throughout his life was to hold onto what had been handed down to him, rather than to try to extend his frontiers. For this reason he conducted no major military campaigns, so this chapter of the Jordan story is almost entirely devoid of bloodshed.

"And Judah and Israel dwelt safely, every man under his vine and under his fig tree, from Dan even to Beersheba, all the days of Solomon."

When God appeared to Solomon in a dream at Gibeon, the young king made one request:

"Give therefore thy servant an understanding heart to judge thy people, that I may discern between good and bad . . ."

In answer to that prayer "God gave Solomon wisdom and understanding exceeding much, and largeness of heart, even as the sand that is on the sea shore.

"And Solomon's wisdom excelled the wisdom of all the children of the east country, and all the wisdom of Egypt.

"For he was wiser than all men . . ."

Rapidly his reputation spread. "And there came of all people to hear the wisdom of Solomon, from all kings of the earth, which had heard of his wisdom."

Early in his regime he established a reputation not only as a patron of the arts, but as a practitioner himself. He was credited with composing three thousand proverbs and one thousand and five songs.

What interested the people of the Valley most was that in the four hundred and eightieth year after the children of Israel left Egypt—in the fourth year of Solomon's reign—he began construction of a great temple at Jerusalem. It was built with cedars cut in Lebanon. Thirty thousand men were drafted in Israel to help with the timber operation. Much stone was also used, which was cut within Israel by some of the hundred and fifty thousand other conscripted men. The labor force was so large that thirty-three hundred foremen were needed. The Temple was to be the crowning achievement of Solomon's reign. Many immense pieces of cedar were carved with elaborate designs. Pure gold leaf was used to cover the entire altar, two giant cherubims, the floor of the Temple, two immense fir doors, and much else in the interior. It took seven years to build the Temple and another thirteen years to finish a palace Solomon built for himself, called the King's House.

All Israelites had some interest, religious or commercial, or both, in the construction of the Temple, but the people of the Valley had a special concern, for great brass foundries were established at this time in the Valley, between Succoth and Zarthan, about midway from the Sea of Chinnereth to the Salt Sea. This location was chosen because the clay here was perfect for casting. Brass was used extensively in the Temple, in making the huge pillars, and the chapiters to set on the top of the pillars, and for lavers, pots, shovels and basons.

In the first chapter of Genesis, the entire creation of heaven and earth, the seas and the sky, the birds, beasts, and humans, is told in 796 words. In The First Book of the Kings, Chapter 7, many more words than that are devoted to a description of the shape, size and design of the brasswork in the Temple. For example:

"And the chapiters upon the two pillars had pomegranates also above, over against the belly which was by the network: and the pomegranates were two hundred in rows round about upon the other chapiter."

In those days the ruler of the neighboring kingdom of Tyre was King Hiram. Through a trade treaty with Solomon, he supplied the wood from Lebanon, and also skilled craftsmen for the construction of the Temple, in return for an annual payment in barley and wine. By coincidence, the man in charge of Solomon's brass foundries in the Jordan Valley was also named Hiram, a widow's son from the Tribe of Naphtali, whose father, a Phoenician, had taught him the secrets of making fine brass. He was "filled with wisdom, and understanding, and cunning to work all works in brass. And he came to king Solomon, and wrought all his work."

The heavy brasswork that came from the foundries in the Valley had to be transported many miles over rough terrain and poor roads to the Temple site, but worse, the trip involved a climb of nearly 4000 feet, for the foundries were located at a point where the Jordan is 1100 feet below sea level, while Jerusalem is 2697 feet above sea level.

Solomon has been called the world's first great "mining magnate," because during his reign the extraction, refining, smelting and fabrication of metal received such an impetus. Deposits of copper were being worked in the Negev. Deposits of iron were discovered on the banks of the River Yabbok, near the Jordan Valley. Metal slag of ancient date has been found in the vicinity of Succoth and, also, farther east of the river, near Ajlun. The presence of metals attracted great numbers of workers to this area in Solomon's time and helped to make the Valley prosper.

During the twenty years that the Temple and the King's House were under construction, a pleasant business and personal relationship was built up between King Solomon and King Hiram of Tyre, who was supplying not only cedar and fir trees for lumber, but also a considerable quantity of gold for decorative use. After the completion of both structures, Solomon, to show his gratitude, gave Hiram twenty cities in Galilee as a gift. It is uncertain how many were in the Upper Jordan Valley, for no precise list has been handed down. The gift was not well received.

"And Hiram came out from Tyre to see the cities which Solomon had given him; and they pleased him not.

"And he said, What cities are these which thou hast given me, my brother? And he called them the land of Cabul unto this day."

This was a play on words. There was a city in the North by that name and it probably was one of the twenty given to Hiram. But the king's ironic use of the word probably rested on its derivation—from the Hebrew word for "as nothing." In effect Hiram was saying:

"Thank you, for nothing."

But apparently his opinion of the gift did not interfere with his continued pleasant relationship with Solomon, because soon thereafter he sent another large shipment of gold to Jerusalem.

The twenty cities were settled by a mixed population and the whole area came to be known as "the District of the Gentile" (Galil) and eventually, therefore, Galilee.

Solomon's control of the picturesque but forbidding land leading to the Red Sea enabled him to build a fleet, to open a profitable trade with distant countries, and to play host to the Queen of Sheba. The visit of the foreign queen was probably the high point of Solomon's career. From the Red Sea harbor in which her ship anchored, the Sabacan queen traveled overland to Jerusalem, by what route history does not say. It is unlikely that she stepped foot in the Jordan Valley, or that she even saw the Salt Sea. The purpose of her twelve-hundred-mile trip is everywhere stated to have been to test Solomon's wisdom by propounding difficult questions to him, but it is likely that she came also to negotiate a trade agreement with Solomon, whose control of the trade routes was probably jeopardizing the income that her kingdom normally received from caravans crossing Sheba, which present-day Ethiopians say was comprised of what is now Yemen and Ethiopia.

One of the myriad legends that grew up about Solomon purports to explain how the curative springs of the Sea of Chinnereth were created in his time.

A company of invalid men from Galilee one day called on King Solomon in Jerusalem and their spokesman, addressing him, said:

"Beloved King, may thou live forever. Thou art wiser above all men. Thou hast adorned Jerusalem with a great Temple to our God. Yet of what avail is all this, if thou canst find no cure for the ills of our bodies, no help for our aching limbs, no remedy for our boils, or the leprosy that plagues us. We beseech thee to help thy poor servants."

So Solomon issued a command to a company of demons, saying to them:

"Hearken, ye demons. In Galilee there is a spring close to a large lake which, like all springs, flows with cold water. Go ye down to the depths of the earth and heat the waters of this spring."

The demons, fearing Solomon, did as he bid and heated the waters to an exceedingly high temperature. As a precaution, Solomon made all the demons deaf, knowing that if they should someday hear the news of his death, they would no longer fear him and might cease to heat the waters of the spring. The legend concludes with the information that although Solomon is dead, the spring is still hot, thanks to the great king's wisdom.

One secret of peace in Solomon's time was his foreign policy of forming friendly alliances with foreign countries; another was his formidable military strength. Throughout his long reign he maintained a sizable conscript army. The backbone of his defensive system was a ring of cities strategically located on the frontiers of Israel and manned by companies of charioteers. One book of the Bible says that in those outposts he had stalls for forty thousand horses, but another book of the Bible makes it four thousand. One of these fortress cities was Hazor, within the Valley and about ten miles north of the Sea of Chinnereth. As early as the nineteenth century B.C. there had been a city at this place, for it was often mentioned in early Assyrian and Egyptian records. During the Israelite conquest six hundred years later Hazor was the most important city in northern Canaan. By Solomon's time there was nothing left of its ancient grandeur, so he ordered a new city built on the remains of the old, and it became one of his most important chariot towns. In Hazor, as well as in Meggido, guarding the Plain of Jezreel, and in many of the other chariot towns, Solomon's engineers built elaborate systems for feeding and watering the horses. This was but one example of the high state of organization that developed in those times in many fields of human endeavor. Another was the efficiency system that was devised for feeding the thousands of people attached in one way or another to Solomon's household. Twelve officers in twelve clearly delineated districts were responsible. Each was required to deliver the victuals for one calendar month of each year, including ten fat oxen, twenty oxen out of the pastures, a hundred sheep, thirty measures of fine flour, sixty measures of meal, "beside harts, and roebucks, and fallow deer, and fatted fowls." Also barley and straw for the horses. One of the twelve, Baana, supplied food from the rich Valley district that lay between Beth-Shan and Abelmeholah, on the west side of the Jordan, as well as from the Valley of Jezreel. Another, Geber, son of Uri, was charged with procuring his one month's supplies each year from Gilead, and transporting it across the Jordan and up the steep way to Jerusalem.

There are no detailed literary, historical, or biblical accounts of what life was like in these times for the mass of the people in the Valley, or in the rest of Israel and Judah, except that most if not all the men of the land were subject to severe taxation and to being drafted for forced labor. A majority if not all the men taken for work in the forests of Lebanon, however, were non-Israelites:

"And all the people that were left of the Amorites, Hittites, Perizzites, Hivites, and Jebusites, which were not of the children of Israel,

"Their children that were left after them in the land, whom the children of Israel also were not able utterly to destroy, upon those did Solomon levy a tribute of bondservice."

The Israelites were also drafted, but apparently were used by Solomon principally as "men of war, and his servants, and his princes, and his captains, and rulers of his chariots, and his horsemen," and also as supervisors and foremen of the vast labor force.

Whatever the condition of the average Israelite, the land prospered under Solomon. In one year he collected six hundred and sixty-six talents of gold from abroad. A talent weighed sixty-six pounds, so his income that year from this single source was $18,480,000, at today's price of gold. The Queen of Sheba, besides bringing to Solomon more spices than had ever been seen before by the Israelites, and great quantities of precious jewels, and numerous other gifts, gave him almost three and a half million dollars' worth of gold. Gold was now so plentiful in Israel that it was used to make three hundred shields for Solomon's bodyguards, and to overlay the king's ivory throne. All the drinking vessels in the King's House were of gold. From all over the world men came to hear Solomon's words of wisdom, and many of them crossed the Jordan or traversed the Valley, their pack animals loaded with gifts for the king: "vessels of silver, and vessels of gold, and garments, and armour, and spices."

Across the river and through the Valley also came women, hoping to find favor in the eyes of Solomon. And many did. "Solomon loved many strange women." In those days an extensive harem was regarded as an important element of royal splendor.

One of Solomon's most noteworthy achievements was obtaining the Egyptian Pharaoh's daughter as his bride. She became his chief queen and had a separate palace of her own. As a result of this alliance, Solomon was able to introduce many Egyptian luxuries into Israel, including horses and chariots. He had twelve thousand saddle horses alone. By establishing a horse market in Israel, he made it unnecessary for princes from surrounding lands to go all the way to Egypt for mounts.

Marriage was one way in which Solomon sealed political and military treaties with his neighbors. During his forty-year reign he had no less than seven hundred wives and three hundred concubines. Some were Moabites from the far side of the Salt Sea, some were Ammonites from over the Jordan, or Edomites from south of the Salt Sea, or Hittites and Zidonians.

Marrying foreign women was politically expedient for Solomon, because each marriage helped to weld another link of mutual self-interest in the chain of friendship that bound Israel to her neighbors. Solomon's marrying propensity was partly responsible for the long era of peace in that part of the world—the Valley of the Jordan included—that for so many hundreds of years had known so much death and destruction. But the marriages brought complications. To placate many of his wives, Solomon joined them in worshiping their pagan gods: Ashtoreth, the Zidonians' goddess of fertility, love and war; Milcom, called the "abomination of the Ammonites"; the Moabites' Chemosh, to whom small children were supposed to be sacrificed by fire. The king built altars to some, and burned incense, and made sacrifices.

By engaging in this syncretistic worship, Solomon was guilty of a serious defiance of Israel's monotheistic ideal.

"And the Lord was angry with Solomon . . ."

As death approached, after a reign of forty years, Solomon knew that punishment would be visited on the house of Israel because of this fatal flaw in his character, although he was told that infliction of the judgment would be stayed until after his death. As a sample of what would happen, several adversaries appeared, even before Solomon's death, to threaten the monolithic Israelite empire, which at the outset of his reign had extended from the Red Sea to the Euphrates, and from the Mediterranean far across the Jordan. Then in his last days Solomon began to hear rumbles of discontent from his own people in the Valley, and across the Jordan, as well as on the west side of the river. His excessive taxation and his harsh policy of forced labor would bear bitter fruit in years soon to come.

The death of the great king is told biblically in one simple sentence: "And Solomon slept with his fathers, and was buried in the city of David his father: and Rehoboam his son reigned in his stead."

Almost at once there was trouble. Solomon had placed in charge of the work force of the northern tribes a young man of humble origin, Jeroboam, who so greatly objected to the king's oppressive practices that he had fomented a revolt. In punishment he was exiled and went to Egypt, where he was befriended by the Pharaoh. Upon Solomon's death he came back home and offered to serve under Rehoboam, if the new king would meet certain conditions. When Rehoboam, after three days' consideration, refused, the people of most of the tribes rebelled. They stoned to death Rehoboam's director of forced labor, and set Jeroboam up as "king of Israel" over all the tribes but Judah and a part of the Tribe of Benjamin which, alone of the other tribes, had remained loyal to the son of Solomon.

Jeroboam built his capital in Shechem, high in the hills to the west of the Jordan, but he crossed over the river to Penuel, which had been destroyed by Gideon, and rebuilt that city, presumably as a defensive point against attacks on his new capital from the east. Jeroboam's next problem was religious. His people were devout, but if they continued to go to Jerusalem to make their sacrifices, he told himself, "then shall the heart of this people turn again unto their lord, even unto Rehoboam king of Judah, and they shall kill me . . ."

Therefore he took counsel and made two calves of gold, and displayed them to his people, saying to them:

"It is too much for you to go up to Jerusalem: behold thy gods, O Israel, which brought thee up out of the land of Egypt."

One of the idols was set up at Bethel, in the far south of the newly delineated kingdom, and the other in the very north, at Dan, the Jordan's headwater city. This was heresy. After the Exodus, while Moses was in the mountains of Sinai, his followers made a golden calf out of their own melted down earrings and began to worship it, idolatrously, with sacrifices, feasting and revelry, in the manner of the pagans. This so greatly incensed Moses upon his return from Mount Sinai that he dropped and broke the two stone tablets, then took the golden calf "and burnt it in the fire, and ground it to powder, and strawed it upon the water, and made the children of Israel drink of it."

Despite the remembrance of this chapter of their own history, many of Jeroboam's followers obeyed his instructions and went "even unto

Dan" to worship the pagan idol. Jeroboam further violated tradition by naming priests from among "the lowest of the people, which were not of the house of the sons of Levi." (By divine command given to Moses, the priests were always to be members of the Tribe of Levi.)

For the next eighty-nine years (from about 931 to about 842 B.C.) the Kingdom of Judah included all the west shore of the Salt Sea, but none of the Jordan Valley, while the Kingdom of Israel included the east shore of the Salt Sea and both sides of the Jordan, from its headwaters all the way down to the Salt Sea, except for the east shore of the Sea of Chinnereth and the upper Jordan Valley, from Chinnereth to Lake Huleh, this territory being held by the Syrians.

When Jeroboam died, his son Nadab continued to maintain the pagan shrines at Bethel and Dan, and "walked in the way of his father, and in his sin."

But in Judah evil was likewise being committed, for they also "built them high places, and images, and groves, on every high hill, and under every green tree." Sodomy became prevalent again, and everywhere there were "abominations."

Nadab was assassinated by Baasha, a man of humble origin, who then proclaimed himself king of all Israel. To do away with any possible future trouble, he exterminated every member of the house of Jeroboam. Judah by now was ruled over by a great-grandson of Solomon, King Asa, who had begun his reign with a partial reformation. He fearlessly abolished cult prostitution, removed all the idols that his forefathers had permitted, cut down the groves in which pagan rites were being held, and instituted a campaign against all unnatural forms of sexual intercourse. When he discovered that his own mother, Queen Maachah, had built an altar in the woods where she worshiped an image of the goddess Asherah, he smashed the idol. Then, with even more courage, he deposed Queen Maachah.

Asa had an army of three hundred thousand Judaeans and two hundred and eighty thousand archers from Benjamin, "all mighty men of valour." In the fifteenth year of his reign, his kingdom was invaded by a hundred thousand Ethiopians and Libyans, supported by three hundred chariots. The Judaeans won an easy victory over the invaders. When the Israelites learned of the defeat of the invaders many, impressed, emigrated to Judah, especially from the tribes of Ephraim and Manasseh, whose land lay along the west bank of the Jordan. These "converts" joined in a celebration that was held in Jerusalem, at which seven hundred oxen and seven thousand sheep—part of the loot—were sacrificed as a thank-offering. At this ceremony a pact was made with

God that "whosoever would not seek the Lord God of Israel should be put to death, whether he be small or great, whether man or woman."

Perhaps to stop the flow of Israelites to Judah, King Baasha built a great fort at Ramah, near Bethel, close to the frontier between the rival kingdoms. This prompted King Asa to take all the silver and gold still in the Temple or in the King's House and send it by servants to Ben-hadad, king of Syria, reminding him that a military pact had been made by their fathers that was still valid, and so would Ben-hadad kindly send a military force to deal with Baasha and the Israelites, who were annoying the true sons of God, the Judaeans. The Syrian complied and his men attacked the north of Israel, concentrating on four cities in or close to the Jordan Valley: Dan, formerly Laish or Leshem; Abel-beth-maachah ("Meadow of the House of Oppression") close to Lake Huleh; Ijon, in the hills of Naphtali, overlooking the sources of the Jordan, and Chinnereth, on the shore of the Sea of Chinnereth. All these cities apparently were destroyed and most of the province of Naphtali was occupied.

Asa ruled over the House of Judah for forty-one long years, but the House of Israel in this time had many monarchs, in quick succession. Two were assassinated. One of the assassins, a young revolutionary named Zimri, proclaimed himself king, but was able to hold power for only a week. His career ended when he burned down the royal palace, destroying the entire contents, himself included.

It was in the time of Ahab, the eighth Israelite king since Solomon's day, that a man of Bethel, Hiel ("Brother of God"), decided to try to rebuild the ancient city of Jericho, although he was well aware of the curse Joshua had uttered:

"Cursed be the man before the Lord, that riseth up and buildeth this city Jericho: he shall lay the foundation thereof in his firstborn, and in his youngest son shall he set up the gates of it."

In the intervening four or five hundred years no one had dared defy the ban. In the time of the Judges, the Moabite king Eglon had temporarily occupied the Jericho oasis—even to having a castle built there for himself—and David had instructed his envoys who lost half their beards to tarry at Jericho until they could appear in public looking normal again, but until now Joshua's warning had been scrupulously heeded. It was brave of Hiel the Bethelite even to think of trying, for he happened to have two sons whom he greatly loved. His firstborn, Abiram, died as the foundations of the rebuilt city were being laid, exactly according to Joshaistic prediction. Instead of giving up, Hiel continued the reconstruction. His youngest son, Segub, died just as the city gates were being put into place.

The Jordan next comes into biblical history with the appearance of Elijah the prophet, who dramatically announced to Ahab, king of Israel:

"As the Lord God of Israel liveth, before whom I stand, there shall not be dew nor rain these years, but according to my word."

Who was this brave man? "Elijah the Tishbite, who was of the inhabitants of Gilead." But what is a Tishbite? No one has as yet been able to discover. There were towns of Tishbeth or Tishbe on the west side of the Jordan in Naphtali, and on the east side in the Valley not far from the river. Elijah was a Gileadite, meaning that he came from the east bank. Archaeologist Nelson Glueck is convinced that Elijah was from Jabesh-gilead, a city that has appeared more frequently in the Jordan story than any other place in the Valley.

The biblical narrative, which is often so painstaking in giving the antecedents of its characters, introduces Elijah at the climax of his career, already an old man. Of his early life we know only that he underwent his training in the wild ravines leading down to the Jordan. But it is no secret why such a man of God would have strong feelings about Ahab, who had married a Phoenician princess, Jezebel, daughter of Ethbaal, priest-king of Tyre and Sidon. She was a fanatical worshiper of the pagan gods, and had four hundred and fifty prophets of Baal on her staff, as well as four hundred prophets of the goddess Asherah. Jezebel was a domineering woman, with so strong a will that she bent Ahab easily to her ways. Because of her influence he gave official sanction to the paganism already being practiced by so many Israelites. Under previous monarchs, an attempt had been made to give the people the impression that they actually were still worshiping Jehovah, the God of Abraham and Moses, even if in a disguised, paganistic manner, but now the open worship of foreign images was ushered in, and Baal took the place of Jehovah. The worship of Baal resembled in no way any present-day religion, in theory, yet in actual practice it was little different from the worship of power, materialism and financial success that dominates much twentieth century practice. Jehovah, the invisible God, represented truth, purity, goodness, intellect; Baal stood for the love of self-glorification and material things that unfits the human soul for any true spiritual experience.

Ahab had established his capital in Samaria, the other side of a mountain ridge from the Jordan. There a magnificent temple was erected, not to Jehovah, but to Baal. In the Vale of Jezreel, leading down to the Jordan, an extensive grove was dedicated to Jezebel's divinities. Lascivious rites were introduced, while rich and ornate vestments were put on the priests. A whole nation was bewitched.

It was in such a time that Elijah came forth and defied the wrath of the king with his warning. It is not difficult to imagine him, even in appearance, as he flung his challenge in the face of Ahab, for he had lived and trained in the rough country across the Jordan. He undoubtedly was a tall, angular man, unkempt to an extreme in outward appearance. He wore his hair long and his principal—perhaps his only—garment was a rough sheepskin cloak with which he sometimes covered even his face. It was tied with a leather girdle in the style of the desert nomads. His language was rude and uncompromising. His whole nature was volcanic. East of the Jordan his appearance and even his rough mannerisms caused no stir, but in Samaria—at the effete court of Ahab and Jezebel—this uncouth and almost violent revolutionary created a sensation as he flung his defiant words at the king. It was the first great rebuke Ahab had experienced, and it was the signal for the start of a long series of personal and national calamities.

The biblical chronicler cheats his readers in not painting the scene as Elijah thundered his prophecy, and in omitting the regal reaction. But it must have been violent, for God immediately told Elijah to flee.

"Get thee hence, and turn thee eastward, and hide thyself by the brook Cherith, that is before Jordan."

Historians, biblical scholars and archaeologists have debated for nearly three thousand years the location of the Brook Cherith. Glueck has written that if scholars and novelists had only read the passage carefully they would not have made so many errors in placing the brook on the wrong side of the Jordan, and to the north or south of where it actually was. In the Bible *"before* Jordan" generally means on the east side of the river, *before* Joshua and his followers crossed over, so the Brook Cherith, says Glueck, must have been in Gilead. Because later in the story the brook dried up, Glueck surmises that it was a small wadi. He also assumes that Elijah would go—or be sent by God—to an area he already knew, near his birthplace, Jabesh-gilead, yet close to the real desert, so Glueck is satisfied that Brook Cherith was a wadi that fed the River Jabesh, which in turn flows into the Jordan—a brook on the banks of which Elijah may have herded sheep in the springtime of his youth.

"And it shall be, that thou shalt drink of the brook; and I have commanded the ravens to feed thee there."

So Elijah turned eastward, crossed over the Jordan, and took up the life of a nomad again on the edge of the Transjordan desert, and there the divine promise was kept.

"And the ravens brought him bread and flesh in the morning, and bread and flesh in the evening; and he drank of the brook."

But the drought that Elijah himself had predicted now began, and the Brook Cherith dried up, and God directed him back across the Jordan to a town called Zarephath, on the Mediterranean coast between Sidon and Tyre.

From now on Elijah fought the stupidities of his time in many localities, in many ways. He would appear suddenly in the most unexpected places—now in Samaria, now in Transjordan, now on the seacoast, now in the Valley, now on the Carmel, now in Beersheba, now at Gilgal, now in such faraway places as Damascus. Wherever he went the ubiquitous prophet performed miracles that were often—like his igniting of the water-soaked logs in the presence of eight hundred and fifty pagan prophets on Mount Carmel—masterpieces of showmanship.

During his time the king of Judah, Jehoshaphat, great-great-grandson of Solomon, and Ahab, king of Israel, temporarily stopped feuding and joined forces for a military venture across the Jordan. Several years earlier, Ben-hadad, ruler of Syria, supported by thirty-two minor kings, had invaded Israel. In one battle alone a hundred thousand Syrian infantrymen had been killed. Although Ben-hadad's army was routed, one Israelite city remained in his hands, Ramoth-gilead, thirty miles or more east of the Jordan, in an area where the desert was formidable. Three years after the end of the war, when Jehoshaphat came on a friendly visit to Samaria, Ahab suggested that they combine military forces and try to take the city. Jehoshaphat's reply was a classic:

"I am as thou art, my people as thy people, my horses as thy horses."

But Ahab was nervous, because a prophecy had been made by Elijah that the dogs of the city streets would someday lick his blood, and "the dogs shall eat Jezebel by the wall of Jezreel," so he called a mass meeting of four hundred pagan prophets and asked their advice. They voted unanimously that Ramoth-gilead should be attacked, predicting that it would be easily taken. Not satisfied with this reassurance, Ahab then called in a "prophet of the Lord," Micaiah, who supplemented his prediction of victory by adding that Ahab would not come back alive. Instead of calling off the operation, Ahab decided to try to outwit fate. He and Jehoshaphat led their combined army across the Jordan. Then he persuaded Jehoshaphat to put on his (Ahab's) royal robes, while he disguised himself as a private soldier. Early in the battle, as Ahab was riding in an ordinary chariot, an arrow, apparently shot at random, struck him between the ribs. His wound bled so profusely that a pool of blood formed on the floor of the chariot, but he remained on his feet, well knowing that those of his own soldiers who knew of his disguise would lose their morale if they thought he had been mortally wounded. But "about the going down of the sun" he died. The offensive was then called off, every man returning to his own country, his own city, his own home.

The body of the king was escorted in sad procession on the fifty-mile chariot trip back across the Jordan to Samaria, the crossing probably being made at Adam, the ford used for most east-west and west-east military operations.

The chariot in which Ahab had been riding when he was killed was taken back across the Jordan to Samaria. While it was being washed of its bloodstains, the dogs of the street lapped up the discolored water. Thus part of the prophecy of Elijah was fulfilled.

A few years later the oasis of Ein Gedi on the west bank of the Salt Sea, which had once been David's hiding place from Saul, again became, momentarily, a spot of historical importance. The king of Ammon, emboldened by the death of Ahab, refused any longer to pay annual tribute of cattle to Jerusalem, so he revolted and sent an army to invade Judah. The invaders reached Ein Gedi before Jehoshaphat was informed of the incursion. As the Judaean army set off to resist the Ammonites, Jehoshaphat appointed a great body of singers and put them at the head of the troops with orders that as they led the foot soldiers into battle they were to sing:

"Praise the Lord; for his mercy endureth forever."

The Judaeans were so victorious and the slaughter was so great that it took three days, after the fighting stopped, just to strip the enemy corpses of their precious jewels and to search the pockets of the dead men's uniforms for other valuables, ". . . the spoil, it was so much."

Elijah was in a cave in the desert when he received three divine commands:

". . . anoint Hazael to be king over Syria:

"And Jehu the son of Nimshi shalt thou anoint to be king over Israel: and Elisha the son of Shaphat of Abel-meholah shalt thou anoint to be prophet in thy room."

The elderly Gileadite was able to carry out only one of these commissions before his death. When he found Elisha, the young man was plowing a field with twelve yoke of oxen—an interesting sidelight on the state of agriculture in the Jordan Valley in those days. As he walked beside the plowman, Elijah threw his own mantle over Elisha and announced to him that he was to start preparing at once to be his successor. The young man advanced no arguments. His only request was that he be permitted to kiss his father and mother good-bye. Then a banquet was held in the partly plowed field, after Elisha had killed and boiled two of his twenty-four oxen.

"Then he arose, and went after Elijah, and ministered unto him." This act in the drama of the Jordan took place at Abel-meholah, Elisha's home and birthplace. But where was Abel-meholah? Authorities agree that it was in the Valley, but some say on the west bank, about halfway between sea and lake, while Glueck and others advance good reasons for believing that it was on the River Jabesh (Wadi al Yabis) not far from where it flows into the Jordan.

Elijah, a grand and awesome character, unafraid of kings and princes, abrupt in his speech, having the manners of a wild Bedouin, appears in marked contrast to his disciple, who was young, effervescent, benign, almost courtly in his speech, yet with few chivalrous or heroic qualities; a much more commonplace character than his master, but at the same time more understandable and familiar. One historian has compared them to two Swiss mountains: Elijah like Mont Blanc, majestic and overpowering; Elisha like tree-covered Rughi, bathed in sunshine and dotted with chalets to the very summit.

Yet a relationship both tender and delightful soon developed between these two disparate men. When it came time for Elijah to take his departure from this earth, he went with Elisha first to Gilgal. Here again the geographers are in conflict, some agreeing that this was a town up in the hills north of Bethel, others contending that it was the same Valley city that had been the Israelites' base of operations immediately after they ended their forty years in the desert by crossing the Jordan. Wherever it was, Elijah had to go from Gilgal to Bethel on an errand and asked Elisha to wait for him in Gilgal, to which the younger man replied:

"As the Lord liveth, and as thy soul liveth, I will not leave thee."

So they went together to Bethel, where Elisha was surrounded by many young prophets who asked if he was aware that on that very day Elijah was being taken from this earth, to which Elisha replied:

"Yea, I know it; hold ye your peace."

When Elijah returned from transacting his business he told Elisha to wait now in Bethel, because it was necessary for him to go to Jericho. Again the younger man replied:

"As the Lord liveth, and as thy soul liveth, I will not leave thee."

In Jericho another group of young prophets flocked around Elisha and asked him if he knew that that day Elijah was being taken away from them, and again Elisha replied:

"Yea, I know it; hold ye your peace."

When Elijah returned, he told his disciple to wait there for him, for "the Lord hath sent me to Jordan." Once more came the simple but determined reply:

"As the Lord liveth, and as thy soul liveth, I will not leave thee."

So together they went down to the river, followed by fifty of the young prophets who stood at a distance while Elijah and Elisha proceeded to the water's edge.

"And Elijah took his mantle, and wrapped it together, and smote the waters, and they were divided hither and thither, so that they two went over on dry ground.

"And it came to pass, when they were gone over, that Elijah said unto Elisha, Ask what I shall do for thee, before I be taken away from thee. And Elisha said, I pray thee, let a double portion of thy spirit be upon me.

"And he said, Thou hast asked a hard thing: nevertheless, if thou see me when I am taken from thee, it shall be so unto thee; but if not, it shall not be so.

"And it came to pass, as they still went on, and talked, that, behold, there appeared a chariot of fire, and horses of fire, and parted them both asunder; and Elijah went up by a whirlwind into heaven.

"And Elisha saw it, and he cried, My father, my father, the chariot of Israel, and the horsemen thereof. And he saw him no more: and he took hold of his own clothes, and rent them in two pieces . . .

"And he took the mantle of Elijah that fell from him, and smote the waters, and said, Where is the Lord God of Elijah? and when he also had smitten the waters, they parted hither and thither: and Elisha went over.

"And when the sons of the prophets which were to view at Jericho saw him, they said, The spirit of Elijah doth rest on Elisha. And they came to meet him, and bowed themselves to the ground before him."

The fifty minor prophets were a little skeptical, however, that they had been witnesses of a real ascension, so they asked Elisha's permission to go and seek Elijah. ". . . peradventure the Spirit of the Lord hath taken him up, and cast him upon some mountain, or in some valley."

Elisha had more faith, but he gave his permission, and for three days the fifty men searched, but they failed to find Elijah. Convinced now that Elijah actually had been taken up to heaven and suspecting that his successor could also perform miracles, they complained to Elisha about the barrenness of the ground around Jericho and the lack of water, whereupon Elisha ordered them to bring him a new jar full of salt. Then, walking to the spring that was the source of Jericho's water, he threw in the salt, saying:

"Thus saith the Lord, I have healed these waters; there shall not be from thence any more death or barren land."

As he left to go up to Bethel a group of children followed him, mockingly shouting:

"Go up, thou bald head; go up, thou bald head."

Elisha at the time was an athletic young man, not over thirty, and was probably wearing his hair cut short, perhaps in an ancient version of a modern crew cut. (Biblical scholars suggest that "bald head" is a mistranslation; that the children were laughing at him not because he was bald, but because his hair was cut so short.) The contrast between him and the man whose place he was taking was obvious, even to the children. The figure of the old prophet was familiar everywhere in the Valley. The young as well as the old had stood in awe of Elijah.

Turning around in the road, Elisha looked angrily at the children and then cursed them in the name of the Lord, whereupon two female bears came running from the woods and attacked the laughing children, clawing to death forty-two of them.

After this, the story of Elisha is principally a record of kindly deeds and great goodwill.

It was only a short time after Elijah's ascension that Jehoram, who had succeeded his father Ahab as king of Israel, was faced with a Moab insurrection. In the farthest part of the Israelite kingdom, the Moabite king announced he was weary of paying an annual tribute of a hundred thousand lambs and a hundred thousand rams. To put down the trouble Jehoram enlisted the support of the king of Edom, and then sent to Jehoshaphat for help. The Judaean king replied in the same words he had used to Jehoram's father:

"I will go up: I am as thou art, my people as thy people, and my horses as thy horses."

As the three armies set off, it was discovered that there was no water for the horses, or for the cattle that were being taken along as a perambulating food supply, so they consulted Elisha, who at first refused to advise them on the ground that they were encouraging or at least condoning pagan worship in their kingdoms, but as a concession to Jehoshaphat, because he was a great-great-grandson of Solomon, he finally agreed. First, however, he insisted that they find a minstrel to play for him. The music apparently induced a prophetic mood, for he then prophesied that although there would be no rain during the campaign, nevertheless there would be plenty of water for both man and beast. Then he instructed them how to store the water by digging deep ditches in the valley where they would be encamped. It happened as he predicted and when the sun shone on the water that miraculously filled the ditches they had dug, the Moabites, seeing it from afar, thought the liquid was blood and decided the three armies had committed harakiri, and now, therefore: "Moab, to the spoil."

The "dead men" not only rose up and smote the Moabites, "but they went forward smiting the Moabites, even in their country." Then, in accordance with instructions they received from Elisha, they laid waste to all the cities, cut down every tree in sight, scattered rocks over all the good farmland, and stopped up all the wells. In a last desperate effort to win the help of his own gods, the Moabite king placed his favorite son on an altar and burned him to ashes, but it was a futile sacrifice.

The story of Elisha had begun on the banks of the Jordan and so it is not strange that many of his miracles were performed on, or in, or near the river. One involved a woman who had a debt she could not pay, so Elisha multiplied her own small cruet of oil until she had oil enough to fill all the empty vessels she could borrow, and with the money received from the sale of the oil was able to pay off her debt.

In the town of Shunem, in the Valley of Jezreel leading down to the Jordan, Elisha assured a barren Shunamite that she would soon be with child. A few years later when the child was old enough to work in the fields, he had a fatal sunstroke and Elisha traveled all the way from Mount Carmel to Shunem to breathe life back into the boy's dead body.

At Gilgal, close by the river, he turned a pot of soup, made in error from poisonous gourds, into a safe and palatable dish.

A man from Baal-shalisha (exact location unknown) brought Elisha twenty loaves of bread and a few ears of corn and asked how he could possibly feed a hundred guests with such scant provisions, whereupon Elisha promised a multiplication of the loaves sufficient to feed everyone, and it happened as he said.

The river itself played a vital role in the story of Naaman, who was a captain in the Syrian army and a favorite of his king, because of his brilliant military record, but was disfigured by the ravages of leprosy. His wife had, as a maid, an Israelite girl who had been taken prisoner during one of the frequent wars between the two countries. One day the girl remarked to her mistress that there was a prophet in Israel who could perform miracles and without doubt, if he wished, could cure the captain. The wife told her husband, and her husband consulted his king, who gave him ten talents of silver (six hundred and sixty pounds), six thousand pieces of gold, ten sets of clothing, and a letter, all of which Captain Naaman was to deliver to the king of Israel.

The route followed by Captain Naaman and the many friends who accompanied him from Damascus to Samaria probably took them across the Jordan at the Bethabara ford, within sight of Beth-Shan, about fifteen miles south of the Sea of Chinnereth.

When Captain Naaman presented the royal letter to the king of Israel, he reacted with indignation, saying:

"Am I God . . . ?"

The king was so convinced that it was a trick by which the Syrians were trying to foment a quarrel with the Israelites that he "rent his clothes." Elisha, hearing of this, asked that Captain Naaman be sent to him. When the Syrian arrived in front of Elisha's house, the prophet sent his servant to tell him:

"Go and wash in Jordan seven times, and thy flesh will come again to thee, and thou shalt be clean."

Naaman was indignant. He had expected that the Israelite prophet at least would invite him into his house, or come out to see him, and that he might place a hand on the diseased parts of his body and make the leprosy vanish. Furthermore, the idea of bathing in such a stream as the Jordan annoyed him.

"Are not Abana and Pharpar, rivers of Damascus, better than all the waters of Israel? may I not wash in them and be clean?"

("Abana" was probably the name then used for the stream later called by the Greeks the Golden River and by modern Syrians the Barada.)

So he left Elisha's home in a rage, but one of his servants reasoned with him, saying:

"My father, if the prophet had bid thee do some great thing, wouldest thou not have done it? how much rather then, when he saith to thee, Wash, and be clean?"

Captain Naaman may not have been convinced, but the journey had been long, so he decided at least not to go home without giving the prescribed cure a try.

"Then went he down, and dipped himself seven times in Jordan, according to the saying of the man of God: and his flesh came again like unto the flesh of a little child, and he was clean."

There are two good reasons to believe that this miracle occurred at Bethabara. First, the captain was so skeptical that he probably would not have wanted to go out of his way, and as long as he was crossing back over the river at this point anyway, on his way home, why not take the cure there? Also, at this point the Jordan, while not as full of life and brightness as the clear rivers of Damascus, at least was not as muddy as it would have been lower down.

This was not the first time the waters of the Jordan had been involved in a miracle, but it was the first time on record that the river had been used for either physical or spiritual cleansing. Although the word "baptism" does not appear anywhere in the Old Testament, there is much about "cleansing," and, at a later date, dipping in running water became a recognized part of the process of purification from defilement. Captain Naaman's cure in the Jordan may, therefore, be considered as the start of the use of holy water for miraculous cleansing. From this day on the Jordan is more than just a river: it is more than just a river of miracles; it is a river that henceforth has an important role to perform for believers, as God's agent in curing the physical and spiritual ills of mankind.

In great excitement over what had happened, Captain Naaman turned his horses around and drove furiously the thirty miles or more back to Samaria, followed by the entire company of soldiers and friends who had accompanied him from Damascus. In joy over his miraculous recovery he tried to shower Elisha with both gifts and gratitude. But the prophet wanted neither, and told the captain:

"Go in peace."

Before he took leave, finally, of Elisha, Captain Naaman said he was now convinced that there was no other god than the god of Israel, and he promised to make no more burnt offerings or sacrifices to other gods. Then he made a request which was not strange, remembering that in those days each land had its god, and the power of each god was believed to be confined to a certain land. Could he have permission to take back to Syria all the earth of Israel that two mules could carry? He wanted it so that when he made sacrifices in Damascus to the god of Israel he could do so literally on the soil of Israel. Elisha made no objection, so it is assumed that Captain Naaman did as he intended, in which case the soil he took must have been from the Jordan Valley, for there would have been no point in burdening the mules with such a load between Samaria and the river, and, also, it is likely that for sentimental reasons he would have wanted to take the earth from the very spot where he had been cured.

Elisha had rejected all of Captain Naaman's gifts, but his servant, Gehazi, ran down the road after the Syrian party. When Naaman saw him, he quickly descended from his chariot and asked:
"Is all well?"
Thereupon the servant, in a great prevarication, said:
"My master hath sent me, saying, Behold, even now there be come to me from mount Ephraim two young men of the sons of the prophets: give them, I pray thee, a talent of silver, and two changes of garments."
Naaman acquiesced at once, putting two talents (one hundred and thirty-two pounds) of silver into two sacks, along with two changes of garments.
When Gehazi appeared before his master, Elisha demanded of him: "Whence comest thou, Gehazi?"
"Thy servant went no whither," Gehazi replied.
But Elisha knew, so he said to his servant:
"Is it a time to receive money, and to receive garments, and olive-yards, and vineyards, and sheep, and oxen, and menservants, and maidservants?
"The leprosy therefore of Naaman shall cleave unto thee, and unto thy seed for ever."
And Gehazi went from the presence of his master with his flesh as white as snow.
Elisha's disciples, who called themselves "the Sons of the Prophets," complained to him one day that they were not happy with their living quarters and would like to build a home for themselves on the banks of the Jordan. (The exact location is nowhere specified.) Elisha approved and agreed to go with them. Each man took tools and a beam of wood. When they reached the river they began cutting trees for more lumber. (It is worthy of note that the trees in the Valley close to the river at this time were large enough to be used for such purpose.)
As one disciple was felling a tree the iron head of his axe flew off the handle into the water and disappeared below the surface.
"Alas, master! for it was borrowed," he cried in dismay.
Elisha asked the man to point to the exact spot where it had gone into the water. Then he cut a small stick and threw it at the spot, whereupon the heavy iron axe head floated up to the surface. (The biblical account says: ". . . and the iron did swim.") It was another miracle in which the Jordan was an active participant.
In these times Ben-hadad and his Syrians came streaming across the Jordan and up the hills to Samaria, determined to starve the city

into submission. They succeeded to the point that an ass's head was being sold in Samaria for eighty pieces of silver, and a pint measure full of dove's dung for five pieces of silver, and a Samarian woman complained to the king that she and a neighbor woman had made a pact: the first day they would kill, boil and eat her son, and the next day they would kill, boil and eat the other woman's son, but, she told the king, on the second day her neighbor had reneged and had hidden her son to save him.

Still Samaria did not surrender.

Elisha predicted to the distressed victims of the siege that the famine would soon end and food would be both plentiful and cheap. Many thought him mad.

One day two lepers sitting outside the city gate debated thus:

If they continued to sit there, they would surely soon starve to death. If they went into the city they would starve, because there was no food to be had in Samaria, unless one were very wealthy. If they went into the camp of the Syrians, not far from the city walls, they might be killed, but it was worth the risk, for they would soon die anyway. So they decided on the third alternative.

When they reached the camp of the besiegers they found it deserted, for the Syrians had heard a loud noise which they thought had been made by thousands of chariots and thousands of horses, and they had convinced themselves that the Hittites and Egyptians must have allied themselves with the Israelites and had come in force to attack the Syrians, so they had fled in fright at twilight, leaving behind their tents, horses, asses, food and personal possessions.

The lepers, after helping themselves generously and hiding their loot, then informed the Israelite king, who ordered soldiers to mount two of the five horses left within the city walls, and to give chase to the Syrians to verify that they had really gone.

"And they went after them unto Jordan: and, lo, all the way was full of garments and vessels, which the Syrians had cast away in their haste."

The road down which this strange nocturnal flight took place was undoubtedly the same route used by Captain Naaman—the road down to the ford at Bethabara.

Elisha's next trip over the Jordan was on his way to Damascus. There King Ben-hadad, being ill, sent an aide, Hazael ("Whom God Beholds") to the Israelite prophet with forty camels loaded with gifts, and with a question he wished answered:

"Shall I recover of this disease?"

Elisha prophesied that he would recover from the disease, but that he would soon die anyway. Then he burst into tears. When Hazael in perplexity asked why, Elisha replied that in a vision he had seen that Hazael would kill Ben-hadad, and would then become king himself, and would thereafter do great evils to the people of Israel. The next day the prophecy was confirmed, at least partially, when Hazael murdered the invalid king by suffocating him in his bed with a thick cloth dipped in water.

The next important crossing of the Jordan was by a messenger carrying a cruet of oil. On the throne of Judah at this time sat Ahaziah, the great-great-great-great grandson of Solomon. (The House of David line was still unbroken, although in Israel there had been no continuity, no stability. Assassination, revolution and suicide had been involved in the contest over who was to be king there.)

At this time the Israelites were still eager to repossess their former frontier city of Ramoth-gilead, so an army under the Israelite king, Jehoram, went across the river and over two ranges of mountains to lay siege to the city. By now Hazael was on the Syrian throne. During one of the battles King Jehoram was wounded and went back across the Jordan to recuperate at his summer palace in Jezreel, up the vale from the river, leaving in charge of his forces Jehu, a bold Israelite general known for his wild horsemanship, as well as for his inordinate ambition. While the king was at Jezreel, he received a visit from King Ahaziah of Judah.

At precisely this time Elisha, remembering the unfulfilled command that had been given to Elijah, called in one of his disciples and entrusted him with a secret mission. He was to cross the Jordan and go to Ramoth-gilead and there, with no witnesses, he was to pour oil from a cruet that Elisha gave him over the head of Jehu, and thus anoint him as the king of Israel.

The disciple carried out his mission successfully. After the brief ceremony was over, Jehu was eager to be the one to break the news to the royal family, so he ordered that no one be permitted out of the camp and then took two fast horses and a chariot and drove madly across the hills, down into the Valley, through the river, and up to Jezreel.

A watchman had been stationed on the roof of the summer palace to give warning in case of a Syrian invasion. When he saw a lone chariot approaching through the pass between Little Hermon and the hills of Gilboa, he passed the news on to the invalid king, who ordered a horseman to meet the chariot and demand of the driver:

"Is it peace?"

Jehu replied:

"What hast thou to do with peace?"

When this message was conveyed back to the wounded king he ordered a second horseman to go out and ask the same question.

Again Jehu replied:

"What hast thou to do with peace?"

By now those in the summer palace suspected who the charioteer was, for only Jehu, son of Mishi, drove like that, so Jehoram left his sickbed and he and Ahaziah, king of Judah, each in his own chariot, went out to meet their visitor.

"Is it peace?" King Jehoram asked, as soon as he was within earshot of Jehu.

"What peace," came back the blunt reply, "so long as the whoredoms of thy mother Jezebel and her witchcrafts are so many?"

When Jehoram saw the wild expression on Jehu's face, he shouted to his brother king:

"There is treachery, O Ahaziah."

Then he tried to wheel around his chariot and escape, but at this instant Jehu drew his bow full strength. The arrow found its mark, killing the Israelite king instantly. Ahaziah fled but was pursued and killed at one of the passes leading from the Plain of Esdraelon up to Mount Carmel. Meanwhile, Jehu had hastened on and entered the city. In a window he saw the queen mother, Jezebel. When she had learned the identity of the man in the chariot, she had hastily gone to her boudoir and with practiced fingers painted her face, made up her eyes, and put ornaments in her hair, hoping to hide the ravages of time, for she was by now far from young. She might have spent her time to better advantage, for Jehu was unimpressed. When she sensed this, she tried logic. From the window she shouted down to the man who had just killed her grandson:

"Had Zimri peace, who slew his master?"

She was referring to one of the early kings of Israel who assassinated King Elah and proclaimed himself his successor, but ruled for only seven days, because his act lacked popular support.

Jehu, with blood already on his hands, was in no mood for logic. Instead of answering the queen mother, he shouted up:

"Who is on my side? who?"

No faces appeared at any of the windows, except those of two or three eunuchs. To them Jehu shouted, as he pointed at Jezebel:

"Throw her down."

"So they threw her down: and some of her blood was sprinkled on the wall, and on the horses: and he trod her under foot."

Jehu then strode into the palace and called for food and drink. But a touch of compunction or compassion came over him and between mouthfuls he said:

"Go, see now this cursed woman, and bury her: for she is a king's daughter."

They went, but they found nothing to bury but her skull, and her feet, and the palms of her hands. When this was reported back to Jehu he remarked:

"This is the word of the Lord, which he spake by his servant Elijah the Tishbite, saying, In the portion of Jezreel shall dogs eat the flesh of Jezebel:

"And the carcass of Jezebel shall be as dung upon the face of the field in the portion of Jezreel; so that they shall not say, This is Jezebel."

King Ahab had seventy sons. Jehu now wrote letters to the elders in each town or city where these sons dwelt, saying:

"If ye be mine, and if ye will hearken unto my voice, take ye the heads of the men your master's sons, and come to me to Jezreel by tomorrow this time."

The recipients of the letters took the instructions literally. During the night wicker baskets, each containing a head, began to arrive in Jezreel. By morning all seventy sons had been killed and decapitated, and their heads delivered to the new king, on whose instructions they were piled up like cannon balls, in two heaps, one on each side of the city gate. Then all the great men, relatives and priests of the House of Ahab were slain. When members of Ahaziah's family arrived to pay their respects to Jehu he had them, too, killed. Then he went to Samaria and under the pretense that he himself was a worshiper of the pagan god Baal, ordered all Baalites in Israel, including those down in the Valley, to assemble in the House of Baal in Samaria. When they came they filled to overflowing the vast building that had been constructed by Jezebel and Ahab; there was not room to wedge in one more human being. Then Jehu appointed eighty men to do the slaughtering, warning them that if a single Baalite escaped, they themselves would be slain.

"Thus Jehu destroyed Baal out of Israel."

But when the blood bath was over and the influence of Jezebel eliminated, Jehu "took no heed to walk in the law of the Lord God of

Israel." He even permitted the worship of the golden calves at Dan and Bethel to continue.

In Jehu's time most of the people of the Valley fell under the foreign yoke when the Syrians, led by King Hazael, conquered and occupied all the lands of the Tribe of Gad and the half-tribe of Manasseh, including half the east shore of the Salt Sea, as far as the River Arnon.

Meanwhile, in Judah, made leaderless by the assassination of the king, Athaliah ("Jehovah Is Exalted"), mother of Ahaziah, who was not of Solomon's line but a daughter of Jezebel and Ahab, occupied the throne. In order to make sure that there would be no family intrigue against her, she killed (or had killed) all her own male children. Or so she thought. But her daughter, Jehosheba, managed to hide in a palace bedroom a baby boy less than a year old, named Joash (or Jehoash), one of the sons of her assassinated brother, King Ahaziah. Some years later, when the boy was seven, he was proclaimed king in a secret ceremony, an event which was followed by the assassination of his grandmother, Queen Athaliah. The House of David line was thus re-established.

Elisha was between eighty-five and ninety years old when word spread throughout the Valley that he was dying of an illness. King Joash, now grown to manhood, hastened to his bedside and wept over him.

Elisha's miracles did not cease, even with his death. Some months later, a band of invading Moabites appeared on the edge of a burial ground as a funeral was in progress. The frightened burial party deposited the corpse, temporarily, in the nearest sepulcher, which happened to be Elisha's.

". . . when the man was let down, and touched the bones of Elisha, he revived, and stood up on his feet."

After the division of the empire of David and Solomon into the separate kingdoms of Judah and Israel, the Jordan, its Valley, and its lakes and sea, were all entirely within Israel, except for the west bank of the Salt Sea and the Jericho area, which were in Judah, and the east bank of the Sea of Chinnereth, and the east bank of the Upper Jordan, which were held by the Syrians.

During the two hundred and ten years that Israel existed as a separate kingdom (from 932 B.C. to 722 B.C.) nineteen Israelite kings held sway. (Twenty, if two kings who ruled simultaneously are both counted.) One ruled for as short a time as seven days; one for as long as forty-one years. Only nine of the nineteen died of natural causes. Seven were assassinated, one committed suicide, one was killed in battle, and one met an uncertain but probably violent fate. The anonymous historian who wrote the account of the Age of the Kings that is read today by Jew and Christian alike as part of the holy writ was most precise as to how long each king ruled, who his mother was, whom he succeeded, by whom he was succeeded, and how he met his death. He also stated bluntly whether the king found favor or disfavor with God. ("Because of the sins of Jeroboam which he sinned, and which he made Israel sin, by his provocation wherewith he provoked the Lord God of Israel to anger.") Not one of the nineteen is listed as a good king or an honorable man. The twenty kings of Judah (only four of whom were assassinated) fare a little better, only eleven being listed as evil.

In reconstructing the life of the people of the Jordan Valley during this period it is well to remember that all thirty-nine or forty kings were not tyrants; that in nearly every case the biblical categorization is based on a religious judgment—whether the king destroyed hilltop shrines, smashed pagan idols, and tried to extirpate Baalism and lead his people back to worshiping Yahweh (Jehovah), or whether he permitted them to make molten images, burn incense in high places, and worship the golden calf.

During the Period of the Kings there were twelve assassinations in the two royal families, counting in that of the mother-queen, Jezebel, but it is to be remembered that this was over more than a third of a millennium—an average of one assassination no more frequently than once every twenty-nine years—and that many of the kings ruled for thirty or forty years (one king of Judah was on the throne fifty-five years) and died in their beds.

In order to cover in forty-eight thousand and fifty-six words the history of a whole people—actually two nations—extending over a period of almost four hundred years (from Solomon's ascension of the throne until the fall of Jerusalem) something had to be omitted from the Bible. Proof that the chronicler knew he was not telling the whole story is the oft-repeated biblical phrase:

"Now the rest of the acts of (here the name of the king is inserted), and all that he did, are they not written in the book of the chronicles of the kings of Israel?" (Or, " . . . the chronicles of the kings of Judah.") The reference is not to the two biblical books called the Chronicles, for they were written, according to Jewish tradition, by Ezra about a century and a half after completion of the books of Kings. The reference is thought to be to two popular histories which, tragically, have never been found, probably having been destroyed in the siege or burning of Israelite and Judaean cities. What is not told in the biblical account—but may have been in the two missing books—is the story of the new cities, highways and bridges that the various kings built, what they did to improve their country's social system, how they labored to modernize agricultural methods and to encourage advances in industry, in the arts, in science, in easing the drudgery of man by the application of simple laws of physics.

Normal, everyday, humdrum, workaday life went on in the Valley, as elsewhere in Israel and Judah, year after year, century after century —the getting and the spending; the planting, plowing and harvesting; the conceiving and the childbearing; the laughing and the crying; the loving, the squabbling and the dying.

The Valley people were removed a safe distance from trouble when it did break out. True, they frequently saw soldiers going back and forth over the Jordan, on their way to battle, cheerful and optimistic. And they saw them return over the river, sometimes with their numbers decimated, their glory gone, their spirits dejected. They saw the river crossed by victorious kings, kings bitter in defeat, and by assassins who wanted to be kings. But these transients always came down one slope of the Valley, forded the river, and then went up the other side and out of the Valley again, and were quickly gone. There was never much north-south or south-north traffic along either shore, and, of course, no traffic at all *on* the river. The glimpses that the Valley people got of history-in-the-making were fleeting, and must have given them somewhat the feeling of watching a parade or a pageant.

However, a locust invasion that destroyed their crops, or a sudden storm that sent the peaceful Jordan raging out of its bed, or, worst of all, an earthquake—these were the events that meant something to every man, woman and child of them.

There are thirty-five references to earthquakes in the Bible, the most poetic being in Psalm 114: "The mountains skipped like rams, and the little hills like lambs." There was one bad earthquake that Valley people who survived it must never have forgotten. It occurred in the eighth century B.C. and was so severe that two of the later prophets, Amos and Zechariah, both made specific mention of it, Zechariah saying, in the course of a thunderous warning that "the day of the Lord cometh":

" . . . ye shall flee, like as ye fled from before the earthquake in the days of Uzziah king of Judah."

The excitement of present-day archaeology in the Jordan Valley, as well as in other parts of the Holy Land, is that what is dug from the earth often proves the historical truth of events narrated in the Bible that may have been looked upon by skeptics as mere mythology. At Hazor ruins have been found of buildings that were, without any doubt, destroyed in the earthquake in Uzziah's time mentioned by both Amos and Zechariah.

Several military events in those days deeply affected the people of the Jordan. In the late eighth century B.C. a strange shift of bedfellows occurred. Far to the northeast, in what is now Iraq, a new force in world affairs was growing strong, the Assyrians. Their capital was an ancient city called Nineveh, a place of splendor, magnitude and luxury that could not be traversed from one end to the other, so it was said, in less than three days. At first the Israelites purchased the friendship of the militant Assyrians with cash tribute, a thousand talents (sixty-six thousand pounds) of silver at a time. To raise this considerable sum, every man of means was assessed fifty shekels (twenty ounces) of silver. But Pekah, who had seized the throne after murdering the incumbent, King Pekahiah ("Jehovah Has Opened His Eyes"), was so frightened by the ever-growing strength of the Assyrians that he made an alliance with the Israelites' mortal enemies, the Syrians in Damascus. Then he suggested that Judah join too. When the Judaean king refused, on the advice of the prophet Isaiah, King Pekah, whose name means "Opening," moved in force against Jerusalem. Although he failed to take the capital city of his brother-king, he killed one hundred and twenty thousand Judaeans in a single day, including the king's son and the governor. Then he headed with his army for Jericho and in that area took two hundred thousand Judaean boys, girls and women of all ages prisoner. (Judah had recently been the victim of human pillage by the Syrians, who took thousands of captives off to Damascus.) Although men were rarely taken prisoner in the biblical wars, it was not unusual to make captives of women, but never before had such a number been seized as Pekah's soldiers rounded up that day.

The task of guarding the Israelites' two hundred thousand prisoners and herding them like cattle along the roads was enough to tax any army, especially an army with sore arms from having slain—presumably with the sword—one hundred and twenty thousand enemy soldiers in a single day. It is probable that they were driven north through the Valley, rather than up over the mountains. Many were old and feeble. Some were barefooted. A number were literally naked. Consider the task of feeding so many, if feed them they did. Consider the human problems of separated families, screaming children, hysterical mothers, ailing infants, angry soldiers, and the agony of those wives who had seen their husbands put to death that day, or who were separated from the rest of their families. The biblical account of the two hundred thousand prisoners mentions none of these matters, but it does tell, in factual little phrases, the story of what was accomplished that day by an Israelite who should be—who *is*—one of the great biblical heroes, a prophet named Oded.

Oded is identified in the Bible only as a prophet. Obviously a minor one. His name had never appeared before. (The prophet Oded who encouraged King Asa of Judah to oppose idolatry lived several hundred years earlier and was probably not even related.) The later-day Oded was obviously a humanitarian and a very brave man, as many of the prophets were. He hastened through the Valley to Samaria, reaching the capital city well in advance of the head of the military column. When the Israelite officers arrived he addressed them—and anyone else who cared to listen—saying:

"Behold, because the Lord God of your fathers was wroth with Judah, he hath delivered them into your hand, and ye have slain them in a rage that reacheth up unto heaven."

At this point the minor prophet Oded could not have been very popular with the foot-weary soldiers and the officers, and especially not with the king, who had ordered it all. But he went on with his straightforward plea:

"And now ye purpose to keep under the children of Judah and Jerusalem for bondmen and bondwomen unto you: but are there not with you, even with you, sins against the Lord your God?"

It is not difficult to imagine the anger of the listeners. Who was this stranger, who dared defy a victorious army and a wise king? But Oded knew he was arguing for the lives of two hundred thousand innocent people and he talked on, his voice undoubtedly rising as he reached his peroration:

"Now hear me therefore, and deliver the captives again, which ye have taken captive of your brethren: for the fierce wrath of the Lord is upon you."

Every man among them, from king down to lowliest private, must have felt that this earnest man of God was fixing him, personally, with the eye of accusation. One by one the city leaders stood up and supported Oded, one of them saying to the army:

"Ye shall not bring in the captives hither: for whereas we have offended against the Lord already, ye intend to add more to our sins and to our trespass: for our trespass is great, and there is fierce wrath against Israel."

The climax is like the ending of some delightful fairy story. Not only were the two hundred thousand innocents set free, but some of the good men of Samaria took some of the loot brought back by the Israelite soldiers—and no soldier likes to lose his loot—"and . . . clothed all that were naked among them, and arrayed them, and shod them, and gave them to eat and to drink, and anointed them, and carried all the feeble of them upon asses, and brought them to Jericho, the city of palm trees, to their brethren: then they returned to Samaria."

The scene that night in the ancient city overlooking the Jordan must have been one of unprecedented joy, as tens of thousands of families were united.

What then of Oded? He never again appears in the biblical chronicle.

But this did not put an end to the troubles of Judah. Now the Edomites came north and did exactly what the Israelites had done, only on a somewhat smaller scale: they attacked Judah and carried off great numbers of prisoners—some of them from the Valley—and there was no Oded among the Edomites, so none of these prisoners was ever returned.

In desperation King Ahaz sent an appeal for help to Tuglath-Pileser III, the Assyrian king who was campaigning at the time in Syria, explaining that he and his people were beset by the Israelites on the north and by the Edomites on the south, and would he kindly offer some assistance? After taking the Syrian capital of Damascus, Tuglath-Pileser III went to Judah's assistance by invading the northern part of Galilee, including the Upper Jordan Valley. First, he besieged, captured and destroyed the cities of Abel-beth-maachah ("Meadow of the House of Oppression"), Janoah ("Rest"), Kedesh, and Ijon which was in the heart of the well-watered area where all four sources of the Jordan spring joyously from the earth. These cities were of importance to the people in the north end of the Valley and their loss must have been a serious blow. Then the invader swept down past the swamps of Huleh to the great stronghold of Hazor.

Those who lived in the far end of the Valley were always concerned about what happened to Hazor. They knew that it was already an ancient city at the time the followers of Moses came out of the desert and crossed the Jordan. Some of their ancestors were present when Joshua stormed Hazor and burned it to the ground. Centuries later other Valley people were conscripted by Solomon to help rebuild Hazor so it could serve as a chariot city. King Ahab, fearing the blows that Israel might someday soon have to withstand from the northeast, greatly strengthened its fortifications. Then came the big earthquake. Now, at the request of the Judaeans, the Assyrians were attacking

Hazor. The year was 732 B.C. When the Assyrians finished with Hazor, the destruction was complete.

Starting in A.D. 1955 a team of Israel archaeologists directed by Professor Yigael Yadin, dug into the post-Solomonic ruins and found them buried deep in ash. Tuglath-Pileser III had done his job well; he had burned as well as smashed. He had left nothing of the greatest city in the Valley, except blackened stones and heaps of ash.

The attack had not been a surprise. For years the people of Hazor had known it was a possibility, so they had prepared as best they could. Once, when there was a report that the Assyrians were actually on the way, they hastily used bricks to block up the big gate on the east side of the city wall. Then they tried to camouflage it on the outside with a thin layer of rubble. When the scare was over the people of Hazor removed the bricks so that farmers' wagons could enter with loads of wheat to be stored in the city's immense silo. On the eve of the actual attack the Hazorites hastily bricked up the entrance again. The silo, incidentally, must have been full at the time of the attack, because Yadin found much burned grain when he unearthed the remains of the silo, more than 2680 years after the event. In a wine jar the excavators found an inscription reading ". . . belonging to Pekah." Archaeology once again had confirmed biblical history.

Many other Israelite cities were besieged and destroyed by the Assyrians, but Samaria was spared for the time, on the understanding that the Israelites pay heavy tribute to the Assyrians. Once, in the days of the Empire, Israel had exacted tribute; now she had to pay tribute.

In 722 B.C., when Israelite King Hoshea failed to make the annual payment promptly, Assyrian King Shalmaneser V began a siege of Samaria that lasted three years and finally was consummated by his successor, Sargon II. The punishment was not a slaughter but something even worse for the Israelite nation: the forced removal of 27,270 (some sources say 27,290) men, women and children from Israel. They and "their gods" were shipped across the Jordan and far to the northeast, and were scattered through cities along the Tigris and the Euphrates, in what is now Iraq and Iran. Once established in this distant place—sprinkled thinly in a foreign land and cut off from any connection with the place of their origin—they gradually vanished—ten of the original twelve tribes. An entire nation was no more.

> Like the dew on the mountain,
> Like the foam on the river,
> Like the bubble on the fountain,
> They are gone, and forever.

The biblical accounts imply that after this wholesale dispersal, there were no Israelites left in Israel:

"Therefore the Lord was very angry with Israel, and removed them out of his sight: there was none left but the tribe of Judah only."

(There is a theory that some of the exiled Israelites later mixed with the Judaean exiles in Babylon and thus remained a part of the Jewish people.)

The total population of Israel could not have been as little as 27,270 or 27,290. Those deported apparently were only the leaders from each town, city or district. The mass of the population must have remained. What really destroyed Israel as a nation was the cleverness of the Assyrians in colonizing the area that was now at least partially bereft of humans. To take the place of the dispossessed, they shipped in tens of thousands of men, women and children from distant places, and scattered them across all of Israel, much as a sower casts his seed on a plowed field. This was indeed a well-plowed field, and it had been fertilized with a great deal of precious blood.

The colonists who arrived did not come by choice. It was an enforced exchange of population, such as Adolf Hitler tried in some of the countries he occupied in eastern Europe in the 1940s. These colonists were all people who were being moved around on the orders of a military dictator. Some, for example, were rebel leaders from Babylon who had led an underground independence movement designed to free their great city from Assyrian domination. They and many other deportees had been leading citizens, with rich homes, servants, important positions in the community, until, motivated by a strong desire for independence, they had organized opposition to their Assyrian occupiers, and had been caught. Now they were being herded, with thousands of others, as if they were cattle, along tortuous, dusty roads, over mountains, down into valleys, across rivers, on and on, toward they knew not what. Many were forced to travel with their families and possessions—if any—a thousand miles or more, and this in a day when walking was the normal way to get from place to place, unless one were a military man or a king and rode a chariot. Three miles an hour. Two miles an hour, if women and children were included. A maximum of thirty-six miles a day, but probably less. Maybe not more than twenty or twenty-five. Forty days it must have taken, at least, to go a thousand miles. Maybe twice that long. They surely were weary and discouraged when they finally reached the Promised Land—only for them there had been no promise, only threats.

Consider those who settled—not by choice—in the Valley. They must immediately have asked: Who called this a river? They knew the great Tigris, father of waters, 1150 miles long in its flow from Mount Ararat to the Persian Gulf, one of the world's oldest rivers. They knew the Euphrates, too, 2235 miles long, formed by a union of the Kur and the Murad. Many on this trek had crossed the Khabur River, which flows into the Euphrates. Some had lived on the shores of the lovely Orontes. On their seemingly interminable journey they had crossed other rivers, maybe not great rivers but sizable rivers: the Abana, the Phorpar, the Ulatha. Who called this piddling stream that a healthy man could jump over a "river"? Most of them probably acquired, at first, sharp contempt for the Jordan. All that had happened until now on its banks or in its Valley—the history that had been written by those who had crossed back and forth—meant nothing to them. They were displaced people; colonists by compulsion, not choice. Their morale must have been low and they could not have been hesitant about finding fault. It mattered no whit to them that the people whose places they were taking—the people who had been born and brought up close to the Jordan —were probably missing it. Everyone misses the familiar. They were missing the Euphrates, the Tigris, and little rivers back where they had come from, just as the Israelites were missing the Jordan. But who had ever called it a "river"?

The newcomers were a diverse, conglomerate people. Those who came the farthest were from Cuthah, in the great valley between the Tigris and the Euphrates, seat of the god Nergal—an ancient city and a large one, by any standards. And ordinarily a happy city. But the Assyrians had come swooping down and had captured Cuthah, so here they were, in this strange place, displaced people. They were only about seven hundred miles from home, had they been birds able to fly across the Arabian desert on a straight line. But the way they had been forced to come, following the Euphrates and circling first north, then west, then south, it had been well over a thousand miles. And now look where they were! The Israelites who had been left behind in the towns and villages—these people among whom they were now being forced to dwell—had never heard of the great city of Cuthah! Not even of the god Nergal ("Lord of the Great City") whose consort was Ereshkigal, and who was the god of hunting, and also the god of the underworld. How could people not know about the great god Nergal, who had connections with Mars; a god so respected—or at least feared—that many people in the valley between the Tigris and the Euphrates joined his name with theirs, by a hyphen, and called themselves Nergal-This, or

Nergal-That. He was worshiped all over Babylonia and Assyria as a powerful force in every man's life, for if he were displeased, he could send down war, plague, flood, earthquake, disaster, havoc, destruction, death. No wonder there were so many temples to him back where they had come from. They must start building temples to him here, quickly, if they were going to be required to make this place their home.

But before they had been long in Israel, Nergal, god of hunting, failed them. Lions suddenly made their appearance in a number of settled places in Samaria, probably coming up from the jungle of the Jordan, which at various times in history has been well known for its lions. (The word "lion" appears one hundred and thirty times in the Bible, and in Hebrew there are nine different words for lion.) The diverse newcomers appealed to their diverse gods for protection against these beasts, the Cuthites making bountiful sacrifices to Nergal, god of hunting, and to Ereshkigal, his consort. But still the lions came. After some of the newcomers had been eaten alive, they sent an appeal to the Assyrian king, saying:

"The nations which thou hast removed, and placed in the cities of Samaria, know not the manner of the God of the land: therefore he hath sent lions among them, and, behold, they slay them, because they know not the manner of the God of the land."

The Assyrian king had a simple, pragmatic solution. He issued an order that one or more of the Israelite priests who had been uprooted and sent to Assyria be brought back at once, and re-established in Israel, to teach the newcomers how to use religion to control lions. It was done as the king ordered, and "one of the priests whom they had carried away from Samaria came and dwelt in Beth-el, and taught them how they should fear the Lord." Apparently there was no trouble thereafter from lions, but the biblical historian adds that the newcomers went right on sacrificing to their old gods, apparently relying on Jehovah only in the matter of lions.

Then there were the people from Babylon ("Gate of God"), which at various times had been called by words meaning "Seat of Life" and "Life of the Trees" and "Place of the Canals." In this part of the world Abraham once lived. When Abraham was young, Babylon was already old. Hundreds of years before Abraham, Ur-Nammu, king of Ur, had begun a zuggurat or temple-tower in Babylon, with terraces of different colors—red, black, blue—at various levels, each terrace planted with immense trees, shrubs and flowers, and on the very top a temple covered with bright-shining silver. But now the Assyrians had taken Baby-

204

lon and made refugees of some of its people, so here they were, not on
the great Euphrates, but on the banks of this struggling stream called
the Jordan, so they must get to work, now that they were here, constructing female shrines, called succoth-benoth, and in them set up
their female images in order not to lose favor with their gods. Some people called them "Booths of Daughters," others bluntly called them
houses of prostitution. What was important was that after the long trip
from Babylon, they must now busy themselves at once with their religious duties.

They came also from Hamath ("Citadel"), people who thought that
their river was the only river—the Orontes. Their god was Ashima, and
they respected no other. They came also from Ava, worshiping Nibhaz
and Tartak, the latter always represented as having the appearance of
an ass, and from Sepharvaim, paying obeisance to the god Adrammelech ("To Carry a King") who also was idolized in the shape of an
ass, and his consort Anammelech, who could be appeased only by the
sacrifice of small children, and so, once again, here in the Jordan Valley and elsewhere throughout Samaria, the innocent young would be
placed on stone altars and roasted alive, to impress angry or inatten-
tive pagan deities.

They came from all the countries of the Assyrian occupation—displaced, unhappy people, few of whom would ever be able to escape
and return to the places they loved. Exactly how many, no one ever reported. What is known is that in the Valley, and in the hills of Israel,
and across the river, monotheism, which had survived for hundreds of
years against such great odds, now was overshadowed by paganism and
almost disappeared. But before monotheism went into a short eclipse,
it had one happy final chapter.

At the southern extremity of the Jordan, around Jericho, and from
there south to the far end of the Salt Sea, and west about two-thirds
the way to the Mediterranean, the Judaeans were still a free and independent people, now ruled by Hezekiah ("Jehovah Is My Strength"),
the best king, some said, since the great Solomon. His personal piety
was as pronounced as his political wisdom and his military fearless-
ness. Aware of how greatly the religious life of his people had been
contaminated by heathen influences over so long a period, he tried to
root out superstition, idolatry, and spiritual blindness. The Temple
was reopened and cleansed, and true worship was re-established. By
word of mouth, the news of these happenings spread from Jericho up
through the Valley—from the shores of the Salt Sea even unto Dan.

Then one day couriers arrived in Israel from Jerusalem with a proclamation signed by King Hezekiah, inviting all true believers, wherever they might live and to whatever tribe they might belong, to come to Jerusalem for celebration of the Passover. From village to village, city to city they went, not only through the Valley, but across Ephraim, Manasseh, Issachar, and Zebulun to Asher and Naphtali, even to the sources of the Jordan at the foot of Mount Hermon. The proclamation began:

"Ye children of Israel, turn again unto the Lord God of Abraham, Isaac, and Israel, and he will return to the remnant of you, that are escaped out of the hand of the kings of Assyria . . .

"Now be ye not stiffnecked, as your fathers were . . ."

In many parts of the Valley the couriers were laughed to scorn and driven away by unbelievers, but wherever they went they made public the invitation from good King Hezekiah.

On the appointed day, people flocked from all corners of occupied Israel—from the Valley, and from the hills; from the villages and from the cities. Apparently the Assyrian authorities took few steps to stop them. There is no record of exactly how many gathered at Jerusalem, but—

"Hezekiah king of Judah did give to the congregation a thousand bullocks and seven thousand sheep; and the princes gave to the congregation a thousand bullocks and ten thousand sheep . . .

"So there was great joy in Jerusalem: for since the time of Solomon the son of David king of Israel there was not the like in Jerusalem."

Before they trekked back home, the people of Israel went from town to town in Judah breaking pagan idols, cutting down groves of trees in which pagan rites were held, and smashing pagan altars. Judah was still a free country, though Israel was part of the Assyrian Empire.

Now a new and menacing figure mounted the Assyrian throne, Sennacherib, whose name has the strange meaning: "Sin Has Increased the Brothers." He personally led his troops against the walled cities of Judah. Carved on a prism of stone, still preserved, is his own report of what happened:

"As for Hezekiah the Jew, who did not submit to my yoke, forty-six of his strong-walled cities, as well as the small cities in their neighborhood, which were without number—by constructing a ramp out of trampled earth and by bringing up battering-rams, by the attack of infantry, by tunnels, breaches, and the use of axes I besieged and took those cities. Two hundred thousand one hundred and fifty people great and small, male and female, horses, mules, asses, camels, cattle, and

206

sheep without number, I brought away from them and counted as spoil. Himself (King Hezekiah) like a caged bird I shut up in Jerusalem, his royal city."

"The caged bird" was saved by what seemed a miracle to the people of besieged Jerusalem. The Assyrian army that surrounded the city—an enormous aggregation of well-armed men—had drunk deep of the heady stimulant of victory. The soldiers were loaded with loot. Self-confidence exalted their spirits. Certainly, tomorrow, in a few hours, the capital of Judah could be obliterated. Then, led by Sennacherib, they would go on to deal with Egypt.

"And it came to pass that night, that the angel of the Lord went out, and smote in the camp of the Assyrians an hundred fourscore and five thousand: and when they arose early in the morning, behold, they were all dead corpses."

Herodotus, the fifth century Greek historian, gave credit for the saving of Jerusalem to "a multitude of field mice which by night devoured all the quivvers and bows of the enemy, and all the straps by which they held their shields. Next morning they commenced their fight and great numbers fell as they had no arms with which to defend themselves."

A less fanciful explanation is that as the formidable foreign army was preparing for its assault on Jerusalem, one of those devastating plagues that were the scourge of the East broke out in the Assyrian camp, causing the hundred and eighty-five thousand deaths and compelling Sennacherib to withdraw to his own capital, Nineveh, with what loot from the plundered forty-six cities his surviving soldiers could carry.

More than twenty-five hundred years later, Lord Byron, in writing his epic poem on the event, accepted the plague version, writing:

> Like the leaves of the forest when Summer is green,
> That host with their banners at sunset were seen:
> Like the leaves of the forest when Autumn hath blown,
> That host on the morrow lay withered and strown.
>
> For the Angel of Death spread his wings on the blast,
> And breathed in the face of the foe as he passed;
> And the eyes of the sleepers waxed deadly and chill,
> And their hearts but once heaved, and forever grew still!

The Israelites remaining in the Valley, who had formed a new emotional link with their Judaean cousins by celebrating Passover with them, and the colonists, who had reason to hate the Assyrians deeply, were not the only ones to rejoice over the outcome of the siege. The destruction of the Assyrian army—whether by Judaeans, mice or plague —filled the countries round about with wonder, and many sent their kings with gifts to Hezekiah, and so, once again, across the Jordan and over the hills to Jerusalem went royal trains, and when Sennacherib met violent death at Nineveh, there was little mourning from Dan even unto Beersheba.

About this time the spotlight focused for a brief moment of history on a Valley city far to the north, Beth-Shan, at the junction of the Vale of Jezreel and the Valley of the Jordan. Since its settlement during the Chalcolithic Age, in the fourth millennium B.C., Beth-Shan had attracted the attention of many races of men. And no wonder! In a land of sand and drought, it was lush, well watered, almost subtropical. Looking down from the height of the city, the Vale of Jezreel could be seen stretching far to the northwest; eventually to the Mediterranean. Below, the thickets of the Jordan, and across the river the uneven skyline of the Gilead hills. The Holy Land's geographer, George Adam Smith, once called Beth-Shan "the farthest-seeing, farthest-seen fortress in the land." Those who farmed its fields boasted about the great fertility of the soil. Because it lay on an important caravan route, it prospered economically. But rival armies were always coming and going, so Beth-Shan was frequently attacked, looted and left in ruins. Once the Egyptians used it as a military base. Joshua failed to take it from the Canaanites, but the Philistines did, and to its walls they nailed the severed heads of Saul and his sons. After the Israelites captured Beth-Shan, they held it for about three hundred years. Then came the Assyrians. But now an entirely new and different breed of men entered the Valley, to play a brief role in the story of the Jordan.

The Scythians were nomad-warriors from western Siberia, who, since about 2000 B.C., had been inhabiting an area just north of the Black Sea. They were noted for their horsemanship and their savagery in battle. Looking at ancient Russian wall hangings depicting Scythian cavalrymen, one has difficulty in deciding which is the more handsome, the horse or the black-mustached rider.

In the late eighth century B.C. the Scythians started to sweep south, but were checked by the Assyrian armies of Sargon II. Herodotus is authority for the story that they drove their way into western Persia, where they remained for twenty-eight years, and then headed for Egypt, killing and looting as they went. When they were bought off from raiding Egypt by the Pharaoh, some of them decided that of all the places they had seen, in their extensive travels, Beth-Shan was the closest to ideal, and there they wanted to settle. So they took Beth-Shan and there they did settle.

Beth-Shan has been translated, variously, as House of Security, House of Tranquility, or, in the bad sense, House of Self-Confidence. Some have even suggested that it originally meant House of the Serpent-God. Now it became simply Scythopolis. Exactly how long the wild horsemen from the plains of Russia remained in the Valley city no historian, not even Herodotus, has told, but even after they left, the place continued to be called Scythopolis.

Nebuchadnezzar (or Nebuchadrezzar, as the biblical writers sometimes spelled it) means "Nabu Has Protected the Succession Rights." The Babylonian king bearing this cumbersome name is known to every Jewish or Christian child who has ever studied the Bible, because of the story of Shadrach, Meshach and Abednego, and how they escaped from the fiery furnace into which they had been thrown because of their refusal to worship the king's golden image. For the people of the Valley at this time Nebuchadnezzar was not a character in a story but a serious threat to their entire way of life.

The Ishtar gate in the city wall encircling Babylon in Nebuchadnezzar's time was decorated with a composite animal in colored tile called a *mušruššu*, having the head of a serpent, the body of a lion, and the claws of an eagle. This represented exactly what a great many people—conquered and yet to be conquered—thought of Nebuchadnezzar at that time. His three driving interests were religion, war and architecture. He was a genius at personal publicity. Not only in the ruins of ancient Babylon, but in the buried remains of at least a hundred other cities archaeologists have found that the bricks used in the construction of public buildings were each one clearly stamped with the word:

NEBUCHADNEZZAR

He made of Babylon the most sumptuous capital of its time, or of any time up until then, with extensive parks, magnificent palaces, and well laid out streets lined with imposing mansions. But in his later years he became the victim of a form of insanity not unknown to medical men then and now: he imagined himself an ox and felt compelled to assume the posture of that animal and to try to live on the grass of the field.

Nebuchadnezzar had no particular interest in the Valley, or in what had been Israel, or even in Judah. His real enemy—his obsession—was

Egypt. But the Judaean king, while at first paying tribute to Nebuchad-nezzar, then threw in his lot with the Egyptians, so the Babylonian monarch sent his army south. Before crossing the Jordan they made certain that there would be no trouble for them on that side of the river. Jeremiah had prophesied Nebuchadnezzar's war on the wandering tribesmen east of the Jordan. It happened exactly as he had said it would:

"Their tents and their flocks they shall take away: they shall take to themselves their curtains, and all their vessels, and their camels; and they shall cry unto them, Fear is on every side."

Then Jeremiah addressed a warning to the people of the Valley: "Flee, get you far off, dwell deep, O ye inhabitants of Hazor, saith the Lord; for Nebuchadnezzar king of Babylon hath taken counsel against you, and hath conceived a purpose against you . . .

"And Hazor shall be a dwelling place for dragons, and a desolation for ever: there shall no man abide there, nor any son of man dwell in it."

There is no evidence, either historical or archaeological, that Nebu-chadnezzar's army went to Hazor, or that attacks were made on any other Valley towns or cities. The goal was Jerusalem. The siege, which began in March of 597 B.C., was quickly over.

Nebuchadnezzar "carried out thence all the treasures of the house of the Lord, and the treasures of the king's house, and cut in pieces all the vessels of gold which Solomon king of Israel had made in the temple of the Lord, as the Lord had said.

"And he carried away all Jerusalem, and all the princes, and all the mighty men of valour, even ten thousand captives, and all the crafts-men and smiths: none remained, save the poorest sort of the people of the land.

"And he carried away Jehoiachin to Babylon, and the king's mother, and the king's wives, and his officers, and the mighty of the land, those carried he into captivity from Jerusalem to Babylon.

"And all the men of might, even seven thousand, and craftsmen and smiths a thousand, all that were strong and apt for war, even them the king of Babylon brought captive to Babylon.

"And the king of Babylon made Mattaniah his father's brother king in his stead, and changed his name to Zedekiah."

Among the deportees was a twenty-five-year-old man, Ezekiel, son of Buzi, a member of the celebrated Zadokite family of priests. Five years after being settled in a village on the Babylonian river of Che-bar, he received his call as a prophet and during the remaining twenty-one years of his life wrote and spoke extensively. There are still scholarly arguments about how much of the biblical book bearing his name he himself actually wrote, some contending only ten percent. Only once in the 1273 verses is the Jordan mentioned, this in connection with Ezekiel's vision of a new and great river that would issue out from under the door of the Temple in Jerusalem, and flow eastward toward the Valley—"a river that I could not pass over: for the waters were risen, waters to swim in, a river that could not be passed over . . . at the bank of the river were very many trees on the one side and on the other . . . These waters issue out toward the east country, and go down into the desert, and go into the sea: which being brought forth into the sea, the waters shall be healed."

As the Salt Sea, in Ezekiel's vision, is "healed" or freshened, it becomes populated by all manner of fish. The prophet even imagines the scene when "the fishers shall stand upon it from En-gedi even unto Eneglaim; they shall be a place to spread forth nets; their fish shall be according to their kinds, as the fish of the great sea, exceeding many."

(By En-eglaim the prophet is believed to have meant a town on the west bank near the north end of the Salt Sea now called Ain el Feshklah. If so, he was envisioning the shore lined for twenty to twenty-five miles with fishermen.)

Then the prophet went back to dreaming about this new river of his imagination, and in his dreaming saw its shores producing not only food but medicines as well:

"And by the river upon the bank thereof, on this side and on that side, shall grow all trees for meat, whose leaf shall not fade, neither shall the fruit thereof be consumed: it shall bring forth new fruit according to his months, because their waters they issued out of the sanctuary: and the fruit thereof shall be for meat, and the leaf thereof for medicine."

The Jordan itself came into the vision only incidentally, as one of the frontiers of the land of Israel.

Although the "mighty of the land" had been taken into captivity, Judah, under her new, enemy-appointed king, continued for ten years to function in about the same way the countries of Europe did under the Nazi occupation in the 1940s. But in 587 B.C., the Valley people saw soldiers of Nebuchadnezzar by the tens of thousands swarming across the Jordan and on toward Jerusalem, armed with instruments of war never seen in these parts before. This time the siege lasted eighteen months. In its final days the princes and elite of the city were reduced to the direst straits; people who had never known want before suffered with everyone else; children were cooked and eaten by the more desperate victims of the famine. What happened in those dreadful days became burned into the national heart and would long be remembered in captivity. It was the culmination of a tremendous tragedy.

On the ninth day of the fourth month, King Zedekiah agreed with his military commanders that the power to resist was gone, so during the night he, his sons, the nobles of Jerusalem, his general staff, and many ordinary soldiers fled through the royal gardens and out of the city by a little-used gate. They headed at once in the direction of the Jordan, closely pursued by Nebuchadnezzar's men (now called Chaldees or Chaldaeans, after the part of Babylonia from which Nebuchadnezzar came).

The feeling of panic must have been great that night on the road leading down from Jerusalem to Jericho. The fugitives knew they were fleeing from what would probably be even worse than death, for the Chaldaeans were not noted for their kindly treatment of prisoners. If only they could escape across the Jordan, and up into the hills beyond, and then finally, if necessary, to the desert!

Zedekiah's men shed, on their way, whatever encumbered them or slowed their speed, for the enemy was close upon them. They had hoped to rest for a while in the gardens of Jericho, before fording the river, but on the Plains of Jericho their doom caught up with them. No one escaped.

Nebuchadnezzar had established his military headquarters for the Judaean campaign at Riblah, on the Orontes River, in what had once been Syrian territory, then Assyrian, and now was part of the extensive Chaldaean or Babylonian Empire. From the king now came orders to transport all the prisoners of importance at once to Riblah, "for judgment." As they had been captured so close to the Jordan, it is possible they were taken through the Valley on their way north; that they forded the river at the Jericho crossing. As they were going over the river someone must have figured out that just six hundred and fifty-three years earlier Joshua had led the people of the twelve tribes hopefully "over Jordan." Now Joshua's descendants were crossing the Jordan again, this time into exile—or worse. Almost everything conceivably possible had happened to the sons of Abraham, Isaac and Jacob in those six hundred and fifty-three years, much of it dire and disastrous, yet nothing—now or ever—could cut the people from their land. Jerusalem had not become the greatest city in the world, yet the tie between Judaeans (Jews) and Jerusalem was now permanent and indestructible. The Jordan might not be the world's mightiest river, but it was their river and ever would be. In exile they would dream dreams and sing songs, and remember.

At Riblah the great Nebuchadnezzar presided over the executions. First, the sons of Zedekiah. Two biblical versions suggest that Nebuchadnezzar himself did the killing. Zedekiah was forced to stand, helpless, and watch as one son after another was slain.

Then attention turned to a fire in which sharp-pointed irons had been heated until they now glowed a bright red. Again the biblical accounts imply that Nebuchadnezzar himself burned out the eyes of the ill-fated king, first one, then the other. After that Zedekiah was taken to Babylon. But not until the executioners had beheaded or otherwise slain "all the nobles of Judah."

Many less-important Judaeans, fearing the worst, had fled from Jerusalem down into the Valley, hoping thus to escape the fate they were certain would be meted out by Nebuchadnezzar to the people of Jerusalem and its environs. Less than one month after the fall of the city, they heard the bitter news of what now was happening up in Jerusalem. Nebuchadnezzar had sent a captain of the guard, Nebuzaradan, with specific instructions on how to deal with the captive city:

"And he burnt the house of the Lord, and the king's house, and all the houses of Jerusalem, and every great man's house burnt he with fire . . .

"Now the rest of the people that were left in the city, and the fugitives that fell away to the king of Babylon, with the remnant of the multitude, did Nebuzaradan the captain of the guard carry away."

Only the peasants were permitted to remain, to care for the vineyards and work the fields. How many? Surely thousands. Perhaps tens of thousands. Possibly hundreds of thousands.

Before setting the Temple afire, the Chaldaeans looted everything of value that could be moved out and transported to the north. The Valley people were especially interested in what happened to all the brasswork in the Temple, for it had been made in the foundries Solomon had established near Succoth, and the Valley people had always been proud of it.

"And the pillars of brass that were in the house of the Lord, and the vases, and the brasen sea that was in the house of the Lord, did the Chaldees break in pieces, and carried the brass of them to Babylon.

"And the pots, and the shovels, and the snuffers, and the spoons, and all the vessels of brass wherewith they ministered, took they away."

Those sent into captivity by Nebuchadnezzar were determined never to forget.

By the rivers of Babylon, there we sat down, Yea, we wept, when we remembered Zion.

We hanged our harps upon the willows in the midst thereof.

For there they that carried us away captive required of us a song; and they that wasted us required of us mirth, saying, Sing us one of the songs of Zion.

How shall we sing the Lord's song in a strange land?

If I forget thee, O Jerusalem, let my right hand forget her cunning.

If I do not remember thee, let my tongue cleave to the roof of my mouth; if I prefer not Jerusalem above my chief joy.

Archaeologists have proof that the Valley in this period went into a decline that lasted for a long time. Elsewhere the world was in a convulsive state. New forces were at work in Athens and Rome that would someday help mold the mind of Western man, and would have a profound effect on the pattern of life on both sides of the river. In faraway Persia, where the people had long worshiped gods of fertility and nature, now appeared Zoroaster (also sometimes called Zarathustra), who proclaimed a religion of lofty moral ideas based on the principle: "Do good, hate evil," a new form of monotheism. In an indirect way, the people of the Valley and their history would be affected by the appearance of Zoroaster in the sixth century B.C.

But despite the dynamic progress in evidence elsewhere, in the Valley the total population decreased, some towns and villages were abandoned, and a tendency developed among the people on both banks to live in strongly fortified cities whenever possible. There was even a decline in the expertness with which the Valley people tilled their soil.

In these times down in Edom something happened that changed the future of the Valley. The people living in the wild country just to the south of the Salt Sea and their cousins the Israelites had been at war, off and on, ever since the Edomites had refused Moses permission to lead his people over their land. Although they were all descendants of Abraham, Esau's line and Jacob's line had been on friendly terms only once during all these centuries—when they joined forces for a joint attack on Mesha, king of Moab. But even this military alliance had lasted for only a short time. After the fall of Judah, the Edomites' rejoicing was so great that the prophets Jeremiah, Ezekiel, Joel, Amos and Obadiah all turned their vocabularies against them, and prophesied a dire fate for Edom.

Jeremiah even brought the Jordan into his prophecy, saying that the Edomites' fate would come upon them like "a lion from the swelling of Jordan against the habitation of the strong." He concluded his prophecy by saying that the fall of Edom would be so horrendous that the noise of the collapse would be heard as far away as the Red Sea.

The descendants of Esau were now being infiltrated if not actually invaded by nomads from Arabia calling themselves Nabataeans. Many Edomites, in the face of this pressure, went north and settled in the lower half of Judah. Some even wandered as far north as the Jordan, adding a new stock to the odd mixture of races in the Valley. The district in which most of the Edomites settled, to the south of Hebron, became known as Idumaea, and the people were called Idumaeans, a new-old race that some generations later would produce Herod the Great.

The people of the Valley—whether they belonged to that remnant of Israelites and Judaeans who had been spared deportation, or whether they were Idumaeans, transplanted Babylonians and Assyrians, or Moabites and Ammonites from across the river, or descendants of the endemic Canaanites—followed the historical developments of this half century with interest, well aware that what was happening in far-off places would inevitably affect their own daily lives. They heard by word of mouth about Cyrus the Great, as he already was being called. This young monarch first defeated King Croesus ("as rich as Croesus") and occupied his kingdom of Lydia (the first country in the world to use coined money). Then he captured Babylon by one of the cleverest ruses in all military history—by diverting the Euphrates, which runs through the center of the city, and then marching his invading troops through the dried-up river bed in an attack that took the defenders entirely by surprise. And that was the end of the empire that Nebuchadnezzar had built! Seventeen days later Cyrus himself walked triumphantly into the captured city amid scenes of jubilation.

The next news that reached the Valley was that Cyrus was going to gather together all the people in Babylonia who were exiles and return them to the lands Nebuchadnezzar had forced them to leave, on the old theory that the enemy of my enemy is my friend. He was especially friendly to the Jews, because they were monotheistic, as the Persians had now become under the influence of Zoroaster. He signed a proclamation declaring that he had received a divine commandment to build a house of God in Jerusalem; to accomplish this objective he was permitting all former inhabitants of Israel and Judah now in Babylonia to return to the land from which they had been exiled. Furthermore, he called on those who might decide not to go to contribute vessels of gold, or goods, or beasts, or other valuables to help finance the rebuilding of the Temple in Jerusalem.

Until now the exile had lasted just short of half a century. During that time the displaced had been living among people who also were Semites, in a land that enjoyed all the comforts and luxuries that civilization anywhere in the world at that time had to offer. The native energy of the race had found many outlets. Protected—in some cases even favored—by their new lords, they had become masters in many arts. Some had done well in business or public affairs, and had acquired property, prosperity and a degree of contentment. Some, like Amos and Nehemiah, had risen to high position. And so, many decided to remain, certain that "back there" would not be like "here," for they had heard reports of what had been done to and in the Promised Land during the half century they had been away. Those who did go were distinguished from their compatriots by their religious zeal, their high moral principles, their vigor, and their willingness to face all the risks that the long journey would involve.

The first caravan from Babylon for Jerusalem set off in the year 538 B.C. It was made up mostly of members of a new generation—young people who were going to see the land of their ancestors for the first time. But there were some sixty years old or more, who could remember, and reminisce, and compare. Altogether there were either 49,897 or 49,942 men, women and children in this new *aliyah* ("going up") to Jerusalem.

Posterity can thank two men for the wealth of detail that has been handed down on this particular trip across the Jordan and into the Promised Land: Ezra and Nehemiah. They were contemporaries, who lived in Persia several generations after Cyrus put an official end to the Judaean exile. Both were excellent journalists and apparently had access to a mass of official documents replete with statistics. In the two biblical books bearing their names they wrote full reports on the 538 B.C. exodus from Babylon that are masterpieces of detail and precision. Yet little is known about the authors themselves.

Ezra is presumed to have held a position in Persia that the modern-day British would call Secretary of State for Jewish Affairs. He served under Persian King Artaxerxes I, as did also Nehemiah, who had the title of the King's Cupbearer, a position of distinction.

Ezra the Scribe, as he was often called, in his report gives some of the actual wording of the proclamation of Cryus, then goes into statistics, disclosing that in the 538 B.C. exodus there were 42,360 men, women and children, plus 7357 servants, male and female, plus 200 "singing men and singing women." They took with them 736 horses,

246 mules, 435 camels, and 6720 asses, for a total of 8136 animals—approximately one riding animal for each six humans.

For posterity's sake Ezra then tells who all these people were, what family or clan they belonged to, and what town or city they came from. Skipping Jerusalem, the greatest number from any one community were from a town called Senaah, which is mentioned nowhere else in biblical or historical accounts of the time. The precise location is unknown but it is thought to have been near Jericho. From Senaah there were 3600 men. (Ezra, in conformity to the custom of the times, lists only the number of men in this detailed accounting. If the average man had a wife and three children, there must have been 18,000 people from Senaah alone.) From the city of Jericho there were 345 men, plus women and children.

Nehemiah's account, which may have been written at quite a different time than Ezra's, agrees in every detail, except that he lists 245 instead of 200 "singing men and singing women," which brings his grand total up to 49,942, and his number for Senaah is 3930 instead of 3630, which was probably a slip of the pen.

Before the trek began, Cyrus appointed Sheshbazzar, a prince, as governor of Judah, and then had his royal treasurer turn over to him 5400 sacred objects that Nebuchadnezzar's soldiers had taken, on the order of the Babylonian king, from the Temple in Jerusalem. During the past half century they had been in a pagan temple in Babylon, being used for what one historian has called "lascivious pagan revelry."

When the people back in the Valley heard that approximately fifty thousand exiles were on their way home, they must have speculated on many matters. Would any of the people of the Ten Tribes sent into captivity in Assyria by King Sargon II come with them? It had been one hundred and eighty-four years since the exile of the Samarians, but what of their descendants? At home the Israelites and the Judaeans had fought what amounted to an almost continuous civil war for centuries, but in exile they must have found more to join them than to separate them, and the Valley of the Tigris to which the Israelites had been sent was not an impossible distance from Babylon, to which the Judaeans had been sent. Besides, there surely would be some Israelites coming from Babylon. In Nebuchadnezzar's deportation, many people from Jericho and from other Valley communities had been rounded up and shipped north, along with the Jerusalemites and the other Judaeans.

What route would they follow on their return? Would they cross the Jordan north of the Sea of Chinnereth and come down the center of the country, stopping perhaps at Shechem, where Abraham had built an altar to God and where Jacob had bought a parcel of ground from the Hittite prince? Or would they avoid the hill country and not ford the Jordan until they came to the Jericho crossing? Coming down through Manasseh and Gad, on the east side of the river, would be a safer, more cautious route. It would avoid humiliation that would be almost intolerable, as they were forced to see what had happened to the best part of their ancient land, now in the hands of idolatrous people.

Abraham's route or Joshua's? The question of which they took is still unanswered, for there is no historical record of how they came. One likes to think, however, that they crossed the river exactly where the Twelve Tribes had crossed, seven hundred and two years earlier. The previous time there had been 601,730 men over twenty years of age able to bear arms, besides all the young and the old, and the women. This time the grand total starting out from Babylon was less than fifty thousand, and many of the elderly might die along the way before ever reaching the river's edge.

That other time they had had millions of animals to get across the river. In one engagement alone, with the Midianites, just before the crossing, they had seized 675,000 sheep. This time the total number of animals listed by Ezra the Scribe was slightly over eight thousand, and they were all for purposes of transportation.

That other time the men composed a well-equipped army—soldiers who knew they would soon go into battle to possess the land that God had promised them. This time the trekkers were going primarily as builders, with the specific assignment from the Persian king to reconstruct the Temple.

That other time they had had to face hostility on all sides. This time they had the blessing of the man who now ruled over the whole vast area, so they would probably not have to fight for the right of habitation.

That other time they had crossed the river easily, thanks to a miracle. This time they might not be able to count on such divine cooperation.

When Joshua led his people across the Jordan there had been no reception committee, but this time the river's banks and the slopes leading down to the Jordan swarmed with people: Valley people and hill people; Judaeans and Israelites. Many were there out of more than idle curiosity; they were looking for friends and relatives from whom they had been separated for forty-nine long years. Then there would be the Idumaeans, Babylonians, Assyrians, Moabites, Ammonites, and others now living here, and who no doubt were a little concerned about what this great new influx would mean for them.

The trekkers who could remember how it had been when they left must have found many changes, especially in the Valley. But they themselves were going to be responsible for still greater changes. They had brought with them some of the culture, the manners and mannerisms, the city ways of a far place, Babylon. Consciously or subconsciously they had been greatly affected by the people among whom they had been living this past half century. Consciously or subconsciously they would impose what they had learned and absorbed onto what already was here.

In the accounts of Ezra and Nehemiah it is made clear that although all the people in the trek were supposed to have come to help rebuild the Temple, they were permitted to go to the localities of their origin. Later, as actual work on the Temple began, many of the craftsmen among them worked in Jerusalem and commuted back and forth to their own towns and villages. Nehemiah explains, for example, that carpenters from Jericho built (or rebuilt) the sheep gate, while men from other Valley places built the fish gate, the dung gate, the Valley gate, the gate of the fountain, and the horse gate. Malchiah, the goldsmith's son, had a big part in building the sheep gate. Everyone receives credit for the work he did. Ezra and Nehemiah set it all down precisely, omitting no one.

Exactly eighty years after the departure from Babylon of the 49,-897 (or 49,942) Israelites and Judaeans, Ezra himself asked his king, Artaxerxes I, for permission to lead another wave of emigration to Jerusalem. Permission was granted. This time about six thousand went. They started on the first day of the first month and arrived in Jerusalem on the first day of the fifth month. Good reporter though he is, in most matters, Ezra fails to tell where they were those four months, what adventures they had on the way (except a slight delay soon after leaving Babylon when Ezra discovered that in his haste he had neglected to bring any members of the Tribe of Levi to serve as priests). Nor does he tell what route they followed. But he does list in great detail the weight and description of the gifts he took to Jerusalem, for the Temple, among them silver vessels weighing 6600 pounds, gold vessels of the same weight, and 42,900 pounds of silver.

Almost immediately upon his arrival in Jerusalem, "I rent my garment and my mantle, and plucked off the hair of my head and of my beard, and sat down astonied." What distressed him was his discovery of a mortal sin the Jews of Jerusalem were committing.

(Ezra and Nehemiah are the first biblical writers to use the word "Jew" extensively. Heretofore in biblical accounts a person was either an Israelite or a Judaean, depending on whether he belonged to one of the ten tribes in the north, or the two tribes in the south. Or he was called a Gadite, or a Danite, or a Benjaminite, referring to his specific tribe. When the word "Jew" was first used it was a synonym for Judaean. But Ezra and Nehemiah—then other biblical writers—popularized its use to describe any descendant of the children of Jacob, regardless of whether he was an Israelite or a Judaean. Henceforth it is used in that sense in this volume.)

The great sin that so disturbed Ezra was that Jews were intermarrying with Canaanites, Hittites, Perizzites, Jebusites, Ammonites, Moabites, Egyptians and Amorites. As part of his campaign to put an end to such intermarriage he compiled a black list of the guilty, with the assistance of a committee of his own choice, and the list was published. On it were the names of singers, sons of priests, and other prominent people. With crusading zeal he induced at least some of them to "put away their strange wives," even if the wives had already borne children.

About thirteen years after Ezra's departure for Jerusalem, Nehemiah approached Artaxerxes at a propitious moment when he saw that the king had a bottle of wine before him and was relaxing from the cares of his office, with his wife beside him, and asked permission to make the same trip Ezra had. The permission was granted.

(A few historians contend that Nehemiah went to Jerusalem before Ezra, while at least one biblical expert believes they went at exactly the same time.)

Nehemiah led a somewhat smaller body of returning deportees than had Ezra. After reaching Jerusalem and spending three days resting from the arduous trip, Nehemiah late one night, accompanied by only a few friends, made an inspection tour of Jerusalem by moonlight, stumbling over heaps of rubbish and debris, all the way to the city limits in the Kedron Valley. He found that the walls had been permitted to crumble, that the gates of the city had been "consumed with fire," and that "Jerusalem lieth waste." Soon, under the leadership of this amazing man, a multitude of workmen, with the vigor of their race, were busy restoring the devastations of a hundred and fifty years, heaving back into place the old blocks of stone that Solomon's artisans had chiseled, rebuilding ancient towers, cleansing from cornices and pillars the black stains left on them by the great conflagration. It took

courage as well as industry, because of the constant danger of attack.
As Nehemiah himself reported:

"They which builded on the wall, and they that bare burdens, with
those that laded, every one with one of his hands wrought in the work,
and with the other hand held a weapon.

"For the builders, every one had his sword girded by his side, and
so builded."

(Twenty-four centuries later some of the ancestors of some of these
people would be doing the same thing, on or near the banks of the Jordan—standing guard and at the same time laboring to restore the place
to its former beauty.)

Among those Nehemiah recruited to help in the rebuilding were
stone masons from Jericho and other places in the Valley—even some
craftsmen from across the Jordan in Gilead. Just as Ezra had listed by
name the Jerusalemites who had taken foreign wives, so Nehemiah
listed by name the goldsmiths, the apothecaries, the governor and his
daughters, and other important people who helped in the reconstruction of the wall.

"Next unto him repaired Uzziel the son of Harhaiah, of the goldsmiths. Next unto him also repaired Hananiah the son of one of the
apothecaries . . . And next unto them repaired Rephaiah the son of
Hur, the ruler of the half part of Jerusalem. And next unto them . . ."

Nehemiah also arranged a drawing of lots whereby nine out of every
ten workmen would be permitted to live down in the Valley or anywhere else they pleased, but the tenth man must live in Jerusalem.
From Nehemiah we learn that the singers who had come on the two
previous treks had formed several communal settlements, one of
them at Gilgal, close to the Jordan. Also, that the ancient Valley city of
Hazor was populated again, for it is listed in his report as one of the
places to which the new rulers of Jerusalem permitted their people to
move.

When the wall was finished, Nehemiah arranged an elaborate dedication ceremony. Crowds came from the hills, from the Valley, and
from over the river. There were musicians with cymbals, psalteries
and harps, sons of priests blowing trumpets, and many choral groups,
with soloists. Ezra the Scribe led one procession; Nehemiah, the King's
Cupbearer, led another. Once again they were able to chant that the
City of David was "a fair place, the joy of the whole world."

A young Greek from the mountains of Macedonia crossed over the
Jordan into Judah in 332 B.C.—and nothing was ever the same after

that. Alexander (soon to be known everywhere as "the Great") was only twenty-four then, but already he had been king for four years, and already he had fabricated a great deal of history. His military successes had been spectacular. For example, he had gone to Asia Minor to liberate some fellow Greeks and had unexpectedly demolished the Persian Empire. This part of the world was accustomed to great warriors. Every country had had them. What distinguished Alexander—and the Greeks—was something else. Everywhere they went they introduced the contagion of all that was meant by Greek culture or Greek civilization. The trip that took Alexander across the Jordan was primarily to visit Egypt, where in that year he founded a great seaport city that would bear his name and would become, after Athens, the greatest Hellenistic cosmopolis of its day. Or any day. But after crossing the Jordan, he stopped in Jerusalem long enough to meet with the High Priest.

Alexander—who is pictured with exceedingly large, searching brown eyes, a long, sharply pointed nose, sensuous lips, a neck like that of a wrestler or prize fighter, and curly hair at least a foot long—left the Jews and their land relatively undisturbed. At least for the moment. Yet his passage through the country did symbolize the start of a new era. The Hellenization of the Middle East was under way. Eventually the empire he was building would extend as far into Europe as the Danube River, as far down into Africa as Syene, on the first cataract of the Nile, and as far east as the Hyphasis River in India. But the Greek culture he was spreading would influence the thinking of man to the far corners of the earth, probably for all time.

After the establishment of Alexandria, and after the sudden death of the man called great—in Babylon, at the age of thirty-three, just as he was planning the conquest of the West—his marshals and generals agreed to recognize the right of his infant son, Alexander the Younger, to the throne, but when the boy was murdered, each marshal tried to take over the empire from his rivals, and thus it was carved up among them. To Ptolemy, also a Macedonian, fell the title of King of Egypt. Under him and thirteen other Ptolemies who followed him, Egypt became again a great power: a Hellenistic monarchy, which at first included all of Palestine.

In this golden age of the Greeks, the mass of Jews retained their Jewishness and were faithful to the religion, the intellectual habits, and even the customs of their forebears, becoming more deeply concerned than ever with the disciplines of the Torah, partly due to the work Ezra had done. But with the so-called elite it was different. For them the

Greeks' exciting new intellectuality, their advanced and courageous culture, and their intense concern with philosophy, literature and the arts was irresistible. The wealthy class soaked itself in the Hellenistic way of life. Many from the Valley, many from other parts of the country, emigrated permanently to Alexandria, where a large and prosperous Jewish community had been built up, with many synagogues, one so vast that it was necessary to use flags to signal to the congregation when they should respond with their "amens." The very word *synagogue* was an example of the Greek influence on Jewish life and language in the Diaspora. Until the Babylonian exile, the Judaeans had always worshiped in the Temple at Jerusalem—and nowhere else. They had been brought up to believe that a temple could be built only in Jerusalem, and that sacrifices (a vital part of their religion) could be offered only in the Temple. Therefore, in the early days of their exile, they built no houses of worship, but instead met on the Sabbath in the homes of their religious leaders and read the sacred books they had brought with them. The Greek word for a "bringing together of people" is *synagogue,* which was used first for the assemblage, and ultimately for the building in which the assemblage was held.

Soon many Jews became so assimilated into their Greek environment that they were no longer able to read the Torah in Hebrew or Aramaic. It was about this time that the Ptolemy who was on the throne asked his librarian to get him a Greek translation of the Bible for the royal library. Having none, the librarian appealed to the High Priest in Jerusalem, who sent seventy-two elders with an official Hebrew text to Alexandria. There, according to one fable, in seventy-two days they made a translation into Greek that was read to the Jewish community, received great applause, and so was presented to the king. From the number of elders and the number of days, it became known somewhat inaccurately as the Septuagint. (*Septuaginta* is Latin for 70.) Another fable has it that King Philadelphus asked seventy Jewish scholars to work independently, each making a translation of the Bible into Greek. When the seventy translations were found to be identical, word for word, the king was convinced they had been divinely inspired.

In these days Jewish poets were even writing about Jerusalem—in Greek. At first there was nothing forced, arbitrary or compulsory about this Hellenization. The Jews who went to Alexandria did so voluntarily, even eagerly. True, there were well-manned Greek garrisons scattered through the Valley, as elsewhere in the kingdom, but soldiers do not make good propagandists for poetry and philosophy, then or now. Not even Greek soldiers.

In Jerusalem, in the towns and cities of the Valley, and in the Judaean hills, the masses of the people remained Hebraic in their hearts, proud, as always, of their prophetic and priestly traditions. But before long Greek colonists began to move in, and their ways were contagious. Along the banks of the Jordan, as well as in the great seaport of Alexandria, Jews began to appear in Greek costumes. Greek slang entered the conversation of the streets. Greek habits were adopted. Greek idioms crept into the thinking as well as the writing and talking of Jews. On the banks of the river and in the market places of the hill towns, debates and dialogues in the Platonic style were now heard. The Temple at Jerusalem began to be rivaled by Grecian gymnasia and theaters. Temples to Zeus and Atargatis appeared everywhere, and statues to Apollo and Aphrodite. In such places as Beth-Shan, Greek gods—Hermes, Athena, Artemis and Demeter—were now being worshiped, as well as Baal, Nergal, Beelzebub, Ashima, Adrammelech, Nibhaz, Tartak, and Jehovah. In the Valley, archaeologists in recent years have dug up handles of jugs that were shipped in at this period from Rhodes full of resinated wine, because the Greek soldiers preferred it to the local wine. Elsewhere the archaeologists have found stone statues of Nabataean gods with pure Greek faces. In several Judaean cities Greek coins were minted.

Gradually in the Valley and in the hills, Hellenism came to terms with paganism. But there was no common ground on which the followers of Jehovah and the followers of the Olympian gods could meet, so in some parts of their own land the Jews became a religious as well as a racial minority.

Toward the end of the third century B.C. Syria decided to enter the international lists again, and a new dynasty arose: thirteen kings in a row named Antiochus, who attempted to become masters of Asia Minor and impose Hellenism wherever they could. It was now a contest between the Ptolemies and the Antiochi, with the land bordering the Jordan as one of the minor rewards for the winner.

The Greeks had built hundreds of shrines in Judah, many of them in or near the Valley, but their own favorite spot was Baneas, at the base of Mount Hermon, where one source of the Jordan bursts forth so joyously, as if from out of the heart of the mountain itself. There they erected shrines to Pan, son of Mercury, the Greek god of the meadows; the protector of hunters, fishermen, and shepherds. They set busts and statues in natural niches in the face of the cliff, and used the caves that were already there for some of the sacred rites they performed in honor of Pan. Often the pipes of Pan made the mountainside, and the Valley below, echo with music. Dances and rites that were as sensual as they were sacred were performed by thinly veiled women and heavily bearded men. Finally the Greeks built a city here and called it, appropriately, Paneas, the city of Pan, after their god of the out-of-doors, and the shrine they called Panion.

Now a new world force began to poke its head over history's horizon. For several generations Rome had been working her way quietly eastward, thus far without a great display of arms. But now Antiochus suffered several embarrassing defeats at Roman hands and was forced to sign a working agreement with them whereby he would continue on his throne, but was forced to pay massive tribute to Rome. He raised some of it by plunder—especially by plundering temples. In the Valley a few pagan temples were plundered. In Jerusalem the great Jewish Temple was shorn of its valuables.

Nearly one hundred and fifty years after the death of Alexander the Great, Antiochus IV, known as Antiochus Epiphanes, came to the throne, and under some pressure from Egypt decided on the forcible conversion of Judah to Hellenism. In a decree dated 165 B.C. he prohibited observance of the Hebraic Sabbath and the practice of circumcisions, on pain of death. In his effort to force the Jews to identify completely with Greek religion and culture, he made participation in pagan rites obligatory. Not only did his soldiers plunder the Temple of whatever wealth had been accumulated there since the days of Antiochus III and his looting, but he set up in the place of the altar of Jehovah, God of the Jews, an altar to Zeus, one of the many gods of the Greeks. On this altar, swine were sacrificed and Jews for whom it was a forbidden animal, were forced to eat of its flesh. Prostitution was also permitted in the Temple, upon payment of a tax to the occupational government.

At first the Jews put up with all the restrictions, insults, and humiliations. Then, one by one, ten by ten, sometimes a score or more at a time, they vanished. This story has never been completely told, and perhaps never will be: a tale of humble men who refused to conform, who wanted only to be left alone while they worshiped God in their own way, as wrong or as peculiar as it might seem to others. So they vanished into the Wilderness. Some found their "wilderness" in the Valley—in what has been called the "jungle of the Jordan" or "the pride of the Jordan." But others, seeking even more solitude, more safety, less possibility of trouble from the Syrian military, left the Valley and went down the west coast of the Salt Sea until they came to Ein Gedi, hiding place of David in his flight from Saul. There they prayed and meditated and studied, while enjoying the "conveniences" of cool caves and the delight of water splashing over rocks into pools of silver foam.

Sometimes, when they left their oasis and went down to the Salt Sea, they would witness one of the minor mysteries of that strange body of water: the sudden appearance on the surface of masses of black bitumen, some of the pieces weighing tons. After Alexander's death, one of his generals, temporarily in charge of this area, had appointed a "Superintendent of the Asphaltic Beds of the Salt Sea," to take charge of salvaging and exporting the black, odoriferous material.

But the Jews themselves were divided. Every slight schism among them was aided, abetted, encouraged and fostered by their Syrian occupiers: division over internal policy, family jealousies, the conflict over what to do about Hellenization.

Antiochus IV, who has been called by some historians "mad, bad, and dangerous," established a custom of selling the high priesthood to the highest bidder. When in 168 B.C. the winner, one Menelaus, was ejected from the Temple by other Jews who were outraged that such a man had been able to purchase the post, Antiochus used the incident as an excuse to sack Jerusalem and butcher great numbers of its inhabitants.

Then one day in 165 B.C. one of his officers went to the small Judaean town of Modin to supervise the sacrificing of swine on the altar of the synagogue there. As the Jewish priest who had been brought to officiate began the ceremony, an aged man named Mattathias stepped forward and killed both the Jewish priest and the Syrian officer. Then he turned to the astonished crowd and called on all believers in the true God to follow him and his five sons—John, Simon, Judas, Eleazar and Jonathan—to the mountains. The Maccabaean Revolt had begun.

Mattathias and his sons were not Valley people. Modin is far from the Jordan, within sight of the Mediterranean. In the early days of the revolt none of the important action took place anywhere near the river. But the Valley people—Jew and pagan alike—watched the struggle nervously, well knowing that it might decide their own personal future, and perhaps the future of this entire part of the world.

At the time the revolt broke out, Judah was a fraction the size it had been in the time of the Twelve Tribes, but it did control the west bank of the Lower Jordan to a point almost as far north as the confluence of the Jabbok and the Jordan, as well as about a third of the western shoreline of the Salt Sea.

When Mattathias died, less than a year after sparking the revolt, his third son, Judas, took over leadership, and from him the rebels received the name by which they have ever since been called, for the nickname of Judas was Maccabee ("The Hammer"), so the rebels were nicknamed the Maccabees, and their fight became known almost at once as the Maccabaean Revolt. (The historian Josephus gives the family name as Hasmon, so the sons and their descendants are often called the Hasmonaeans. But in song, in legend, and in the Apocrypha they are simply the Maccabees.)

While the father was still alive, he and his sons were joined by thousands of Hasidim, religious zealots who sincerely, passionately wished to avoid armed struggle by withdrawing into the Wilderness, and who had no sympathy for the nationalistic aims of the Maccabees, but were driven into militaristic action by the extremism of the Hellenizers.

Judah was a perfect land for guerrilla warfare. For three years the Maccabees were in action in the deep gullies, the dried-up wadis, the burning desert, the barren mountains and the desolate Wilderness they knew so well. Again and again a handful of them would win against Syrian forces ten, twenty, fifty times as numerous. Perhaps no army in the world has ever had such high morale. It is true that Antiochus was busy with larger troubles, bigger wars elsewhere, yet it was a humiliation that he was forced to conclude a peace treaty with a band of rebels and order the withdrawal of the abominable decree of 165 B.C.

There was rejoicing among the Jews of the Valley—among Jews everywhere—when Judas, his brothers, the Hasidim and the other guerrillas marched back into Jerusalem, cleansed the Temple, and reinstituted the worship of God in their own place, in their own way. Only enough oil was found to keep the lamp before the Ark of the Covenant burning for one night, yet, miraculously, the light burned for eight days and nights, and so it is, when the victory of the Maccabees over the Syrians is celebrated throughout the Jewish world in a winter feast called Hanukkah, one candle is lighted each night for eight nights.

The Maccabaean success led to cruel persecution of Jewish minorities outside Judah, causing Judas to raise the battlecry: "Fight this day for your brothers!" While brother Simon went up into Galilee to deal with the situation there, brothers Judas and Jonathan led another part of their army across the Jordan (probably at the Jericho fording place) to do battle with Timotheus and his Ammonites in order to relieve the plight of their fellow Jews on that side of the river. Again, their daring was great and their military success phenomenal.

But Judas despaired of his people across the river being able to enjoy freedom after the Maccabees retired, so he organized a great exodus, gathering together "all of Israel, them that were in the land of

Gilead, from the least unto the greatest, and their wives, and their children, and their stuff, an exceeding great army, that they might come into the land of Judah."

The crossing used on this occasion was the one at Bethabara, for the refugees from Ammon were heading for the city now popularly called Scythopolis, but still referred to in the biblical account by its old name. It was another mass migration, with those in charge undoubtedly having great difficulty getting thousands of children, invalids, the aged, sheep, goats, donkeys, asses, even camels safely across the river, even if it was midsummer when the river would have been passably low.

". . . and they went over Jordan into the great plain against Beth-shan."

After five years of successful revolting, Judas was killed in battle and was succeeded by brother Jonathan. In Jonathan's time one battle was fought on the Jordan the tactics of which are not clear from the record. Apparently the fight was on the west bank, but the Maccabees, in attempting to escape from their Syrian enemies, swam to the other side.

During most of the seventeen years that Jonathan led the Maccabees his activity was limited to guerrilla action, but he greatly increased the territory of Judah, adding all of Gilead on the east bank of the Jordan up to the Jabbok River, and twenty-five more miles of the western shoreline of the Salt Sea.

Jonathan became such a power that he was appointed high priest, and three years later military and civil governor. But in 143 B.C. he was treacherously murdered by a pretended ally. For the next eight years another brother, Simon, was high priest and the unchallenged ruler, adding still more land to Judah's total area. According to his custom he was traveling through the country holding court, when one night in the fortress of Doc, near Jericho and within sight of the Jordan, he and two sons were slain at a banquet by his son-in-law, Ptolemeus, who had been their host. (All five sons of Mattathias died violently, two in battle, one in ambush, and two by murder.) Simon was succeeded by his son, John Hyrcanus, who ruled for thirty-one years and on his death left a country that was larger than it had ever been, except under Solomon. His son, Aristobulus, added Galilee. He died within a year, after having imprisoned his own brother, Alexander Jannai. The widow of Aristobulus brought about Alexander's release, then married him and had him made both king and high priest. During his twenty-seven-year rule he further extended the boundaries. Now the Jordan, and all its headwaters, and both its banks for the river's entire length, as well as the shores of the Sea of Chinnereth (now being called the Sea of Galilee) and all the shores of the Salt Sea were within the kingdom of the Maccabees. Alexander Jannai is now believed by archaeologists to have been the one who first fortified the great natural fortress of Masada. (Previously credit had been given to Jonathan.) This immense rocky promontory, two thousand feet above sea level, could be approached from the sea side by a single, narrow, tortuous path; from the back side—the Wilderness—only by way of a narrow neck of land, the top of which was four hundred feet lower than the plateau of Masada. Here was a natural fortress that needed little work to make it impregnable. The top was flat, about half a mile long and a quarter of a mile wide, covered in those days with rich soil. And on all sides, a steep, almost perpendicular drop, varying from one to almost two thousand feet. Whoever it was who first fortified Masada created a few additional man-made hazards for any enemy that might try to besiege a Jewish army encamped on the plateau.

A woman was responsible for the golden age of the second Kingdom of Judah. When Jannai died, his widow, Alexandra, succeeded him on the throne. She turned out to be the wisest, most capable, and most enlightened of all the Hasmonaean rulers. She instituted many social reforms, established free elementary schools, and introduced the principle of compulsory primary education, not only for boys but for girls as well, thus putting Judah at the forefront of all Middle Eastern countries in the matter of both education and equality of the sexes. The Jordan Valley was one of the areas that most benefited by Queen Alexandra's reforms. She was popular from the Salt Sea to the slopes of Hermon. But when she died her sons, Hyrcanus II, a Pharisee, and Aristobulus II, a Sadducee, fought so bitterly for the throne that civil war ensued, with first one son then the other inviting the Romans to come in, on his side. They finally did. But on their own side. In 63 B.C. Pompey occupied Judah and put an end to seventy-six years of independence under the Maccabees.

The Valley would never be the same again, nor would the rest of Judah.

5

Was Herod son of Antipater one of the great kings of his epoch, or was he a dangerous despot who should be ranked with history's worst villains? Was he an egotistical, self-centered, vainglorious politician, or a suave statesman of world significance? Was he, as one modern Jewish writer has called him, "radiant . . . resplendent . . . dynamic" or, as another has written of him, "insane, murderous and ignoble"? Was he "one of the greatest ambassadors to the Gentiles the Jews ever had" or did he ultimately do their cause great harm? When he ordered monuments, buildings and even cities named after members of his own family was it out of love and respect? When later he ordered some of those same people murdered was it out of hate or fear? Is Archaeologist Glueck correct in calling him "a champion of the Jews, a friend of the Romans, and an admirer of the Greeks"? Were the many years of peace in Palestine in his time proof that he was a brilliant diplomat who knew know to manage the people of Palestine over whom he ruled, as well as the emperors in Rome who ruled over him?

However those questions are answered, Herod son of Antipater is the most important single character in the life story of Jordan to date. His paternal grandfather was an Idumaean convert to Judaism. His mother was a Nabataean princess, from a wealthy family, for the Nabataeans in these days were powerful merchant princes controlling all the important caravan routes east of the Jordan. His father, Antipater, was the power behind the throne of the last of the Maccabaean kings and was named procurator of Judah by Julius Caesar in 47 B.C. He thereupon appointed his son, Herod, governor of Galilee, later adding Samaria to his hegemony. After three years of rule Antipater was poisoned by members of his own family, while having dinner with his concubines, and died. His son fared better, not only living until he was sixty-nine—a rare old age for a monarch in such murderous days—but winning the favor of those mightier than he. In 40 B.C. he was named king of Judaea by the Romans, but because of his political orientation, his character, and his immoral behavior, and above all not being a legal king, he was not accepted by the Jews and bitter civil war flared for three years. During that time Herod "discovered" Masada. His opposition was headed by Antigonus, the last of the Hasmonaeans, who was popular with his fellow Jews because he was a great-grandson of a nephew of the illustrious Judas Maccabaeus, and because of his undisguised antagonism to Rome. When Antigonus drove the Romans out of Jerusalem and was proclaimed king, Herod, with an entourage of close to a thousand men, fled down into the Valley, and then south to Masada. After a short period of safety on the plateau, which, ironically, had been strengthened by one of the original Maccabaean kings, Herod left to seek political support. He found it in Rome and in 37 B.C. returned with two Roman legions to lay siege to Jerusalem. At this critical moment in his career Herod married the last Hasmonaean princess, Mariamne. If he hoped that this would win him Jewish support, he was disappointed. The Roman legions, however, were more effective. In five months they managed to take Jerusalem. Herod, now king in fact as well as in name, thereupon not only put Antigonus to death but ordered the execution of members of the Sanhedrin, that body of Jewish intellectuals and distinguished citizens which acted as a senate and supreme court combined.

It is significant—and a vital part of the Jordan story—that one of his first acts was to send work battalions down to Masada to make the plateau even more impregnable than it already was. Over a period of several years he enclosed the entire mountaintop with a nineteen-foot casemate wall of white stone, with thirty-seven towers, each one hundred feet high, so Josephus reported. (Archaeologists consider the figures somewhat exaggerated.) He also constructed storage places in which enough grain, corn, wine, dates, pulses, and oil could be stored to last an army during a long siege. Gardens were laid out on the plateau to supplement what was in the magazines. He also built barracks, workshops and arsenals—a complete fortress.

The work on the top of that remote, almost inaccessible plateau must have involved more difficulties and complications than building a lookout station on the sharp peak of a Swiss Alp, yet in the thorough manner that characterized most of what he did, Herod ordered that neither time nor money, labor nor materials be spared. Large square blocks of cut stone were used for most of the construction. The walls of all the buildings were plastered inside and out.

Out of the solid rock Herod had his workmen hew twelve deep cisterns, with a capacity of more than thirteen million gallons (fifty thousand cubic meters). Josephus said: ". . . by this prudent measure he was able to provide the inhabitants with water as if they had springs at their disposal." The cistern walls were plastered smooth with hydraulic cement. Water was channeled in from a nearby wadi.

But Masada was built to be more than a fort. This was a royal hideout and so there was a palace, and a building to serve as a residence for visiting dignitaries, or perhaps as a living place for ministers of the court.

The palace itself was amazing in conception. Instead of standing in the most commanding spot on the plateau, as a French château would have, it was part way down the northern face of the mountain, at three different levels, looking somewhat like a three-layer wedding cake, each of the three buildings partially cut into the face of the cliff, partially resting on a ledge of its own—an engineering feat remarkable in any age. The three separate buildings were connected by a staircase, yet each was self-contained. The only outside access was from the summit. On the highest level, just below the flat surface of the plateau, there was a building with an impressive semicircular verandah, its four rooms flanking a courtyard. Its floors were of mosaic that had been made in a special workshop up on the plateau. This first building may have been started by Alexander Jannai. If so, Herod decided to leave it for members of his court and palace guards, and sent his builders still lower on the face of the cliff to construct his quarters. The building on the middle level, sixty feet down from the summit, is circular, with two concentric walls of masonry and a wide verandah from which a magnificent view can be had of the Salt Sea, Ein Gedi on the left shore, and then, at the far end of the sea, the start of the Valley. On this level were two pools, both plaster lined, one square, the other semicircular. The square pool may have been a reservoir, to assure the establishment of an ample supply of water at all times. The other must have been a bathing pool, for there are steps leading down into it.

The third structure is another forty feet down. To create the ledge or platform on which to erect this part of the palace, it was necessary to build strong buttresses. Here again was engineering of a high order. The building itself was square, with an open court, surrounded by four porticoed cloisters. The fluted columns—as elegant as if they were in

Rome, instead of two thousand feet above the shores of a desolate sea far off in the Near East—were set on Attic bases and crowned with Corinthian capitals. The walls on this level were covered with three layers of plaster, the final coat having a surface as smooth as glass. The walls were decorated with green, painted panels, bordered in black, then made brilliant with stripes of red, all done in tempera. Some panels were painted to resemble marble; others were purely geometric in design.

Modern-day visitors who work their way to the top of Masada often contemplate why the ruler of all he surveyed in that first century B.C. would have chosen a place so blisteringly hot most of the year for a palace. Was the climate any different then than now? Meteorologist-historians do not think so. Was it because Herod was so eager to get away from his subjects, his enemies, his rivals, his friends, that he chose a place to which they were not likely to go? Possibly. Was it because this was by nature one of the most inaccessible spots anywhere in Palestine, and by his work he had made it even more so? Probably. Josephus explained that:

"Herod might have suspended his magnificent palace between heaven and earth in order thereby to ensure himself a fortress against his foreign enemies, or a refuge from his own people. On the other hand, this king who in his cruelty brought terror upon the Hasmonaeans, his own family, and all who opposed him, may merely have been looking for a spiritual sanctuary in which he could escape from the very violence he had created."

Herod's love of the Valley was beyond any question. No one before him had done so much to make it powerful, prosperous, resplendent, and secure. It was part of his general plan for the entire land of the Jews, but the Valley seems to have been especially favored.

Here, as elsewhere in the country, he managed to make the roads safe for travel by night as well as by day. Brigandage was not eliminated, but it was somewhat controlled. Under Herod for many years this area that had known so much bloodshed was at least temporarily at peace with its neighbors, and with itself—more or less. If there was a famine, as there was in 25 B.C., Herod saw that most of the people were somehow fed, even if at his own personal expense.

Like Solomon, Herod had a passion for construction. Building a new city gave him intense delight. Public works were his joy. Josephus wrote in high praise of his "waterworks, baths, and large and beautiful piazzas and cloisters." He built a line of fortresses up and down the entire length of the Jordan—from the foot of Mount Hermon to the Salt Sea;

from Paneas to Jericho. Then he began building villages, towns, cities. He concentrated first in the Lower Valley. On the west side of the river, opposite Adam, he built an immense fortress on top of a hill from which the entire Lower Valley could be observed, and called it Alexandrium. Josephus described it as "a stronghold fortified with the utmost magnificence." It was to play a major role in the Valley's future military history. On the same side of the river and just a little to the south, he built a new city, which he called Phasaelis, in memory of a brother. Josephus said that by building Phasaelis, Herod "rendered the neighboring country more fruitful by the cultivation its inhabitants introduced."

South of Jericho, back some distance from the Salt Sea yet commanding a good view of that strange body of water, Herod leveled off the top of a mountain until it looked like a volcano crater and there built a fort that he named after himself, Herodium. From this stronghold he had a road built directly to Masada, the bastion of them all. On the opposite side of the Salt Sea he rebuilt a fort called Machaerus that originally had been constructed by Alexander Jannai, the mad Maccabaean king, and was later destroyed by a Roman general; a fort that would one day serve as prison for a man who would become even better known to future generations than Herod himself. Machaerus was one of Herod's favorite forts because not far away, in Wadi Zarqa Ma'in, were the hot springs of Callirhoe which he enjoyed so much that they came to be marked on maps as "Baths of Herod."

The Valley, of course, was not the only area in which the constructive genius of Herod found an outlet. He turned Jerusalem into a Greco-Roman metropolis, surmounted by a new Jewish Temple built in the manner of a Greek temple and decorated with a great eagle, a bird that never had had much connection either with matters Hebraic or matters religious. Josephus was bold enough to suggest that Herod's obsession with the Temple was more out of desire to leave a lasting stone monument to himself than from any intense piety or interest in the religion of his converted grandfather. However, Herod took great care not to offend the susceptibilities of the Jews. For example, he trained a thousand priests as stone masons, to work on the shrine.

Although the Temple itself was officially declared completed in ten years (9 B.C.) work continued on it and contiguous buildings for another seventy-three years. Herod ordered the entire Temple area enclosed with a wall made of massive stone blocks up to fifteen feet in length. It is a portion of this wall—which escaped unharmed when the Temple was later destroyed—that today is called "the Wailing Wall."

Herod was extremely adept at winning friends in high places. No matter what cataclysmic development occurred in Rome's power struggle, he always seemed to be a close friend of the winner. Thus he became the greatest of Rome's regional kings. In rapid succession he ingratiated himself with Cassius, Antony, and Augustus. Yet at one period it seemed that he had met his match—a woman, the brilliant but unscrupulous Cleopatra, last of the Ptolemite rulers of Egypt. She was four years Herod's junior and four times as wily. Or so she thought. Her aim was to see that Judaea and Coele-Syria to the north were made part again of the Ptolemaic Empire. On a visit to Jerusalem she sought to win Herod over by her usual tactics, which included a generous and unashamed use of the feminine appeal she knew she possessed in such ample measure. After all, had she not succeeded so well with Marc Antony (Marcus Antonius) that he had bestowed upon her as small tokens of his affection innumerable geographical favors, including the Salt Sea; Paneas, on the slopes of Mount Hermon; the seaport of Joppa (Jaffa), and the Valley city of Jericho? So she visited Jerusalem. But there she found a difficult opponent. Herod was not at all the pliant man Antony had been. He refused, flatly, to trade geography for feminine favors. He even contemplated—although, of course, Cleopatra did not know it at the time—having her killed, thinking that this would solve not only some of his own problems but some of Marc Antony's as well. (At many times in his career Herod could think of no better solution of a problem than murdering someone.) On this occasion friends advised him against such volatile action, one suggesting that he could get more from Cleopatra alive than dead. So Herod treated his Egyptian visitor with courtesy, gave her a few gifts, agreed to rent her land at Jericho for what would amount today to about $150,000 a year, gave her some good advice about her Salt Sea holdings, and then saw that she got safely home to Egypt. Herod's advisers were probably right. He lived twenty-six years longer than Cleopatra, and prospered most of the time. The Salt Sea, Joppa, Paneas—all those geographical gifts she had received from her lover—eventually, one by one, fell into Herod's possession.

Cleopatra apparently cared little about the aromatic balsams, the fertile fields, and the rich date and palm groves of Jericho; therefore she had been happy to rent Antony's gift for a good cash income, but Herod had a finer sense of appreciation. As the Valley was his favorite area in the ever-growing territory over which he was privileged to rule, so Jericho now became his favorite spot in the Valley. The climate of Jericho pleased him. It was close enough to Jerusalem so he could make quick, commuter-like trips back and forth, yet it was removed enough to provide a degree of security that the capital city lacked, and security was always one of Herod's considerations, for he had enemies—and he knew it; as many enemies, perhaps, as any Roman ruler ever had or would have.

As if showering a woman he loved with jewels, Herod began bejeweling Jericho, first with a magnificent theater, then with a hippodrome in the Roman style, then with a citadel he named Cypros in honor of his mother, then with a tower he called Phaseaelis after his brother. There in Jericho he built himself a winter palace and inaugurated a vast irrigation project. Most of the buildings constructed in this Herodian period were placed a considerable distance from the Jericho that Joshua had kept in ruins for so long with a single curse.

The Valley at this time was the most densely populated area of Palestine, even without the considerable number of Roman soldiers stationed there. Whenever given the opportunity they flocked to the new Jericho, to visit the hippodrome and the great amphitheater. To Jericho also came the aristocracy of Jerusalem, who made it their favorite winter resort. Once a year, at Passover, Jews from the Valley made their annual pilgrimage to Jerusalem, many of them taking the route that led through Jericho. They traveled in large groups, carrying all their provisions for the round trip, singing, laughing and telling stories as they went.

In 31 B.C. two events of importance to the Valley occurred, one a conflict of humans, the other a conflict of nature.

"Then there was an earthquake in Judah," reported Historian Josephus, "such as had not happened at any other time, and which earthquake brought destruction upon the cattle of that country. About ten thousand men perished by the fall of the houses." (Apparently Josephus did some further investigating after the book containing this report was published, for in a subsequent work he placed the death toll at thirty thousand.)

The conflict of humans was between Octavius Caesar (Caesar Octavianus) who would henceforth be known as Augustus, and Marc Antony, with Augustus winning, after which Herod, who once more had somehow managed to be on the winning side, was confirmed as ruler of his corner of the world by the new master of the Roman Empire. In gratitude, Herod began honoring members of the Roman imperial house by building harbors, temples, and even cities which he named in their honor, not only at home but as far abroad as Syria and Greece. When Augustus extended Herod's territory to the Mediterranean, Herod constructed on the seacoast an impressive city and port he called Caesarea Maritima. When Augustus gave him the territory at the base of Mount Hermon—which Cleopatra had once owned and had rented to a robber chieftain named Zenorodus—Herod demonstrated his appreciation by building at Paneas a temple of snow-white marble to the Emperor's glory. Now Caesar and Pan could be honored simultaneously.

The last years of Herod's life were marred by family friction, illness, murder, regret for murder, more murder, frustrations, agony, and then, finally, death.

The homicidal episodes began in the year 29 B.C. when, in a fit of rage, he ordered the execution of his wife, Mariamne. She was his one real link with the Jewish people, for she had been born a Jew, and, more than that, a Hasmonaean. His disposal of her by slaughter did not tend to increase Jewish affection for him. It was not until after it was too late that he discovered he had erred, that Mariamne had been innocent of the charge he had placed against her, and that he had really loved her after all.

Next came Alexander and Aristobulus, sons by Mariamne, who had been brought up in Rome and were heirs to the throne, both highly acceptable to the Jewish people, for, by rabbinical definition, a Jew is one whose mother was a Jew, and that made Alexander and Aristobulus Jews. But their half brothers by other wives of Herod were jealous and poisoned their father's mind against them, so, in 7 B.C., Alexander and Aristobulus were executed.

The conniving against Alexander and Aristobulus had been led by Herod's eldest son, named Antipater after his grandfather. But Herod became suspicious of him, too, and so ordered him put to death. The execution took place in 4 B.C. just three days before Herod's own demise.

The final chapter of this tortured man's life is properly set in the Valley. He went to his favorite city, Jericho, to die: Jericho of the scented balsams, the soft nights, the rustling palms, where he had built a palace to his own somewhat pagan taste; Jericho, near the river for which he had shown as much affection as he ever showed for anything —or anybody; Jericho, the city of the thunderous curse and the home of Rahab, the clever harlot, where the most awesome event in biblical history had occurred when the city walls were tumbled down by shouts and trumpet blasts. There, now, in the elegant surroundings he had created, Herod met a foul and festering end, his body riddled with an incurable disease, his mind crazed with pain.

It was told that in his dying days he tried to figure out how to make the Jews mourn his death and decided to issue an order that instantly upon his own demise, hundreds of distinguished Jewish citizens should be rounded up and slaughtered, so that ever after, on the day of his (and their) death, there would be national lamentation.

Once when the pain became almost unbearable, he attempted suicide, but unsuccessfully. Five days later he died as a result of his malady. His body was moved from Jericho to Herodium with great pomp.

One story, published long after his passing, linked the past and the future. Matthew alone tells it. Neither Mark, nor Luke, nor John confirms it.

In 40 B.C. the Senate in Rome, upon the advice of Antony and Octavian, had conferred on Herod the title, King of the Jews, and until his death thirty-six years later he called himself, and he liked others to call him, King of the Jews. But several years before his death he was informed by three wise men from the East that a Jewish child had been born in Bethlehem who, it was said, was the Messiah and who was already being called King of the Jews.

"When Herod the king had heard these things, he was troubled, and all Jerusalem with him.

"And when he had gathered all the chief priests and scribes of the people together, he demanded of them where Christ should be born.

"And they said unto him, In Bethlehem of Judaea: for thus it is written by the prophet . . .

"And he sent them (the wise men) to Bethlehem, and said, Go and search diligently for the young child; and when ye have found him, bring me word again, that I may come and worship him also."

But Joseph, warned in a dream that Herod would try to kill the infant, took both mother and child from Bethlehem to Egypt.

"Then Herod . . . was exceeding wroth, and sent forth, and slew all the children that were in Bethlehem, and in all the coasts thereof, from two years old and under, according to the time which he had diligently enquired of the wise men.

"Then was fulfilled that which was spoken by Jeremy the prophet, saying:

"In Rama was there a voice heard, lamentation, and weeping, and great mourning, Rachel weeping for her children, and would not be comforted, because they are not.

"But when Herod was dead, behold, an angel of the Lord appeareth in a dream to Joseph in Egypt,

"Saying, Arise, and take the young child and his mother, and go into the land of Israel: for they are dead which sought the young child's life."

Even without this mass killing, Herod's almost insane suspicions had driven him in his late years to such murderous extremes that he would be remembered by many even more for his homicidal outbursts than for his administrative ability. It would have pleased his vanity had he been able to know that most historians would differentiate him from all the Herods who would follow him, by calling him Herod the Great. Yet, 1967 years after his death, an eminent American Jewish historian, Max Dimont, would write (in *Jews, God and History*):

"It may be clear to others why Herod has been called 'the Great' but to the Jews it has always remained a mystery. Herod was the archmurderer of his time. He murdered 45 members of the Sanhedrin, reducing that formerly independent judicial body to the status of a rubber stamp. He intimidated the High Priests into subservience with threats of assassination. He murdered his rivals, his favorite wife, and several of his sons, and according to the Gospel of St. Matthew, he imitated the Biblical Pharaoh by ordering the execution of all male infants in Bethlehem, because he feared a prophecy that a rival to his throne would be born there."

But in the days of Herod all was not building and killing. The Valley knew in that time men whose influence on the thinking and behavior of the world would still be felt centuries after Herod's buildings had crumbled. One such was Rabbi Hillel; another, Rabbi Shamai. These scholarly giants headed two opposing schools of Mishnah. Since the start of the era of Greek enlightenment, Jews down in the Valley, in the rest of the land, and even in places of the dispersal, regardless of their public attitude toward the Greeks, zealously studied Greek philosophy and used much of what they learned to further their own intellectual and religious development, and also in interpreting the laws set down for them to follow in the Torah (the first five books of the Bible). Mishnah (from the Hebrew "to repeat" and therefore "to teach, to learn") was a method of interpreting Hebraic law, as well as an actual code based on decisions of the rabbis, which became the authority for further opinions and decisions. Because certain rabbis feared that the Mishnah might eventually rival the Torah itself in authority, they forbade it to be put into writing, so it became known as the Oral Law.

Rabbi Shamai gave the law a narrow, conservative and legalistic interpretation, stressing property rights. Rabbi Hillel's viewpoint, both liberal and universal, stressed human rights. Rabbi Shamai's followers respected him for his toughness; Rabbi Hillel's praised him for his gentleness.

Rabbi Hillel for years served as the Nasi or prince of the Sanhedrin. He was looked upon by many as the exponent of Judaism at its purest. Up and down the Valley, which he often visited, he was known as "the Great Teacher." More than that, he practiced as well as preached a way of life embodying gentleness, kindness, charity, humility, and deep piety. Many of his words of wisdom had echoes, two or three generations later, in the New Testament. Once when an impatient man asked Hillel to teach him all the fundamentals of Judaism while standing on one leg, the great rabbi replied:

"Do not unto others what you would not have others do unto you."

Another translation of what he replied puts it thus:

"What is unpleasant to thyself, that do not do to thy fellow man. This is the whole law, all else is but exposition."

On another occasion he said:

"Judge not thy fellow man until thou art in his place."

A story handed down for centuries tells how the wise men of that day were once assembled at Jericho, when a voice from heaven announced:

"Among those present here there is one who deserved the Holy Spirit to rest upon him, if the age in which he lived had been worthy of it."

The eyes of all present turned toward Hillel.

After Herod the Great, the Valley people were ruled over by two of his sons. In his will Herod had bequeathed Galilee and Peraea to Antipas, his youngest son, who came to be known as Herod the Tetrarch ("Petty King"). Peraea was the name given in that time to a district on the east bank of the Jordan, about ten miles wide, corresponding roughly to the western edge of Gilead, from the River Arnon to a point somewhere between the Jabbok and the Yarmuk. The Valley people living on the west side of the Jordan, in Judaea and Samaria, fell under the rule of an older son, Archelaus. He was given the title of ethnarch (governor) instead of king. During the ten years that he ruled he acquired the worst reputation of all Herod's sons. First, he offended Jewish susceptibilities by marrying Glaphyra, the widow of his half brother, and then by becoming such a repressive and arbitrary administrator that the people of Judah urged Augustus to depose and banish him, both of which Augustus did. From then on Judaea was nothing more than a Roman province, ruled by procurators appointed by the Emperor.

Yet the Valley during the Roman period prospered, perhaps more than at any other time in its long history. The network of roads and the considerable number of forts established near the river kept the nomad tribesmen at bay. In a previous period great quantities of spices from South Arabia had passed through the Valley on their way to Damascus, Aleppo and the north. Now, in the Roman period, the Valley became the route for the shipment of a wealth of goods from India to Rome.

At this time an amazing race of Arabs enters the Jordan story—fleetingly—the Nabataeans, who at different periods of their relatively short history were unscrupulous plunderers, efficient engineers, excellent architects, sculptors, builders, agricultural scientists and irrigationists, makers of fine pottery and glass, and the most practical Utopians in that part of the world. Archaeologist Glueck has called them "one of the most remarkable people in history" and has likened the short but spectacular role they played in the history of the area to "the brilliance of a meteor flashing briefly across the skies to blazing extinction." At the height of their power the Nabataean kingdom extended from Damascus in Syria to Medain Saleh in Saudi Arabia.

Although they are always referred to as an Arab tribe, they were direct descendants of Abraham, grandfather of the founder of the Twelve Tribes of Israel. One of Abraham's sons was Ishmael, born to him by Hagar, his wife's Egyptian maidservant. When, at Sarah's insistence, Abraham invited mother and child to leave his home at once, they fled to the desert, where they were dying from thirst when an angel appeared and guided them to a well. Ishmael, who was nicknamed "the wild ass among men," and lived to be one hundred and thirty-seven, married an Egyptian girl who bore him twelve sons and a number of daughters, one of whom married her first cousin, Esau. This made the twelve princes of the House of Ishmael brothers-in-law of Esau, as well as his first cousins. One of these twelve princes was Nebajoth, who is called by some biblical historians the founder of the Nabataeans.

During their early existence as a tribe, the Nabataeans lived a considerable distance east and south of the Jordan, in Arabia, astride the main trade routes from the Orient to the Mediterranean. There they plundered the spice and incense caravans as fast as they came by, which was frequently. As they grew more powerful, they levied a toll on each caravan, in return for a guarantee of safe conduct.

One of their tribal laws commanded them "neither to sow corn, nor to plant any fruit bearing trees, nor to use wine, nor to build a house." Later, however, the ban on the use of alcohol was lifted and the drinking of wine became an important part of their religious rituals.

They lived a simple life, free of taxes, tensions and troubles. Year by year they pushed farther northward and westward, finally establishing a capital in one of the strangest spots on earth—a canyon fifty miles south of the Salt Sea, which the Nabataeans believed was the ancient home of their pagan gods. This oasis, in a wilderness of sand, barren mountains and stark cliffs, is almost invisible from a plane. It can be reached only on foot, or by riding a horse or donkey for more than a mile through a twisting corridor that is little more than a crack in the rocks, sometimes as narrow at the bottom as three yards. Hundreds of feet overhead the rock walls on either side seem almost to touch, thus keeping the corridor in eerie shade most of the time. Footsteps echo, as in a hollow cave. Birds that resemble bats occasionally fly by. Now and then, along the way, some ancient sculptor, perhaps just practicing, chiseled in bas-relief a head or an entire figure from the living rock, sometimes on the left cliff, sometimes on the right.

Suddenly the pathway makes a sharp turn and the visitor is almost blinded by the sun as the corridor ends in a great open space. This is Petra ("Rock"), a natural fortress that a handful of men could hold against an entire army, just by defending that corridor.

At first this was merely a base from which the caravans could be attacked and to which the loot would be brought. Later, as the Nabataeans came under Greco-Roman influence, they made of Petra a place of breathtaking beauty. The walls of the canyon are of red, pink, white, brown and even violet limestone. Instead of quarrying the stone and then using it in constructing buildings, the Natabaeans decided to carve public and private buildings out of the living rock. This meant first hollowing out a small or large room or series of rooms; then, in bas-relief, creating an ornamental façade, often with great stone pillars. When the task was finished, no roof was needed; there was no danger of damage or destruction from storm or earthquake, and the structure was there for all time, an integral part of its setting and its background. In this manner they built many temples, tombs, a theater, a treasury building, a palace, public baths and private homes.

As the prospering Roman world became an ever and ever better market for spices, silks and other luxuries from India and China, the Nabataeans decided to give up plundering and collecting tolls, and become traders themselves. Soon they were doing a thriving export-import business with cities as far off as Rome. By the time of Herod the Great they were in control of most of the important trade routes, east to west, south to north.

Petra was still their capital, but by now it had become a depot for converging caravans and so important a spot in the economy of the Middle East that one historian called it "the most outstanding commercial city of the world at that time."

In this period a sprinkling of Nabataeans began to appear in the Valley, bringing with them an entirely new social and political order. There were no slaves and no poor among them. Their social system was so democratic that everyone, no matter how wealthy or high placed, was required to take his turn at performing public services, such as cleaning the streets, doing police duty, and standing guard over the city's water supply. As a result, classes did not exist in their society, nor were there any family distinctions. All were equal, in practice as well as in principle.

Wealth and prosperity were considered by the Nabataeans as civic virtues, but as such they carried with them duties, especially increased civic responsibility. As the Roman historian Strabo put it:

"The Nabataeans are temperate and industrious, so that a public penalty is imposed on him who lessens his property, but to him that increases it, honors are given . . . they serve themselves, and the custom extends even to the kings. They form 'messes' of thirteen men each and two singing girls to each mess. The king in his great house holds many 'messes.' No one drinks more than eleven cups, in one and then another golden beaker. Thus the king is a democratic one, so that in addition to serving himself he sometimes even himself serves others. He often also submits his accounts to the people, and sometimes also the conduct of his life is inquired into. Their dwellings are extensive structures of stone, and their cities are unwalled on account of peace. Most of it abounds in fruit except the olive; they use oil made of sesame. Their sheep are white haired, their oxen large; the country does not produce horses; camels render service instead of them. Even the kings go without tunics in girdles and slippers, but they go out in purple . . . They think dead bodies no better than manure: as Heraclitus says, corpses are more to be thrown away than dung heaps. Wherefore they bury even their kings beside their privies. They honor the sun, setting up an altar in the house, making libation on it daily and using frankincense."

This Nabataean social system made little lasting impression on the way of life either in the Valley or elsewhere in the Middle East. Of far greater lasting importance was the Nabataean contribution to the world's knowledge about the conservation, collection, storage, and the most efficient use of water.

Because they had once been a race of nomads, they knew the desert and its ways, and they understood how to make the desert work for them. They made a science out of irrigation and raised agriculture to the highest level it had ever known in that part of the world.

Until the Nabataeans became agronomists, the custom in this region of vast deserts was for people either to be nomads, constantly on the move, from oasis to oasis, or to settle sedentarily in some spot like the Valley of the Jordan or the Vale of Jezreel, where fresh water was plentiful. The Nabataeans instead took over barren desert areas that other people considered worthless because of lack of water. There, working on the principle that there might be enough water if not a drop were ever wasted, their engineers perfected a collection, storage and irrigation system that conserved all the scanty rainfall. No one before or since has ever been so successful in storing up so close to one hundred percent of all available water, especially the torrents that come roaring down the wadis during a flash flood—water that generally goes to waste by being funneled either directly into the Salt Sea, or via the Jordan into the Salt Sea, where, by becoming mixed with the contents of that salinized lake, it becomes worthless for agricultural purposes. Many of the cisterns and reservoirs the Nabataeans built more than two thousand years ago have recently been discovered by archaeologists and some have actually been put back into use again.

Sometimes the Nabataeans enlarged a natural cave, thus creating an immense cavern for the storage of water. More conventional cisterns were hewn out of the limestone strata of hillsides. The openings were left narrow, to prevent the bright sun from causing excessive evaporation. Always there was a trap near the entrance of the cistern to collect sedimentation.

The Nabataeans were also pioneers in the science of terracing to prevent erosion.

Thus they were able to wrest a livelihood out of many areas of the desert that had never before been permanently inhabited by human beings; areas which soon, thanks to their genius in so many fields, became outposts of an advanced civilization.

The Nabataeans were at the height of their cycle in the time of Herod. Their own most powerful king, Aretas IV, began his reign just five years before Herod's death. Antipas, the son to whom Herod left Galilee, married the daughter of this Nabataean king. They were later divorced. Although the Nabataeans spoke a dialect of Aramaic, they developed a distinctive script of their own. Many also spoke and wrote Latin and Greek.

Their pottery was so fine that it resembled good porcelain. Their architectural sense was well developed, and their sculptors were in a class with the Greeks. The pagan gods they worshiped represented the weather, springs, the sun, water, fertility, joy, and sexual pleasure. Their chief god, Dushara, was always represented by a block of stone or an obelisk, but they made realistic statues of their other deities. Atgargatis, goddess of fertility, was represented as a beautiful mermaid. Wherever Nabataean traders went, they carried their gods with them, so they could worship them in such distant places as Naples, just as well as at home in Petra.

Antigonus, the Greek ruler of Syria after the death of Alexander, sent two expeditions to Petra to try to suppress the Nabataeans. On the first occasion all the young men of the city happened to be away at a fair, so there was little resistance as the Greek soldiers occupied the canyon, killed most of the women and children, and hurriedly left with a large loot of frankincense and myrrh, and five hundred talents (thirty-three thousand pounds) of silver. When the men of Petra returned and discovered what had happened, they gave chase, caught up with the Greek army, and massacred 3950 of the 4000 Greek soldiers. The other fifty somehow managed to escape. The second attempt also resulted in a victory for Petra. The Nabataeans bribed the Greek commander with costly gifts to leave without attacking.

The Valley had for long been accustomed to seeing a strange variety of men go south—sometimes to the shores of the Salt Sea, sometimes farther on into the great Wilderness lying west of the sea. Generally they went individually, occasionally in pairs, now and then in large groups. They might be rebels against the existing government, or individuals who wanted to lead a solitary life for a wide variety of personal reasons, or members of religious groups who wished to retire from the world's wickedness. In these times there was an especially large exodus. The men going south through the Valley now—Jews, all of them—were not running away from life. They were neither habitual hermits nor escapists, but sincere seekers after truth, who hoped to found a new society. They were more interested in individual perfection than they were in politics. They wished to seclude themselves from the evils and frustrations of city life. They were in rebellion against the priesthood and the authority of Jerusalem. They felt themselves to be the select and privileged few to whom the Law in all its purity had been committed.

The largest group called themselves Essenes ("Healers"). The Jewish philosopher Philo of Alexandria, who may have the right to the title of "the first theologian in the world," described the life of the Essenes in his great work, *Concerning the Contemplative Life*. He said there were four thousand Essenes living in villages, working hard at agriculture and similar pursuits, but devoting much time to the communal study of moral and religious questions, including interpretation of holy books. All their property was held in common. They abstained from animal sacrifice, practiced celibacy, kept no slaves, had a good system of social security for their aged and community medical care for the sick, swore no oaths, took no part in any commercial activity, and abhorred militarism in any form. Philo also said of them:

"They accumulated neither silver nor gold, nor did they acquire lands in order to procure large income for themselves; but they toiled merely to secure the necessary means of supporting life. They are practically the only men who possess no property, not because of the mischance of fortune, but because they do not strive after riches, and yet they are, in truth, the richest of all, for they count as riches the absence of needs and contentment . . . The manifestations of love of mankind are benevolence, equity and community in goods, which cannot be praised too highly . . . None has a house which does not belong to all. In addition to the fact that they dwell together socially, every house is open to comrades who come from a distance. Also, the storehouse and the provisions contained therein belong to all, as well as the articles of clothing; likewise the eatables are available to those who do not observe the common mealtime . . . dwelling, eating and living together socially has, among no other race, been carried to such a high degree of perfection as among these men. For they do not keep for themselves what they have earned during the day, but put it together and offer it for general consumption. The sick and aged are treated with the greatest care and gentleness."

Philo also said of them:

"Among them is no maker of weapons of war . . . nor do they follow any occupation that leads to injustice and covetousness."

The Roman scholar Pliny wrote extensively about the Essenes, who, he said, had renounced women and money, yet maintained the strength of their community on the shores of the Salt Sea by taking in an ever-increasing number of men who came to join them in their solitary existence, or by the adoption of children from the outside world who were trained in the ascetic ways of the Essenes.

The Roman historian Josephus said the Essenes were to be found not only living a monastic life in the Wilderness on the edge of the Salt Sea, but also in Jordan Valley cities, and elsewhere in Judah.

Josephus reported that when they lived by themselves in isolated communities their day began before sunrise with morning prayers addressed to the sun, "as though entreating him to rise." Then each man went to his assigned task, under the direction of an overseer, and worked until noon. Then all members bathed and ate a simple meal together. They worked all afternoon and had their second meal of the day in the evening, again after a bath, again in common. They adhered strictly to their principle of self-labor, neither using slaves, ever, nor employing laborers. Silence was maintained during all meals. The Essenes were punctilious about cleanliness, not only in the preparation and serving of the food, but in all other departments of life.

They believed in immortality, in resurrection, in the concept of the Messiah, in the punishment of the wicked in an eternal hell, and the reward of the good in an everlasting heaven. Josephus said "they reject pleasure as an evil, but esteem continence and the conquest of our passions to be virtue."

They developed elaborate purification rites, including ceremonial immersion in water for the remission of sins and the entrance into a new life. They also held "friendship meals," which could be attended only by the initiated. Although neither the ablution nor the meal had the sacramental significance that later-day Christian baptism and the Eucharist would take on, the Essenes' cleansing by immersion was a forerunner of the baptismal rites which before long would be taking place in the Jordan. A novice had to serve a three-year novitiate and during that time was not permitted to eat with the full members.

One group of Essenes, seeking an ideal spot in which to live a life of contemplation and meditation, went to Wadi Qumran, which leads from the northwest down into the Salt Sea at a point just seven miles on a straight line south of Jericho. On a height close by the wadi they found the ruins of a fort built in the Iron Age and decided to rebuild it into a monastery. The spot was known as Khirbet Qumran. (Khirbet is Arabic for "ruin" but the derivation of Qumran is to this day still in doubt.) Some scholars once argued that Qumran was the site of Gomorrah, destroyed along with Sodom and the other Cities of the Plain because of their wickedness, but no credence is now given to this theory.

The spot had been ideal for a fort. It was now ideal for holy men wanting seclusion. It was protected on the south by a steep drop into the wadi, on the west by a cliff leading to the Judaean desert, and on the east by a slope leading two hundred and fifty feet down to the sea. Even from the north, access was not easy. For the Essenes, it was ideal in other ways. There was nothing here to aid or abet soft living. The landscape is one that encourages sharpness of thinking and depth of contemplation. For some it might appear a spot "as inhospitable as a lizard's nest" and the cliffs might seem "black and ugly" and the sea resemble "the pit of Satan." Yet a romantic Irish writer did see here "a peculiar beauty about the desolate grandeur of the sandy wastes and the cliffs" and did write of the "soft radiance and gentle glow, as an eastern sunset suffuses the countryside with a pink flush, and the hills turn violet and mauve, and darkness swiftly descends." The Essenes found it ideal for their ascetic purpose, so they built their monastery here and as their numbers grew—ultimately to more than five hundred—they added additions to their buildings until they had a completely self-sustaining community that included potters' kilns, metal workshops, a smelting furnace, flour mills, stables, a laundry, ovens, storage bins, kitchens, an elaborate system of cisterns, and a scriptorium in which many scribes sat endlessly copying scrolls, which served as the books of that age.

At Khirbet Qumran the Essenes lived for more than a hundred years in contemplative retirement from the noisy world of Jerusalem and the other cities of Judah. They put their beliefs down in manuscripts that have lately been found. They believed in the divinity of a Messiah whom they called the "Teacher of Righteousness" and who met a violent death at the hands of the "Sons of Darkness." They called themselves the "Elect of God" and their community the "New Covenant." They expected that soon a new age would commence that would put an end to the present "Epoch of Wickedness." They attempted to win divine favor by diligent study and obedience of the law, and hoped to be appointed by God as judges of the ungodly when the "End-Time" came. They held that the priests in Jerusalem were unfit to hold their sacred offices and called one of them the "Wicked Priest." They believed that the "End-Time" would be marked by the arrival of not one but three Messiahs: a prophet resembling Moses, a Messiah like unto David, and a great priest.

There were more than five hundred documents in the Qumran community library. Whenever danger threatened they would be quickly hidden in nearby caves, for safekeeping. Some of the members of the community also lived in these caves that faced out onto the Salt Sea. Here in this scorched part of the land, each man of the community worked at cultivating the soil, as well as his soul. They lived lives of equality and purity, and adhered to the strict Essene code of asceticism, without interference from any outside quarter—until a whim of nature brought their idyllic life to a temporary end.

Josephus reported that when Herod was in Jericho in the spring of 31 B.C., an earthquake so violent that it caused panic among his troops shook the entire Jordan Valley. This was apparently the same quake that hit Khirbet Qumran. The main building was split in two, one half sinking almost two feet. Apparently the Essenes abandoned Khirbet Qumran at once, for while many coins have been found bearing dates up to 31 B.C., none has ever been uncovered for the years 31 B.C. to 4 B.C.

But after twenty-seven years, at least some of the Essenes apparently returned, cleared away the debris of buildings that had been too badly damaged to be repaired, and reopened their monastery. They dumped the debris they removed at the edge of the wadi, where it remained for almost two thousand years, until British and American archaeologists poked into it.

In these times there were at least a million and a half people in the Valley or on the heights overlooking the Valley. Many lived in cities as elegant as any in the world at that time. Here there was prosperity for the few, and a good life—by the standards of that time—for the many. Wheat was so plentiful that it was exported to Rome. Except during a great drought there was no hunger in the Valley in those days for anyone.

Since the time of Alexander the Great there had been a steady immigration of Greeks to this part of the world, encouraged by the dynasties that Alexander's generals had founded in Egypt and Antioch. Wherever they settled, the immigrants brought in Greek ways of life, Greek thinking, and Greek ideas about civic organization and democratic rule.

On the east side of the Jordan, between the Yarmuk and Jabbok rivers, they founded a city they named Pella, after Alexander's birthplace in Macedonia. Pella, once called Pihilu, has been compared to an eagle's nest on a mountain ledge. It was difficult to reach from above, or from below, or from anywhere, except by a single road that connected it with cities to the north and south. On the sides of its steep slopes were innumerable bubbling springs that sent water tumbling to the floor of the Valley far below, and ultimately to the Jordan. No wonder the Greeks settled there.

Thirty miles up the Yarmuk they founded Dion, also named after a Macedonian town. (About the "Fatal Well of Dion" there was an epigram that read: "Sweet is the water of Dion to drink, but drink it and thou losest thy thirst—and also thy life.")

They rebuilt Rabbah-ammon—there is no record of what had happened to the immense iron bedstead of the Giant Og—and called it Philadelphia, City of Brotherly Love.

Much closer to the Jordan were the twin cities of Hippos, just north of the Yarmuk, and Gadara, just south of the Yarmuk.

Altogether in this small area on the east side of the Jordan there were more than a dozen cities of size and importance. Directly across the river from them was Scythopolis. In 63 B.C. Roman General Pompey seized Scythopolis, Hippos and Pella from the Jews and annexed them to his Syrian province. Ultimately they were given a degree of communal freedom. Some time later ten of these cities in the Valley or to the east of it banded together and formed what they called the Decapolis (League of the Ten Cities) for trade and mutual defense against nomadic tribes. The exact date of the founding is uncertain, but as Augustus had given two of the cities, Hippos and Gadara, as gifts to Herod, it is likely that the league was not formed until after his death, when these cities regained their independence. It is also uncertain which were the original ten, but this is unimportant, for the league soon grew until there were many more than ten.

The cities of the league had much in common. The Greek influence —and later the Roman—predominated in all of them. They enjoyed— although not always at the same time and not always in equal measure —a degree of independence. They had their own councils, the right to coin money, the right to grant asylum, and the right of association with each other for defensive and commercial purposes.

Each city was unique in many ways, yet they were far more alike, architecturally, than San Francisco and New York, or London and Leeds. The people were of mixed nationalities and religions but the cities were all Greek in style: a main street lined with great stone columns, fountains, a forum, an immense stone arch, one or more temples, a theater, public baths, and a mausoleum, all Doric and Corinthian. The eye of a visitor as he approached one of these cities was first caught by the cluster of majestic stone columns. The skyline would also be broken by the lines of the great amphitheater. The streets were paved with large slabs of basalt, laid so squarely, so tightly, that two thousand years later there would still be no unevenness and still no space between slabs, although their smooth surface would be deeply rutted by the iron-rimmed wheels of all the chariots that had gone over them through the centuries. The road from the Valley zigzags for eight miles up to Gadara and in that distance climbs two thousand feet, twisting and turning over a stratum of crumbling limestone, yet that road, like many others hereabouts, is still paved today with great blocks of basalt—an index to the iron-hearted purpose of the men who built well, even while engaged in the Herculean task of attempting to conquer the world.

In the cities of the Decapolis that lacked water there was always an aqueduct running parallel with the road. The great aqueduct through which Gadara received its fresh water supply came from a source more than thirty miles to the east. With all these aqueducts, the water ran through sections of pipe hewn out of solid basalt, with flanges fitted together as tightly as if they were of cast iron.

In Gerasa, on the west side of the Jordan, almost down to the Jabbok, a thousand immense stone columns lined the main street, on which there were many public and private buildings, all with impressive façades. Shops and bazaars were on side streets. In each city the most beautiful building was the temple, while the best preserved was generally the amphitheater, with benches of stone seating up to seven thousand people, and subterranean rooms for actors, wild beasts, and the prospective victims of wild beasts. In some of the Decapolis cities the theaters were built into the side of a hill. Also, for amusement, any city fortunate enough to have a stream it could utilize created an artificial lake, surrounded by seats for spectators, on which naumachias would be staged. These were sea circuses, or sham naval battles. Thus a seafaring people brought their ocean to the desert. In the temples of the Decapolis, even in Roman times, the gods that were worshiped were the gods of the Greeks. One of the few non-Greek deities to whom shrines were built was Astarte, the Phoenician goddess of fertility and sexual life. Each city had its own local god of civic fortune, often unnamed. The people of Scythopolis were devoted especially to bearded Dionysus (also called Bacchus), the Olympian god generally pictured with ivy entwined in his hair, who was worshiped in rites that were especially orgiastic. The pagans of Scythopolis believed that in their city, so close to the Jordan, Bacchus as a child had been nursed by nymphs from the forest.

The Greeks brought to the Valley a high degree of culture, as evidenced by the epigrams and verses they carved in stone: reflections on death, a paean to beauty, a few phrases of prose made deathless by being chiseled in stone. The Decapolis turned out its own writers, poets and philosophers. Gadara alone produced Philodemus the Epicurean, a contemporary of Cicero; Meleager the epigrammatist; Menippus the satirist; Theodorus the rhetorician, and others. Gerasa was the birthplace of many great teachers.

The three most important roads connecting the cities of the Decapolis all began at Scythopolis, crossed the Jordan, and then extended fanwise eastward across the Palestinian desert. Because traffic moving west across the river converged at Scythopolis, this city became in many respects the key to the entire Decapolis network. Each city of the Decapolis had control not only of its immediate suburbs but of considerable outlying territory. As the cities were in all cases less than twenty-five miles apart, their lands actually touched.

The Greeks had chosen which spots to populate after lengthy consideration. Each had been picked because of some specific advantage. Hippos had no water but stood on a commanding height overlooking the Sea of Chinnereth, athwart the highway leading to Damascus. Gadara, looking down on the Jordan, was a formidable fortress because of the steepness of three of its four sides. From almost anywhere in the city the beauty-loving Greeks, and those who came after them, were able to get a spectacular view of lake and Valley. Gerasa, Philadelphia, Abila and Kanatha were all situated on ridges, close to streams at least ten or twelve feet wide, with plenty of good farming land nearby.

Of all these cities Scythopolis was the largest and the richest. Its land stretched all the way down to the Jordan, and in all the other directions of the compass as well. Many of its citizens were wealthy and the degree of culture in Scythopolis was high. Its amphitheater was immense, the best seats facing the hills of Gilead across the river. The linen manufactured here was exported to all parts of the civilized world and was well known for its high quality.

What a panorama of history this city had seen! Through its streets already had marched Canaanites, Egyptians, Hittites, Assyrians, Babylonians, Philistines, Israelites, Scythians, Persians, and now Greeks and Romans. In the next two thousand years many more races would discover Scythopolis, many other armies would come, many other battles would be fought in or near the city. There was still much history to be written at this crux of the Jordan.

6

A great many important events of the New Testament occurred either in the Valley, or around the shores of the Jordan's three bodies of water —Lake Huleh, the Sea of Galilee and the Dead Sea. Some took place actually on or in the waters themselves.

The localities in which Christ was born and spent His early years— Bethlehem, Nazareth and Jerusalem—cannot by any stretch of geographical imagination be claimed as Valley cities, yet it is likely that He spent more of His earthly life in the Jordan Valley, or around the shores of its three lakes than anywhere else. It was on the banks of the Jordan that John the Baptist inaugurated the rite of baptism, and after Christ Himself was baptized, the Jordan became a holy river for Christians. Later Christ spent much time at one of the sources of the Jordan. Three important events in His life occurred on mountains looking down on the Jordan.

However, the most important Christian area was the Sea of Galilee, which, curiously, had played no great role in the Old Testament story. Now it became what several theologians and historians have called "the birthplace of Christianity." Of the thirty-three miracles, nineteen were set in Galilee, most of them in the lake area. This was Christ's lake. He walked on its waters, calmed its storms, ate its fish, and preached to its people from a boat. Here He rebuked the wind, warned the wicked, cured the sick and tried to teach a new way of life. Here He fed thousands with five loaves of bread and two fish. Here He transferred demons from the bodies of men to the bodies of swine. During His lifetime Christ is known to have visited fifteen towns and cities, five of them either on the shores of the lake or close by. Six of His twelve apostles were from the lake area, as were three of the "many women who followed Jesus from Galilee ministering unto him."

The New Testament chapter of the Jordan story properly commences with the birth of John the Baptist to an elderly couple, Zacharias, a priest, and his wife, Elizabeth, who thought she was far too old to bear a child. The exact place of his birth is unknown. The biblical accounts state only that it was in the hill country of Judaea, but it was probably not far from the Valley, for he grew to manhood in the Wilderness. One theory (discounted by many biblical students) is that he lived for years in an Essene community, perhaps in the large monastery at Qumran. If so, his ultimate decision to go forth "and make ready a people prepared for the Lord" must have involved a break with the Essenes. He spent many years in the Wilderness fasting, meditating, and contemplating the task awaiting him. He dressed as other hermits of that day, in a single garment made from goat's hair, tied at the waist with a leather girdle. His food was locusts and wild honey, and thus he followed a tradition of his ancestors, for the Jews who had been led through the desert by Moses also lived for a time on locusts, although in Egypt, where they had come from, locusts were eaten only by the poorest beggars. Yet throughout the Middle East there were nomads so simple that they rejoiced over plagues of locusts—manna from heaven—and in some towns locusts were sold by the measure in public market places to Arabs who threw them alive into well-salted boiling water. After being cooked for a few minutes, they were put to dry in the hot sun, then their arms, legs, wings and feet were torn off, and the remainder of the dead bodies stuffed into sacks that were placed on the backs of camels or asses, and served as a readily available source of food for the nomads, who boiled them in butter and spread them on unleavened bread. John the Baptist violated no religious law by eating locusts, for the rule about clean and unclean animals promulgated by Moses said:

"Yet these ye may eat of every flying creeping thing that goeth upon all four, which have legs above their feet, to leap withal upon the earth;

"Even these of them ye may eat; the locusts after their kind, and the bald locust after his kind, and the beetle after his kind, and the grasshopper after his kind."

It was in the fifteenth year of the reign of Tiberius Caesar—A.D. 29 —that John the Baptist came down from his Wilderness retreat to "the country about Jordan" and began preaching "the baptism of repentance for the remission of sins." By now he was at least in his middle thirties.

There is no certainty about exactly where on the Jordan the baptisms took place. St. John says it was at Bethabara ("The Place of the Ford"). But where was Bethabara? It has been located at various places on various maps by various authorities. It is certain that it was on the Lower Jordan between the Sea of Galilee and the Dead Sea. Many believe it must have been at the Jericho crossing, called in Arabic Makhadet Hijlah, five miles north of the Dead Sea. Others place it at Adam just south of Succoth. Still others think it was the ford leading across the river from Scythopolis. Still others say it was near the Arab village with such an odd name, Tell Abu el Kamel ("Mound of the Father of Lice").

Some of the people who flocked down to the Valley to listen to John the Baptist were drawn by curiosity, but many went in sincere response to his call for national repentance. Day after day, addressing the crowds, he attacked the established order, calling the current religious leaders a brood of "vipers" and denying that there was any certain and absolute value in the bare fact that a person had descended from Abraham. A new start, he told them, was essential; the revival of a truly spiritual approach to life, symbolized by baptism.

The cleansing of sins by submersion in water was a new religious doctrine. The Jordan had, of course, been used by Elisha in curing the Syrian captain, Naaman, of leprosy, but this was hardly the same thing as baptism, a word derived from the Greek *baptein:* to dip in water. Some theologians see a connection between baptism and the manner in which Noah and his family, safe in their ark, were tided over into a new world by the waters that destroyed the wicked. The spiritual significance of baptism has also been likened to the spiritual significance of Jewish circumcision. Many of those who flocked down to the Jordan were somewhat bewildered by this innovation, but others apparently had such faith that they readily submitted to complete immersion, while they repented publicly of their sins and promised to lead a new life.

One day Christ came to the place where John the Baptist was preaching and expressed a desire to be baptized. The four gospels agree in what few details are given of the event, but writers and artists for more than nineteen hundred years have been disagreeing, in prose and in pictures, about details not mentioned in the four accounts. A painting in the Louvre by Rubens, "The Baptism of Christ," shows Him in ankle-deep water. Ravenna in his painting called "The Baptism of Jesus" portrays Him in water up to His waist. Other artists, as well as thousands of writers, have given the world other imagined details.

After the baptism, Christ went up from the Valley into the Wilderness and fasted for forty days and forty nights. At the end of this time, when He was suffering intensely from hunger, He was visited by Satan, who first tempted Him to turn stones into bread, then took Him to the pinnacle of the Temple in Jerusalem, urging Him to throw Himself to the ground to prove His divinity, and finally led Him to "an exceeding high mountain and shewed Him all the kingdoms of the world and the glory of them," and said to Him:

". . . all these things will I give thee if thou wilt fall down and worship me."

Towering over Jericho is a mountain called Jabel al Quruntul (Jebal Qarantal), believed by some to have been the Mountain of Temptation. From a fortress on the summit Christ and Satan could have had a splendid view. In the immediate foreground was the new city of Jericho, built by Herod the Great, with its magnificent palace, theaters, baths, hippodrome, and an immense pool Herod had had constructed to hold water for the irrigation of his extensive gardens. If the day was clear, Mount Hermon's white crown could have been seen, far off on the northern horizon, glittering in the sun. In between was the green Valley, snaking its way across the landscape. And a short distance back from the river, the cities of the Valley. And in the distance, to the south, the deep colors of the Mountains of Moab.

One biblical authority, the Reverend Canon René Leconté, brushes aside centuries of argument over which mountain was the one on which the temptation took place by writing:

"The evangelist (St. Matthew) is purposely vague about the spot where the temptation took place. It would be as useless to try to find the exact spot as to wonder how Jesus Christ succeeded in getting up to the pinnacle of the Temple . . ."

Soon after successfully resisting all the blandishments of the devil, Christ returned to the Valley and there learned that John the Baptist had been seized and imprisoned, because he had aroused the suspicion of Antipas, youngest son of Herod the Great, who had inherited part of his father's kingdom. It was the religious activity of the man from the Wilderness that apparently had frightened him. He was naturally suspicious of anything that might develop into a revolt. The mass following that this strange man had already attracted was cause enough for alarm. Obviously he was a potential danger. The reports Antipas received of what the evangelist was telling the people who streamed down to the river's edge sounded to him like treason. Even worse, John the Baptist had dared criticize the personal life of Antipas, who had divorced his first wife, a daughter of the Nabataean king, Aretas IV, to marry Herodias, a woman both beautiful and clever. She was the daughter of Aristobulus, whom Herod the Great had had executed. First she became the wife of her uncle, Herod Philip, by whom she had a daughter, Salome. (As soon as Salome was of age, she married her grand-uncle, another Philip, known as Philip the Tetrarch.) Meanwhile, Herodias had become the wife of her first husband's half brother, Herod the Tetrarch, more commonly known as Antipas. This brought a denunciation from John the Baptist, who declared in his preaching that the second marriage was both illegal and illicit.

For such a combination of reasons, the man in the camel's hair robe was seized and incarcerated in the fortress of Machaerus on the west side of the Dead Sea, which had been built by Alexander Jannai, the last of the Maccabees. His imprisonment was a signal for the start of Christ's ministry in Galilee, which at this time (about A.D. 31) was one of the most cosmopolitan areas in the world. Here there was a unique mingling of many races, many religions, many cultures. Here were Jews and Nabataeans, men from the East and Greeks from the cities of the Decapolis, Roman soldiers and Herodian officials, farmers and fishermen, Pharisees and Sadducees, people speaking Aramaic, Hebrew, Greek and Latin in dozens of dialects, with a hundred different accents. Galilee, at this decisive moment in world history, was a great meeting place of races. The monotheism of the Jews had survived the attacks of Greek and Roman paganism, yet around the shores of the lake, and up and down the Jordan, there was evidence that the art of the Greeks and the ways of the Romans had made more than a slight imprint.

If Josephus is to be believed, two hundred and four cities and towns now lined the shores of the lake, the smallest of them having a population of fifteen thousand. Even if there were no large cities—and we know there were—and even if all two hundred and four towns were of that minimal size, Josephus is telling us there were more than three million people living at that time around the edges of the Sea of Galilee, which has a perimeter of thirty-three and a third miles. If three million people were to stand close, shoulder to shoulder, on the shoreline of the Sea of Galilee, they would form more than thirty concentric thirty-three-and-a-third-mile circles of tightly packed humanity. Josephus obviously was exaggerating—as he was wont to do—yet from other sources and from archaeological findings it is confirmed that the lake region in the time of Christ was more heavily populated than ever before—or since.

This place at this time was vibrant and alive, but Christ did not choose one of the teeming cities as His new home. Instead He went directly to Capernaum, at the northwest corner of the Sea of Galilee, about two miles from the point where the Jordan flows into the lake. Not far off is the Plain of Chinnereth (Gennesaret), so fertile, so lush that Josephus once called it "the ambition of nature" and wrote that here there is a "happy contention of the seasons" and that here "nature forces those plants that are natural enemies to one another to agree together . . . it supplies men with grapes and figs continually during ten months of the year, and the rest of the fruits as they ripen together throughout the whole year."

Capernaum is nowhere mentioned in the Old Testament. It was of no great historical importance, but after the dismemberment of the kingdom of Herod the Great, Capernaum was close to the frontier dividing the territory of Antipas and the territory of Archelaus Philip, and so here a customs post and a tax collector's office were established, and a small garrison of Roman soldiers in charge of a centurion (captain) was brought in. But it was still, essentially, a community of fishermen.

Capernaum contrasted greatly with Bethsaida, also close to the inlet of the Jordan, but just across the frontier, at the northeast corner of the lake. Bethsaida, hometown of three of the twelve apostles, had also once been a village of simple fishermen, its name literally meaning "House of Fishing." But Philip had rebuilt it into a Greco-Roman city of such elegance that it was renamed Julias, in honor of Julia, daughter of Emperor Augustus.

There was great contrast, also, between Capernaum and Tiberias, ten miles to the south. When Christ was twenty-seven years old, which was long before He commenced His Galilean ministry, Antipas began building a great new city midway down the west shore of the lake on the debris of an ancient city called Rakkat, and he called the new place Tiberias, in honor of Emperor Tiberius, the dour and unimaginative stepson of Augustus Caesar. He chose this location because of its defensive advantages and also because nearby were some already-famous springs. The water of the springs, with a constant temperature of 136 to 144 degrees Fahrenheit as it comes from the ground, is characterized by a repugnant, sulfurous smell, and is so nauseous that no one could possibly drink it, yet in those days it was reputed to have medicinal qualities that would cure almost all the ills to which the human body is ever subject. Even before Herod's time, the lame, the halt, lepers, and those with withered limbs would flock to the baths and sit in water almost hot enough to cook an egg, in the hope of a cure.

Ancient Rakkat had been a few miles south of the springs. There Herod built a palace that he hoped would stand forever and be considered one of the wonders of the land. He also built many other noble structures: temples, a fortress, baths, a stadium, a forum and a theater, all in the lavish style that came to be known as Herodian. The new city was adorned with many statues. Herod intended Tiberias to be not only the principal city of Galilee, but the capital of his entire kingdom.

Without waiting for the city to grow naturally, Herod issued an imperial edict requiring thousands of people residing in other parts of Galilee to move immediately to Tiberias, thus making it a metropolis overnight. He even moved in many slaves. One nineteenth century Christian authority accused him of populating Tiberias with "all the riff-raff he could induce to go there," and added that Tiberias therefore became "a pagan and disreputable place." But whoever the inhabitants were, Tiberias soon was being much talked about, much written about. No other city in Galilee is so often mentioned in the writings of Josephus.

Because Tiberias was built on an area that had been a graveyard and because some of the sepulchers were actually uncovered while workmen were digging the foundations for new buildings, the new Roman city was considered "unclean" under Jewish religious law and no Jew was permitted to enter the city, so it automatically became in its early days an exclusively Gentile community. This explains why Tiberias is mentioned only once in the entire New Testament, and why Christ, as far as the written record shows, never set foot in the city.

There is no mention in the Old Testament of boating or fishing on the lake, whereas in the time of Christ it was alive, day and night, with boats being used for pleasure, or as a means of transportation, or for fishing. Several days after His arrival, as Christ was walking along the waterfront, He saw two brothers, Peter and Andrew, fishing with a net and said to them:

"Follow me, and I will make you fishers of men."

They dropped their net and obeyed, thus becoming the first of His twelve disciples. A short time later He saw two other brothers, James and John, in a boat mending their nets and He enrolled them, also, as disciples. From Capernaum He traveled around many parts of Galilee, preaching, teaching, and curing illnesses.

". . . and they brought unto him all sick people that were taken with divers diseases and torments, and those which were possessed with devils, and those which were lunatick and those that had the palsy; and he healed them."

As His fame spread, more and more people followed Him wherever He went, some of them from the other side of the Jordan, many from the Valley itself, and others from the cities of the Decapolis.

"And seeing the multitudes he went up into a mountain . . ."

With those ten words St. Matthew commences three memorable chapters on the Sermon on the Mount, which included the Lord's Prayer, the Beatitudes, and many words of great religious and philosophical wisdom.

There is scholarly uncertainty over where "the mountain" was, with some contending it was no mountain at all; that Christ stood on a hill not more than twenty or thirty feet high and from such a pulpit delivered his sermon. Others believe he spoke on a 1187-foot, two-peaked mountain called the Horns of Hattin, directly behind the city of Tiberias. One biblical commentator, favoring the Horns of Hattin, wrote:

"At its foot, as if to show how little men regarded such precepts (as were enunciated in the sermon) was fought one of the most dreadful battles recorded on the pages of history."

Still another theory is that the sermon was preached from a gentle hill just behind the lakeside town of Tabigha, a short distance west of Capernaum. In the still of an evening, any words uttered from the summit could have been heard distinctly at the foot of the hill.

After returning to Capernaum, Christ and some of His disciples went in a boat onto the lake.

"And, behold, there arose a great tempest in the sea, insomuch that the ship was covered with the waves: but he was asleep.

"And his disciples came to him, and awoke him, saying, Lord, save us: we perish.

"And he saith unto them, Why are ye fearful, O ye of little faith? Then he arose, and rebuked the winds and the sea; and there was a great calm.

"But the men marvelled, saying, What manner of man is this, that even the winds and the sea obey him!"

(The use of the word "ship" in the King James Version of the Bible is misleading. It was probably little different from the fishing boats used on the lake today, twenty or twenty-five feet long at the most, capable of holding perhaps a dozen men. The Bible indicates how small the Sea of Galilee boats were when it tells how close the fishermen came in to shore to load and unload.)

Such sudden storms as the one described are no rarity on the Sea of

Galilee, even today. One moment the surface of the water is as smooth as glass. Then suddenly a wind begins to blow from the northeast through the wadis, ravines and gorges that act like great funnels, as they draw the cold winds from the mountains and deliver them down to the lake, almost seven hundred feet below sea level. Such winds are not only violent, but they come with no warning. Suddenly the whole lake is lashed into a frightening fury and even the most experienced fisherman would not try to bring his boat to shore, for fear it would be pounded to splinters on the rocks.

After the sea grew calm they proceeded and on the far shore entered "the country of the Gergesenes," where they were met by two men possessed of devils who came out of a tomb, looking "exceeding fierce," and blocked their way. A conversation took place between Christ and the devils, the latter suggesting that if Christ cast them out of the two men He should make them enter the bodies of a herd of swine feeding in a field nearby.

"Go," Christ commanded.

"And when they were come out, they went into the herd of swine: and, behold, the whole herd of swine ran violently down a steep place into the sea, and perished in the waters."

The Galilean episodes seem to have constituted the quieter, happier part of Christ's life, and no wonder, for there was much here to recommend itself to a sensitive person. The hills behind Capernaum were laced with mysterious beauty. Sunshine and shadow played on the surface of the lake, making the water glitter and sparkle. Sometimes it would seem to be deep blue, sometimes pale green. On occasion, when a cold wind blew down from snow-capped Mount Hermon, the lake would suddenly get dark and boisterous, and heavy waves would beat against the stony shore, and the water would seem to be inky black. Often, it is true, the heat was oppressive because of how far the lake is below sea level, yet generally in the evening refreshing breezes blew in and brought relief. On certain days it was possible to see the Jordan River flowing right through the center of the lake, rapidly, from north to south, because of the difference in the smoothness and roughness of various areas of the lake's surface.

Christ had obvious affection for Capernaum, where He felt at home among the simple fisher folk, yet because they failed to take His advice about repenting of their sins, He warned them that dire punishment would be inflicted upon them:

"And thou, Capernaum, which art exalted unto heaven, shalt be brought down to hell: for if the mighty works, which have been done in thee, had been done in Sodom, it would have remained until this day.

"But I say unto you, That it shall be more tolerable for the land of Sodom in the day of judgment, than for thee."

At the same time He warned Bethsaida and Chorazin, a town several miles northwest of Capernaum, that they, also, would be punished because their people had not repented.

During the year or more that Christ stayed in the fishing village, He traveled widely about that part of Galilee, but He was rarely out of sight of either the Jordan or the Sea of Galilee. Besides curing the sick and casting out demons, He spent much time teaching and training His twelve disciples. In one talk to them He again made reference to those cities that had once stood at the other end of the Jordan, saying:

"And whosoever shall not receive you, nor hear your words, when ye depart out of that house or city, shake off the dust of your feet.

"Verily I say unto you, It shall be more tolerable for the land of Sodom and Gomorrha in the day of judgment, than for that city."

In Capernaum Christ lived in the home of His disciple Peter, who had been a fisherman. One day He left the house alone and sat by the edge of the lake. It was probably the Sabbath, when all good Jews, fishermen included, abstained from any work. The street along the waterfront was crowded. The day was warm, the sun bright, and the lake calm, with the water shimmering as if its surface were made of millions of diamonds, their facets reflecting the brightness of the daylight. Lovers walked past, hand in hand. Fishermen stood in groups, talking of yesterday's catch, tomorrow's plans. Now and then a single Roman soldier passed, whistling or humming a marching song, or a group of Roman soldiers, laughing raucously, perhaps at a new piece of ribaldry some soldier just in from Rome had told them. A few men gathered around Christ, knowing about the sick He had cured, the lepers He had made normal again, the devils He had cast out of madmen. He began talking quietly to them, in a soft voice, yet with an intensity that compelled everyone who passed by to stop and listen. Then, the presence of so large a group of people attracted those who were merely curious. Soon the crowd was of sizable proportions. Then it grew into such a multitude that those on the periphery could neither see nor hear the man who was speaking. Christ tried standing on a rock. Then someone made a better suggestion and a fisherman waded out to where his boat was anchored, brought the craft in to shore, rowed Christ out a short distance from the land, and then moored his boat. Now all could see Him. As He began to speak again, the multitude grew silent. He spoke entirely in parables. All his similes referred to the sea and to fishing, or to the land and farming. His first story was about a farmer who was planting a field, and some of his seeds fell on stony places, or were devoured by chickens, or were choked to death because they had taken root among thorns. As He finished this story, His disciples, attracted by the size of the crowd, came down to the seashore and asked Him:

"Why speakest thou unto them in parables?"

Christ replied that He was certain that this was the most effective way of conveying great religious and philosophical truths to the simple folk of Capernaum. Then He explained the parable of the sower. Next, He told a parable about another sower whose enemy, while he slept, came and scattered the seeds of weeds in his newly planted wheat field. Then, a parable about a mustard seed.

By now the sun was high in the heavens and it was hot, and Christ was probably weary from standing in the open boat talking to so large a crowd, so "he sent the multitude away and went into the house." His disciples followed Him and one of them asked Him to explain the parable of the enemy who sowed weed seeds in his neighbor's wheat field. Christ did, and then told the disciples, among whom were four fishermen, a number of additional parables, including one likening the way the good and the wicked will be separated at Judgment Day, to how fishermen separate the good from the bad when they draw in their nets.

As reports of Christ's preaching and His miraculous cures spread through Galilee, the crowds that swarmed around Peter's cottage grew larger and larger. One day four men arrived carrying a bed on which lay a victim of palsy. Unable to get anywhere near the place where Christ stood, because of the great press of people, they climbed to the top of the house and made a hole in the roof large enough to admit the bed, which they then lowered into the house.

The reaction of Peter, whose house it was, is not recorded. Christ, however, was so impressed by the ingenuity and the faith of the four men that He told the victim of palsy:

"Son, thy sins be forgiven thee."

When certain scribes who were present criticized the wording of His blessing, He turned again to the palsy victim and said:

"Arise, and take up thy bed, and go thy way into thine house," which the man did.

The scene shifts, now, from this village by the Sea of Galilee to the opposite end of the Valley—back to the fortress of Machaerus, on the west side of the Dead Sea, where John the Baptist had been imprisoned for so long. The normal procedure in those days throughout the Roman Empire—as well as in many other parts of the world in many eras, before and since—was to inflict the death penalty, without much hesitation and without many formalities, on anyone guilty of the crime of high treason, or even suspected of it. But Herod the Tetrarch, better known as Antipas, was afraid to have John the Baptist executed. At many times in history this has been the problem of men with apparently unlimited power: their fear of using such power because of the likely reaction. Thus John the Baptist's crime seemed to be his salvation: he had a following, and Antipas knew it.

"And when he would have put him to death, he feared the multitude, because they counted him as a prophet."

This fear even outweighed his desire to please his wife, Herodias. Her indignation over John the Baptist's criticism of their marriage had been greater than his. It was she who had demanded his arrest and imprisonment. But this alone did not satisfy her. Her passion for revenge was so great that she, personally, wanted to kill the man who had talked so disrespectfully of her. Such a pleasure Herod thus far had denied her, "for Herod feared John, knowing that he was a just man."

Then came the night of the fatal party. It was in celebration of Herod's birthday, and was a gala affair, for the guests included all the high-ranking officers of the Roman Legion, and many other important people from all parts of the extensive territory over which Herod ruled. The account of the party specifically mentions that many of the guests had come the long distance down the Valley from Galilee, probably crossing over the river into Peraea at the Jericho ford.

There was much to eat and more to drink—wine from the great vineyards in the Valley of the Jordan. The principal entertainment was dancing by the daughter of Herodias by Herod Philip, who, by an odd twist, although now no longer her husband, had become her brother-in-law when she married Antipas, which was what had caused all the trouble. Salome was beautiful and her dancing must have been both provocative and intoxicating, for when she finished and curtsied, the applause was thunderous, especially from those sitting close to Antipas, who was so deeply affected that he called the girl over to him and in congratulating her made an offer that was dangerous for any man, under any circumstances, to have made to any woman:

"Whatsoever thou shalt ask of me, I will give it thee, unto the half of my kingdom."

Salome hesitated. Then she fled from the great banquet hall to where her mother was waiting for her, certain that Herodias would advise her.

"What shall I ask?" she inquired of her mother.

Herodias knew what *she* wanted.

"The head of John the Baptist."

Salome not only agreed to ask, but—

"She came in straightway with haste unto the king, and asked, saying, I will that thou give me by and by in a charger (a large, flat silver platter used for carrying meat) the head of John the Baptist."

Antipas now realized how reckless his offer had been. Yet he had sworn an oath and, for a Roman, an oath was an oath. Those around him had heard what he had said to Salome. Many were officers of the Roman Legion, and owners of great estates; all were important people. It would not do for him to lose face in front of such a group.

And so—

"Immediately the king sent an executioner, and commanded his head to be brought: and he went and beheaded him in the prison."

While Antipas, Salome, Herodias and the others waited, word of the girl's strange request was whispered from guest to guest, until all in the great banquet hall knew. Some, who had drunk too deeply, must have made ribald jokes. Others probably expressed curiosity. Perhaps here and there someone was embarrassed or revolted.

Then suddenly the doors of the great banquet hall were flung open and a servant appeared bearing an immense silver platter. On it—as ordered—was the head of the bearded prophet. Slowly, so the macabre object would not fall to the floor, the servant carried it to his lord and master. Antipas took it and solemnly handed the platter to the girl dancer. Surely with nervousness—if for no other reason than that she knew the eyes of so many men were upon her—Salome walked slowly from the room bearing the platter, and gave it to her mother. What Herodias did with the head, the accounts do not tell.

When the story of John the Baptist's tragic fate reached his disciples, they hastened over the Jordan to Machaerus and asked for the remains. Mournfully they carried the corpse back across the river and gave it a decent burial.

When Christ heard the news, He was deeply affected. He immediately told His disciples that He wished to go to some desert place, to be alone with His thoughts. They went by boat from Capernaum a few miles across the north end of the lake, and then by foot up into a wilderness belonging to the city of Bethsaida, now called Julias by the Romans. Two accounts say they went up a mountain; two others say they went onto the desert. But wherever it was that they went, they found no solitude.

"And when the people had heard thereof, they followed him on foot out of the cities."

Instead of meditating, Christ spent the day preaching and healing. Then when evening came, His disciples suggested that He dismiss the multitude so the people could go from the desert to the villages to buy food for their evening meal.

"But Jesus said unto them, They need not depart; give ye them to eat.

"And they said unto him, We have here but five loaves, and two fishes.

"He said, Bring them hither to me.

"And he commanded the multitude to sit down on the grass, and took the five loaves, and the two fishes, and looking up to heaven, he blessed, and brake, and gave the loaves to his disciples, and the disciples to the multitude.

"And they did all eat, and were filled: and they took up of the fragments that remained twelve baskets full.

"And they that had eaten were about five thousand men, beside women and children."

Finally, as it began to grow dark, Christ told His disciples that He wished them to return to the other side of the lake, while He went alone up onto a height to pray. As they put out in their boat, a sudden wind blew with such force that they were unable to make any progress against it. In the fourth watch of the night (the last three hours before morning) Christ came down from the mountain and began to walk across the surface of the lake to the other side. As He passed the motionless boat loaded with His disciples, they cried out in fear, thinking He was a spirit. Immediately He spoke to them, identifying Himself. At that precise moment the wind suddenly stopped, so He entered the boat and they all went together to the Gennesaret region, a few miles down the lake from Capernaum.

It was now full daylight. When the people of this lakeside district saw Him, they recognized who He was and many families went home and got their sick and their dying, and carried them in their beds to where Christ was, "and besought him that they might touch if it were but the border of his garment: and as many as touched were made whole."

Wherever He went thousands followed Him. After three days He expressed concern that the multitude had not eaten, and when He found that the disciples had seven loaves of bread and a few fish, He repeated, here on the west side of the lake, the miracle of the loaves and the fish He had previously performed at Bethsaida. This time four thousand men, women and children were fed, and what was gathered up after the meal filled seven baskets.

After sending away the crowd, Christ and His disciples went by boat to Magdala ("Tower"). This town, on the western side of the lake between Capernaum and Tiberias, was more Greek than Jewish, but it was the birthplace of Mary Magdalene, who would play a major role in a later chapter of the story.

The entire Magdala area is honeycombed with caves hewn from the rock. For many years they were inhabited by robbers, who defied any attempt to rout them. Josephus in one of his historical works tells how they were finally dislodged:

"These caves were in mountains exceedingly abrupt, their middle no other than precipices with entrances into the caves; in these did the robbers lie concealed. But the King caused chests to be made and be let down with iron chains by an engine from the top of the mountain, it being not possible to get up to the robbers' caves by reason of the sharp ascent, nor to creep down from above.

"Now these chests were filled with armored men who had long hooks by which they might pull out such as resisted them, and then tumble them down and kill them by so doing. But the letting the chest down proved to be a matter of great danger because of the vast depth."

Josephus spends pages telling of the slaughter, as the Roman soldiers succeeded in "hooking" many of the astounded robbers. After a considerable number had been dropped to their death on the sharp rocks below, the Roman commander of this strange enterprise offered an amnesty to those still in the caves and still alive. One woman with seven children agreed to accept whatever the terms might be, but her husband, an old man, refused to permit her to surrender and when she persisted he threw her and all seven children out of the cave to their death below. The report does not tell what eventually happened to the husband, but in this manner "all these caves were at length subdued."

From Magdala, Christ crossed the lake to Bethsaida again, and then went up through the Valley on the east side of the river, past Lake Semochonitis to the slopes of Mount Hermon. At the spot where the pagan god Baal had been worshiped in early Israelite days, and where the Greeks had erected shrines to Pan, and where Herod the Great had built a marble altar to honor Augustus, one of Herod the Great's sons, Philip the Tetrarch, had recently made a magnificent city out of the inconsequential mountainside town of Paneas. There he built a splendid palace for himself and the place became his capital city and he called it Caesarea, after the Emperor, and then added Philippi, to differentiate it from his father's Caesarea, on the Mediterranean coast.

Philip the Tetrarch was an amateur scientist and the first person of importance to expound the theory that the water gushing from the side of the mountain at Paneas—one of the chief sources of the Jordan— came not from hidden springs but through a natural underground tunnel from a strange lake on top of a mountain peak some distance above Paneas, Lake Phiala. Few men at that time had ever seen it, for it was in a relatively inaccessible place. It lay in what resembled a great soup bowl, thought to have been the crater of an extinct volcano, about three miles in circumference. Its water was dark-colored and motionless, except for the ripples made by thousands of frogs that filled the nights with their deep-throated croaking, and the slithery movement of millions of leeches that lived in the lake but fed on grass around the shoreline. A few ducks floated lazily on the murky surface, and hawks circled constantly overhead, swooping down now and then to pluck a meal of frog meat from the lake. It was a place of mysterious solitude and oppressive desolation. The oddity of Lake Phiala, however, was that it had neither ingress nor outlet. No stream ran into it, and none left it. Yet, despite the intense heat of the sun and the resulting rapid rate of evaporation, the level of the water in this mountaintop soup bowl was always exactly the same, suggesting that it must have been fed by strong springs beneath the surface.

Philip paid a visit to Lake Phiala and tried to prove his theory by tossing handfuls of chaff into the lake. He claimed that later he saw the same chaff come out at Paneas. This experiment was reported by Josephus as "proof" that Philip was correct in his theory. Other amateur scientists pointed out that the volume of the flow at Paneas would have soon exhausted the contents of such a small lake as this, and— even more conclusive—the water of Lake Phiala was hot, brown and flat, while the water that gushed out below was cool, crystal clear, bright as sunshine, and almost sweet to the taste. Also, there were no leeches in the water at Paneas. Nevertheless Philip was the tetrarch (ruler of the district) and Josephus was one of the most respected historians of his time, and so some credence was given in those days to the theory.

By now Christ had traversed much of the Jordan Valley and also knew intimately the lake through which the Jordan flowed, but this visit to the river's principal source was taking Him farther north than

He had ever been before during all the thirty-nine or forty years of His life. Up here He was as yet little known and therefore had nothing to fear from the Roman authorities. This may have been one of the reasons He selected the Mount Hermon area to visit.

The disciples who accompanied Him must have been awestruck by what they saw. None of them had ever before viewed anything like this place of pagan temples, deep grottoes, rugged cliffs, solemn groves, gushing fountains, rushing streams, laughing brooks.

Christ and His disciples remained in the Mount Hermon area for a week. There is no account of how the time was spent, but if any parables were uttered here, instead of being about fishing and farming, they must have been concerned with forest and woods, springs and streams.

Christ had already tried to teach His disciples to come near to nature, not with the licentious revelry of the pagans, nor with the superstitious awe of those who were afraid, but with calm joy and tranquil confidence in the essential goodness of nature.

One day in Caesarea Philippi, Christ, while discussing with His disciples a problem that was greatly troubling Him, asked them:

"Whom do men say that I the Son of man am?"

One of them replied:

"Some say that thou art John the Baptist: some, Elias; and others, Jeremias, or one of the prophets."

To which Christ replied:

"But whom say ye that I am?"

Simon Peter replied:

"Thou art the Christ, the Son of the living God."

Christ congratulated him on his perception, adding:

"And I say also unto thee, That thou art Peter, and upon this rock I will build my church; and the gates of hell shall not prevail against it."

(Because the Bible nowhere explains that Caesarea Philippi, where the incident occurred, had been built on an immense black rock, the subtle play on words has been lost to most Bible readers.)

It was then and there that Christ made the decision to tell His disciples that He would soon have to go to Jerusalem and "suffer many things of the elders and chief priests and scribes, and be killed, and be raised again the third day."

When Peter protested that this must not be permitted to happen, Christ replied with two, long-to-be-remembered sentences. First He turned to His disciple and said:

"Get thee behind me, Satan . . . "

Then He concluded a brief discourse on the value of human life by saying:

"For what is a man profited, if he shall gain the whole world, and lose his own soul? or what shall a man give in exchange for his soul?"

After six or eight days (St. Matthew and St. Mark say "six"; St. Luke says "eight"; St. John omits the account entirely) Christ took Peter, James and John, His closest disciples, "and bringeth them up into an high mountain apart." That is all the identification there is, but most biblical scholars agree that it was Mount Hermon they climbed, although some years ago Mount Tabor, bordering on the Great Plain of Esdraelon, was honored by Christian pilgrims as the location of this event, but probably for a very simple reason. In those days travel was still difficult and Mount Hermon was relatively inaccessible. The pilgrims were already in the area of Jerusalem, Bethlehem and Nazareth, commemorating other events in Christ's life. Mount Tabor was nearby, and it was a mountain much easier for the pilgrims to climb than Hermon would have been. There are many reasons why Christ and His disciples, having spent a week at the base of Mount Hermon or on its slopes, would not have crossed the Jordan and traveled fifty or sixty miles—a journey of several days on foot—in order to climb Mount Tabor. The overriding reason, which the pilgrims may not have known about when they picked Mount Tabor, is that in Christ's day the slopes of Mount Tabor were a military zone, with a Roman fortress at the peak. This made it about the last place in the land that Christ and His disciples would have picked for this particular purpose.

Christ wished to be alone, except for the three disciples who were closest to Him. On Mount Hermon He could find the serenity He sought. Besides, this snow-capped peak had always had a special meaning for Jews, and He was a Jew. It dominated their Promised Land. Its summit could be seen from most parts of Samaria and even from Judaea. It was looked upon by many as the dwelling place of the Lord. Several Psalms had been inspired by its snowy crest, often lost in the clouds. It was on this high place, under the quiet stars, that Christ made His decision to return to Jerusalem and face the fate He knew awaited Him. There one more miracle occurred.

"And as he prayed, the fashion of his countenance was altered, and his raiment was white, and glistening."

Then before Christ and the disciples appeared two figures out of their religious past: Moses and Elijah (who is referred to as Elias in all three accounts of the transfiguration), and a voice from out of a cloud said:

"This is my beloved Son, in whom I am well pleased; hear ye him."

When they reached the base of the mountain again, they found a great crowd of people, including many scribes, waiting there, with the other nine disciples.

Then they returned by way of the Valley of the Upper Jordan to Capernaum. There, when Christ was told that the local collector was demanding payment of the taxes they owed as residents of Capernaum, He told Peter to go to the lake and fish with a line and hook, and to be sure to look in the mouth of the first fish he caught, for there he would find a piece of money of sufficient value to pay the taxes for both of them. And it happened as he had said—the penultimate Galilean miracle.

One version (St. Matthew's) indicates that after leaving Capernaum, Christ and His disciples crossed to the east side of the Jordan at some point, and followed the Valley until they came to Peraea, the province opposite Jericho. Crowds followed them wherever they went, just as in Galilee. When the disciples scolded those who brought small children to see Him, Christ replied:

"Suffer little children, and forbid them not, to come unto me: for of such is the kingdom of heaven."

It also was there that He advised a wealthy young man to sell all his worldly possessions and give the money to the poor, for—

"It is easier for a camel to go through the eye of a needle, than for a rich man to enter into the kingdom of God."

After crossing back over the Jordan, they went to Jericho, followed by an immense crowd. As they drew near to the city more and more people added themselves to the procession.

In Jericho an incident occurred involving a man named Zacchaeus, who was the chief publican of Jericho, meaning that he was the tax collector for the entire city. This made him an important and extremely rich man, for in those days collecting taxes for the Romans was big business. It was done on a contract basis, with the publican or tax collector retaining a goodly percentage of all he took in. The publicans had subcontractors working under them, and all of them—the collectors and their subcontractors as well—engaged in such malpractice and extortion that the very word "publican" had become odorous. The main contractors were generally foreigners to the area, while the subcontractors might or might not be local men, but all were despised and hated. This quite natural feeling was aggravated for Jews because the

272

publican was considered ceremonially unclean, on account of having contractual connections with Gentiles. This uncleanliness led to the use of the expression "publicans and sinners," which appears half a dozen times in the Bible, and "publicans and harlots" which is also to be found in the New Testament.

Zacchaeus was in this enviable or unenviable position of being the chief publican of the rather large city of Jericho. But he was a little man, so small of stature that when he rushed out into the road upon the approach of Christ, he was unable to see anything, everyone else being taller than he and blocking his view, so he dashed ahead and climbed a large sycamore tree close by the highway down which Christ was approaching. From this vantage point, small though he was, he would be able to get a good bird's-eye view of the man who had already become celebrated for the miracles He had performed.

As Christ passed the sycamore tree He looked up, saw the tax collector, and said to him:

"Zacchaeus, make haste, and come down; for to day I must abide at thy house."

So Zacchaeus came quickly down and rushed to his home to prepare a reception for his distinguished guest. The crowd was stunned with surprise.

"And when they saw it, they all murmured, saying, That he was gone to be a guest with a man that is a sinner."

When Christ arrived at the tax collector's home, Zacchaeus greeted Him by saying:

"Behold, Lord, the half of my goods I give to the poor; and if I have taken any thing from any man by false accusation, I restore him fourfold."

Christ said this showed Zacchaeus was a true son of Abraham and henceforth salvation would come not only to him personally, but to his entire household. Some self-righteous people present were critical, but Christ answered them by saying that His mission was to seek out and save the lost.

After preaching for some time in Jerusalem, Christ again crossed over the Jordan to avoid capture by those who wished to destroy Him.

". . . but he escaped out of their hand.

"And went again beyond Jordan into the place where John at first baptised; and there he abode."

But after a short time He received news of the critical illness of Lazarus of Bethany, brother of Mary, who later anointed His feet with a pound of expensive spikenard ointment and then wiped His feet dry with her hair, and Martha, her sister. So Christ and His disciples crossed back over the Jordan once more. When they reached Bethany they found that Lazarus had been dead and buried for four days. Christ brought him back to life, and then went on to Jerusalem, aware of exactly what His fate was going to be there.

Neither the Jordan, nor its Valley, nor its lakes figured in any way in the story of the arrest, condemnation and crucifixion, except that people everywhere in the area were affected or involved, in one way or another; the believers and the disbelievers; those who considered Him a dangerous agitator and a threat to Roman rule; those who looked on Him as a wise teacher; those who had faith that He was far more than that—that He was the true Messiah.

Only one of the four New Testament chronicles (The Gospel According to St. John) tells the story of Christ's appearance some time after the resurrection at an unnamed fishing village on the Sea of Galilee. Seven of the twelve disciples were there. They had spent all night fishing with a net but had caught nothing. Now it was morning and they were pulling in to port when a man on shore asked them if they had had any luck. When they replied in the negative, he shouted to them:

"Cast the net on the right side of the ship, and ye shall find."

They did, and the net was immediately filled with so many fish that they were unable to pull it in.

As they were only a hundred yards from shore, some of them put out in a small boat and dragged the net to shore. When they counted their catch they found they had one hundred and fifty-three fish, all of a considerable size. Then they discovered that the stranger had prepared a meal for them of cooked fish and bread, so they all ate together, close by the waterfront. As they did, they realized that they had been witnesses to the final miracle of their resurrected Lord.

There is no further reference, after this, anywhere in the Bible to the Jordan, or to its three lakes, yet they did not stop playing important roles in the lives of the people whom Christ had left behind.

Throughout the length of the Jordan Valley, from Dan to the southernmost extremity of the Dead Sea, there was tension in the early spring of A.D. 66—a foreboding of cataclysmic developments.

Nero was on the throne in Rome, monstrously sinister yet feeble, devoting more attention to winning prizes at literary festivals than to keeping an empire together. He had already had his own mother done to death and had ordered many Christians burned alive in public on the trumped-up charge that they had tried to destroy the Roman capital by fire.

Most of the Jordan Valley and the shores of its three lakes were in charge of a procurator sent out from Rome, but the east bank of the Upper Jordan and about a quarter of the Sea of Galilee's shoreline were ruled over by Herod Agrippa II, great-grandson of Herod the Great. When Nero increased the area of his territory, Agrippa changed the name of his capital—originally Paneas, then Caesarea Philippi—to Neronias. Then he rebuilt the city so the emperor might be doubly pleased.

In Jerusalem each new procurator seemed more incompetent, more mendacious than the last. Many behaved as if convinced that the solution of any problem was slaughter; that the perfect way to kill an idea was to lop off a head.

Finally Nero sent Gessius Florus as procurator. This man's sole qualification seemed to be that he had a sister who was not only beautiful and witty but knew how to buy what she wanted with her favors, and one thing she wanted was an important post for her brother. Florus was as stupid as his sister was clever. During the Passover celebration he was responsible for the seizure of the vestments of the high priest in Jerusalem. When a committee of moderate Jewish leaders appeared before him to protest, he had them seized and massacred. He found ways to violate most of the sacred beliefs of the Jews with both arrogance and obscenity. He demanded payment of tribute valued at half a million dollars, out of Temple funds, for protection—protection from his own officials.

Most of the subjects of Procurator Florus were supporters of either of two parties, the Zealots, called "the War Party" because they advocated defiance of Rome, or the Peace Party, which considered such defiance to be folly. The membership of the Zealots increased daily, as Pharisees, Essenes, Sadducees and others joined their ranks.

One of the first events in the total war against the Romans was set in the Valley, as were many later episodes. A band of Zealots led by Menahem, son of Judas of Galilee, in a military operation as reckless as any in history, attacked and succeeded in capturing the impregnable fortress of Masada, on the west shore of the Dead Sea, which contained an immense store of food and arms, both greatly needed by the rebellious Zealots. Now tension gave way to open defiance, not only from Dan to the Dead Sea, but all over Judaea, Galilee, Samaria, Peraea and Udumaea.

This was David against Goliath. The Jews were united and had help from their own people in the Diaspora, but they were defying the mighty Roman Empire. All the world was watching, for if the revolt succeeded and spread to other countries, there might soon be no Roman Empire.

A Roman general was sent post haste from Syria with thirty thousand men. He had some successes in the upper reaches of the Jordan and in other parts of Galilee, but when winter came he was forced to retire. This gave the Zealots a chance to organize for the approaching conflict. Galilee was placed under the military direction of Joseph ben Matthias, who would become known as Joseph Flavius, historian, or simply Josephus. He was the son of a Jewish priest in Jerusalem and a descendant of the Maccabees. As a very young man he had lived three years in the Wilderness, associating with the Essenes. At nineteen he joined the Pharisees, that minority group of Jews who stressed ethical rather than theological concepts. At twenty-six he went to Rome and became so impressed by the strength and magnitude of the Empire that he returned home strongly opposed to the Jewish revolt that was already taking shape. Yet, strangely, in the winter of A.D. 66 he was placed in charge of all Jewish forces in Galilee; strangely, because of his emotional and intellectual attachment to the Romans, and because he was only twenty-nine, had never held office of any kind, had never been either a soldier or a statesman, and had no apparent qualifications for such a post.

As governor of Galilee he organized the first Jewish navy on the Sea of Galilee, consisting of two hundred and thirty "ships." (Probably nothing more than converted fishing vessels.) They were assembled at a seaport Josephus called Tarichaea, on the west shore of the lake. Some maps and some historians locate Tarichaea at the point where the Jordan flows out of the lake. One historian insists the city was on an island in the Jordan just after the river leaves the lake. The more likely location is five miles north of Tiberias. Possibly Magdala, home of Mary Magdalene, and Tarichaea were one and the same place.

Wherever it was, Josephus made it his headquarters. There one day some young rebels appeared at his office with a wealth of silver goblets, gold coins, clothing and other valuables they had seized after waylaying an important Roman minister. Josephus took the loot from them, indicating his intention of restoring it to its rightful owner. The next day a crowd of a hundred thousand armed men—the figure is Josephus'—held a mass meeting in the hippodrome of Tarichaea and demanded that Josephus be stoned or burned alive. He appeared with his clothes torn and his head covered with ashes to show his repentance, then declared that he never had any intention of returning the stolen goods; he was going to sell them and use the proceeds to strengthen the city wall. This satisfied all but two thousand men, who stormed his house. Josephus mounted the roof and addressed the mob, suggesting that they appoint a delegation to enter his house to talk things over. When they did, he flogged the committee members "until their innards were visible," then flung open his front door and pushed the blood-drenched victims into the street. His own story is that this so terrified the rest of the two thousand that they fled.

The first time the navy of Josephus went into action was the day he heard that some of the men of Tiberias were organizing a revolt against him. He put a crew of four into each of his two hundred and thirty boats and sailed down (or up) the coast to Tiberias. There he ordered the boats to stay far enough out from shore so that those on land would not be able to see how few men were in the crews. He and a bodyguard of seven went ashore, where they found that the ruse had worked: the Tiberians, convinced that the boats were packed with well-armed soldiers, threw down their weapons. Josephus asked for a conference with the ten most important citizens of Tiberias. As they stepped into his boat, they were taken to sea. Josephus returned with other half-empty boats and asked for a conference with the fifty leading senators. They, likewise, were kidnaped. In this manner the entire senate—many hundreds of men—as well as two thousand other leading citizens, were made prisoner and taken to Tarichaea.

Some days later Josephus was told that a young Jew named Clitus had been the leader of the revolt. He went by boat to Tiberias, had Clitus brought down to the water's edge, and there ordered one of his guards to cut off both the young man's hands. When Clitus begged the governor to spare one hand, Josephus agreed on condition that Clitus draw his own sword with his right hand and cut off his left hand himself, which he did. Such conduct on the part of Josephus is explained by one of his biographers, G. A. Williamson, in these words:

"Of course it was a savage world in which Josephus lived, and he was only doing the sort of thing that others had done before him; but he so often takes credit for mercy, generosity, and piety that we cannot but wonder at deeds like these, deeds which gave him feelings not of shame but of immense self satisfaction. He wrote so eloquently in praise of Moses and his enlightened legislation; but what would Moses have thought of conduct such as his?"

In February, A.D. 68, Nero sent an experienced officer, Vespasian, to take charge in Judaea and save the empire from the humiliation of any more defeats at the hands of so small a rebel force. Vespasian in turn sent his son Titus to Alexandria to fetch the powerful Fifteenth Legion.

One story that has come down to us about Vespasian tells that when he finally reached the Dead Sea with some of his troops, he was so bewitched by the discovery that human bodies floated in the salt water that he lined up his troops on the shore and ordered all who could not swim to advance two paces. About half of his force responded. At his order these men—many hundreds—were then bound hand and foot with stout rope, taken out in small boats, and thrown into the sea at its deepest point. Then the general, who would some day be supreme ruler of the world's greatest empire, stood on the shore roaring with laughter as he watched his victims "tumbling about in the great cauldron of bitter brine in helpless perplexity."

When Vespasian started his spring campaign in Galilee, one of the first cities he occupied was Scythopolis. He had little if any Jewish opposition, for a short time earlier the Greco-Syrian community of Scythopolis had engaged in a pogrom, murdering most brutally thirteen thousand Jewish men, women and children of the city and plundering all their property.

Then Vespasian turned his attention to Jotapata, some fifteen miles due west of the Sea of Galilee. Josephus staked his military reputation on his conviction that he could hold this strategic fortress. He did hold it—for forty-six days.

One of the defenders' great problems was their desperate shortage of water. The Romans knew it and Josephus knew the Romans knew it, so, as the situation grew desperate, he had his soldiers wash their shirts—using most of the remaining water—and hang them up, dripping wet, in sight of the Romans below, in the hope of confusing them, which it did.

On the forty-seventh day Titus led his Romans over the wall and into the city. Then a two-day massacre of the inhabitants began. Josephus estimated that the dead, from the start of the siege to the finish, numbered forty thousand. More than twelve hundred Jewish women and children were sent into captivity. Josephus himself escaped by a secret passageway to a cave well stocked with provisions, where forty other important people of Jotapata were already in hiding. When the Romans sent word they would spare the life of the young governor if all surrendered, Josephus was eager to accept the offer, but the other forty reproached him for his cowardice and threatened to kill him if he tried to leave. Then someone suggested a suicide pact. Josephus opposed it and delivered a speech condemning the very idea of suicide as a sin against God and a crime under the laws of Moses. The others pointed out that *he* had a choice; *they* were all going to die, one way or another. Josephus then proposed that they draw lots and kill each other in turn. Whoever drew the first lot would be killed by whoever drew the second, and so on. They agreed, and one by one they went to their deaths, until there were just two men left. In commenting on the fact that he was one of the two, Josephus in his life story asks the question: "Shall we put it down to divine providence or just to luck?" In the Slavic edition of the same work, this sentence, now in the third person, reads: "He counted the numbers cunningly and so deceived them all."

Taken before Vespasian, Josephus managed to ingratiate himself with the general by predicting—as if he were a prophet—that Vespasian before long would become emperor. This bit of cunning probably saved his life.

Another strong point Vespasian attacked was Tarichaea, which he ultimately seized, but not without terrible casualties on both sides.

Many of the defenders, when the loss of the city appeared certain, tried to escape onto the Sea of Galilee in the two hundred and thirty boats. What followed has been called "a naval battle" by some historians. The Romans built rafts, loaded them with heavily armed soldiers, and attacked the Jewish boats, killing off the fugitives with no difficulty and sinking their boats one by one until the total of dead, says Josephus, numbered seven thousand, and the Jewish navy lay at the bottom of the lake.

Those who attempted to escape by land were driven in the direction of Tiberias. There they were easily captured and herded into a stadium to be "sorted out," much as Jews taken to extermination camps in Europe during World War II were "sorted out" by the Nazis. On order from Vespasian twelve hundred old and "useless people" were murdered, six thousand strong young men were sent as a gift to Nero, for use as slave labor in digging the Corinth Canal in Greece, and the rest of the thirty-five thousand were sold as slaves to the highest bidder.

Less than a year later—in the summer of A.D. 68—Nero committed suicide. As there was no obvious successor, four generals each tried to seize power. When Vespasian won, he remembered the prophecy of Josephus, who was thereupon released and put on the Roman headquarters staff. He eventually took on the emperor's family name, Flavius. During the rest of the war he served as a combination military historian, front-line war correspondent, and interpreter for Titus. Thus he was able to describe subsequent events as an eyewitness.

In those days most Valley people regarded Josephus as the worst sort of traitor, although present-day Jewish opinion is divided, some arguing that even though he worked to please his new masters, and did describe many events prejudicially, from the Roman point of view, nevertheless he filled in for posterity a large gap in the annals of his time, thereby making an important contribution to history, and often wrote understandingly, even sympathetically, about Judaism and Jews.

When Vespasian returned to Rome to don the imperial purple, he appointed Titus commander in chief with the task of completing the subjugation of the Land of the Jordan.

The last Jewish stronghold besieged by Titus before he began his attack on Jerusalem was Gamala, on the east side of the Sea of Galilee. Even after Jotapata and other Galilean strongholds fell, Gamala held out, relying on its almost impregnable position about a thousand feet above the level of the water. The word Gamala means "camel's hump," an appropriate name because of the shape of the mountain ridge on which the fortress-city was situated. Josephus tells of deep valleys on all sides, of the "frightful precipices" which made an approach from any side "quite impossible." The fortress was further protected by walls, towers and ditches.

The attack was made by three Roman legions toward the end of September, A.D. 69. The Fifteenth pitched camp on a ridge to the east and the Fifth to the north, while the Tenth worked on filling in ditches that had been dug to protect the fortress on the south side. When this had been accomplished, battering rams were directed at three spots in the defensive walls. The walls soon gave way and ironclad legionnaires poured through the three gaps "with a mighty sound of trumpets, and noise of armor, and shout of soldiers." The desperate Jews threw themselves at their enemies and beat them back by main force, while other defensive forces rained down stones and darts from high towers onto the heads of the attackers. To escape these missiles, the Roman soldiers took refuge in a line of houses balanced precariously on the edge of the cliff. The weight of the Romans was so great that one after another the foundations of these dwelling places gave way, and the buildings—as well as their human contents—fell into the abyss. As they did, they knocked over houses on a lower level, compounding the Roman disaster and crushing to death a goodly number of the attacking force. Thus it happened, reported Josephus, "that a great number were ground to powder by those ruins, and a great many of those that got from under them lost some of their limbs, but a still greater number were suffocated by the dust that arose from those ruins."

Vespasian himself barely escaped being killed and finally fled with the remnant of his army to the Roman camp below, while the Gamalites celebrated victory with extravagant rejoicings. But their triumph was brief. Vespasian delivered a speech to his surviving soldiers, telling them that the honor and reputation of the Roman Empire was at stake and that when they attacked again there must be no turning back. Either by accident or because of some clever demolition work, the next day, as the attack was renewed, a high tower on the Gamala wall collapsed "with a prodigious noise." The Romans rushed through the gap in the wall and "everything gave way, and went down before the tenfold fury of the onset—the outer city first, and then the wonderful château itself was taken."

Josephus claims that the Roman victory was achieved as the result of a strange phenomenon of nature. As the defenders were shooting darts down at the attackers, a fierce wind peculiar to this area blew up. "There arose such a divine storm against them (the Jewish defenders) as was instrumental in their destruction. This (the wind) carried the darts which they threw back and drove them obliquely away from them. Nor could the Jews, indeed, stand upon their precipices by reason of the violence of the wind."

The Romans put nearly all the inhabitants of Gamala to the sword, even the helpless women and children. "Five thousand of those miserable people, seeing escape impossible, destroyed themselves; husbands threw their wives over the walls; parents seized their children and leaped madly from the ramparts and were crushed into hideous masses on those yawning gulfs below." So fell Gamala on the twenty-third of October, A.D. 69, after a siege of twenty-nine days. Of the entire population that thronged the city and citadel, only two women escaped.

The fall of Jerusalem on September 26, A.D. 70, is not part of the Jordan story, but it is worth mentioning that Titus had to use fifty thousand Roman soldiers to take the city, which was defended by only twenty-three thousand Jewish soldiers. Caesar had used only twenty-five thousand legionnaires, some historians reported, to conquer all of Gaul and invade Britain.

After the fall of Jerusalem the scene shifted to the Valley again. Now just three strongholds remained in Jewish hands: Herodium, near Bethlehem; Machaerus, the fortress in which John the Baptist had been beheaded, and Masada, on the opposite shore. First Machaerus surrendered, then Herodium. But Masada held out, thus becoming the only Jewish military possession left in the world.

Counting the women and children, there were just nine hundred and sixty defenders of Masada. Among them were men who called themselves Sicarii or Sicarians ("Dagger Men"). All were zealous patriots, determined to oppose the conquerors to the very end and never to become Roman captives—which they knew would mean either being brutally slain, or being sold as slaves. They were led by Eleazar Ben Yair, member of a Galilean family celebrated for turning out warriors.

Using Masada as their base, the Sicarii harried and harassed the Romans for seven years. Then Titus ordered the Roman procurator of Judaea, General Flavius Silva, who had taken part in the siege of Jerusalem, to move against Masada in force and end this final embarrassment to the Romans. Silva went into action at the head of the crack Tenth Roman Legion, supported by many auxiliary troops and a supply force of tens of thousands of prisoners of war who were used to haul water, food, timbers, and other provisions and supplies. From their vantage point on high, the nine hundred and sixty Jews watched the massive preparations to force their surrender. Seeing how much in earnest the Romans appeared, they began to ration their limited supply of water and food.

First the Romans tried to storm Masada, but they were easily driven back. Then they began to make preparations for a lengthy siege. Eight or ten separate Roman camps were established at the base of the great mountain. Then a siege wall two miles long was built around the base and a twenty-four-hour guard was established to make sure that no one came or went from the plateau. Next, on the west side, the Romans began construction of a solid ramp of beaten earth and rocks, leading from the Wilderness behind Masada to the plateau. This was a Herculean task, but because of the immense labor force available, rapid progress was made. As soon as the height of the ramp approached the height of Masada, the Romans moved up the incline an iron-protected siege tower and a massive battering ram. From the top of this tower immense stones were catapulted into the fortress and arrows were fired at any defenders who dared show themselves. The battering ram finally succeeded in making a breach in the defensive wall. The Masada refugees, however, quickly built, at the point of the breach, a barrier of timbers and earth. Josephus, in telling what happened next, reported:

"Silva, finding that the battering with his machines did not produce the consequence he expected, ordered his soldiers to provide themselves with firebrands to destroy the works of the enemy. The new wall immediately took fire, and the flames raged with the utmost violence. But the wind being at north it drove the fire with such rapidity on the Romans that they expected the almost instant destruction of their machines. But just at this juncture, the wind veered to the south, and beat so violently on the wall that the whole of it was in flames in a moment. The Romans, grateful for this providential stroke in their favor, returned to their camp full of spirits, and with a fixed determination to attack the enemy by break of day on the following morning; and, in the meantime, to place strong guards, that their opponents might not escape in the night."

Eleazar Ben Yair knew that the end had arrived. It would be futile to try to throw up new defenses. And there was no hope of relief from any quarter. Just two alternatives remained: surrender or death. For him the decision was not difficult to make. Yet he felt that each of his almost one thousand companions had a right to make his or her personal choice, so he called them together and while the night sky was still red with the fire of the burning wall and the air was thick with smoke, he delivered a speech that ought to be rated as one of the classics of all time. Josephus gives these quotations from it:

"Will anyone who is not destitute of the common spirit of man wish to view the rising of another sun? Nay, would he wish it even if he might live in safety? Can anyone have so little regard to his country, so mean, so contracted a soul as not to regret that he has survived to behold this fatal day? Happy would it have been for us if we had all been sacrificed, rather than to have witnessed this sacrilegious destruction and to have beheld Jerusalem itself become a pile of ruins.

"While hope remained, however, our courage did not fail, and we despaired not of a happy change in our affairs. But as we have now no further reason to expect so auspicious a circumstance, and as we are urged by an invincible necessity to this step we ought now to take, it becomes us to have some regard to our wives, our children and ourselves; and in the plan of our proceedings we should be expeditious, while the means are yet in our power. All men are equally destined to death; and the same fate attends the coward as the brave. Can we think of submitting to the indignity of slavery? Can we behold our wives dishonored and our children enslaved? Nature has not made this necessary; and if the evil arises, it must be from the force of cowardice and the fear of dying when we have it in our power. We had courage to abandon the Romans, to defy those who called themselves our masters, to reject their offered terms of quarter and pardon, and to refuse an indemnity when they besought us to accept it . . . While freedom is our own, and we are in possession of our swords, let us make a determined use of them to preserve our liberties. Let us die free men, gloriously surrounded by our wives and children. And let us be expeditious. Eternal renown shall be ours by snatching the prize from the hands of our enemies, and leaving them nothing to triumph over but the bodies of those who dared to be our executioners."

Josephus indicates that when Eleazar finished there was no great round of applause, only silence—silence for many moments while each man thought, considered, weighed his life in the balance. Finally, however, they voted for self-destruction. The decision was unanimous. When there had been some hope, they had fought. But now . . .

The morning had begun to dawn. The red in the sky from the flames was supplanted by red in the sky from the morning sun. Already, down below, there were indications that the Romans were stirring. There was no time to be lost.

Each man embraced his wife and his children for the last time. A great sound of wailing filled the early morning air as each father and husband stabbed to death those he loved most dearly.

"There was not one man wanting in the necessary courage," reports Josephus.

Next, the men collected all their personal effects, and put them into one great heap, and set them afire. The food and water—a considerable quantity of each—were not destroyed, in order to let the Romans know that the defenders had not been starved into submission.

Now they cast lots to pick ten men for the grimmest task of all. After the ten had been chosen, all the other men lay down beside the lifeless bodies of their wives and children, while the ten executioners went down the line, stabbing the other men to death.

Now the ten cast lots, to see which one of them would kill the other nine. When it was decided, the nine lay down beside their families, awaiting their coups de grâce. When the tenth man was certain that he had done his job well and that all nine were dead, he set fire to the palace of Herod the Great, and then plunged his bloody dagger into his own body and fell to the ground.

It was only a short time later that the Romans down below girded on their armor and prepared for the final assault. They approached the plateau warily. There was no sound but the crackling of the flames. No movement. They shouted a demand of surrender. No reply. Finally two terrified women appeared, followed by five small children. They had horror in their eyes and could hardly speak. Somehow they had escaped the fate of all the others. From them the Romans heard the entire story and from them Josephus obtained a synopsis of the speech their commander had made.

After extinguishing the flames, the Romans went to the scene of the mass suicide and there found bloody confirmation of the story that had been told them by the two women.

"Far, however, from exulting in the triumph of joy that might have been expected from enemies, they united to admire the steady virtue and dignity of mind with which the Jews had been inspired, and wondered at the generous contempt of death by which such numbers had been bound in one solemn compact."

Thus did Josephus, who at heart was as much a Roman as a Jew, try to explain the reactions of General Flavius Silva and his Tenth Legion.

With Masada conquered, the Romans could now claim total victory, and so Titus, the emperor's son, went to celebrate at what had once been the playground of Pan and his nymphs, but now was called

Neronias, after an emperor who was dead and whom many wished to forget.

For twenty days he was the guest of Herod Agrippa at the head-waters of the Jordan. For twenty days in feasting and drinking they celebrated the wisdom, the military ability and the political genius of the Romans. Part of the celebration consisted of performances in the theater of Neronias, during which those in charge "gratified the ferocity of the inhabitants by gladiatorial exhibitions, in which captive Jews were turned into the arena to fight against wild animals."

Sparkling spring water still bubbled from the side of the mountain at Neronias, and the Jordan that had seen so much strange behavior by mankind still followed its serpentine course down to the marshes of Huleh, then through the Sea of Galilee, and finally to the Dead Sea. Nature was normal. To the eye, little had changed. But for the people of the Valley these were sad days. An ominous calm settled over the land. Tacitus, the Roman historian, estimated that six hundred thousand helpless civilians had been slain in the aftermath of the siege of Jerusalem. Hundreds of thousands of others were shipped off to Rome to be paraded like captured animals through the streets in a triumphal procession, and then to be sold as slaves—or to meet a worse fate. It was the same Tacitus who said of his own people, the Romans: "They make a desolation and call it peace."

So there was peace in the Valley now, but an uneasy, unhappy peace. Everywhere in the Valley the population had shrunk. Some villages had been entirely abandoned. Few people were prospering; many were experiencing hunger for the first time. In Rome, Hadrian succeeded Trajan as emperor. After promising the Jews that they could rebuild their destroyed Temple, he changed his mind and decided to make Jerusalem into a great Roman city, Aelia Capitolina, crowned by a new temple, but a temple in which sacrifices would be made to Zeus, god of the Romans, rather than to Jehovah, god of the Jews. Then, in a supreme effort to suppress Judaism entirely, he issued a series of decrees forbidding all the fundamental Jewish religious practices, especially circumcision. More than anything else, these decrees fanned the embers of revolt that had never been really extinguished—embers that began to glow again with an intense heat.

Two heroic-sized figures now enter the Jordan story. Much is known about one; almost nothing about the other.

Rabbi Akiva ben Joseph was an almost illiterate shepherd boy when he fell in love with Rachel, heiress to a considerable fortune. After bearing him a son, she persuaded him to go to school with the child, while she managed the home. At forty Akiva began learning the alphabet. By fifty he had become a respected biblical scholar. At sixty he was surrounded by disciples who listened in awe to his erudite words. At seventy he was considered one of the great scholars of the day, his poverty matched by his profundity. At eighty he was honored for his intellectuality, even by those who disagreed with him. He was almost ninety when he solemnly proclaimed that the Messiah whom all Jews had been awaiting for so long a time had finally arrived.

Shimon Bar Kosiba for more than eighteen hundred years has been a man of great mystery. Even his exact name was in doubt. In the Talmud, in history books, in literature, he was sometimes called Bar Kochba, Ben Cozeba or Bar Kohba. But in a cave by the Dead Sea in 1961 letters on parchment were found settling at least that one question. His name was Shimon Bar Kosiba, although admirers called him, more familiarly, Bar Kochba ("Son of a Star"). Almost nothing is known about his early life, where and when he was born, who his antecedents were, what his early life was like or what he was by profession. It is known only that in A.D. 132 he streaked across the sky like a meteor—and in so short a time was gone. His nickname was appropriate. He has been called a "military Messiah" and "the Messiah on horseback" and, by a Roman historian, "in actuality . . . nothing more than a murderer and a bandit."

There is ample evidence, however, that his personality was magnetic, his enthusiasm contagious, his optimism pervasive, and his ability to inspire blind devotion almost beyond measure. He was a natural-born leader and as he went around preaching defiance of the Romans, he enrolled recruits by the thousands.

It had been sixty-two years since the destruction of the second Temple and the fall of Jerusalem. Few now alive knew about the carnage there had been in Jerusalem, except as an awful story they had heard from eyewitnesses when they were young. But they did know, themselves, that just twenty-two years ago a second revolt had begun in Babylon and had been taken up by Jews in many other parts of the Empire: in Egypt, Antioch, Cyrene, Cyprus—and here. They knew that that revolt had been kept alive for three years, with the final outcome often hanging in the balance, but that finally the Jews had been forced by scarcity of arms and lack of men to capitulate. It was a second bitter defeat. Yet when Bar Kosiba appeared they were suddenly imbued with hope again; with not just a willingness but an eagerness to join his secret, underground army; with hope enough to make one more struggle for their freedom—for their right to worship as they pleased, for their right to be something more than the slaves of an empire whose capital, however magnificent, was nearly two thousand miles from them geographically, and even more distant ideologically, psychologically and emotionally. Rome now was the memory of the great humiliation to which Jews and Christians alike had been subjected. In Rome there were now two great stone reminders: the Arch of Triumph, built to commemorate the crushing of a little people by a mighty empire, and the Colosseum, which would always serve for Christians as an apparently indestructible symbol of bestiality—the bestiality of the spectators who had applauded, even more than the bestiality of the animals that had done the devouring.

The response to Bar Kosiba was one more proof that hope is probably the strongest element in the human makeup. This was where Emperor Hadrian made his great mistake: not realizing that the martyr race would once more rise up in its dedication, as it had before under David and Judas Maccabaeus and under Eleazar Ben Yair.

Bar Kosiba's freedom fighters quietly left their homes and vanished. At first they hid in some of the caves that nature and man had carved out of the cliffs lining the Lower Jordan. Then they began, by prearrangement, to assemble in desert gorges and in other secret places in the Wilderness. Their numbers grew, first by arithmetical progression, and then by geometric progression. The total number of men under arms went from thousands into the tens of thousands, and then into the hundreds of thousands. They had the religious and nationalistic fervor of the Zealots, yet, because of their devotion to a single leader, they seemed to be imbued with an additional quality that made them dare to undertake what had twice been proved utterly impossible.

There is no historic record of how arms were obtained, how men were trained, or where the main centers of resistance were established. But it is certain that much of the action was played out in the Valley and in the Wilderness to the west of the Dead Sea. At first they operated in the manner of any underground army, in any age, in any land, harassing the occupational forces in a hundred and one ways. Many advantages were on their side. Soldiers on a foreign soil are always handicapped. They are not as well acquainted with the terrain as their opponents. They are unhappy to be away from homes and families. They instinctively question the importance of capturing or holding a particular geographic place remote from where they live. From contact with the indigenous people, to whom the land really belongs, they often develop a feeling for them that may be considerably less than the necessary hatred. Most important, they have none of the patriotic fervor that comes from defending one's own soil against theft and seizure by foreign aggressors. And so Bar Kosiba's men harassed and stole weapons and undermined Roman morale, from Dan down to the southernmost tip of the Dead Sea, and in many other parts of Galilee, Samaria, Judaea, and Peraea.

Bar Kosiba's rebels were aware that they were heirs of a proud tradition. Eleazar Ben Yair had been dead long enough to have become a national hero, and his heroic speech of abnegation and decision was already a Jewish classic. He, as well as the very much alive Bar Kosiba, served as inspiration.

Their leader now signed himself, "Shimon Bar Kosiba Nasi al Israel." The Hebrew word *nasi* may be translated in many ways. It can mean simply "chief" or "head," but it was often used, also, for "prince," and in modern Hebrew it is the word for "president."

What gave Bar Kosiba's revolt the greatest impetus of all was Rabbi Akiva's announcement that in his opinion the young revolutionary leader was the long-awaited Messiah, come to lead his people to their final victory.

For the Jews this pronouncement by a man who then was being hailed as the greatest scholar and theologian of his day was almost as influential as the blessing of the Pope would have been for Roman Catholics in later centuries. Akiva was that much respected and revered.

There was now a great increase in enlistments from all groups except the Christians, who were put in a difficult position, for, despite their hatred of the Romans, which was equal to if not greater than that of the Jews, they had already accepted Christ as the true Messiah, so they could hardly also acknowledge Bar Kosiba's claim.

Bar Kosiba was no ordinary underground leader, and his movement was unlike any other underground enterprise in history—before or since. He not only inspired, recruited and organized, but also ruled as if he were a duly appointed or elected civil official, paying precise attention to the most minute details—even concerning himself about whether a group of his people in this place or that place had all the items necessary for the celebration of their various religious rites. He decreed punishments, dispensed justice, tried to settle civil disputes, and complained if exact accountings were not forwarded to him when due. He ruled from his place of hiding with a firm hand, demanding strict obedience of orders, and denouncing in strong language any subordinate commanders who might be derelict in their duties. And all the while his force grew and grew in numbers.

At least one center of the rebellion—perhaps *the* center—was in the Wilderness of Judaea, and so it is possible to imagine streams of volunteers making their way, perhaps from as far north as Dan, down through the Valley to Jericho, and then up into the Wilderness. Many came from the far side of the Jordan, for the geographical limits of the revolution were extensive.

Ein Gedi is often mentioned in the documents of those days. Two of Bar Kosiba's principal lieutenants were stationed in this key rebel spot, which—whatever else it may have been—at least was a supply base to which foodstuff was brought from north and south, and then distributed to the volunteers wherever they were stationed.

No battle-by-battle account of the progress of the revolt has ever been found, and none may exist, even in unexplored caves.

Although the Romans had seen preparations taking place for the revolt and knew about Bar Kosiba, the first serious attacks on Roman strongholds by the freedom fighters took them by surprise. They had underestimated both the size and the spirit of this rebel army.

In response to an emergency call for help, the Twenty-second Legion, Deiotariana, was sent in from Egypt. (At this time five legions in all were concentrated in Judaea.) The Twenty-second was almost immediately cut to pieces by the rebels.

Town after town held by the Romans fell to the rebels. Before long Bar Kosiba's men controlled the entire Valley, from Masada and Ein Gedi all the way to the river's headwaters. Then they took their real objective, Jerusalem. Bar Kosiba immediately made it his capital and ordered work to start at once on the construction of a third Temple. There in Jerusalem he established a highly centralized, extremely socialistic government. He exerted a tight control over the wealth of the area he had liberated, confiscated land when he felt it necessary, coined money that bore his name, regulated agriculture, and rationed food. Many social reforms were imposed by edict. Life in the Valley underwent drastic changes. Now there was bright hope.

It was to be expected that he would incur the opposition of the Establishment. The Sanhedrin, the seventy-one-man Supreme Council, disapproved of him and promptly and unanimously disallowed his claim to Messiahship. Some were annoyed by what appeared to them to be his irreverence. On one occasion, with something less than humility, he had prayed in these words:

"Lord, don't help us, but don't spoil it for us."

By now more than fifty important towns and cities were in rebel hands and there were somewhat over a half million men in Bar Kosiba's army.

In Rome, Hadrian finally began to worry, so he summoned from Britain his most able general, Julius Severus, who was attempting—thus far without success—to put down a revolt of the Celts. The emperor told him that the British situation was a far less serious threat to the empire than what was happening in the Holy Land. Severus started east at once, with thirty-five thousand crack troops. When this fresh army was defeated in its first engagement with the freedom fighters, Severus decided on a brilliant tactic: a scorched earth policy. Wherever his soldiers went they were instructed to put the torch to anything they could not make use of themselves. Thus towns, villages, houses, barns, clothing, furniture, and even ornaments were reduced to ashes. At the same time, all animate objects were slaughtered: children as well as cattle; mules as well as men; women as well as beasts of burden. This might not have been the way to quick victory, but it was a certain way to bring about the eventual destruction of a stubborn race. Or so the Romans thought.

Then, in the summer of A.D. 134, Hadrian himself arrived in the land of the Jordan, with an overwhelming force, and methodically proceeded with the extirpation of the Jews. Jerusalem was recaptured. Romans were soon in control of the entire Valley again. The last great battle of the revolt took place at Beitar (now called Bittir by the Arabs), a hill a few miles southwest of Jerusalem. Bar Kosiba had led the remnant of his army to this place after their loss of Jerusalem. Talmudic descriptions of Beitar and of the battle defy explanation. One reference says that in the village on the top of this smallish hill—a village that today numbers a few hundred inhabitants—there were seven hundred schools, and in each school were seven hundred teachers, and each teacher had seven hundred pupils, thus making the school-going population of the village 343 million, a figure in excess of the total population of the entire world at that time, which is estimated to have been 250 to 300 million.

The description of the blood that flowed at Beitar also sounds slightly exaggerated. Dio Cassius, a non-Jewish Roman historian, who was just as inclined to the use of hyperbole and just as adept at multiplicaton as Josephus, said the Roman horses were "up to their girth in gore"; that blood flowed in a mighty river all the way to the Mediterranean; that 580,000 were killed by the sword alone.

But despite the historical exaggeration of Dio Cassius, it *was* a cataclysmic battle. It was the last time that Jews would fight for their liberty on their own soil for another 1813 years, except for sporadic and localized uprisings.

Hadrian now decided to extinguish forever the hopes and aspirations of the Hebrew nation, so Jerusalem was leveled, with the ancient equivalent of bulldozers, until it was almost everywhere a flat waste. Not on the exact same spot, but somewhere nearby, a new city would be built, and no Jew would ever be permitted to enter it, on pain of death. Even the word Jerusalem must henceforth never pass the lips of anyone. Thus a city would be obliterated, not only physically, not only from sight, but from the memory of man. So the Romans planned. And Judaea would henceforth be called Palestina, after the Philistines, who at one time had been Israel's greatest enemies.

Bar Kosiba himself was killed at Beitar, thus proving that he had not been the Messiah, and a short time later his patron, the aged rabbi who had had such faith in his divinity, was put to death by the Romans in a most cruel manner.

And that would seem to be the end of the story. But it was not. There was one more short episode.

In a series of caves on the west shore of the Dead Sea, between Ein Gedi and Masada, some of Bar Kosiba's people took refuge—soldiers, their wives and their children. It is not certain exactly when they went there, except that it was in the dying days of the revolt. They took with them the sort of objects normal people in any age in any country might have taken: their jewelry, some feminine ornaments, cosmetics, preserved food, domestic utensils, and many documents, such as leases, bills of sale, and deeds. Maybe it was foolish to burden themselves with so many scrolls, so many pieces of papyri, for they, the owners of these documents, would probably all soon be dead, and yet, they were still motivated by that strange human ingredient, hope, and hope commanded: "Take them, just in case . . ."

One proof, in addition to the dates on some of the documents, that they went into hiding late in the war is seen in some of the Roman objects they brought with them: souvenirs, many of rare beauty, that Bar Kosiba's soldiers must have picked up when they captured towns that had been under Roman military occupation or when they attacked and defeated Roman units.

Two of the caves in which they hid were three miles north of Masada, seven miles south of Ein Gedi. They were near the mouth of a great canyon, high up on the face of a cliff, about one hundred and fifty feet below the lip of the summit and seven hundred to eight hundred feet from the floor of the gorge. They could have been reached only by ropes, or perhaps by narrow goat paths that have since been obliterated by erosion. In any case, they were as safe as any hideout that man could have found anywhere, except that some of the refugees may have fallen to their deaths in attempting to get up or down the face of the cliff.

From the openings of the caves Bar Kosiba's people could look out onto the dead stillness of the Dead Sea. It was not a hope-inspiring vista. Their food supply was limited. Soon it began to run out. One by one they died of starvation. As fast as they did, the others would bury the dead bodies under a little sand in the floor, at the rear of the cave. Finally all life in the caves ceased. Now the silence was again as great as ever, in this forsaken spot on the edge of a forsaken sea.

Always, the report that a Roman commander sent back to the Roman senate, after fulfilling a mission, followed a certain formula. But Hadrian's report to the Roman senate on the suppression of the Bar Kosiba revolt deviated from the formula by omitting one customary sentence:

"I and my army are well."

The Roman casualties had been too heavy for him to say it.

Yet, now, at last, the revolt of the Jews could finally be called finished. Even the tiny remnant of that once mighty rebel army led by a man hailed as the Messiah was dead—of starvation. Judaea as a nation had now been extinguished. The illustrious race that had produced the splendor of Solomon and the wisdom of the sages would now be scattered and would become, for the next eighteen centuries, the only people in the world without a homeland.

Almost at once the Lower Valley began to take on a new character. Most places destroyed in the fighting were not immediately rebuilt. Scattered through the Valley now were many ghost towns whose people had either all been killed, or had fled. Few Jews were left south of the Vale of Jezreel. In their place came strangers from abroad—people from many parts of the empire who drifted in and out of the Valley, crossing and recrossing the Jordan, until they found locations that pleased them.

No longer did the Lower Valley at Passover echo with the laughter and talk of crowds of pilgrims on their way south to Jericho and thence into the hills to Jerusalem, to take part in the ceremony of the unleavened bread. In days past they had made their joyful way along the banks of the river and up to the city of peace to give thanks to a kind God for making the earth bloom again, and for having freed their ancestors from cruel bondage. Such pilgrims no longer came. The Temple in which they had been wont to pray was gone, ground to dust, and besides, there was a law now: No Jews permitted here.

Many fled from the Lower Valley to far-off Mesopotamia, because the new Parthian rulers there were behaving toward Jews with tolerance. Others moved no farther north than Upper Galilee, remaining still within sight of the wide green Valley.

Now that all hope of reviving a Jewish kingdom had been killed, the Jewish intellectual drive turned inward, to study and worship. The center for such activity became Tiberias. In all three revolts this city on the west shore of the Sea of Galilee had escaped general destruction. Most other towns and cities in this area had been smashed by Vespasian and Titus, yet Tiberias had been spared, because of its adherence to the Romans. As a reward for this submission, Tiberias had not only been permitted to retain its population and privileges, but in the face of national havoc it had acquired additional wealth and honors, becoming known as a city of refuge. It even had a coinage of its own, one of the most reliable indications of the importance of a city. Hadrian himself, although occupied with the problems of an entire empire, personally ordered the immediate rebuilding of a palace in Tiberias that had been burned during the Bar Kosiba revolt.

Such was the city by the edge of a lake into which the refugees now came streaming. They made no attempt to convert Tiberias into a new Jerusalem. No Temple was built here, or even contemplated. But Tiberias did become the spiritual center of what was left of Judaism. It was strange that this particular city should have been selected, for it had played no role whatsoever in centuries of Jewish history; lately it had been a predominantly Roman city, built by Romans, and named in honor of one of the least distinguished of Roman emperors, and it was technically an unclean place in which Jews were forbidden to set foot. Yet now the Jewish sages and scholars flocked here and soon Tiberias became the seat of great academies of rabbinical learning. A way was even found to explain the name of the city without mentioning the stepson of Augustus Caesar. The Hebrew word for "navel" is *tabur*, and so, they said, Tiberias means the city that became the "navel" or "focus" of Jewish life in the land.

Although the lake had been almost ignored by biblical historians —except in the time of Christ—the sages now began to express affection for it, one of them coining the saying:

"Jehovah hath created seven seas, but the Sea of Galilee is his delight."

Now that the Temple in Jerusalem no longer existed, and now that the Jews were being dispersed, it became necessary, if the race and the religion were to survive, that the tenets of the faith be codified and put into writing. It was on this task that the scholars worked at Tiberias for the rest of the second century. About A.D. 200 they completed what they called the Mishnah, the oral law organized in six classifications: Seeds, Seasons, Women, Damages, Holy Things, and Purities. Here were the rules of life that the good Jew must follow: dietary regulations, civil and criminal law, and rules governing the produce of the field, religious festivals, and the conduct of family life.

After the Mishnah was completed, the sages at Tiberias continued to discuss and debate the meaning and all possible interpretations of the various laws, sentence by sentence, word by word. A record was kept of these conversations and two hundred years later the Mishnah was republished, along with the two-hundred-year running commentary, plus many fascinating fantasies, such as the one about the 430 million school children in the village of Beitar. This monumental work, originally in sixty-three tractates running to many millions of words, is unique; no other religion in the world has ever produced anything even remotely resembling it. It contains such a wealth of intellectual material that it has been compared to a sea in which a student can swim all his life without ever reaching or even approaching the far shore.

The passages dealing with the law, or *Halacha,* contain lengthy and erudite discussions of such fine legal points as that raised in the theoretical case of a woman whose husband died, and so, following Mosaic law, the oldest brother of the deceased married the widow, and then he died, so the next oldest brother married her, and this happened four more times, until finally the woman herself died; "therefore, in the resurrection whose wife shall she be of the seven, for they all had her?"

The passages dealing with *Aggada* or "narration" contain brilliant philosophical discussions of morals, ethics, and conduct.

The passages called the *Midrash* contain sermons that are sprinkled with fables, parables, and wise sayings.

There was intellectual stimulation for everyone in the pages of the Talmud, for the comments on ethics and morality quickly led to a discussion of subjects as varied as astronomy and personal hygiene; economics and poetry. No wonder that men could study the Talmud for a quarter of a century, a half century, and still be intrigued and stimulated by it. It sharpened the wits of its readers and made them better doctors, lawyers, astronomers, businessmen, philosophers, poets, and even grammarians. It can be argued that the intellectual alertness resulting from the introduction of "study" as a part of Judaism's religious routine was the secret of what not only kept so small a group of people alive for eighteen hundred years, despite the lack of a country of their own and repeated attempts at their extermination, but was responsible for their making contributions in every field of human endeavor all out of proportion to their numerical strength.

One of the early scholars in Tiberias was known as Rabbi Meir Baal Haness, *meir* meaning "giver of light" and *baal haness* being Hebrew for "maker of miracles." He was said to have been so brilliant that he "gave light" even to the sages, and his miracles were reported to have been many. After Rabbi Akiva was tortured to death by the Romans, his remains were brought to Tiberias. Later the city became the final resting place of many other great religious and intellectual figures.

In A.D. 199 the Jordan Valley received an imperial visit, from Lucius Septimius Severus, the fifty-three-year-old Roman emperor. This progressive and in some ways amazing monarch kept statues of both Moses and Christ in his private chapel in Rome. During his six years in power he showed great interest in Palestine, especially in the extensive road-building projects his immediate predecessors had inaugurated.

(Although "highway" appears often in the King James Version of the Old Testament, the word is a translation of the Hebrew for "heaped up" and often meant nothing more than a temporary road, built quickly for some state occasion—such as the visit of foreign royalty—by heaping up earth or gravel. In the New Testament, there is little indication of vehicular traffic anywhere in the Valley. The single reference to horses or chariots is to the chariot of the eunuch treasurer of Queen Candace of Ethiopia, who paid a visit to Jerusalem "by chariot.")

Many new villages were built by the Romans at this time to the east of the Jordan, some of them embellished with theaters, temples, aqueducts and colonnades. To connect these new communities and to serve their military, commercial and administrative needs, the Romans built a splendid network of roads on that side of the river. Two Roman-built roads crossed the Jordan in an attempt to bring east-bankers and west-bankers closer together, one leading to Tiberias, the other a repaving of the old Amman (Philadelphia)–Jerusalem road that had already been in use for many centuries.

Under the Romans, Christianity crossed the river and became firmly established even among the nomad peoples, the most notable of whom in these days were the Ghassanites, who had streamed north from Yemen shortly after the time of Christ and had displayed such orderliness and efficiency that the Romans made them wardens of the eastern country. Many Ghassanites were converted to Christianity. They eventually established a civilized and powerful kingdom to the east of the Jordan, extending up as far as Damascus, which flourished for hundreds of years. Many prominent twentieth century Christian Arab families in Jordan, Syria and Lebanon are believed to be descendants of these early Ghassanites.

During the Hellenistic Period, which is regarded as lasting until A.D. 325, when Christianity became the state religion of the Roman Empire, the Valley that had already seen the flowering of two great religions was witness to the outcropping of an antireligion that more than a millennium and a half later would appear to be as powerful an influence in the lives of at least some western men as the two religions themselves.

Anti-Semitism took many forms in the days of its origin. Among upper-class Greeks and Romans in Egypt, Syria, and Asia Minor there was an intellectual snobbism that contended the Jews had no right to consider themselves the cultural equals of the Gentiles. Also, the Jews were deemed to be arrogant in that they refused to give up their monotheism and worship the pagan gods; what was religion for them was called superstition by the Greeks and Romans. Also, Jews were looked upon as a disturbing element in the Hellenistic world. Also, in the Hellenistic cities of Egypt, Syria, and Asia Minor there was a feeling that the Jews had been given more civil and political rights than they deserved. Also, and especially, the Jews served as an outlet for the resentment the unhappy populations felt toward their rulers, yet did not dare express; anti-Semitism became then, as today, a convenient way in which to release frustrations. In two respects, however, this Hellenistic anti-Semitism differed from the present-day disease: it was not based primarily on either religious or economic hostility.

By the time Emperor Severus paid his visit to the Valley it had been sixty-four years since the defeat of Bar Kosiba, yet in all that time the Jews had been denied the right to erect new buildings or even to reconstruct buildings that had been destroyed, but now Severus—and later his son, Marcus Aurelius Antoninus Bassianus (more often known simply as Caracalla)—encouraged the Jews to revive a complete communal life. As a result they again began to prosper economically and flourish culturally, one of the visible signs being the many synagogues they constructed during this period, some of the finest of them in the Valley. On the very edge of the water at Capernaum, close to where Christ had lived in a fisherman's cottage, the Galilean Jews erected an impressive, two-story, white stone synagogue that stood out dramatically against the black basalt of the area. No building in the entire length of the Valley contained better examples of the stone sculptor's art. Besides conventional carvings of trees, flowers, grapevines, seashells, eagles with spread wings, seven-branch candlesticks, and the shofar or ram's horn used in sacred festivals, the Capernaum synagogue contained a curious interpretation of the Ark of the Covenant in the form of a Temple on chariot wheels. Perhaps only by coincidence another splendid synagogue was built about the same time at Chorazin, the town just to the north of Capernaum, also intimately associated with Christ's preaching and miracles. This one was of black basalt, and contained a bas-relief depicting the signs of the Zodiac, and a chair magnificently carved out of a single block of stone, called "the chair of Moses," reserved as a seat of honor for the head of the community.

The Romans themselves were also engaged in a frenzy of building at this time on the west side of the Jordan, the most impressive project of the period being a Roman theater at Beth-Shan hollowed out of the side of a hill, the lower tiers of white limestone, the upper of black basalt. The auditorium, built to seat five thousand people, was semicircular, instead of being completely circular, as were the seats in the old Roman amphitheaters. At Beth-Shan the crowd would be viewing theatrical productions instead of gladiator exhibitions. Another sign of the times was a special section of seats in front of the theater reserved for the elite or for distinguished visitors. On the level of row fourteen of the public tiers were nine exit tunnels that the Romans called *vomitoria*. (*Vomere* in Latin means "to vomit.") The immense stage, all of stone, had a ceiling or roof supported by a row of magnificent columns, topped with Corinthian capitals.

In the rebellions against the Romans the Jewish population of Beth-Shan had been put to the sword, but in the fourth century this Valley city was made the capital of *Palaestina Secunda* ("the Second Province") that included all of Galilee, the Vale of Jezreel, and the Jordan Valley.

One Jordan Valley personality who straddled the third and fourth centuries was known simply as Eusebius, a Christian theologian and church historian who often wrote about the headwaters of the Jordan. One of his books contains this story:

"At Caesarea Philippi, called Paneas by the Phoenicians, there are springs at the foot of Mountain Panius out of which the Jordan flows. They say that on a certain festival day a victim was usually thrown in and that this victim, through the power of a demon, in some wonderful way disappeared. The thing was a wonder to all that were there to see it.

"Astyrius (a pious Roman of senatorial rank) happening to be present once at these rites, and seeing the multitude astonished at the affair, pitied their delusion. So, raising his eyes to heaven, he implored the God over all through Christ to refute this seducing demon who deceived the people, and thus put an end to the delusion of the people. As soon as he had thus prayed, it is said that the victim immediately floated on the stream and that thus this miracle vanished and no such wonderful miracle was ever after performed at this place."

The same Eusebius makes a revelation about the woman who went to see Christ at Capernaum because she had "an issue of blood for twelve years" and had spent all her money on physicians' fees without relief, but was miraculously healed by touching the hem of Christ's robe. Eusebius says she had gone to Capernaum from Caesarea Philippi, her hometown, and adds:

"At the gates of her house, on an elevated stone, stands a brazen image of a woman on bended knee, with her hands stretched out before her, like one entreating. Opposite to this there is another image of a man erect, of the same materials, decently clad in a mantle, and stretching his hands out to the woman. This, they say, is a statue of Jesus Christ; and it has remained even until our times . . ."

A later historian, Theophanes, reported that these statues were smashed in anger by Emperor Julian on a visit to Caesarea Philippi. This was the emperor who became known as Julian the Apostate because he renounced Christianity, forbade the practice of that religion, and tried to turn his empire back to paganism.

By the fourth century Christianity had spread to far parts of the world. One result was that a never-ending parade of pilgrims began to arrive in Palestine, especially in the Valley. Some came without pretext or pretensions. Others were pseudoscientists, amateur adventurers, or writers so unqualified for their task that they accepted fable as fact, exaggeration as truth, legend as actuality. Those who succeeded in having their observations published were often responsible for spreading and popularizing myths, which might live for generations in the respectable guise of truth.

The earliest pilgrims appear to have been more attracted by the

Dead Sea and the Lower Jordan than by the Sea of Galilee—despite its many sacred sites. The first published report of record was by an anonymous observer who signed himself simply "Bordeaux Pilgrim." His visit was in A.D. 335, just a few years after Emperor Constantine had declared Christianity the official Roman religion. He claimed that at Jericho he saw the sycamore tree that the tax collector Zacchaeus had climbed to catch a glimpse of Christ, and the house of Rahab the Harlot, which, he said, was still standing and in good repair. In describing the Dead Sea he said the great difficulty a bather encountered was that "the water turns him over."

Fifty-five years later a Spanish lady identified as Silvia Aquitana, or simply as Etheria, made two expeditions to the Valley. She claimed that Zoar, the only City of the Plain that was spared, still stood, and she reported that with her own eyes she had seen the ruins of Sodom, Gomorrah and the other cities that had been destroyed. The pillar of salt into which Lot's wife had been converted was not visible, she said, because the water of the Dead Sea has risen so greatly that it now covered Mrs. Lot. On her second trip the Spanish adventuress traveled up the right bank of the Jordan, "a very beautiful and pleasant valley, abounding in rivers and trees, for much excellent water was there."

8

It all happened in Arabia, almost a thousand miles to the southeast of the Jordan, yet it had as great an effect, in some ways, on the Jordan story and the lives of the Jordan people as the crossing of the river by the Twelve Tribes of Israel, or the founding of Christianity, or anything else that had occurred—or would occur—on or in or near the river itself.

"The Year of the Elephant" was the way the desert people referred to A.D. 570, because that was the year of an invasion by the Abyssinians, who brought with them the first elephant ever used in Arabia in a military operation. (Ultimately the Abyssinians were defeated, so legend says, because a flock of immense birds dropped boulders on them at a critical moment in the battle: the first aerial bombardment in history.)

On the thirteenth day of the month of Rabia in the Year of the Elephant, an event occurred in the great trading center of Mecca that ultimately changed the course of human affairs throughout most of the civilized world, with the Jordan Valley one of the first areas affected: a son was born to an Arab trader who was so handsome—if one is to believe local tales—that on the night he consummated his marriage, "two hundred virgins of Mecca expired of jealousy and despair."

The father died either just before or just after the birth of the boy, who was given what at that time was an extremely uncommon name, Mohammed ("the Praised One"). Members of the tribe into which he was born, the Quraish, worshiped stone idols, engaged in blood sacrifices, and followed a custom of burying alive a certain number of female children each season. Every village had special gods, inhabiting rocks, shrubs, trees, caves, springs, wells and mountaintops, and all of them were treated with superstitious reverence.

Mohammed's life story has been written by hundreds of biographers and most agree that little is definitely known of his youth, yet this has not prevented Arabic literature from fabricating innumerable legends. One of the strangest tells that one day while the boy was tending a herd of goats, two men, who appeared in white robes bearing a golden platter of snow, made an incision in his belly, extracted his heart, took from it a lump of black, congealed blood which they threw away, then washed his heart with the snow until it was pure white, and put it back. Then they weighed him, with a hundred of his own people on the other side of the balance and found the boy to be the heavier; then with a thousand, and still he was heavier. One of the men finally said:

"Leave him, for if you were to weigh him against his whole nation he would still outweigh them!"

Mohammed, who apparently was subject as a child to epileptic fits, was cared for in infancy by a Bedouin wet nurse with whom he lived on the desert for several years. Before he was six his mother died and he was brought up first by his grandfather, then by an uncle, Abu Talib, both of whom neglected to see that the boy learned to read and write. This did not dim his intellectual curiosity. He was intrigued, for example, by the talk he heard at the great Town Hall of Mecca, where either a fair or a religious meeting was nearly always in session. Often he loitered on the edge of the crowd listening to Jews discuss Jehovah, as well as Abraham, Isaac and Jacob, and Christians telling about miracles performed in the Valley of the Jordan. The Jewish patriarchs became his boyhood heroes.

Abu Talib had a clothing store in Mecca and sold perfume in the harems, but occasionally made a caravan trip to the north, to trade hides, raisins and silver, for oils, perfume and manufactured goods. When Mohammed was twelve his uncle took him to Damascus on such a trip. One biographer declares that on the way they passed close enough to the Dead Sea for the boy to see where Sodom and Gomorrah had once stood. It is not impossible that the caravan went up the east side of the Dead Sea and within sight of the Jordan, but this is unlikely, for other biographers tell of a stop at Bosra, on the Wadi Ez Zeidi, which feeds into the Jordan but is considerably east of the river. If they followed this route they never came within fifty miles of the Jordan.

In Bosra they stopped for food at a Nestorian monastery. Mohammed, being the youngest, was left to guard the richly laden animals, while the men went inside to eat. At dinner Bahira, the senior monk, announced that he had had a vision just before their arrival in which he had been privileged to greet the prophet of Allah, who was recognizable because a cloud hovered over him, protecting him from the burning sun. When they went outside, they found Mohammed thus shaded by a cloud that protected him alone. Then the monk discovered on the boy's back, between his shoulder blades, "the seal of prophecy." Other biographers mention this mark, identifying it as a large brown mole the size of a pigeon's egg and the shape of a pear.

Mohammed's first experience with military matters came when another uncle, Az Zubeir, an army commander, took him along when he went to fight that year's round in a perennial war between the Quraish and the Al Fifar tribes. Each year they fought for a limited number of days, previously agreed upon, and when the period was up declared a truce until the same time the next year, when the war was resumed. Mohammed's task was to run around the battlefield picking up the enemy arrows that had not found their mark and delivering them to his uncle.

Some accounts of his life say that he spent his entire young manhood as a traveling salesman and leader of caravans, frequently traveling back and forth between Mecca and Damascus along roads to the east of the Jordan, and that on these trips he came into close association with musicians, storytellers, poets, philosophers and religious men with whom he would often discuss profound subjects; that he saw the caves in which the lost tribe of Beni Thomud had lived before the time of Abraham; that he visited a town near the Red Sea where the Jews had profaned the Sabbath by fishing on the holy day and as punishment had been transformed into red monkeys; that he was shown caves long ago inhabited by a proud tribe of Arabs who killed a sacred camel that had been in the habit of giving enough milk to feed the whole tribe, and in punishment had all been obliterated by pagan gods. On these trips Mohammed was protected not only by the special cloud that always hovered directly above him, but once as he sat under a withered tree it miraculously put out leaves and blossoms to provide additional shade, and when the sun was especially hot an angel flew over him, shielding him with its immense wings.

In those days the entire Jordan Valley and all the rest of Palestine were included in what was called Syria. Several biographers declare that on these trips Mohammed developed a mysterious reverence for

Syria, principally because it was the land to which one of his heroes, Abraham, had gone to live.

"Joy be to the people of Syria," Mohammed is quoted as saying, "for the angels of the King God spread their wings over them."

When he was twenty-five he came to the attention of a wealthy widow of Mecca, Khadija, who has been variously described as the city's wealthiest heiress, a merchant princess, and Arabia's principal importer-exporter. She had already buried two husbands, one a wealthy merchant, the other a banker. The fortunes they left her she had considerably augmented by her own astute commercial activities, investing money that others entrusted to her in caravans, and when they made a profit she divided it with her investors. Because of Mohammed's reputation for honesty and veracity, she engaged him to take charge of a caravan to Syria. He traveled in her employ for two or three years. Once, as he was returning from a trip, Khadija happened to be on the roof of her home and saw him approaching under the protection of two immense angels who were shielding him from the sun with their wings. Although she was then forty-two and fifteen years his senior, she offered herself to him as a wife, and he accepted. After their marriage they discovered they had had the same great-great-great-grandfather. Polygamy was the custom, but during almost a quarter of a century, until Khadija's death, Mohammed had no other wife. She bore him two sons who died in their youth and four daughters, one of whom, Fatima, married Ali, a son of Mohammed's favorite uncle, Abu Talib. Fatima and Ali, in turn, had two sons. Muslim families in many parts of the world today trace their lineage back to Mohammed, claiming descent from the sons of Fatima and Ali.

After his marriage Mohammed often disappeared for long periods into the wilderness, just as Moses and Christ had done in their time. One day in his forty-first year he went alone onto Mount Hura, a few hours' journey from Mecca, and when he returned home reported to Khadija in great excitement that he had had a vision: in a cave on the mountain the angel Gabriel had appeared before him, holding a tablet on which were written words Mohammed could not comprehend, being still illiterate.

"Read!" commanded Gabriel.

"I know not how to read," he replied.

"Read!" commanded Gabriel again.

Suddenly, miraculously—so he later reported to Khadija—he was able to read every word. The message said Allah was the true god and

Mohammed was his prophet. Gabriel then instructed him to proclaim Allah's will to the people.

Khadija was Mohammed's first convert. She was convinced from the start. Then he won the support of a rich merchant, Abu Bakr, and of Omar, a city leader. Then many aunts, uncles and cousins became disciples. His first large group of non-family converts were Arab slaves. The public at large scoffed at him or stoned him. There were many parallels between Christ and Mohammed. Both were considered radicals by the established order; both were accused of being a threat to the economy of their times. For twelve years in Mecca, Mohammed continued to preach a doctrine of complete submission of body and soul to Allah. (*Islam* is the Arabic word for "submission.") Because the Arabs were divided into many tribes hostile to each other, Mohammed dreamed of becoming, like Moses, a unifier. Because they worshiped many idols, he stressed the first commandment and taught his followers to chant: "There is no god but Allah." Gradually he developed a religious code involving forgiveness, kindness, aid to the poor, protection of orphans, honesty in business, decent treatment of slaves, prohibition of alcohol, faithfulness to promises, and an abhorrence of money lending. His followers scratched the words he uttered on animal bones, dried skins and palm leaves. Eventually this wisdom was gathered together and consolidated in a book called the Koran.

At first the desert people took him for a *kahin* or soothsayer, one of those Arabs claiming to be in receipt of divine messages which they translated into rhymes that they mumbled half aloud to anyone who would listen. Mohammed hardly conformed to the pattern. He neither mumbled, gasped, rolled his eyes, nor performed feats of magic, and his words did not rhyme. For a long time he greatly puzzled his own people.

Once Mohammed brought the Jordan into his preaching, when he made this promise:

"If you follow me you will become princes of both Arabs and non-Arabs, you will be resurrected after death, and you will be given gardens like the gardens of Jordan."

He was fifty-two when the feeling against him in his native city of Mecca became so great that he fled to Medina, an Arabian city which at that time was so Jewish in character—due to the great number of Jews who had settled there as far back as the first century—that it was then called (and has continued since then to be known to the outside world) by its Hebrew name, Medina, rather than by its true Arabic name, Yathrib.

Mohammed's long trek to Medina gave history—or legend—a memorable anecdote. One of his first converts, Abu Bakr, went with him on the flight. To outwit a mob of Meccans who were pursuing them, they hid in a cave. Trembling with fear, the wealthy merchant said:

"We are but two, against so many of them!"

To which Mohammed quietly replied:

"That is not true. We are three, for God is with us."

While they were hiding, a spider spun a web over the entrance of the cave. As the Meccans passed the spot, one of them suggested searching the cave, but the leader pointed to the spider's web, and also to a pigeon sitting quietly on its nest at the entrance of the cave. The crowd understood and went on. Thus the prophet's life was saved.

The Muslim calendar begins with A.D. 622, the year of Mohammed's *hegira* (the Arabic word for "flight") from Mecca.

By the time of Mohammed many people had crossed the Jordan, or been baptized in its waters, or been cured of physical ills by its miraculous power. From the banks of the Jordan, Elijah had been taken aloft by a chariot of fire drawn by celestial horses. But no one had ever had the experience in the sky over the Jordan that Mohammed had. One of his biographers has called it "the greatest and most stupendous event that ever befell any of the posterity of Adam." The details are not in the Koran, yet the legend is believed in its entirety by most devout Muslims.

One morning Mohammed awoke his wife and told her that during the night, while he was sleeping, the angel Gabriel had come and kicked him with his foot, vigorously, three times, and then had ordered him to accompany him. Mohammed observed that it was one of the darkest, most silent nights he had ever known. Neither dogs, owls, cocks, nor wild beasts were making a sound. Even the waters had ceased to murmur and the wind to whistle. All nature was motionless and quiet. Outside his dwelling Mohammed found a white female beast, part mule, part donkey, unlike any animal he had ever seen. It had a human face, the ears of a horse, eyes like stars, and the wings of an eagle. Gabriel said its name was Al Borak ("Lightning"). He ordered Mohammed to mount. On the flight over Arabia, Al Borak confided that he had once flown Abraham on a visit to his son Ishmael— an episode unrecounted anywhere.

When Gabriel commanded the animal to land, Mohammed demanded to know why, and where they were.

"This is Mount Sinai, where God communed with Moses."

The second landing was at Bethlehem, where two voices asked Mohammed to tarry, the second being that of a girl of ravishing beauty. Gabriel explained that the first was "the voice of the Jews and if you had listened, your whole nation would have been won over by Judaism," and the second was the voice of Christianity, "and if you had listened your people would have been inclined toward Christianity."

The next stop was at Jerusalem, where they entered the Temple and joined Moses, Abraham and Jesus in prayer. Then a ladder appeared leading to heaven. Mohammed ascended with the speed of lightning to the First Heaven, made of pure silver, decorated with stars hanging from golden chains, each containing an angel. Here he was greeted by a decrepit man whom Gabriel identified as Adam. In Second Heaven, of polished steel, they met Noah and saw a cock so huge that it was a five-hundred-day journey from its head to its feet. Its wings were covered with carbuncles and pearls, and it crowed so loudly that it awoke the entire universe, except the fairies. In Third Heaven, studded with precious stones too brilliant for mortal eyes to gaze upon, there was an angel whose eyes were seventy thousand days' journey apart. Here, also, was the Angel of Death, entering the names of children as fast as they were born and erasing other names as fast as people died. In Fourth Heaven they met the Angel of Tears, weeping rivers over the sins of the world. In Fifth Heaven they saw the Angel of Fire in whose eyes all lightning originated. In Sixth Heaven they met John the Baptist and Moses, who wept as he told Mohammed that he, Mohammed, was destined to conduct more of his nation to Paradise than Moses had been able to conduct of his people. In Seventh Heaven they met Abraham, who had seventy thousand heads, each with seventy thousand mouths, and each mouth had seventy thousand tongues, and each tongue spoke seventy thousand languages. From there they went to the House of Adoration where they met Allah, with twenty thousand veils over His face, otherwise no one would have been able to gaze upon Him. He gave Mohammed fifty prayers for his followers to use, but later, after hearing Moses' advice that fifty were too many for any mortal man to say, Mohammed asked God to reduce the number to five, which was done.

In all the various heavens Mohammed had noticed illuminated signs reading:

THERE IS NO OTHER GOD BUT ALLAH
AND MOHAMMED IS HIS PROPHET

Gabriel accompanied Mohammed back to Jerusalem, thence to

Mecca. On the return trip they flew over Jericho, the lower end of the Jordan, the Dead Sea, and then northern Arabia.

The claim of the Muslims that Jerusalem is a holy city for them, as well as it is for Jews and Christians, is based on the belief that Mohammed left the print of one of his feet on a rock in Jerusalem, as he vaulted onto the back of Al Borak for his return flight. To preserve the memory of his miraculous voyage through the air, a mosque was built on the rock.

Many Muslims down through the centuries have believed the story literally; others have called it a heavenly dream. One fable designed to prove how miraculous the trip was narrates that as Mohammed and the angel were leaving his bedroom, one of Gabriel's wings brushed against a vase and knocked it over, but the trip to heaven and back was made so rapidly that upon their return Mohammed caught the vase as it was still falling, and before it had struck the floor—even before a drop of water had been spilled.

When Mohammed told his wife of the night's adventure, she begged him not to repeat the story to anyone, for fear he would be derided, but he ignored her advice, only to discover that she had been right after all; he *was* derided.

"It takes a full month for a caravan to go from Mecca to Jerusalem," some of his followers argued. "How could Mohammed have gone there and back in a single night?"

The argument split the ranks of the believers. Abu Bakr, who had once been to Jerusalem, asked Mohammed to describe the city to him and then passed judgment, saying:

"You have spoken the truth!" Then he joined the ranks of those who took Mohammed's word literally.

On the basis of his personal encounters with God's Chosen, Mohammed described Moses as a tall, dark, lively man, with curly hair and a long nose, and Christ as being of medium height, with flowing hair, and a countenance that was so shining, Mohammed said, that He looked as if He had just come out of a bath.

Early in his career Mohammed was a little uncertain what his attitude should be toward war, but later he made each follower take an oath to fight when called upon. He later devised a code about plundering. Whatever loot was taken was to be divided: four parts for the soldiers, one part for Allah, and one part for the Prophet.

Khadija lived to be sixty-six. One month after her death Mohammed married Aisha, the seven-year-old daughter of his convert, Abu Bakr. Although he permitted his followers a maximum of four wives, he now took thirteen for himself, in addition to many concubines. Aisha was described as "the only unspotted virgin in his life." Most of the others were widows. Two were Jewish: Rihanah, whom he married immediately after his followers had massacred a considerable number of Jews, including her husband and other members of her family; and Safya, wife of Kinanah, whom he married after his men had killed her husband in battle.

Now, when Mohammed went on a journey, he drew lots to see which wife to take with him.

Not only had the Jewish patriarchs been Mohammed's boyhood heroes, not only had he been attracted by the gentleness and humility inherent in Christianity, not only did he call Abraham his ancestor and talk often of Moses and Christ, but he saw no reason why Jews and Christians should not accept his leadership in a joint fight against the forces of paganism. When he moved to Medina he also expected the financial support of the great number of wealthy Jews there, who controlled most of the business life of the city. When they failed to show any inclination to abandon their religion for his, he developed a deep hatred of them, finally ordering all of them to leave the city within twenty-four hours or face execution. Many of them put up a resistance but were defeated. Some of the survivors found refuge in Yemen. Others fled north, returning to the land from which they had come. A majority resettled in Jericho. Others scattered themselves through the Valley and in the hills of Judaea.

Mohammed's new militarism began with attacks on caravans going to Mecca. It continued with the destruction of the Jewish town of Banu Kuraiza, where his commander forced seven hundred Jews to dig a deep trench, then to stand beside it while his soldiers beheaded them.

Mohammed's destruction of the large Jewish town of Khaibar had two oddly contradictory repercussions. On the battlefield he married the Jewish wife of the Jewish commander—and at the same time he incurred the undying enmity of another Jewish woman, Zainab, who, in revenge for the killing of all the male members of her family, somehow managed to poison a piece of meat being prepared for the dinner of Mohammed and his friends. The prophet took one bite and then spat out the meat, shouting:

"This bone informs me that it has been poisoned!"

Others in his party were not so perspicacious. At least one of them died.

After confiscating the wealth of Medina's Jews, Mohammed was able to equip an army of ten thousand men for a march on Mecca. It was during the eighth year after his Hegira that he returned to the city of his birth, a conqueror. Within two years he was the supreme leader of all Arabia. Success was indeed crowning the efforts of the illiterate shepherd boy.

But in A.D. 632 Mohammed fell ill. He was convinced that it was a result of the attempt to poison him, even though he had not swallowed a single morsel of the meat. He had a violent fever, burning pains in the head, and a great dizziness. For hours at a time he would be in a state of delirium. Certain that he was going to die, he asked his twelve other wives for permission to have Aisha with him. His child-wife was not yet quite twenty. The others assented. Once he got up from his sick bed, his head swathed in a great wet bandage, and appeared before his followers at prayer. Then he returned to his bed. While youthful Aisha ministered to him, the other wives stood in a circle in the room discussing his illness. Finally they decided he had pleurisy and should be given a certain bitter medicine. He was now in a coma, but they forced some of the medicine past his lips. Suddenly the sixty-three-year-old prophet revived enough to demand why they had done this to him, and when he received their reply shouted at them:

"Pleurisy is one disease with which Allah has not inflicted me!"

Then he ordered all twelve meddlesome wives, as punishment, to swallow some of the bitter potion themselves. A short while later he died, on the breast of his child-wife.

Someone then remembered that he had once said that a prophet ought to be buried where he died, so the bed was moved aside, a hole was dug in the ground, and his remains were interred directly under the spot where he had drawn his last breath.

Mohammed left behind a greatly changed Arabia. He had gone far in abolishing differences of caste, class, color, and racial distinction. He had made humility a virtue, covetousness an evil, and greed a vice. He had stressed ethical obligations and, against great odds, had championed monotheism. When his army took Mecca, he had smashed with his own hands three hundred and sixty idols, declaring:

"The truth has come; falsehood has vanished."

He had established a religion, created a nation, and laid the foundations for an empire. In the sixth century his people had been unknown desert nomads. Now, a third of the way through the seventh century, they were becoming a force to be reckoned with. In the eighth century they would spread their rule across three continents. In the ninth they would create a distinguished civilization.

All this was of imminent consequence to the people of the Jordan Valley, for soon they were to feel, acutely, the effects of this Muslim dynamism.

Since man learned to obtain what he wanted at the point of a sword —or by the use of even more lethal inventions—there have been a certain limited number of military engagements that have settled the pattern of life for a considerable percentage of mankind for the next few centuries. Some historians limit the number of these epochal military encounters to ten or a dozen. Others have a longer list. But all lists include the Battle of the Yarmuk (also spelled Yermouk).

The Yarmuk River, the Jordan's most important tributary, drains the land once ruled by Og, giant king of Bashan, and is fed by numerous streams flowing through southern Syria and the northern part of what in the time of the battle was called Gilead. Before it flows into the Jordan, a few miles below Lake Tiberias, it serves, today, as the natural frontier between Syria and the Hashemite Kingdom of Jordan, and between Israel and Jordan. On part of its long journey westward it flows wildly, impetuously through a great canyon of rocks made black by volcanic action, then the canyon vanishes, the river broadens to a width of thirty feet, and just before joining the Jordan flows through a valley of its own noted for its pleasant groves and for what one geographer has called "the sweet salubrity of the delicious air that wafts over the delightful banks of this pleasant stream."

The battle named after this heretofore unhistorical river grew out of the political and religious ambitions of Mohammed. At the close of the fourth century, the Roman Empire had been divided in half, with the eastern countries falling under the rule of Byzantium, later called Constantinople, now Istanbul. Byzantine rule continued for several hundred years, except for a brief holiday from cruelty, intolerance and persecution—for Jews and Christians alike—during the fifteen years the Persians were in control of this part of the Near East.

The Battle of the Yarmuk was cataclysmic because it was Islam versus Christianity, Arabia versus Europe, the desert versus the city, the East versus the West, the new versus the established. It was a contest between an amazing vitality that had come sweeping up from the Arabian desert and creeping decadence.

Mohammed had had plans for extending his political and religious hegemony, but death put an end to his dreaming and scheming. His immediate successor, Abu Bakr, was busy during his two brief years in power as caliph (Arabic for "one who replaces") consolidating gains already made. But when Omar, in A.D. 634, became caliph, Muslim armies began to sweep northward, like a series of tidal waves. Omar was so committed to the militaristic approach that it was said of him that his only notion of how to deal with an infidel (that is, anyone not subscribing to the beliefs of Islam) was to kill him. Under Omar the building of an empire really began.

Almost every Arab with a horse or a camel was conscripted into Omar's army. Their orders were to fight a humane war. Women, children and the aged were not to be put to the sword, if they agreed to "embrace the true faith and render tribute." But if they refused, "be sure you cleave their skulls." Cornfields, cattle and fruit trees were not to be destroyed under any circumstances.

Bosra ("Tower of Strength"), the city some distance east of the Jordan that Mohammed had visited many times during his caravan days, was one of the first places sacked. Its wealth of merchandise quickly found its way down to Mecca. There were several other small preliminaries to the Battle of the Yarmuk. One city, Arrestan, was taken without any loss of life on either side by a ruse reminiscent of the Trojan horse trick. Omar decided that this Christian city was too heavily fortified to be taken in a normal manner, so he sent word to the local king that his army would be passing that way soon, en route to somewhere else, and he would like to store a few cumbersome articles in Arrestan and pick them up on his army's return journey. After the king had innocently agreed, twenty large chests were left. The next day, while most of the devout Christian population of Arrestan were in church, twenty Muslim soldiers made their way out of the twenty chests, imprisoned the adult population of the city simply by locking the church doors, then opened the city gates to admit the rest of Omar's army. By the time the church service was over, the Christian city of Arrestan had been made safe for Islam.

Damascus was the next goal, but as Omar's soldiers marched north toward that great metropolis, news came that they would probably be met along the way by the Byzantine army of Emperor Heraclius. He had assembled by sea and land, from various parts of Europe and Asia, a force of eighty thousand. Many had been landed at the seaport of Caesarea. Some already had crossed the Jordan; others were already in the Valley of the Yarmuk. There they were joined by sixty thousand Ghassanites, Arab converts to Christianity, who were already on the east side of the Jordan. The Byzantine commander, Manuel, advanced slowly, leading an exceedingly well-armed, heavily equipped force. The Muslim commander, knowing that he was going to be outnumbered, sent a distress call to Mecca, where Omar made a public appeal for more men to fight for "the glory of Allah and His prophet, Mohammed." Eighty thousand more men volunteered and started north. On their way they met five thousand Christian soldiers from Amman, whom they killed to the last man, then decapitated. Not many hours later the new Muslim volunteers joined forces with the rest of Omar's army. Each of the first five thousand men in the column had a Christian head impaled on the point of his lance, which, as one account put it, "was of great encouragement to Abu Obediah." (Abu Obediah was second in command of Omar's army.)

It was now November, A.D. 636, the fifteenth year by the Muslim calendar.

As the hour of battle approached—a battle that would decide the fate of the Near East and ultimately the destiny of a great part of Europe, Asia and Africa—Khaled Ibn-Walid, who had been put in charge of the entire operation, sought to instill fighting spirit in his Arab troops with an address in which he said:

"Paradise is before you; the devil and hell behind you. Fight bravely and you will secure the one; flee and you will fall into the other."

But Khaled had less confidence in the effect of his oratory than in a trick of his own invention. With the Islamic army were many women—wives and concubines of the soldiers. It was natural that as battle lines were formed they were placed to the rear. To the surprise of many, the second in command, Abu Obediah, was put in charge at the rear. As the fighting began, the women, under his direction, attacked any of their own soldiers who showed anything less than enthusiasm for the cause by trying to flee. The women attacked first with words of scorn and reproach. But if such vocal assault was not convincing, Abu Obediah gave them the signal for physical attack. Some of the women had armed themselves with tent poles. After being beaten over the head by a number of tent poles, in the hands of women so robust that they were quite properly called viragoes, most soldiers decided it was better to take their chances facing Greeks and Romans than their own women.

Three times the soldiers of Omar were beaten back. Three times they attempted to retreat. Three times Abu Obediah's viragoes stood firm and forced the fleeing Arabs to turn and face the enemy again. At the end of the first day's fighting, the women became nurses and cared for the wounded.

The second day's battle was as fierce as the first. Seven hundred Arab soldiers lost either one or both eyes as a result of the expert marksmanship of enemy archers. That day went down in history as "the Day of the Blinding." Those who lost eyes were afterward especially honored "and they gloried over their wounds, as trophies of having struggled for the faith." On the second day the women again rallied their menfolk, with words and with tent poles. Some of them even joined in the battle and "smote off the heads of some of the Christian enemy." The battle lasted as long as it was light enough to distinguish friend from foe.

It may be only a battle fable, but for more than thirteen hundred years the story has persisted that what finally gave the Muslims their victory was a fortuitous sandstorm. It began blowing up at a moment when the two armies were locked in deadly combat, when the losses on each side were about equal and when valor too seemed equal. But the Arabs were to the windward of the storm, which meant the sand blew full in the faces of the Greeks and Romans, who ducked their heads, turned their backs to the wind—and to the enemy—or actually quit the fight, because of the cutting sand.

As the Byzantine soldiers fled, some were overtaken in mountain passes and slain. Others were drowned trying to cross the Yarmuk or the Jordan. There must have been some survivors, but history books say that all eighty thousand were killed.

In dividing the loot, each Muslim foot soldier was given one part, each horseman two parts, with a third part for his mount. Arabian horses were assigned a double portion.

After searching the uniforms of the dead for valuables, the Muslims began to bury their own victims. But now a great problem arose. Many soldiers on each side had been decapitated and head and torso were often nowhere near each other on the ground. Because of the lack of uniforms or distinguishing costumes, it was difficult, without a face to study, to tell Christian foe from Muslim friend, and thus to decide whether to bury or not to bury.

Now the Irresistible Tide, as the Muslim force was called, rolled on. It rolled first down the Valley of the Yarmuk to the Jordan, then south in the Jordan Valley in the direction of Jericho and Jerusalem. Wherever they went, the Arabs were welcomed by Jews and Christians alike, for the feeling was almost unanimous that nothing could possibly be as bad as it had been in recent years under Byzantine rule.

The siege of Jerusalem followed no pattern. The Christian garrison had been reinforced by refugees from Yarmuk and other towns taken by the Arabs. During four winter months intermittent skirmishing went on, until finally the patriarch, Sophronios, mounted the Jerusalem wall and addressed a rhetorical question to Abu Obediah, who was in charge:

"Do you know that this is a holy city?"

The Arab commander replied:

"We know it to be the place where the bodies of our prophets lie buried. (He was referring, of course, to the Jewish prophets.) We know that it is the place from which our prophet Mohammed made his nocturnal ascension to heaven. We know that we are more worthy of possessing it than you are, nor will we cease our siege until Allah has delivered the city into our hands, as he has done in other places."

The patriarch offered to surrender Jerusalem on condition that Caliph Omar himself come from Mecca to sign the articles of surrender. Abu Obediah agreed. So did Omar.

Accounts written in the Middle Ages describe the caliph's long trip. It is possible that he crossed over the Jordan at the Jericho ford and went up to Jerusalem that way. He traveled the thousand miles on a red camel, his saddlebags full of dried fruit, barley, rice, wheat and dates, with containers of water dangling from the saddle. He was a simple man. He shunned regal frills, eating with his fingers from the same dish as his attendants and sleeping in a tent of black goat's hair, as the simple desert nomads did then—and still do today. He wore a robe of coarse wool, patched in several places with pieces of sheepskin. Wherever he went he encouraged the people in Muslim-held communities to come to him with their complaints, which he tried to settle.

When he arrived at Jerusalem, his appearance and behavior astonished the patriarch and his followers as well. They had expected elegance, pomp, ceremony. Instead, here was this bald-headed man who seemed to be the essence of humility.

The peace terms Caliph Omar offered Patriarch Sophronios were magnanimous in the extreme, considering what the victor generally did to the vanquished in those times. The people of Jerusalem were guaranteed protection of life and property. (This was a concept virtually unknown in military history up to this time.) The Christian churches would not only not be destroyed but they would be permitted to continue to function. However, the Christians must agree to these conditions:

No new churches would be built, church bells could no longer be rung and the cross must no longer be displayed, anywhere. Henceforth every Christian would be forbidden to: sell wine, use a saddle when riding an animal, shave the front of his head, chant in a loud voice at a funeral, carry a religious image in public, discourage anyone from con-

verting to Islam, give sanctuary to a spy, build a house taller than surrounding Arab buildings, employ as a servant someone who had previously worked for a Muslim, and dress in the manner of an Arab.
Among other requirements: Christians must wear girdles, jump to their
feet if an Arab entered the room, and entertain any Arab traveler who
passed by, without charge for the first three days. Oddly enough, nothing was said in the long list of prohibitions about Jews. Mohammed's
personal and brief hostility toward Jews, which had been for strictly
political reasons, had by now almost vanished from the behavior of his
successors.

The patriarch had no choice but to accept the terms. His relationship
with the caliph was apparently pleasant, even if a little strained, as is
likely the case between the leader of the victors and the leader of the
vanquished. He showed his visitor around the city, but before he would
permit the caliph to enter the Church of the Resurrection he insisted
that respect of God required the Muslim leader to make himself a little
more presentable in appearance. Obliging, the caliph borrowed some
fresh garments to replace his patched and tattered robe. When the
Muslim hour for prayer arrived, the caliph demanded:

"Where can I pray?"

"You may use the Church of the Resurrection," the patriarch replied.

Omar shook his head.

"Then you can spread your prayer mat on the floor of the Church
of Constantine."

Omar rejected that suggestion too. Instead he made his prayers to
Allah on the steps of the church, later explaining to the patriarch that
he had done the Christians a great favor by his action.

"Had I prayed in either of your churches, as you suggested, the Muslims surely, after I left, would have taken possession of the building
and consecrated it a mosque."

Then Omar asked to see the sacred rock said to bear the footprint
of Mohammed. He found the entire area covered with years of rubbish
and debris, which he ordered cleared away. Then he made plans for
the construction on the spot of an unpretentious place of Muslim worship. (It was not until fifty-four years later that the Great Mosque of
Omar was built.)

In the years that followed the fall of Jerusalem, one of the matters
that interfered slightly with the onward sweep of Islam was a quarrel
between Aisha, in whose arms Mohammed had died, and Ali, Mohammed's son-in-law. Aisha, now a mature woman of forty-two, felt she
had been offended by her deceased husband's favorite daughter's hus-

band, so she decided to make war on him, personally leading a strong Muslim force into battle. She rode in a scarlet pavilion, protected with chain armor, fastened to the back of a camel. Before the fight was over the pavilion bristled with darts, arrows, spears and javelins that had been hurled at Aisha by brother Arabs fighting for her kinsman, Ali. The chain armor, fortunately, saved her. Ali won the brief civil war and sent Aisha back to Medina, a prisoner, in disgrace yet still alive. In fact she lived another twenty-two years, until she was sixty-four, which was a ripe old age for a woman to attain in those days—especially a woman who had been married at the age of seven! She died with the satisfaction of knowing that in a hole in the ground under her bed lay the remains of not only Mohammed the Prophet, but also his first two successors. (After the grave had been opened twice—to permit the interment of Abu Bakr and Omar—it was decided to forbid any further burials under Aisha's bed.)

In the years following the Battle of the Yarmuk and the fall of Jerusalem, the young politico-religio giant grew rapidly in power and dominion, and the Great Rift, from the Red Sea up to Syria, filled up with Arabs on the move. The cities of the Decapolis lost their importance. European influence was quickly stamped out. Everywhere the call of the muezzin replaced the sound of church bells. Each day news from places far distant from the Jordan told of more and more Muslim military victories. Finally the empire was extended all the way from the Pyrénées of Spain to India in the east. Two thirds of all Christians were converted to Islam. At one time a seventh of the population of the world professing any religion at all subscribed to the tenets of Islam, believing that Allah was the only God and Mohammed was his Prophet.

Under domination by the Muslims, life improved for the masses in most places they took over. The new culture out of the East made greater contributions to the world's knowledge of medicine, chemistry and mathematics than had any other civilization to date. A new sort of literature flowered. Islam was responsible for the Alhambra in Spain and the Taj Mahal in India. Beauty was not only recognized but created. Some observers even went so far as to say that Islam helped inspire the European Renaissance.

(It has been pointed out that a majority of the great Muslim philosophers, geographers, scientists, architects, illuminators, astronomers and other intellectuals and creators who thronged the courts of the caliphs were Levantine Greeks, Syrians, Persians or Jews, more often than they were Arabs. Nevertheless, it was an empire of enlightenment for having encouraged—or even permitted—the flowering of such a culture.)

And the Jordan rolled on, watching them all come and go. So far, she had been crossed, forded, bridged, recrossed, traversed, bathed in, baptized in, cursed or blessed by Canaanites, Israelites, Phoenicians, Moabites, Amalekites, Nabataeans, Amorites, Hittites, Hivites, Horites, Egyptians, Ghassanids, Persians, Philistines, Mongols, Greeks, Romans, Samaritans, Chaldaeans, Nestorian Christians, Abyssinians, and now dark-skinned men from the south of Arabia.

But the Jordan story was not nearly over. It had only really begun. A great deal more was still to happen on or in or near this river of history.

9

In all the thousands of years of the Jordan's history no single incident outside the Middle East had had such long-range importance to the river and its people as the gathering of high church officials at Clermont, on the edge of the Auvergne mountains in France, late in November 1097. There Pope Urban II called for the recruitment of a papal army to try to recover possession of Jerusalem, city of the Holy Sepulchre. He prefaced the appeal with a vividly descriptive account of atrocities currently being committed by Muslims in the land of the Jordan. ("Even now the Turks are torturing Christians, binding them and killing them with arrows, or making them kneel, bending their heads, to try if their swordsmen can cut through their necks with a single blow of a naked sword. What shall I say of the ravishing of the women?")

The inflaming words Urban II uttered on that cold day in 1097 set off a series of chain reactions which kept exploding for almost two hundred years. Tens of millions of people scattered over three continents became involved, somehow, in the half-dozen military expeditions called Crusades, either as protagonists or antagonists, beneficiaries or victims. The map of the Middle East was redrawn. The social, political, religious and economic life of whole races was revolutionized. Yet the Jordan felt it more than any other single region. As a result of the Crusades, even the appearance of the Valley underwent the most considerable physical change in its history.

It really began long before the council meeting at Clermont, and the man almost as much responsible as Urban II was Abu Ali al-Mansur al-Hakim, sixth caliph of the Fatimid dynasty, one of the strangest personalities in Islamic history. He ascended the throne at the rare young age of eleven. In 1009, by his order, all who were not Muslims were required to announce this fact frequently, blatantly, and humiliatingly. For example, there was no prohibition against non-Muslims using the public baths, but each Christian who did so was required to wear around his neck an immense five-pound wooden cross; each Jew, an immense five-pound wooden frame hung with jingling bells. Part of the Valley and all of Jerusalem were within the realm of the Mad Caliph— as he came to be called—and so when he decreed the destruction of Christian places of worship, the holy city and the Valley echoed loud and long with the crash of sledgehammers against stone. Hakim's destruction of the Church of the Holy Sepulchre was one of the prime acts that inspired the First Crusade.

Another cause was the molestation of pilgrims. Constantine's declaration, making Christianity the official Roman religion, started the influx. They came from all corners of the world, some spending months on the way. Nearly all wandered through the Valley, or at least went down to see the river and visit the place of the baptism. A few put their impressions into writing. About A.D. 680 Bishop Arculf, a Frenchman, dictated to a British monk a report on what he had seen. He said he had found Jericho entirely uninhabited except for one house, which he was assured had belonged to Rahab the Harlot. However, between Jericho and the river were many well-populated villages. The good bishop was especially impressed by the number and immense size of the palm trees he saw close to the Jordan. To mark the spot where Christ had been baptized a wooden cross had somehow been made secure in the bed of the river, with a stone causeway leading to it, so pilgrims could walk out and actually touch the cross, or put a toe into the water.

Half a century later, Bishop Willibad of Eichstatt in Bavaria made a long pilgrimage and reported he had seen two springs named Jor and Dan, that gave the Jordan its water and its name. He also told of the wooden cross to mark the baptismal spot, but instead of a stone causeway there now was a rope, one end fastened to a tree on the shore, the other to the cross, so that pilgrims could immerse themselves up to their necks in the water of the Jordan at the very spot of Christ's baptism, while holding onto the rope. He said most of those who immersed themselves were invalids or barren women, hoping to be cured or made fertile.

In the early days of Arab rule, the Valley had enjoyed an amazing degree of freedom. In Jerusalem the Jews had even been permitted to build a synagogue in the Temple area near the Wailing Wall. But when more and more land-hungry desert tribesmen poured in from remote places, their demands were satisfied by giving them Jewish farms. In A.D. 670 most Jews in the Valley had been engaged in agriculture, but as their land was seized they became merchants and artisans, thus partially accounting for the high degree of commercial and industrial life in the Valley at a time when Europe was still primarily agricultural. It was not at all unusual for most of the bankers, assayers of coins, traders and artisans of a community to be Jews, the physicians and scribes to be Christians, and the Arabs to be the landowners, large and small.

As the complexion of the population changed, so did the degree of safety the pilgrims enjoyed. At first they had had no hesitation about going singly to the holy places, but then they were warned to travel at least in pairs, and finally in large groups, with any straggler being almost certain to be waylaid and, at the least, robbed. Hair-raising are some of the published accounts of what befell innocent pilgrims seeking only to see the spots where holy events had occurred, or perhaps to gain some divine blessing by the reverent act.

Conditions for the pilgrims grew worse after the Mad Caliph destroyed the churches. They grew still worse when the Seljuk Turks, late in the eleventh century, became temporary masters of the Holy Land, and often swept back and forth across the Jordan, or up and down the Valley. They also hated Jews and Christians with equal venom. They massacred with little discrimination or hesitation.

The Valley was especially concerned about what happened to the pilgrims, because nearly all of them, after praying in Jerusalem, went to the Sea of Galilee, to visit the scenes of so many Christian miracles; then to the baptismal spot and the place where the Twelve Tribes had crossed, and finally to the Dead Sea, with the more adventurous even looking at the various possible sites of Sodom and Gomorrah.

The pilgrims were a source of revenue, and not only for souvenir merchants. Brigandage became a major industry in the land lying between the river and the Mediterranean. Bandits hid in every defile leading from the seacoast to the holy places. They seemed to infest every large clump of trees. They were as cold-blooded as they were bold.

A French pilgrim, Hugh de Payen, a Burgundian knight, was so incensed by the attacks which he personally witnessed that he and eight other knights banded together to protect those coming from abroad on pilgrimages. They were granted office space in the Temple area of Jerusalem and thus became known as the Knights of the Temple, or, later, Knights Templar. They took monastic vows of poverty, chastity and obedience, and wore white robes with a red cross on the left breast. The order grew rapidly and was joined by many young knights of wealth and position from abroad. Because pilgrims were often wounded in attacks by Arab brigands, another society was founded, the Knights of St. John, to care for the sick and the injured. Their costume was a black robe with an eight-pointed white cross. Both orders eventually became military organizations, acquired large estates, and built immense castles, some of them in or near the Valley.

But the dangers to pilgrims grew greater and greater, with Urban II in his blunt, almost gory address at Clermont declaring:

"Think of those who have crossed the river as pilgrims. If they carried wealth, they were forced to pay toll and tribute every day, at the gates of cities . . . If they were accused of anything, they were forced to buy their freedom again. And those who had no money, trusting in their poverty—what of them? They were searched, and even the calluses were cut from their bare heels to see if they had sewed something there. They were given scammony (a powerful cathartic made from the root of an Asiatic plant) to drink, until they vomited or burst their bowels—lest they had swallowed coins. More, their bowels were cut open with a sword, their intestines pulled forth and slit, so that what was hidden there could be disclosed. Who can relate this without sorrow?"

And so the treatment of pilgrims was one of the reasons Urban II gave for raising an army to march on Jerusalem.

What was life like at this time in the Valley, and in the neighboring hills that were now sacred to the people of three religions? The Arab geographer, el-Mukadassi, in 985 wrote this obviously exaggerated yet vivid description of life in the Valley city of Tiberias:

"For two months in the year they gorge themselves upon the fruits of the jujube bush, which grows wild and costs them naught. For two months they struggle with the numerous flies that are rife. For two months they go about naked, because of the fierce heat. For two months they play the flute. (This was a reference to the short pieces of sugar cane that the people sucked, which somewhat resembled flutes.) For two months they wallow in mud, for the rains make their streets impassable. And for two months they dance in their beds, because of the legion of fleas with which they are inflested. It is even said that the king of the fleas holds his court in Tiberias."

It was more than a year and a half after Pope Urban II's call to arms that the first Crusaders were seen in the land of the Jordan. The actual number of them was never known for certain. One estimate was that seven hundred thousand started out, but that only a quarter of a million finally reached Constantinople, and many of them were killed, or fell ill, or returned home. By the time the armies reached the land of the Jordan, there were no more than thirty thousand, only half that number fighting men. They were of diverse nationalities, but, more than that, they were of many types. Some were intensely devout Christians whose motive was totally, unquestionably and purely religious—men whose emotions had been inflamed by stories of what was happening to places of Christian significance now in the hands of "the infidel" who was desecrating them. Some of these devout men actually sought the touchstone of immortality through physical contact with the Holy Land, perhaps by immersing themselves in the water of the Jordan.

Others, however, had joined up for different reasons. Merchants, traders, exporters and importers, bankers, and promoters had money they wished to put to work and all had selfish mercenary reasons for supporting an army that might be able to open up new territory for them.

There were young squires and nobles who sought free land.

There were peasants from many countries who could no longer wrest a living from their overworked soil and so had little to lose—except their lives—by joining in this search for new fields.

There were serfs who would become free men if they settled on foreign soil, and criminals who would avoid imprisonment and even execution if they were able to slip through the fingers of the law.

There were wild young adventurers whose imagination had been fired by thoughts of the excitement that lay in store for them in what they had been led to believe was an exotic land of castles, mosques, and harems.

There were even hardened sinners who had been promised complete forgiveness and eternal reward if they endangered their lives in the holy cause.

These were the men who now came pouring in, seeking loot, blood, real estate, adventure, religious inspiration, forgiveness, eternal reward, sanctuary—or even perhaps relief from boredom.

The Jordan during its long history had seen widely divergent types, men of many races, people oddly contrasting in appearance, race, color, creed, occupation, mentality and culture. Yet never had the Jordan seen such men as these. Most of the thirty thousand were unable to converse even with many of their fellows. One of the Crusaders explained:

"Who ever heard so many languages in a single army? We were

Franks, Flemings, Gauls, Bavarians, Lombards, Normans, Angles, Scots, Italians, Lotharingians, Bretons, Greeks and Armenians."

But the confusion of language was not nearly as great as the conflict of character, background, and motivations.

The Crusaders reached the environs of Jerusalem on June 7, 1099. Their first discovery was that the perimeter of the city was much greater than their military leaders had been led to expect. Because of the limited number of soldiers available, it was impossible to surround the city. Bitter disagreement broke out among the commanders about which side was the most vulnerable. A more serious discovery was that the city wall, part of which had originally been built by Solomon out of immense blocks of stone, in order to resist just such attacks as this, was thicker and stronger than had been reported. At first scaling ladders made of palm stems and twisted trunks of olive trees were used, and crude ramps. But such efforts were like mosquitoes biting an elephant.

No battering rams or catapults had been brought; the Crusaders had come armed principally with swords and spears, which were of little avail against Solomon's stone. Wood was needed to build siege machines. But there was no wood in sight. The city was surrounded by what the Muslims called the Valley of the Damned.

Crusader morale was low at this point. Food was scarce. Frequent storms drove sharp grains of sand into eyes that were already sore and down throats that were already raw. Worst of all was the water situation. Cisterns were empty. Streams had been dammed. The Muslims had cut off all possible water supplies. The Crusaders' animals made known their thirst by incessant lowing and bellowing that soon got on the nerves of the distraught soldiers. Then a happy discovery was made. The Muslims had left the Pool of Shiloam unblocked, unpolluted. Half-crazed men fought with each other to get to the water's edge. They also had to beat the animals out of the way. Those too feeble or ill to fight for a place at the pool took handfuls of mud and tried to suck the water from it. Many men collapsed close to the water that might have saved their lives.

Daily the heat grew more intense. Then came the *khamsin* or sirocco, a wind from the desert with such a peculiar barometric quality that it warps the mind as well as it torments the body, even of an otherwise normal man. It blew for days and some Crusaders went literally mad.

Many men, knowing a little about the geography of the area, deserted their units long enough to make the trek down to the Jordan. Some went for religious reasons: to sanctify themselves in the holy water at the place of the baptism, or to pray at this sacred spot, asking

God for victory in the coming battle with the infidel. But others went to slake their thirst or to immerse their bodies in the water for physical rather than spiritual reasons. A few had desertion frankly in mind. Raymond of Aguilers tells it bluntly:

"Despairing of God's mercy, some of the men went to the plains of the River Jordan, collected palms, and were baptized in its waters. They did so chiefly with the intention of abandoning the siege, to go home by whatever means they could."

The Crusaders had had many disillusionments so far. Those who had been fed on stories of an exotic land romantically different from anything they had known at home found the difference principally in the excessive heat, filth, squalor and privation of this semidesert place. The great wall of Jerusalem was impressive, but from what they could see, on the outside looking in, the towered city was not much like the one that had been pictured in paintings or even in the imagination. And now came the shock for many of discovering the truth about the Jordan.

June is one of the worst months of the year to see any river in the Middle East—especially the Jordan—for the flow is feeble, the width slight, the depth shallow, the color not especially attractive, and the temperature tepid, except at its very sources. In June the Jordan is not a river to inspire poetic rhapsodies, or to give pleasure to those merely seeking relief from the heat. Yet many made the trip from Jerusalem down to Jericho and thence to the Jordan. At least they were able to clean the dirt from their filthy bodies, while some, at the spot where the wooden cross was still implanted in the middle of the stream, found spiritual cleansing as well.

The Valley was also visited by searching parties sent there by military commanders to scout for timber. Much wood was needed to construct siege machines large enough and powerful enough to breach the Jerusalem wall. Some scouts went up into the hills on the hunt for large trees, others down into the Valley looking for whatever they could find, even slim saplings.

It was the end of June before enough timber had been brought in to begin construction of the war machines. Some was hauled by mules and camels; some on the backs of men. Soon siege towers three stories tall were ready, as well as catapults that hurled great boulders—an eleventh century version of heavy artillery.

Details of the successful attack on Jerusalem's walls have little to do with the Jordan story. At 9 A.M. on July 15, ten thousand Crusaders went through the gates of the Holy City, after the war machines had breached the wall. But what then happened is of definite concern to the river. The story was first told by a few refugees from the horror that was Jerusalem on that awful day, and it was retold for decades and centuries. They had fled from carnage such as the Land of the Jordan—in all its bloody history—had never known. Harold Lamb, a chronicler whose account is largely sympathetic to the Crusaders, gives an idea what happened when the blood lust was finally unleashed:

". . . and the Crusaders ran into the houses, cutting down the wailing women who shrank back from them. Behind them lay the broken bodies of children and young girls lying with sightless eyes. Blood dripped from the stairs and stained the white walls . . . The hour of retribution had come, and death for the unbelievers . . . the horsemen (Crusaders) slashed with axe and swordblade until the fountains turned red and frantic horses slipped upon the hot, wet stones and fragments of human flesh . . . Old men stood, with the calm of fatalists, and saw the heads of their sons roll to the musty carpets. They in turn were struck down, their skulls shattered by axes or their bowels cut open by a sword's edge. Women clung to their bending knees, screaming and panting, until steel wrenched open their soft bodies and they cried out no longer . . . The Crusaders rode through human blood above the fetlocks of their horses. Blood splashed the knees of the horses and the reins . . . utterly weary they put down their weapons and washed their hands and arms. Taking off their armor, they put on clean mantles and walked through the littered streets (littered with bodies of the men, women and children they had slain) to the narrow entrance of the little Church of the Sepulchre. The anger had left and they were filled with happiness . . . Surely God had willed it."

But the next day new throngs of Crusaders entered the city and the slaughter began again. "The streets were obstructed by piles of bodies that had lost all human semblance. Horses trampled on severed hands and heads in the gutters . . ."

What this chronicler does not tell is that although the Crusaders' war was against the infidel Muslim, the Crusaders also unleashed their fury on the relatively few Jews present in Jerusalem, who had been innocent bystanders in all that had happened. Down by the river's edge, other Jews huddled in terror as they heard the story of what had been done to their kinsmen who had been trapped inside the wall that Solomon had originally built. It was a tale of horror almost beyond belief. On the blood-drenched day of July 15, 1099, at about 9 A.M., the Crusaders herded all Jews, Karaites and Rabbinites, into the synagogue near the Temple area, then barred and locked the doors, and set fire to the building. No one escaped. The smell of burning human flesh permeated the area for hours.

Now that the stated objective of the Crusade had been achieved, official leave was given to soldiers and officers to make authorized pilgrimages to Jericho and the Jordan. By the thousands they streamed down to the river's banks. It was at this time that a tree covered with sharp thorns received the name it has carried ever since, *spina Christi* ("the thorns of Christ"), for the Crusaders were sure that it was from branches of such trees that the crown of thorns must have been made that was placed on Christ's head.

Baptism is a rite normally performed only once in a person's life, but during these Crusader days a strange new custom was inaugurated —of being rebaptized, regardless of age, in the Jordan. Raymond of Aguilers wrote:

"We proceeded to dress only in a shirt and new breeches, as we had been commanded about baptism . . ."

After recovering from their terror over what had happened, many who dwelt along the Jordan decided to commercialize on the desire— apparently almost as strong eight hundred and sixty-six years ago as it is today—for souvenirs. They sold the Crusaders bouquets of reeds gathered on the edge of the Jordan, and containers of Jordan water, and even plaited branches of *spina Christi*. (Some of the Crusaders, to save money, tried breaking off branches of the thorny tree themselves and got well scratched for their trouble.)

Before returning home many soldiers took the time to go down the Valley to the Dead Sea. One who made the trip, Fulcher, a French historian attached to the Crusades as the counterpart of a modern war correspondent, wrote:

"Verily here is now the great lake, which they call the Dead Sea because it does not rise. It is so salt that no animals will drink it; nor will birds. I, Fulcher, made trial of it, climbing down from my she-mule and drawing some water up in my hand. I tasted it and found it more bitter than hellebore. Nor is it easy, even by force, to submerge anything in its depths.

"I believe that this saltiness of the lake comes from one of two causes. Near it rises a solitary mountain, great and high and encrusted with salt. Either rainfall, streaming down the ravines of the mountain, brings the salt, or an underground channel . . .

"Circling the south of the lake we found a village most pleasantly situated and abounding in the fruit of the palm, which they call dates— which we ate all day and enjoyed. We came upon other remarkable things there. The Saracen inhabitants had fled, except some people blacker than soot, whom we spared to carry loads of seaweed from the lake. Among the trees I saw some bearing apple-like fruit. However, when I gathered them, wishing to know what sort they were, I found when the shell was broken only a kind of black dust out of which puffed a lifeless black smoke."

The Crusaders' visits to the Dead Sea revived the Sodom-Gomorrah mystery. The one wicked city that was saved, at the specific request of Lot, is called Zoar in the Bible. Although there is no trace today of Zoar and archaeologists have no positive knowledge where it was, apparently it was still standing in 1099 and was called Zughar, or Aughar or Sukar. One account says:

". . . the neighboring people call the town Sakar, i.e., Hell; its water is execrable; no place is equal to it in evil climate; its people are black-skinned and thick-set; its waters are hot, even as though the place stood over hell-fire; its trade is lucrative . . . much arable land . . . and its markets are greatly frequented. The Arab writers identify it with Lot's Zoar. Crusaders knew the place as Segor, but themselves called it Palmer." (With all its other names how it came to be called Palmer is not explained.)

In the record of the Crusades, this part of the world is officially called *Terra Sancta* ("the Holy Land") yet the men who took part called it *Outremer,* a French expression meaning "Beyond the Sea" that became popular even with those who spoke no French. Outremer officially extended only to the Jordan.

As word reached Europe that Jerusalem had fallen, those who had been too old, too young, too ill, or too little interested in things military to join the armies of the Crusaders now came on pilgrimages from all points of the compass, and soon the Valley was teeming, the river at times being so crowded with holy bathers that they had to await their turn to immerse themselves. The pilgrims now included ladies in bright cloaks and rich people with servants, as well as black-robed monks and poor people who carried all their worldly possessions in a small bundle.

By now most of the Crusaders had had enough. Like any soldiers in any epoch, after the war's end their principal desire was to return home. Most did. They had endured hardships beyond their own previous imagination. They had fulfilled their vows and they knew fresh recruits were on the way to take their places. Finally only two hundred soldiers of the original liberating force remained. They called themselves "the Exiles."

Gradually for many Valley dwellers life returned to something approaching normal. Caravans began to stream across the river at the various fording places. Trade was lively now. Armenians and Syrians appeared with olives, dried figs, silk, cotton and glassware to sell. Once more the Jerusalem-Jericho district began exporting cotton, sugar cane and other products of its soil. Down from Damascus streamed pack animals loaded with carpets and manufactured goods. A truce was signed with some of the coastal cities still in Muslim hands and trade agreements further accelerated the flow of goods.

Week by week the number of pilgrims increased. Three years after the capture of Jerusalem a convoy of thirty ships—many loaded with pilgrims—arrived in Jaffa harbor just as a storm broke. Twenty-three of the vessels were wrecked and the shore was strewn with the bodies of more than a thousand victims. One of the survivors, signing himself merely Saewulf of Worcester, left a lurid description of conditions in Outremer. It took him two days and two nights of hard travel to make his way from the coast to Jerusalem and he found the route lined with decomposed or partially decomposed bodies of Christian pilgrims who, he surmised, had been slain by Saracen robbers.

As soon as the military had finished its work by planting the Crusader flag along the coast and over many inland cities, those with an economic interest in the Crusades assumed control. The occupied territory was divided between a number of powerful European barons and princes, who established a system of rule and exploitation known as feudalism. On some commanding height, each lord built a castle, partly as a regal dwelling place, but principally as an impregnable fortress— a substantial way of announcing to one and all that the Crusaders, now here, intended to remain.

The villages round about each castle supported his lordship through the payment of taxes. Taxation laws varied from area to area, but a common rule was that each peasant paid to his lord one third of the profit from his land, besides certain extras in the form of eggs, cheese, fowls and animals. There were also head taxes, import and export duties, tolls for the use of certain roads, and taxes on manufacturing. In return, the peasants were supposed to be protected from harassment by the vassals of any other feudal character. If an argument broke out between rival barons, the peasants were conscripted to give their services and often their lives in a quarrel they might not in the least understand.

Most of the Jordan Valley on the west side of the river fell to a feudal baron who called himself the Prince of Galilee and the Lord of

Tiberias, while the Dead Sea area and the territory across the Jordan were given to the Lord of Mont Réal.

Just as the Gothic cathedrals of western Europe were the principal architectural contribution of a certain age, and the American skyscraper of another age, so the particular architectural contribution at this time and in this place was the great stone Crusader castle. No two were exactly alike, yet all were impressive, if for no other reason than because of their bulk, and the sense of permanency and solidity they inspired. They were as remote in architectural concept as possible from the delicate beauty of a minaret, or the sparkling white charm of the Taj Mahal.

Soon after the end of the fighting, tens of thousands of men were conscripted for work on these massive edifices that began to crown the rocky summits of isolated hills all the way from Shobek, considerably to the south of the Dead Sea, to Antioch, in what is now Turkey. The Valley received its full share of them, for not only was this an area well worth exploiting, because of its water and fertility, but if Outremer was to be held, the Valley must be held, so the military routes that crossed the Jordan were of vital importance.

The easternmost castle was at el-Kerak, three quarters down the east side of the Dead Sea, on the route used by caravans going north to Damascus, and by religious Muslims going south on the pilgrimage to Mecca that each person is supposed to make at least once in his life. In French this spot was called *La Pierre de Desert* ("the Stone of the Desert"). English-speaking Crusaders nicknamed el-Kerak "the Crack of the Desert." It was a massive building with a great square tower. Its subterranean passageways, with high vaulted ceilings, were masterpieces of medieval construction. The great wall of el-Kerak was twenty-six hundred yards in circumference and enclosed an entire Arab village, as well as churches, a convent, a mosque, the castle itself and many sub-buildings. From el-Kerak a road was built not only to the Dead Sea but all the way up to the Jericho crossing of the Jordan. Proof that there was considerable shipping on the Dead Sea at this time is extant documentary evidence that the castle of el-Kerak had the right to impose a shipping tax on each vessel each time it put in to a Dead Sea port.

Of even greater strategic importance was the castle called Kaukab al-Hawa by the Arabs, and Beauvoir or Belvoir by the Crusaders. It was built on the west side of the Jordan at a great altitude just a few miles south of the Sea of Galilee, to guard the entire Valley, in both directions. It boasted one of the most beautiful views the Holy Land offered. From its magnificent height much of the Jordan Valley could be seen. From up there, 1020 feet above sea level, Lake Tiberias seems a resplendent green gem, in a setting of dark gold.

Castles were built on many other heights overlooking the Valley, as well as on the edge of the lake, and on the Jordan itself at the only point in its entire length where the river flows for a brief distance at exactly sea level.

As soon as the castles were even partially completed, life took on great glamour for the feudal barons. This was a period of prosperity, in which they had the best of two worlds: from the East came fine silks, rare perfumes, precious stones, delicately fabricated jewelry, exotic spices, rich brocades, each caravan bringing new wonders and delights; from the West, shipments of a more practical nature. The men spent much time at indoor and outdoor sports. Hunting was a popular pastime and many of the titled gentlemen kept falcons.

Most of the castles had open courts containing fountains, Greek and Roman sculpture, and a wealth of mosaics.

Between the feudal lords there was rivalry over which could entertain in the most spectacular manner. Betrothals, weddings, hunts, and even birthdays were excuse enough for celebrations that kept members of this new Valley aristocracy rushing from event to event, from castle to castle—from the headwaters of the Jordan to the lower end of the Dead Sea.

One contemporary account said:

"We who had been westerners now became easterners . . . We are beginning to forget the places of our birth. We have homes here and servants; many have taken wives . . . some already have grandchildren here. Those who had spoken different languages now use the speech of all. One cultivates vines, another the fields. Many who had been poor at home are now rich."

There was periodic military action, sometimes in the Valley itself. The fortress at Banias changed hands several times, with bloody battles being fought once more on the slopes of Mount Hermon. In 1157 there was a battle near Lake Huleh. Later there was fighting on the banks of the river itself, near where the Bridge of Jacob's Daughters would later be built. Twice the Crusaders went over the Jordan to attack Bosra, the rich commercial city to which Mohammed had been taken as a boy by his uncle. Both times the Muslims managed to recapture it. But in general it was a period of calm and peace, at least compared with some of the bloody eras the Jordan had previously seen.

One of the most vivid characters in the entire long Jordan story was thrust up by history at this period, and for a brief time played a dominant role in shaping the future, not only of the Valley and Outremer, but of the entire Middle East. He was an "infidel" by Crusader terminology and yet many Christian writers, after it was all over, paid him higher tribute for his bravery, his military brilliance, and his honesty than they bestowed on their own heroes.

The Crusaders called him Saladin ("Honor of the Faith"). In Arabic his name was Yusuf ibn-Ayyub Salah-ed-Din. He was a Kurd from distant Mesopotamia. Both his father and an uncle had been generals, Saladin himself rose quickly through officer ranks until at the age of thirty-three he was made sultan of Egypt and four years later sultan, also, of the extensive area called Syria. The primary achievement of his career, from the Muslim point of view, was that he brought about in the Islamic world the greatest unity it had known up until that time—and perhaps since. Also, he was looked upon as one who exemplified in his own person all the highest virtues of Islam. They respected him for his piety, sense of justice, wisdom, and excessive humanitarianism. During his time not only were his Muslim subjects relatively happy and prosperous, but so were hundreds of thousands of Jews who lived under his rule—Jews who heretofore had been persecuted by both Muslims and Christians, yet now found asylum and a certain amount of fair treatment in Saladin's realm.

Some of his followers believed that Allah had granted Saladin a charmed life. He came close to death many times, once at the hands of a secret brotherhood called the Assassins, an organization of fanatics that had its origin in the streets of Cairo but spread up through the entire Middle East, including the Valley, until there were members even in Persia. They removed their enemies by the use of the dagger, after bolstering their courage with hashish. They were therefore called *Hashishin,* or "users of hashish," and from hashishin ultimately came the English word "assassin." They warned each prospective victim by leaving two loaves of bread by his head while he slept. This was an invitation to meet all demands for tribute or be visited by an execution squad. The Assassins, operating in groups of three, would disguise themselves as beggars, camelmen or merchants, hiding their long knives under their cloaks. The first would make an attempt at swift murder. If he failed, the second would rush up and in the confusion attempt a deathblow. If he also failed the third would emerge from hiding and do the killing. Those Assassins who performed exceptionally daring deeds were rewarded by a visit to a mountaintop in

Persia where the master of the order lived in a paradise of women, song and exotic splendor.

When the attack was made on Saladin, the first and third Assassins were intercepted by guards, while Saladin himself, although wounded, grappled with the second until assistance came.

One of Saladin's most bitter opponents was the châtelain of one of the Valley's great châteaux, Raynald de Châtillon, who had been captured by the Saracens in a minor engagement in 1159 and had been held prisoner for seventeen years. Upon his release he married Stephanie, a beautiful woman whose husband had died, leaving her not only the castle of el-Kerak, but also one at Mount Royal farther south. Raynald at once began building a Red Sea fleet to harass Saladin's shipping, with the ultimate objective of attacking Mecca. When most of his ships were captured by Saladin's sailors, he turned from buccaneering to brigandage, making frequent raids on the caravans that passed his castles on their way to and from Damascus. In 1183 Saladin sought to put an end to this harassment by ordering a full-scale attack on el-Kerak. It happened that at the time the castle was full of musicians, jesters, and guests attending the marriage of Raynald's stepson to the daughter of the king of Jerusalem. One legend has it that the timing of the attack was entirely accidental; that Saladin was unaware of the wedding feast; that when he was told in which tower the bride and the bridegroom had taken shelter he ordered that they remain unmolested.

In 1185 famine swept most of the Middle East, so Saladin and Raynald made a four-year truce. The lord of el-Kerak kept his word for one year. Then his spies informed him that on a certain day an especially rich caravan would be passing by and that one of the passengers would be Saladin's sister, so he ordered an attack.

In Islamic law there is provision for what is called a *jihad,* or "holy war." Any soldier killed while serving Allah during a jihad is supposed to go immediately to his heavenly reward, no matter how great the sins he may previously have committed, and without having to await the judgment day. Goaded by Raynald, Saladin now declared a jihad against all Christians in the Holy Land. At the same time he took a personal vow: death for Raynald.

For almost a year Saladin bided his time. Then, during the early summer of 1187, he personally led twenty thousand Muslim soldiers across the Jordan just below the Sea of Galilee and attacked the city of Tiberias. The small body of Templars and Hospitallers defending the seaport were cut to pieces.

At this point one of those colossal military blunders was committed that can—and in this case did—change the history of the world. The king of Jerusalem—the ranking monarch of the entire Crusader empire —was a headstrong young man named Guy who had gained the throne a year earlier by a clever marriage. Realizing that a crucial battle was shaping up, he dispatched the Crusaders' entire military might to the north. Encampment was made about fifteen miles due west of Tiberias, close to the abundant springs of Tsipori (Sepphoris), which during the first four centuries A.D. had been the largest and most important city in Galilee, home of many celebrated Talmudic scholars, seat of several great academies, and spiritual center of the Jewish people. The name of the city was said to have been derived from *tsipor,* Hebrew for "bird," because the city was perched like a bird on the mountaintop. (The Arabs called it Saffuriya, and on Roman coins it was Dio-caesarea.)

The two armies that soon were to clash were about equal in strength, for nearly twenty thousand Crusaders were encamped by the springs of Tsipori.

Among the feudal barons there were many jealousies, even bitter animosities, the greatest feud being between Raymond III, Count of Tripoli and Lord of Tiberias, and Raynald of el-Kerak. Raymond cautioned King Guy against taking too great a risk at this particular time and in this particular place. Raynald insisted that the entire Crusader army be sent immediately on a forced march across the waterless hills that lay between Tsipori and Tiberias. King Guy took Raynald's advice. In a wasteland just south of the two-pronged mountain called the Horns of Hittin, because it resembles the profile of an animal's head, Saladin's men were waiting.

The battle began on July 2, 1187, and lasted just three days. Many of the Christian soldiers wore heavy armor that protected them against the missiles of the enemy yet greatly accentuated their suffering from the weather. The metal drew the heat like a magnet and became blisteringly hot to the touch. Both sides had cavalry units. The clouds of dust stirred up by the horses made the air so thick it was almost impossible for men or beasts to breathe. Parched throats were as raw as if they had been sandpapered. Just a few miles below, the soldiers could see the sparkling blue of two lakes, Huleh and the Sea of Galilee, connected by a ribbon of cool-looking green—the Jordan. Some of the Christian soldiers had bathed at one time or another in the river or the lakes. They knew how refreshing the water could be.

Nature now played a cruel trick: a sirocco began to blow, adding mental depression to physical suffering.

July in this region is the hottest, driest month of the year. The earth is so scorched that all nature seems dehydrated and brittle to the touch. At the spot where the two armies met, the ground was covered with a deep carpet of dead grass and dry reeds. One of the Saracen commanders, seeing that his troops were windward of the enemy, conceived a brilliant tactic: he ordered his men to set fire to the undergrowth. The sun already was imposing a temperature almost beyond the endurance of the Christian soldiers. The fire augmented it by a few more degrees. Even worse, the acrid smoke that was driven into the faces of the Christian soldiers by the sirocco blinded them temporarily and made them gasp for breath. Foot soldiers dropped their weapons, broke ranks, and fled. Knights, in armor that was now impossibly hot, tried to get out of their metal uniforms, even if it meant certain death from enemy missiles. Here and there a valiant group tried to resist sword, sun and smoke, only to be ridden down by Saracen cavalrymen, swinging their great scimitars.

In Galilee, where Christ had spent so much of His ministry preaching His philosophy of pacifism, a Christian army that had taken to the sword perished by the sword on this hot summer afternoon.

One report of the debacle said:

"As a result of a frivolous decision, born of long-standing animosities, a splendid army was annihilated."

Among the few prisoners taken were Raynald and King Guy. Saladin had Raynald brought to his tent and after rebuking him at great length for his treachery, made him a sporting proposition: if he would renounce Christianity and convert to Islam, his life would be spared. When Raynald refused, he was executed. One account says that Saladin himself administered the coup de grâce.

Summarizing the defeat, the Reverend George Adam Smith, British ecclesiastical authority on the history and geography of the Holy Land, used these caustic words:

"A militant and truculent Christianity, as false as the relics of the 'true cross' round which it was rallied, met its judicial end within view of the scenes where Christ proclaimed the Gospel of Peace, and went about doing good."

Dr. E. W. G. Masterman, writing in 1905 in the *Biblical World,* a Christian publication, referred to the men defeated at Hittin as "a corrupt power aggressively flaunting a cross, the essential teaching of which it despised . . . "

Because King Guy had made the colossal error of committing almost his entire military strength in the Battle of Hittin, and because this force was annihilated, Saladin had little trouble taking over the other Crusader holdings. Jerusalem fell that autumn. One by one the castles surrendered. Finally only Belvoir, perched so high above the Valley, held out, her red banner flying defiantly from her battlements over an otherwise Saracen world. After eighteen months of heroic resistance, Belvoir too finally fell, in January 1189.

The wealthy Franks bought their freedom and left for Europe. Only those too poor to pay the asking price were forced to remain.

There were other Crusades, either eight or nine in all, depending on which authority makes the count, but the invaders never again got into the Valley. The story of the Crusades, as far as that story affected the Jordan, was over, although the truce that Saladin and Richard the Lion-Hearted signed permitted Christian pilgrims to visit Jerusalem, some of whom, of course, found their way to the river.

The account of a post-Crusade pilgrimage made in 1232 by a German Dominican named Borcard or Burchard gives an indication of what was already happening in the Valley. He described Capernaum as "once a noble city, but now an exceedingly mean one, scarcely containing seven houses of poor fishermen." The entire Dead Sea area by his time had already become a place of desolation, except for Ein Gedi, with its "exceedingly noble vinestocks."

An era had ended. Solomon's Jerusalem was no more. The Greco-Roman cities of the Decapolis were on the road to oblivion. Beth-Shan and Jericho, once so magnificent, would never be so again. Dark days were ahead for the Valley.

10

Strange people poured through the Valley during the thirteenth century: Mongols, Kwariziminians, Tatars, Mamelukes, Turks. Their arrival helped put an end to an empire that had given the world many magnificent cities, had honored learning, encouraged scholarship, developed distinctive artistic and architectural forms, and spread the knowledge of other races, such as the Hindu system of numbers and the Chinese secret of paper. The Muhammadan Empire would not die quickly; empires seldom do. But the end of the golden Muhammadan Age was precipitated by Genghis Khan, who, with little show of modesty, announced that he had been commanded by "the eternal blue sky" to conquer the world—a command he came very close to obeying.

Genghis Khan died in 1227, before he could get as far as the Holy Land. The role he did not live to play in the Jordan story was acted out by a grandson, Hulagu Khan, brother of Kubla Khan, known to most English-speaking people because of a single line in a celebrated poem. Hulagu's first accomplishment was wiping out the Assassins, who in his day were still the greatest band of international criminals the world had ever known. Then he and his horde swept down in the direction of the Mediterranean and the Red Sea. (It is significant that Mongolian soldiers are seldom called an "army" or a "tribe"—always a "horde," indicating how loosely organized and undisciplined they were.)

They reached Baghdad on the fourth day of the month of Safar 656 by the Islamic calendar (A.D. 1258). The caliph, accompanied by three thousand priests, secretaries, aides and other attendants, went out to meet the visitor. Hulagu treated the caliph with suave gentility. He had only one request:

"Would you be so kind as to ask your subjects to put aside their weapons for one day, so we may be facilitated in taking a census?"

As soon as the disarming had taken place, Hulagu ordered a massacre in which eight hundred thousand men, women and children were put to death. Then the city that had been one of the great show-places of the Middle East was converted into a place of desolation. The irrigation system was destroyed. Artistic and cultural centers were burned and wrecked. The greatest loss to posterity was the city's library of hundreds of thousands of hand-inscribed volumes—reduced to ashes.

Then the horde swept on to Damascus. Then over the Jordan. Down the Valley. Across Galilee. Wherever they went they murdered and plundered, destroying church, mosque and synagogue indiscriminately.

The Valley had never seen such men as these. They were more animal-like than human. They ate anything that lived: rats, lice, cats, dogs. Their favorite drink was blood, preferably human blood. When they went to war they took wives, children and cattle with them, but they left these encumbrances behind when they made raids by fast ponies on places far distant from their base of operations, seizing the loot and making off with it at such speed that they were out of sight before an alarm could be raised. Their officers lived in gold-colored tents, which led to them eventually being called "the Golden Horde." When they killed they did it by decapitation. They always made a neat pyramid of the heads, and another symmetrical stack of the rest of the corpses.

At this time up from the south came a new force: men known as Mamelukes. They were white-skinned Circassian slaves—victims of the Turkish system of seizing, after each military victory, as many young boys as possible, to be converted to Islam, then trained as slaves. (The word *mameluke* is Arabic for "slave" or "one possessed.") In those days the Mamelukes rebelled against their Turkish-Egyptian masters, seized power, marched north, and made the land of the Jordan their own by defeating the Mongol hordes in a battle at Ein Harod, in the Vale of Jezreel, within sight of the Jordan.

The Mamelukes turned out to be better soldiers than masters of an empire. In two hundred and sixty-seven years there were forty-seven Mameluke rulers, the average remaining in power little over five years. The change in leadership was generally brought about by assassination.

When the Mamelukes took Acre in 1291, they brought the era of the Crusades to an end, less than two hundred years after Urban II's bold call at Clermont for war on the infidel. Now, once again, the people of the Valley heard the sound of sledgehammer against holy buildings, as Christian churches everywhere were destroyed. However, during the Mameluke period Christian pilgrims were still permitted to come and go. One of them, Sir John Mandeville, after a trip in 1322, described the Jordan as "no great river but it has plenty of good fish." Then he put into circulation a great deal of nonsense about the Dead Sea, including the classic of all: that a piece of iron thrown onto the surface will not sink.

After two and a half centuries of Mamelukes, the Valley saw still another breed of men, the Ottoman Turks, who came sweeping in to defeat the former Egyptian slaves and in 1516 take control for the next four centuries. At first this was a regime of great enlightenment, and the people of the Valley were happy. Manufacturing, commerce and intellectual pursuits were all encouraged. Tribute was exacted, tax money flowed to Constantinople and the local pashas were all appointed by the sultan, but the great corruption for which the Ottoman Empire eventually came to be known did not develop immediately; it appeared later, as a creeping malady, attacking one limb at a time, until finally the whole body-politic was diseased.

The zenith of Ottoman days came in the middle sixteenth century under a sultan known as Suleiman the Magnificent. He took a deep interest in the entire Valley, as well as in Jerusalem. Soon after coming to power in 1520 he ordered the walls of the Holy City rebuilt, a symbolic gesture the people appreciated.

Now a unique figure enters the Jordan story—João Miguez, a Spanish Jew. In these times of fanaticism and persecution, the Jews of Spain were given the choice of becoming Christians or leaving the country. Those who underwent conversion were called *Conversos* ("converted") by the Spaniards or *Marranos* ("swine" or "pig") by other Jews. Many Marranos rose to positions of power and intermarried into noble Spanish families, some even becoming Catholic bishops, but others abandoned Judaism only on the surface, taking great risks to observe their religion secretly. Some were caught, tried by the Inquisition, and put to death. Others fled abroad to be able to practice their religion openly, among them members of the Miguez family, who moved to Portugal, then Antwerp, then Venice, publicly professing they were Jews and changing their names. Thus João Miguez became Joseph Nasi ("prince" or, in twentieth century Hebrew, "president").

Soon after Suleiman the Magnificent came to power, Nasi, now a wealthy banker, won the sultan's confidence and when two of Suleiman's sons bitterly contested the right of succession, Nasi backed the elder. After the younger, along with four sons, was murdered, Nasi was named a member of the surviving son's bodyguard and was given a title, Duke of Naxos. As a further gesture of goodwill Suleiman made him a present of the ruins of Tiberias, and seven other Galilean communities, all either in or near the Valley.

(The last time Tiberias had come to world attention had been in 1204, the year of the death of Moses Ben Maimon, commonly known in the western world by his Greek name, Maimonides, the most important Jewish philosopher of the Middle Ages, as well as being a medical man of such note that he was named personal physician to the court of Saladin. Of Maimonides it was said: "Verily, if the moon would submit to his art, he would heal her of her spots!" and "From Moses to Moses there is none like unto Moses." Although he spent much of his life in Morocco and Egypt, he asked that he be buried in Tiberias. One legend tells how, as his coffin was being transported north across the desert, the funeral party was attacked by Bedouins who, once they discovered the name of the deceased, returned the loot they had collected and accompanied the coffin, as an honor guard, the rest of the way to Tiberias.)

Nasi had some grandiose ideas for Tiberias. He knew that during the Spanish Inquisition close to a hundred thousand Jews, whose Spanish ancestry dated back a thousand years or more, had been forced to flee their native country and had scattered over Turkey, Africa, Egypt and various parts of Europe. Since then many other Jews had been forced to flee from many other countries. To help them find permanent homes in the land of their forefathers, Nasi devised the first Palestine colonization scheme, under which these displaced persons would be enabled to settle in Galilee, where there had always remained, throughout the centuries, at least a small Jewish population. First he sent agents to Tiberias with adequate funds to rebuild the city. (While clearing up the rubble that past conquerors had left, workmen discovered a flight of steps leading down into an old church vault full of marble statues and three ancient church bells.)

Nasi met his worst opposition in the Valley itself from people already established there who resented the idea of great numbers of refugees being brought in and did much to obfuscate his colonization plan.

Nasi wanted his Jewish colony to be self-supporting, so he imported thousands of mulberry trees, hoping the newcomers would be able to raise silkworms and make not only exportable silk but also wool material that would compete with the fine wools being manufactured in Venice. He issued a proclamation to the Jews of the world, announcing that any who had been expelled from lands of their residence and were willing to become farmers or artisans would be welcome in the city he was rebuilding in the Valley of the Jordan. Especially welcome would be Jews from Romano Campagna, who at that time were enduring considerable persecution under Pope Paul IV. When Nasi learned that thousands of Marranos had been imprisoned in the Adriatic seaport of Ancona, he persuaded Pope Paul to release those who chanced to be Turkish subjects, on his promise to transport them to Tiberias in his own ships. Later various technicalities were raised by the Holy See and none of these people ever saw Tiberias. Next, the entire Jewish population of the small town of Cori, in the Romano Campagna, accepted Nasi's offer and sent agents to Jewish communities in certain large Italian cities to raise funds for their trip. Either the funds were never forthcoming or the people of Cori changed their minds, for few if any ever reached the Valley. Then from the Adriatic city of Pesaro a ship loaded with one hundred and two Jewish emigrants, all eager to settle in Tiberias, set out for Venice. It was boarded at sea by pirates from Malta who kidnaped all one hundred and two passengers and sold them into slavery. From start to finish the Tiberias colonization plan was beset by troubles.

In 1597 the first production of Shakespeare's historical drama *Henry IV* was given, a play containing an indirect reference to the Jordan more amusing than significant. In the first scene of the second act of Part One, two messengers are discussing the inn in which they are staying and how run down it has become since the death of the manager. One messenger complains:

"I think this be the most villainous house in all London road for fleas; I am stung like a tench."

His companion agrees. The first messenger then adds:

"Why, they will allow us ne'er a jordan, and then we leak in your chimney; and your chamber-lie breeds fleas like a loach."

In Shakespeare's time a jordan was a chamber pot, often spelled jordain, or jurdaine, or jurdan, or jurden. It had acquired its name in a roundabout way. Many pilgrims to the Holy Land, starting with the Crusaders, had wanted to take some Jordan water home with them, and so a thriving business grew up in Palestine of supplying bottles for transporting the water. Most of the bottles were of a peculiar design, with a large neck, and came to be known in Great Britain, Europe and America as "Jordan bottles." Later the name was applied to a pot or vessel with a large neck used by alchemists and doctors. Then, finally, to a chamber pot.

(In the nineteenth century it became British slang to use the expression "Jordan over" to mean dead, while "this side of Jordan" meant alive. "Jordan" also came to mean "a blow with a staff," but there is no record of the derivation. There is also a verb "to jordan," meaning to refine something in a jordan, which in this case is a machine used in manufacturing paper pulp, named after its nineteenth century American inventor. Also, there is Jordan's Law, a biological theorem bearing the name of the American naturalist who devised it.)

The apparently erroneous idea that the remains of Sodom, Gomorrah and the other cities destroyed for their wickedness lie at the north end of the Dead Sea only slightly below the water's surface was first circulated in 1697 by the Reverend Henry Maundrell, an English chaplain who explored the Valley with fourteen countrymen and later reported that "reliable men" had declared they had seen in the water "several pillars and other fragments of buildings" that apparently were the ruins of the Cities of the Plain.

In 1759 the Valley came to world notice when an earthquake convulsed the whole area, causing great damage and loss of life.

Late in the eighteenth century the land of the Jordan was at its nadir. A traveler in 1785 reported there were three hundred thousand people in Acre and its environs, two thousand in Jerusalem, and only thirty thousand scattered through all the rest of Palestine. The Valley itself was more thinly populated than it had been since prehistoric times. It was described by one contemporary observer as a place of "misery, corruption, ignorance, and scant population."

Two characters of storybook fame now enter the Jordan story. One represented the East, the other the West. Each was a hero to his own part of the world.

Ahmed Pasha, popularly known as El Djezzar ("the Butcher") was the Ottoman ruler of Syria, which then included the present-day states of Syria, Lebanon, Jordan and Israel, divided into five provinces or pashaliks. El Djezzar had his headquarters in Acre, on the Mediterranean coast. He had been born in Bosnia (now Yugoslavia), and had become a slave in Egypt, but he committed so many crimes there that he took refuge in Palestine, and gradually became the ruler of a sizable territory. He seemed to like his sobriquet; at least he lived up to it. Legends of his bestiality are plentiful. Once he had the living bodies of a considerable number of Greek Christians cemented, standing up at regular intervals, into a five-foot wall being built in his palace. Only their heads were visible. This enabled El Djezzar to watch their death agony. One of his lesser forms of torture was to have the noses and ears of his victims amputated with a sword. In his defense it was said that he was so kind that he always found new husbands for the widows of men he ordered executed. He was well known as a Francophobe, offering the equivalent of a dollar for the decapitated head of any Frenchman brought to his palace.

It is little wonder that Napoleon, who recently had been victorious in Egypt, bore no great friendship for El Djezzar. But there was a stronger motive than this personal feeling behind Napoleon's decision to march into the land of the Jordan. He wanted to deny Palestinian seaports to his great naval enemy, the British, and to head off a Turkish army he feared might march south to try to take Egypt away from him. So, personally at the head of 12,975 troops, plus a considerable number of Egyptian and Arab servants, camel drivers, interpreters, laborers, and French medical men, he started north, first across the desert, then up the Mediterranean coast. The army was equipped with forty-nine guns, ranging from five-inch mortars to twelve-pounders, and started out with five thousand camels, donkeys and mules. It was a strange army in many respects. Some of the French officers had been given permission to bring along their wives; others brought their mistresses. They had more personal luggage than any army ought to carry, including especially fancy tents for the women, beds, mattresses and even carpets. One brigade had the wife of a general as its commander.

Reporting on the trip across the desert, Napoleon told Paris:

"We have crossed seventy leagues of sand . . . and we have had to eat dogs, donkeys and camels."

One night a cavalry officer left his stallion tied to a hitching post. The next morning it was gone. His soldiers admitted having killed and eaten the animal, but said "it had an ugly disposition anyway," and promised not to treat his mare to a like fate.

Napoleon had a low opinion of the land of the Jordan in those days.

"Cities are crumbling into ruins, ports are silting up, the roads are disappearing, the swamps are rendering the plains unwholesome. Nevertheless, the country retains its character."

Then he quoted an Arab writer:

"Egypt is a farm, but Syria is a garden."

The French army took El-Arish and Gaza without incident, but what happened after the capture of Jaffa added one more bloody chapter to the sanguinary chronicle of the area. There was excessive looting, cruelty, murder. Most of the city's population—women and children included—was killed. One report said:

"Blinded with a passion for killing, deaf to the remonstrances of the generals, the men (Frenchmen) painted the streets with blood."

Napoleon is pictured by one of his friendly biographers as sitting on a sea wall with his head in his hands brooding over what was going on and remarking to an aide:

"Never did war seem to be so barbarous."

Two thousand unarmed Jaffa-ites took refuge in several large buildings near the sea. As a mob of Frenchmen—maddened by their blood lust and perhaps also influenced by wine they had discovered in a cellar—were preparing for a massacre, an officer on Napoleon's personal staff appeared and made an impassioned plea to them, then promised the two thousand that if they filed quietly from the building their lives would be spared. When Napoleon heard that these people, plus one or two thousand other enemy soldiers, had been taken prisoner, he is reported by several of his biographers as saying:

"How do you expect me to feed so many extra mouths?"

Therefore—presumably on Napoleon's order—they were all taken down to the beach and killed. To save bullets, the execution squads were ordered to kill by the bayonet, with Napoleon quoted as saying:

"Remember, the bayonet has always been the weapon of the brave."

From Jaffa the Napoleonic army marched north to attack the fort of Acre. It soon became evident that this stronghold would be taken only after a long siege, if at all. But to buoy up hopes at home Napoleon sent a message to Paris that was about ninety percent false:

"The Army of the Republic is mistress of the whole of Palestine."

(He had taken just three cities along the coast.)

The day the army left Cairo he had sent his Directory in Paris a message:

"It is likely enough that when you read this letter I shall be standing on the ruins of the city of Solomon."

(Actually, the closest he and his army ever got to Jerusalem was Jaffa, nearly fifty miles away.)

When Napoleon heard that "the Butcher" had ordered the Pasha of Damascus to send an army across the Jordan to Acre to assist in the defense of the seaport, he decided to meet these reinforcements head on, so he dispatched a small force in charge of General Murat, a cavalry officer, with orders to take the fortress of Safed, high in the hills eight miles as the bird flies west of the Jordan, in order to keep a lookout from that height on any Turkish troop movements across the river north of the Sea of Galilee. Then he dispatched Brigadier General Junot to take Nazareth and watch for troop movements across the river south of the lake. The two officers carried out their missions, but within a few days Murat reported that a large Turkish force was encamped on the east bank of the Jordan, near the Damascus-Safed road, preparing to cross. Junot sent even worse news: a Turkish force had already crossed the Jordan south of the lake and had occupied Tiberias. Junot, with only three hundred infantrymen and one hundred and sixty cavalrymen, had gone down into the Valley to meet this army, but after a brief engagement had retreated to Kefar Kana, just four miles from Nazareth, formerly called Cana, the town in which Christ had performed the wedding feast miracle. Napoleon sent General Kléber with reinforcements for Junot.

The next message received at seacoast headquarters said the Turks had taken up a position in the Vale of Jezreel, not far from the slopes of Mount Tabor. Some reports said twenty thousand Turks, some thirty thousand. The ratio of Turks to Frenchmen was placed as high as seventeen to one. Napoleon made a quick decision. At noon on April 15 he started out at once from the seacoast, personally leading a cavalry division equipped with eight pieces of moderately heavy artillery. While he was on his way Kléber and his men fought a ten-hour battle, from 6 A.M. until 4 P.M. That night one of the French privates wrote in his diary:

"We'd gladly give up the little bread we have for some bullets and gunpowder. We've had no time to eat. We are so worn out with thirst and fatigue we couldn't even speak. At a short distance there was a lake, which the division was unable to reach, so there was no way to refresh ourselves."

One of Napoleon's more romantic biographers tells how a fierce cavalry battle was taking place between Turks and Frenchmen as Napoleon's force approached, and how, before his men even got within sight of the field of combat, he ordered one of his larger artillery pieces fired. Thereupon, according to this fairybook version, "the Ottomans panicked and fled at the sound. Seeing this, the French commander ordered another shot fired and the rout was complete."

A more plausible version says:

"Napoleon formed his troops in three squares four thousand yards apart and advanced rapidly against the enemy. The Turks, after a short resistance, fled to the Jordan, pursued by the French cavalry."

What happened at and in the river—a river sacred to Christians and Jews, even if not to the Turks—is told in a report written by a French schoolmaster who took part in the Mount Tabor battle as a private:

"We were dying of thirst . . . but our thirst for vengeance had put out our thirst for water and had kindled our thirst for blood . . . Indeed, here we were, wading up to our waists in the water, the same water which only a short time ago we craved to drink. But we no longer thought of drinking but only of killing and dyeing the water red with the blood of those barbarians, who only a moment before had hoped to cut off our heads and drown our bodies in that same water, where they themselves were drowned and which was now filled with their corpses."

After committing this carnage at and in the Jordan, the Frenchmen then crossed over and looted a camp in which the Turkish forces had left tents, surplus arms, ammunition, and a goodly quantity of personal possessions. One account says they spent hours "swapping loot."

After the battle, General Kléber embraced Napoleon and exclaimed: "General, how great you are!"

That night Napoleon and some of his officers and men were the guests of a monastery at Nazareth. One account of the evening tells how at dinner several antireligious jokes were made by slaughter-weary French soldiers, who were each time quickly silenced by Napoleon. The next day Napoleon took part in a christening service, and one of his soldiers who had had a finger slashed off during the previous day's battle and who for some macabre reason had saved the object, obtained permission from the holy fathers to bury the severed finger in the monastery's cemetery, with appropriate services.

"I don't know what will happen to the rest of my corpse," he told his comrades, "but at least I'll have a finger in the Holy Land."

That day, as the Te Deum was being sung in the monastery, some of Napoleon's soldiers, on orders, burned down two villages and the town of Jenin, lying between Nazareth and Nablus.

That same day Napoleon conferred fur-rimmed caftans on three Muslim chieftains of the Valley who had been friendly to the French, one of them one hundred and one years old and reputed to be unable to utter a single sentence without including in it a quotation from the Koran.

After the Mount Tabor victory, Napoleon hastened back to Acre and almost immediately ordered his commanders to give up trying to take the fort and prepare to return to Egypt. When plans for the evacuation were complete, the troops that had been left at Nazareth and

Safed to keep an eye on the Jordan were ordered to join in the retreat.

On their way south along the coastal route, the French burned the towns and villages they passed through, and also destroyed any crops already harvested. Many of the French soldiers were victims of the plague. One story told by many of Napoleon's biographers is that he personally distributed containers of poison to the ailing men so they could take their own lives; another, that he ordered his doctors to give them fatal doses of narcotics. Napoleon later denied both stories, and he may have been right, but he certainly was wrong in reporting to his Directory in Paris that his total casualties in the Palestine venture had been five hundred dead, a thousand wounded. The consensus of military experts is that fewer than half the 12,975 men who started out returned alive.

From the Jordan's point of view the best summarization was by a contemporary commentator who wrote:

"The French invasion brought Tiberias to European notice once more. After the French retreat, it sank back into its old obscurity, and now it must await another change, of good or evil fortune, to become known again."

11

In other parts of the world during the nineteenth century there were cataclysmic conflicts between empires, civil wars, and other sanguinary strife, yet this was a long era of relative tranquility for the land of the Jordan, emphasizing again the soundness of the bridge-highway theory: that this has always been an area of transit for foreign armies or a barrier between rival powers, and that the Valley's fate has thus depended throughout much of its history on whether or not those to the north, south, and east were in foment against each other.

However, while there were no great military activities in the Valley during the nineteenth century, the entire area suddenly became of considerable geopolitical as well as religious interest. The second half of the century saw the growing internal disintegration and international decline of the Ottoman Empire. The Balkan provinces broke away. The Crimean War was touched off, supposedly out of a dispute over the holy places. European economic and political penetration began, especially to the south, in Egypt, as evidenced by European control of the Suez Canal. Again, the Valley was the bridgehead.

During the nineteenth century, all this outside interest resulted in the river and its lakes being visited, investigated, and written about as never before. So many pilgrims, explorers, amateur and professional scientists, and writers concentrated their attention on the river that during the nineteenth century the outside world really became acquainted with the Jordan.

It began with a Swiss explorer-scientist-writer, John Lewis Burchardt. In 1812, while crossing the trans-Jordanian desert, he wandered quite by accident through a long slit in the rocks that led him to the remains of the rose-red city of Petra. He was the first outsider to see it in almost seven centuries, as far as anyone knows. Its location had remained a mystery since the time of the Crusades, its very existence doubted. The story of how the Swiss stumbled upon it and his reaction to the architectural wonders that ancient sculptors had carved out of the living rock are not part of the Jordan story, for Petra is far south of the Dead Sea, yet the Nabataeans who created those temples and tombs, the hippodrome, forum and triumphal arch, have already played a small role in the river's history. Also, Burchardt's discovery had much to do with encouraging others to come streaming through the Valley looking for historical and archaeological secrets.

On his way home from Petra, Burchardt followed the river to Tiberias, where he had the following experience:

"As we approached the city of Tiberias, our mind dwelled already with joyful anticipation on a good dish of fishes out of the Lake which we would have for our evening meal. We had heard a great deal about the tastiness of these fishes, and had gone without fresh fish for quite a long time. But who can describe our great disappointment that, when we finally came, late in the afternoon, to Tiberias, we had to learn that the last and only boat had broken apart from decay back in 1811 and up to now no new one had been built. Such is the lassitude of the people there! A good-willing man, seeing our disappointment, waded up to his waist into the quiet waters of the Lake and cast a line. He brought us some small fishes which bore no resemblance in form or in tastiness to those we had heard about."

The first recorded attempt to descend the Jordan by boat was made in 1835 by a twenty-five-year-old Irishman, Christopher Costigan of Dublin, a candidate for the priesthood who, before he set out, tried to read everything that had ever been written about the Jordan and the Dead Sea. Yet he made the error of beginning his adventure in August, one of the hottest months, when the river would be at its shallowest. He had his boat transported by camel from Acre to Tiberias. Then, accompanied by a Maltese servant, he started to traverse the Lower Jordan as far as the Dead Sea. For three days he struggled to get his craft through rapids, around landslides, over waterfalls, and across shallows. As a result, he was more often in the water than on it. When the servant lost his nerve the young Irish explorer was forced to abandon his attempt to navigate the river. He proceeded down the Valley on horseback, after hiring Bedouins to transport his boat by camel. On the way a band of Arab brigands waylaid him. His horse panicked and galloped full speed directly at the attackers, who apparently decided the wildly gesticulating rider was a madman, so they fled. Costigan arrived at Jericho tattered and bedraggled, but still undaunted.

Late in August, accompanied by the same Maltese servant, Costigan started on what he intended to be an eight-day scientific voyage the length and width of the Dead Sea, during which he would take soundings and study the sea's eccentricities.

A north wind carried them easily down as far as the great promontory El Lisan ("the Tongue"). Then they started back. It was logical to row by night, when it was cooler, but they found they could make no progress at all then, because of the strong north wind, so they were compelled to row by day, when the sun beat down on them unmercifully. One day, while Costigan slept, the servant, tired of rowing so heavy a boat, tried to lighten his labors by throwing overboard the entire supply of fresh water. Their suffering now became intense. They dared not land at two or three green spots they passed, where they might have obtained water, because of their fear of nomad tribesmen. On the fourth day the servant contracted such a severe fever that he lay tossing on the bottom of the boat while Costigan, who had had no previous experience at rowing, had to work the oars. On the seventh day their bodies broke out in enormous blisters from having poured sea water over their clothes to get relief from the heat. On the eighth day they tried to make coffee from sea water to assuage their painful thirst. Finally they reached the north end of the lake, and the servant set off on foot for Jericho to get help for Costigan, who was now the more gravely ill of the two. The servant, who fainted seven times along the way, returned some days later with horses he had rented and took his master to an Arab hut in Jericho, where Costigan with difficulty wrote a note to a British priest he knew in Jerusalem:

> My Dear Sir:
> For God's sake send me some medicine and emetic above all things. I cannot rise from my bed, and if I pass two such nights as the last without aid or medicine, you will have to do something else for me!
>
> (Signed) C.C.

The priest rode all night to Jericho and found the young Irishman lying in the open air, delirious. An improvised bed was made on the horse's back out of sacks of straw, a fur coat, and two cushions, and at 9 P.M. the procession left Jericho, with one Arab leading the horse and two others holding Costigan's legs so he would not fall off. It took them eleven hours to reach Jerusalem. Three days later Costigan died.

It was a story of bravery and suffering, but the two-man expedition had contributed little to scientific knowledge, for Costigan left behind only a few illegible notes on the margins of books he had taken with him, and the Maltese servant could only report that at one place where they took soundings their line, although ten hundred and fifty feet long, had not reached bottom. Otherwise, he said, the maximum depth was about four hundred and eighty feet.

The headstone over Costigan's grave on Mount Zion sets forth that his ambition had been to increase men's knowledge of the holy places; that he died despite the efforts of a "good Samaritan."

Less than two years later two Englishmen, Moon and Beke, became the first men in the long expanse of time to tell the world the true distinction of the Jordan and the Salt Sea into which it empties. Since the days of Abraham, men of many races, some of them scientists and mathematicians, had gone up and down the Valley, and back and forth across the river, apparently without even suspecting that this stream differed from all others in the world in one specific respect. Greeks, Romans, Jews, Christians, Muhammadans, Crusaders and desert nomads had become acquainted with every nook and cranny of its winding course, yet had failed to realize that it flowed for most of its length below sea level and emptied into the lowest spot on the earth's surface. Moon and Beke made the discovery by the crude method of timing how long it took them to boil water, and came to the conclusion that the Dead Sea was five hundred feet below the level of the Mediterranean, which they reported that year (1837) in the *Journal* of the Royal Geographical Society. They were between seven hundred and eight hundred feet wrong, but at least they had finally brought to light the great geographical peculiarity of the Jordan.

The year Moon and Beke made their report the Victorian Era officially began when eighteen-year-old Victoria became Queen of England. It was the start of the most peaceful decades the world has ever known. But not in geographical circles. For ten years a fierce controversy spluttered over heretofore ignored questions about the Jordan and the Dead Sea: whether the river actually did meander; what the sea level was at various points. Late in 1837 a Frenchman said he had barometric proof that the Dead Sea level was −600 feet. Early in 1838 a German said −1332 feet. Some said Lake Tiberias was lower than the Dead Sea. Others said the Jordan could not possibly make such a drop as reported if it meandered. The president of the Royal Geographical Society in his annual address in London in 1842 declared officially and unequivocally that the Dead Sea level was −1,311.9 feet. In his address the next year he amended the official and unequivocal measurement to −1,312.2.

In 1847 Dr. Edward Robinson of New York read a paper before the Royal Geographical Society entitled "The Depression of the Dead Sea and Jordan Valley" in which he questioned the correctness of every one of the figures thus far announced and called on "all European governments to combine their resources to solve this burning problem," adding that "the matter must not be permitted to rest another year." Then in a final burst of oratory he said that public attention must be aroused. Those in power, he prayed, would "speedily cause the questions raised to be put to rest forever."

That same year the captain of a British frigate, HMS *Spartan*, which had put into port at Haifa, Palestine, suggested to his officers that someone ought to "undertake to examine the course of the Jordan, as well as of the valley through which it runs, and especially to measure the depth of the Dead Sea." Immediate interest was expressed by a young Shropshireman, Lieutenant Thomas Howard Molyneux, who by coincidence was exactly the age Costigan had been. Three sailors, who had had some exploration experience in Australia, also volunteered, and the captain put the ship's dinghy at their disposal. At Acre they rented three horses and four camels to carry the boat and their supplies. They also took along Toby, a dragoman from Beirut, who brought with him two more horses and some camping equipment.

Lieutenant Molyneux was a serious young man and kept a detailed diary, but it reads more like an adventure story than the account of a scientific expedition. On the overland trip to Tiberias he had considerable trouble with the obstreperous camel that was hauling on its back the ship's heavy dinghy. The camel kept "roaring and coming to his knees." Molyneux's entry for Sunday, August 22, 1847, begins:

"At 11h. 30m. arrived at the top of the last ridge of hills overlooking the Lake of Tiberias and the Valley of the Jordan, and enjoyed a magnificent view. Jebel Sheikh, smothered in clouds, was distinctly seen, bearing NNE; before us were the blue waters of Tiberias, surrounded by fine ranges of hills; to the left the ruins of Safed, perched on a hill (both Safed and Tiberias had been hit ten years earlier by an earthquake that had killed thousands of the inhabitants and left both cities in ruins); and near the northern end of the lake a gap in the mountains, with a green patch, which pointed out the spot where the Jordan discharges its waters into Tiberias, as well as the ruins of an ancient town which stands a short distance from its embouchure.

"At 12h. 50m. a great crisis took place. We had experienced some difficulty in descending the upper part of the hills above Tiberias, but by degrees the road became so steep that we were obliged to hold the boat by ropes, till at length we arrived at a point beyond which the camels could not proceed, and to return was impossible; the stones, when started, rolled to the bottom; the camels began to roar; then followed the usual trembling of the legs—the certain precursor of a fall; and in short to save the boat it became necessary to cut the lashings and let her slide down on her keel to the foot of the hill. There we again harnessed the unfortunate camels, and proceeded without further mishap to Tiberias."

The next day Molyneux decided the lake had been made too small on all maps he had ever seen and he ascertained that the hot springs had a temperature of one hundred and thirty degrees.

Soon after starting down the Jordan the boat came to a spot where an ancient arched bridge had toppled into the river, completely blocking passage. Here, for the first time—but not the last—the boat had to be emptied of all its contents and carried along the bank past the obstruction. In many places they found the river split into so many small streams that there was not water enough in any one of them to float their dinghy. There were also innumerable weirs running across the river—loose walls of stone, mud and turf, designed to turn the Jordan's water into fields for irrigation purposes. Arab shepherds by the dozens, sometimes by the hundreds, followed the boat along the shore, and whenever Molyneux's men tore down a weir to allow their boat to pass, they would refuse to permit them to go on until they had rebuilt the obstruction.

The expedition was plagued by Arab tribesmen the entire way. Describing one attack, Molyneux wrote:

"At this time I had just shot a very beautiful kind of kingfisher, and most of my other barrels had been discharged at an animal we saw on the banks of the river, which the guide called a boar, but it appeared to me more like a gigantic fox, when Toby called out to me to load my pistols. On looking up I saw the camels and muleteers surrounded with a cluster of spears."

The Arab chieftain told Molyneux that this was his territory; that it was customary for all travelers to pay a toll; that if payment was not made at once they must turn back.

"The sheikh insisted on being paid 600 piastres; he said his country extended two days' journey down the Valley, and that if I would pay him, he and his men would go with us and see us safely to the country of the next sheikh. Circumstanced as we were . . . I saw it was necessary, if possible, to come to some terms with these people and therefore offered the sheikh 100 piastres . . . This proposal he treated with the most perfect contempt."

A compromise was finally reached at 200 piastres. But each day a new Bedouin sheikh would appear making more demands. Molyneux was kept busy bargaining and negotiating.

"I saw today in the jungle a large wild boar, and a small herd of gazelles, as well as great numbers of jackalls; and also doves, eagles, and vultures innumerable; but I had too many other things to do to trouble myself about them, and indeed I was afraid to discharge my barrels."

When they reached Beisan (ancient Scythopolis or Beth-Shan) Molyneux wrote in his diary:

"I think the view from this point over the Valley of the Jordan was one of the finest things I had seen—an abundant vegetation extending up the slopes of the eastern hills, which are crowned with trees to the summit."

That same day, when trouble with the Arabs threatened again, the young naval officer shot two doves with one bullet from the back of his horse, which so impressed the tribesmen that they lowered their demands for money—slightly.

"I had hoped to get down to the Dead Sea in four or five days, but it was like moving an army in an enemy's country—not only looking out for positions where we could not be taken by surprise, but anxiously looking out also for supplying our commissariat, for though the muddy Jordan is throughout full of small fish, yet we began to fear about our provisions, and determined to rely more on our guns for something to eat, so that we might save what we had for the Dead Sea . . . The Bedouins will sell nothing; indeed they appear to have little to spare, rich as the country appears to be."

In each day's entry Molyneux recorded the temperature inside the tent at various hours of the day and night. It was nearly always over one hundred.

The camels and horses traveled as close to the river as possible, but often the only pathway was at such a distance that those on foot and those in the boat lost sight of each other. On the sixth day Molyneux was with the animals and the three sailors were in the boat, when they thus lost contact. That evening when there was still no sign of the boat Molyneux sent his dragoman back to investigate. He found the boat bobbing around in the river, empty, and the guide stripped naked. The guide said they had been attacked by fifty fierce nomads. One of the British sailors had been struck over the head when he attempted to raise a rifle; all had been searched and robbed; the three sailors had vanished, he knew not where. Molyneux spent some days searching for his lost crew. Then, accompanied by his guide, his dragoman and a Greek he met in Jericho, who claimed to have had years of experience at sea, he set sail on the Dead Sea, which he called in his diary "this vile place" and "this misty furnace." The Dead Sea water he said was "destructive to everything it touched, especially metals . . . everything in the boat was covered with a nasty slimy substance; the iron was dreadfully corroded and looked as if covered with patches of coal-tar, and the effect of the salt spray upon ourselves, by lying upon the skin, and getting into the eyes, nose and mouth, produced constant thirst and drowsiness, and took away all appetite."

Then Molyneux scotched several old canards:

"As to the alleged destructive effect of the Dead Sea on birds flying over its surface, we killed some which were actually standing in the water; and on Saturday, while in the very center of the sea, I three times saw ducks, and some other fowl, fly past us within shot. I saw no signs, however, of fish, or of any living things in the water, although there were many shells on the beach."

Then this report on a mystery:

"I must mention a curious broad strip of foam which appeared to lie in a straight line nearly north and south throughout the entire length of the sea. It did not commence, as might be supposed, at the exit of the Jordan, but some miles to the westward, and it seemed to be constantly bubbling and in motion, like a stream that runs rapidly through a lake of still water; while nearly over this white track, during both the nights that we were on the water, we observed in the sky a white streak, like a cloud, extending also in a straight line from north to south, and as far as the eye could reach."

More fortunate than Costigan, Molyneux found a favorable breeze for his return from the Lisan. The temperature one day at noon stood at one hundred and thirty degrees. When he returned to Jericho he learned that the three seamen had made their way back to Tiberias and thence to Jaffa. When he reached Jerusalem he laughingly said to the British consul:

"I am doing well now—no fever yet—but when I am on board and the excitement is over, I shall catch it!"

He did. He died of fever three weeks later.

After no one had responded for almost ten years to the plea made before the Royal Geographical Society in London—for "all European governments to combine their resources to solve this burning problem" —the government of the United States took a hand in the matter. As Lieutenant William F. Lynch of the United States Navy told it later in his official report:

"On the eighth day of May, 1847, the town and castle of Vera Cruz having sometime before surrendered, and there being nothing left for the Navy (U.S.) to perform, I proffered an application to the Honorable John Y. Mason (Secretary of the Navy) for permission to circumnavigate and thoroughly explore Lake Asphaltites or the Dead Sea."

Two months later Lynch, a forty-six-year-old Virginian who had served twenty-eight years in the Navy, received such permission and in October was ordered to take command of the American storeship *Supply,* formerly the *Crusader,* and was given a staff that included a doctor, a botanist, another lieutenant, a midshipman, and ten able seamen, one of whom was a trained mechanic. They landed on March 31, 1848, at Acre, where they were joined by two American volunteers, a Syrian dragoman, an Arab cook, a nobleman from Mecca who claimed to be the thirty-third lineal descendant of the Prophet, and an Arab sheikh who wanted to go along for the trip. The procession from Acre to Tiberias was an impressive sight. On wagons drawn by three camels each there were two boats that had been built in the United States especially for the expedition: the *Fanny Mason,* of copper; and the *Fanny Skinner,* of galvanized iron. Over each boat flew a large American flag. Then came the officers, the seamen, the American volunteers, the direct descendant of the Prophet Mohammed, and the Arab sheikh, all mounted on horseback. Then a long line of camels loaded with supplies, their attendants and the household staff. Lynch had wisely put himself under the protection of the principal Bedouin chief of the day, Arkely Aga, who had more power in the Valley than the entire Turkish administration. His men, with tufted spears, brought up the rear. The horsemen numbered thirty and the camels twenty-nine. When they reached Tiberias they found it "a very dirty town" populated by a thousand Jews and a few hundred Arabs. There was only one boat on the lake, a small wooden craft, which they purchased for twenty-one dollars. They christened it the *Uncle Sam* and added it to the flotilla.

As the boats were launched, Lynch reminded his men that "since the time of Josephus and the Romans no vessel of any size has sailed upon this sea, and for many, many years but a solitary keel has furrowed its surface."

Some Arabs at Tiberias, when told that Lynch was on his way to the Dead Sea by official order of the United States government, expressed the conviction that he must have committed some terrible crime, to be punished in this way by a normally benevolent government.

Describing the start of the voyage on April 10, Lynch wrote:

"We bade adieu to the last outwork of border civilization and steered direct for the outlet of the Jordan . . . With awnings spread and colors flying, we passed comfortably and rapidly onward . . . Gallantly marched the cavalcade on land, and beautiful must have appeared the boats on the water. Little did we know what difficulties we might have to encounter. But, placing our trust on high, we hoped and feared not."

Lynch was not placing his trust exclusively "on high." He had asked for—and received—from the U. S. Navy: one blunderbuss, fourteen carbines with bayonets, fourteen pistols, ten bowie knives, swords for the officers, and a few miscellaneous pieces of armament.

The *Uncle Sam* came to grief almost immediately, trying to navigate the first of twenty-seven major rapids Lynch counted along the river. She was abandoned.

On the third day they came to the confluence of the Yarmuk with the Jordan; on the fourth night they camped just above a dangerous rapid where the Wadi al Yabis joins the Jordan; they spent the sixth night at Adam, by the remains of a Roman bridge; on the eighth day they entered the Dead Sea. Despite all the rapids, dams, landslides, stone weirs, cataracts, waterfalls and other impedimenta—natural and man-made—the *Fanny Skinner* and the *Fanny Mason* made it without a mishap.

The Jordan deeply impressed Lynch with its charm and its mystery, "seeming as if desirous to prolong its luxuriant meanderings in the calm and silent Valley, and reluctant to pour its sweet and sacred waters into the accursed bosom of the bitter sea."

On the Dead Sea they immediately ran into a tempest so furious that it seemed as if the bows of the boats "were encountering the sledge-hammers of the Titans, instead of the opposing waves of an angry sea."

"Camp Washington" was the name they gave their Dead Sea base of operations, set up near the oasis of Ein Gedi. Lynch insisted on scaling ancient Masada to see the ruins of Herod's castle and at the extreme south end of the sea they found a round pillar of solid salt which they called on their maps "the Pillar of Lot's Wife." Commenting on the tongue of land, jutting out from the east side of the sea, El Lisan,

Lynch said the human mind cannot conceive "a more dreary scene or an atmosphere more stifling and oppressive." He named two spots on El Lisan "Point Costigan" and "Point Molyneux." The temperature mounted so greatly that men with spectacles were unable to wear them, because the frames burned their ears and noses. The heat caused drowsiness, which in turn increased the danger of fever, because the men were too lackadaisical to fight off the malarial mosquitoes which, "as if their stings were envenomed by the heat, tormented us almost to madness."

Writing about the men in his own boat, Lynch said:

"My companions had yielded to the oppressive drowsiness, and now lay before me in every attitude of a sleep that had more of a stupor in it than repose. The fierce angel of disease seemed hovering over them, and I read the forerunner of his presence in their flushed and feverish sleep. Some, with their bodies bent and arms dangling over the abandoned oars, their hands excoriated with the acrid waters, slept profoundly; others, with heads thrown back and lips cracked and sore, with a scarlet flush on either cheek, seemed overpowered by heat and weariness even in sleep; while some, upon whose faces shone the reflected light of the water, looked ghastly, and dozed with a nervous twitching of the limbs."

Meanwhile, what the expedition was accomplishing was explained by Lynch later in his report:

"We have carefully sounded this sea, and determined its geographical position, taken the exact topography of its shores, ascertained the temperature, width, depth and velocity of its tributaries, collected specimens of every kind, and noted the winds, currents, changes of weather and all atmospheric phenomena. These, with a faithful narrative of events, will give a correct idea of this wondrous body of water."

After a rest in Jerusalem, Bethlehem, Jaffa and Acre, Lynch then explored the Upper Jordan, Lake Huleh and the sources, even scaling Mount Hermon. (His own stamina was amazing, considering he was past forty-five and had been ill most of his twenty-eight years in the Navy, according to his service record.) He even insisted that his men accompany him to Damascus and then to Baalbek. They were to meet their ship at Beirut, but before they could get to that seaport (they were traveling by horses) the young American lieutenant who was second in command died of fever in an Arab village.

But the expedition was a phenomenal success. Lynch wrote an official report of 235 oversized pages, with several hundred plates, and then what he called "The Narrative," 509 pages, that eventually went

360

into eight editions. But he felt that the public, especially in the United States, had not appreciated what they had suffered and what they had accomplished. "There was little evidence of curiosity respecting us or the labor in which we had engaged." And so in his preface he wrote this rather strange sentence:

"I had an abiding faith . . . that a liberal and enlightened community would not long condemn an attempt to explore a distant river and its wondrous reservoir, the first teeming with sacred associations and the last enveloped in a mystery which had defied all previous attempts to penetrate it."

Not only has history not condemned Lynch, but more than a century later he is recognized as a true pioneer: the first man ever to descend the Jordan by boat and explore the Dead Sea. The charts and maps his expedition produced, and the geological, meteorological and botanical observations they made became the foundation on which all subsequent knowledge of the river and its Valley was built and until the 1930s remained the main source of technical information on both the Jordan and the Dead Sea. His Dead Sea soundings are still the only ones available for the bathygraphy of the Dead Sea as a whole.

Twenty years after publication of *The Narrative* a forty-four-year-old Scotsman, John MacGregor, who had made canoe trips in many parts of the world and was called "the father of canoeing as a modern sport," took his already famous *Rob Roy* and went to explore the Upper Jordan, Lake Huleh and the river's sources. The *Rob Roy* was made of oak with cedar siding, was fourteen feet long, twenty-six inches wide, twelve deep, could hoist sails that were a deep blue, flew a golden ensign and weighed only seventy-two pounds. MacGregor started at the Hasbani springs, then made side trips up and down the Leddan and the Banias. On the way down to Lake Huleh he encountered Arabs who had never seen a boat of any sort and at first were astonished, then bewildered, and finally angered. Dozens of them waded into the Jordan, seized the canoe, lifted it high into the air—with MacGregor still in it—and carried it to the tent of their sheikh. Some had rifles and pistols with which they repeatedly threatened to blow his head off. Through his guide-interpreter he managed to persuade the sheikh to release him.

MacGregor's exploration of Lake Huleh and its swamps added much to the outside world's understanding of that strange stepchild of the Jordan.

"I think that by a cutting four hundred yards long, and twenty feet deep, at the end of Hooleh Lake (that was his Scottish spelling!) the whole of the marsh and lake would be made dry in a year, and an enormous tract of land would become productive and salubrious," he wrote in his diary.

That was in 1869. Eighty-two years later the drainage of Lake Huleh was actually undertaken.

After leaving Lake Huleh, MacGregor found that the current was often so rapid that the *Rob Roy* had to be portaged. Whenever he was forced to leave the river he at least tried to keep it within sight. His most painful experiences were transporting the *Rob Roy* over "stony hills and dizzy precipices, where not one single inhabitant is seen for miles, and not even an Arab's tent for days."

The book that came from the adventure was entitled *The Rob Roy on the Jordan*. Along with his lectures, it earned him almost a half million dollars between his return to Britain and his death twenty-two years later, all of which he gave away for religious and philanthropic work. At his death he was better known by the name of his canoe than he was as John MacGregor.

Then there were the pilgrims. By the early nineteenth century, members of the Orthodox faith in particular were making annual pilgrimages in great numbers to the baptismal spot on the Jordan during the Easter and Epiphany seasons. Quite by chance the Lynch expedition had arrived at this place in the river in April 1847 just in time to witness the arrival of a column of such pilgrims. In *The Narrative* Lynch described what he saw at five o'clock one morning:

"Copts and Russians, Poles, Armenians, Greeks and Syrians, from all parts of Asia, from Europe, from Africa, and from far-distant America! On they came, men, women and children, of every age and hue, and in every variety of costume; talking, screaming, shouting, in almost every known language under the sun. With their eyes strained toward the river, heedless of all intervening obstacles, they hurried eagerly forward. Dismounting in haste, and disrobing with precipitation, they rushed down the bank and threw themselves into the stream. They seemed to be absorbed by one impulsive feeling, and perfectly regardless of the observations of others. Each one plunged himself, or was dipped by another, three times, below the surface, in honor of the Trinity; and then filled a bottle or some other utensil from the river. The pageant disappeared as rapidly as it had approached and left us once more the silence and the solitude of the wilderness."

Another observer described the procession in these words:

"The pilgrims wore costumes of every shade of the rainbow. Included were Muhammadans, Druses, Catholics, Armenians, Copts, Syrians,

362

Jews, Episcopalians, Lutherans, Presbyterians and Methodists. Even infidels. Many had joined the procession just because of the excitement; some because they misunderstood its purpose. As the mass of humanity moved toward the Jordan during the night the camels often stampeded, while the Turkish soldiers would fire off their muskets at the slightest excuse."

About this same time, David Roberts, a distinguished British artist, went to Jericho to paint the scene of a pilgrimage. The Reverend George Croly, a British clergyman, who accompanied him, wrote this description of what they saw:

"At Easter the neighborhood of Jericho is frequented by pilgrims who come to cleanse themselves in the River Jordan, but the land retains its ancient character for lawlessness, and the devotees are escorted by a strong military force under the direction of the Governor of Jerusalem, Achmet Aga . . ."

Describing the encampment of the pilgrims on a height overlooking the river, he wrote:

"It is a strikingly Oriental scene . . . the numerous tents . . . the pilgrims in the costumes of various countries; men, women, and children, some praying . . . officers of the escort galloping in all directions . . . some amuse themselves throwing the *djerrid*, others target practise at full speed . . .

"Our encampment was soon buried in sleep as the night came on, though occasionally I caught sounds of the song and the dance, either from the tents of the pilgrims or our Arab guard. The night was one of the most beautiful I had seen ever in that country, and the moon was reflected in all its brightness on the silent waters of the Dead Sea. I lay down in my tent with the door open watching the lights glittering from tent to tent and wondering at the combination of creeds gathered together, to visit scenes so dear to the memory. Near me sat a black group of Abyssinians in their blue turbans. Many, also, were from the Russian Empire.

(The revolution in Russia in 1917 put an end to any further pilgrimages from that country until 1964, when fourteen clergy and theology professors arrived in Jerusalem for the first Russian pilgrimage in forty-seven years.)

"Before two in the A.M. the whole host of pilgrims was aroused and at three a gun gave the signal that the Governor was on horseback and had moved forward. We followed and overtook him. Lights were carried before the Governor. We moved on in silence and the heavy tread of the dense mass was the only sound that broke the stillness of the desert.

"As we approached the brink of the Jordan a general rush took place and women broke into a shrill cry of joy. Even camels heavily loaded could scarcely be restrained. The Governor's carpets were spread on a high bank close to the river where he could command a view of the whole scene. The military band and colors were brought round him and seats were assigned to our party. One of the achievements is to be the first to plunge in. On this occasion a young Greek was swept away by the rapid current and unfortunately drowned before our eyes. Young and old, male and female, were soon in the stream, in one promiscuous mass, some in imminent danger of being drowned . . . This extraordinary display lasted about two hours, when the whole returned, the Governor now bringing up the rear."

Another description of the Easter pilgrimage about this same time said:

"As the river is approached in the early hours of the morning, to avoid the excessive heat of the day, guards go forward with torches of turpentine and old rags. A pilgrim from Poland fell behind the rest and was robbed and stripped naked. As we reached the river the pilgrims rushed into the water, one undistinguished mass. The haughty Turk (the Governor) sat on his horse and looked with scorn on the Christian dogs. But the pilgrims were highly delighted with their bath. Men ducked the women, as farmers do their sheep. Children were carried to the river and dropped in. Some had water poured on their heads in imitation of the baptism of Christ. The Latins maintain the baptism took place farther up stream, so they bathe there. Today two Christians and one Turk were drowned (at the Orthodox spot) without possibility of rescue. Also, an Arab guard fired a pistol in error and killed a woman pilgrim."

Some years later an even more detailed description was published by Stephen Graham called *On the Banks of the Jordan,* in which he explained that the intense interest of the Russians in the pilgrimage was based on their theory that "it is chiefly necessary to die well," their religious thoughts centering almost exclusively on death and resurrection. Accordingly they came thousands of miles, bringing death shrouds which they wore when they immersed themselves in the holy water of the Jordan and then took home and guarded carefully so their bodies could be clothed in these sanctified garments upon their death. (Some pilgrims, wishing to do a charitable act for friends or relations, would wear not one shroud into the Jordan but maybe as many as a dozen, one on top of the other.) Each pilgrim also took home some soil from Jerusalem to be put in his coffin. They had their arms tattooed with the word Jerusalem and with a likeness of the Virgin Mary, certain that when they arrived in heaven these markings would set them immediately apart as deserving of special treatment.

The day before the caravan left Jerusalem for Jericho, the pilgrims would cut pieces of linen in the shape of the Stone of the Anointing which stood outside the Church of the Sepulchre. They would then place these pieces of linen and their shrouds on the stone for blessing, with the idea that they were doing—in advance—for their own dead bodies what Joseph of Arimathaea had done for the body of Christ. The night before departure was always a busy one, with the pilgrims cutting up their pieces of linen, procuring shrouds, getting them blessed, and searching for containers in which they could bring back Jordan water.

There were generally one to two thousand men, women and children in a pilgrimage. In the procession would be hundreds of asses and donkeys, for those too ill or feeble to walk. Some pilgrims wore large wooden crosses hung from their necks on pieces of rope.

In those days nothing remained of Jericho but a small Arab hamlet called Erikha, with hovels enough to house a mere two hundred people. A Russian shelter there had accommodations for only fifty, but it did serve a thick green soup in metal washbasins for as many pilgrims as wished it. Ten or twelve men and women would eat from each basin with wooden spoons.

The thousands of scuffling feet kicked up a great white cloud of stifling dust. As the river came in sight, a few rushed ahead to be the first to experience salvation, but most waited for the priests and monks from a nearby monastery to go down and consecrate the water. Hawkers near the baptismal spot sold soap stamped with pictures of Jesus Christ and John the Baptist, as well as rosaries, crosses, and empty bottles.

By now it was sizzling hot. As soon as the pilgrims arrived at the river they began to get undressed and put on their white shrouds. Soon all the women were in what looked like long white nightgowns, while the men wore thin cotton trousers and white shirts. Some women as well as men stood naked. Now the priests began the service of the sanctification of the water.

"Come ye thirsty and take water gladly from the river of salvation," one of the priests chanted.

Candles were passed around and lighted. Then the multitude joined in singing a hymn that began: "They baptized Thee, in Jordan, O

Lord." The priest dipped a gold cross swathed in towels three times in the river. This was taken as a signal for the pilgrims to jump in. For at least an hour the scene was one of confusion, especially after they came out of the water. Few had brought towels. Some took off their shrouds and hung them on thorn bushes and walked around naked waiting for them to dry. Many sang and kissed each other. Some had lost their clothes. Despite the Turkish guard there were many thefts. The Russians had a custom of always drinking a glass of vodka after coming from the river. Hawkers sold small glasses of a colorless Arab liquor called *araq* (raki) to those who had forgotten to bring vodka or had already drunk what they did bring.

Before returning home many pilgrims visited the Dead Sea to take a bath in the salt water, in the belief that while immersion in the Jordan had benefited them spiritually, immersion in the Dead Sea would cure them physically. Some even tried to drink the Dead Sea water, slightly diluted with fresh water from a well. Some took bottles of Dead Sea water back home to use against their enemies. One story the pilgrims told each other was about a Russian witch who asked a pilgrim to bring her back some Dead Sea water. The night it was delivered to her all her cattle died.

Many of the Jordan pilgrims also visited the Monastery of St. Guerassim, where it was possible to obtain certain ecclesiastical benefits for people back home. The legend of St. Guerassim—a variant of the St. Jerome and Androcles stories—is that one day Guerassim, then a young monk, met a lion in the Jordan Wilderness and pulled a thorn from the animal's paw. In gratitude the lion followed him back to the monastery and served him faithfully for years, even doing domestic labor. Guerassim finally gave the lion the task of keeping watch on the monastery's ass, while it was grazing. Once the lion was negligent and returned at night without the ass, so in punishment the monk put the ass's panniers on the lion and made the king of beasts meekly haul water up from the Jordan and lead pilgrims to the monastery. One day the lion returned from the river to find Guerassim dead. There was no joy left in the animal's life and when the monk was buried, the lion stretched out on the top of his tomb and promptly died. At the St. Guerassim Monastery the monks prayed continuously for people whose names were shouted out to them by the pilgrims, in return for contributions to maintain a monastery named after a man who had befriended—and then punished—a lion.

It is sad to be compelled to conclude the story of the nineteenth century in the Jordan Valley with an episode involving bloodshed. This has been one chapter—one epoch—with little violence and few deaths.

The ugly incident of the century occurred in 1860 at Hasbaya, a town close to one of the happy, bubbling sources of the Jordan. Hundreds of Christian Protestants had settled in this place so near the majesty of Mount Hermon and so well favored by nature. But there were violent religious conflicts. First, there was the animosity between Christians and Muslims. Then there were the Metawilehs, a heretical sect, followers of Mohammed's son-in-law, Ali, who hated Christians with such a vengeance that no matter how poor, they would smash and destroy any jar, dish or cooking utensil that might—even accidentally—have been used by someone professing Christianity. Also there were the Druses, members of the most peculiar religious group in the Valley. They were remarkable in many ways: strong, virile, individualistic. Everything about their religion was supposed to be secret. Their sanctuaries were called "solitudes." They had no known form of prayer, no exact time or precise place for worship, and no acknowledged priesthood. They practiced polygamy. A few of their customs and beliefs probably came from Persia. Some scholars believe that they are descended from Canaanites who lived to the north of the area settled by the Twelve Tribes of Israel.

Murders, robberies and outbreaks of violence became common around Hasbaya. The fanatical spirit of the Muslim population was secretly fomented by Turkish pashas and the Muhammadan religious body called the *ulema*. Turkish troops sent to Hasbaya occupied the old palace and when the town was suddenly surrounded by Druses, Othman Aga, Turkish military commander, offered to protect the Christians if they would surrender their arms and take refuge in the palace. They did both. The Druses were then permitted to burn and pillage the town. For eight days the hundreds of Christian refugees were without food. Then on June 11, 1860, by which time most of them were so weak they could hardly lift an arm, the Turks threw open the palace gates, and the Druse horde rushed in. A description of what the attackers did with swords, axes, hatchets, guns, pistols and their bare hands has been preserved. Not even in horror-fiction is there anything comparable. Turkish soldiers were stationed on the stairways leading up from the Great Court where the prisoners had been confined, and when any Christian attempted to flee up the stairs the soldiers would pitch him down to the butchers below, who would catch the body on the points of their bayonets.

Some weeks later an English traveler visited the palace and saw what he estimated to be twelve hundred corpses lying in that improvised slaughterhouse, just as they had fallen, body upon body, heap upon heap.

Yet, then as now, clear, sparkling water flowed joyfully from the springs of Hasbaya and went cascading down to help form a holy river.

12

It is doubtful whether there had ever been, anywhere, a land as sick as the Jordan Valley was late in the nineteenth century. An area that had once happily supported a million and a half people now had only a few thousand inhabitants. Within sight of Lake Tiberias there had been some of the most beautiful cities of the Greek and Eastern Roman empires. Now around the lake there were only six sad-looking settlements, each housing less than two hundred and fifty persons, with the single exception of Tiberias. The Valley of Ginneisar (Gennesaret), northwest of the lake, was ravaged by malaria. Almost none of the Jordan Valley was under cultivation. There was not a single bridge intact between Lake Tiberias and the Dead Sea. When the river level was high, voyagers had to travel all the way to Adam (Damiya) and take a ferry boat that was pulled back and forth by ropes. Often the boat was disabled. Much of the rich soil of the Valley had relapsed into barren, rocky wasteland. There were a few scattered, impoverished communities here and there; otherwise the population was made up of nomad tribesmen.

A report to the Royal Asiatic Society said:

"The present inhabitants are Bedouins and a mongrel, miserable, sickly-looking race of Arabs called 'the Men of the Ghor.' They live in movable tents of reeds. At Jericho dwell twenty or thirty families. They live mostly on fish caught in the river and lakes . . . they sell reeds, melons, canes, charcoal and firewood. They are despised and oppressed by the regular *fellahin* (peasants) who descend to the Ghor looking for pastureage . . ."

As a result of the ravages of war and centuries of Arab neglect, the great cities had crumbled, dikes and dams had been destroyed, canals were clogged, and overgrazing had left the hills denuded, thus encouraging destructive erosion. A once proud people had sunk into hopeless poverty.

But by the start of the twentieth century a movement had begun that was destined to change both the geography and the history of the entire Valley. A Budapest-born, Viennese journalist-playwright, Theodor Herzl, in 1896 wrote an eighty-six-page book, *The Jewish State,* in which he advocated an orderly exodus of Europe's Jews to a land of their own in which they would govern themselves. He spent years obtaining private audiences with Baron Edmond de Rothschild, the king of Italy, the German kaiser and the sultan who ruled the Ottoman Empire, trying to persuade them to use their influence to enable at least some of Europe's Jews to return to the banks of the Jordan. He made only one visit himself to the Holy Land, where he conferred with Kaiser Wilhelm, who was then visiting the country. Although Herzl never crossed the Jordan and never walked along its banks, he did see it. In his diary for November 2, 1898, he wrote:

"We climbed the Russian Tower (on the Mount of Olives), myself only as far as the first level, because I got dizzy, the others to the very top. Incomparable view of the Jordan Valley, and its mountain slopes, the Dead Sea, the mountains of Moab . . ."

About his audiences with the kaiser he wrote:

"I pointed out what could be done with the water power of the Jordan . . . The Kaiser eagerly took up the subject and developed the idea."

Reporting on an audience with King Victor Emmanuel III of Italy, he wrote in his diary:

"First, I told him I would like to win over the Sultan.

" 'The only thing that has any effect on him is money,' the King replied. 'If you promise him, in return for the Jordan, half the profit it yields, he'll let you have it.' "

Herzl spent the first year of the twentieth century finishing a novel, *Altneuland* ("Old-New Land"), which was published in 1902. It was the story of a Viennese Jew and a retired German army officer (a Christian) who lived twenty years on a desert island, then in 1923 visited Palestine and found in existence there a Jewish State so Utopian they decided to remain and become citizens. The novel was amazingly prophetic. Herzl foresaw much of what would happen half a century later, when a Jewish state finally would be proclaimed. Here is his fictionalized description of Lake Tiberias as he envisioned it might be in 1923:

". . . and there it lay in the afternoon sun, the lovely Plain of Kinnereth and its lake. Friedrich (the German) could not repress a cry of delight at the sight of this unexpected magnificence. Many boats, large and small, left their luminous trail on the broad surface of the Lake of Tiberias. Sails shimmered and the brass of motor boats sparkled in the sun. The eastern shore and the newly wooded slopes were dotted with white villas. And here was Magdala, a sparkling new town with fine houses and colorful gardens . . .

"Tiberias was a favorite with rich Americans and Europeans who, to escape the winter of their own lands, had formerly gone to Sicily and Egypt. As soon as the first good hotels had been established in Tiberias, the stream of visitors began . . . driving through Tiberias from north to south they saw neat little lanes and quaint squares and beautiful residences, and little harbors, noisy and busy. They passed stately mosques, churches with Latin and Greek crosses, and magnificent stone synagogues . . . Far away to the north end of the lake was the mouth of the Jordan and, beyond, the snowy majesty of Mount Hermon, towering over the low hills and the rejuvenated land like a benevolent giant . . . and everywhere greenery and flowers and a lovely fragrant world.

"'It is truly the Garden of Eden!' Friedrich said softly, and feeling Miriam close to him, involuntarily touched her hand and pressed it, as if to thank her for all he saw and felt."

Elsewhere in the book a university professor explains to the visitors:

"We have a warm climate, especially here in the Jordan Valley. That's why we have taken a special interest in refrigeration . . . if you enter one of our houses in summer you'll see a cooling block of ice in the middle of the sitting room . . . and if you want to pay for it, you can even have a bunch of flowers frozen into a block of ice standing on your table."

In Herzl's Utopia, chemical works were constructed on the shores of the Dead Sea, a railroad was built the length of the Valley with tracks on either side of the river, and a canal was dug from the Mediterranean to the Dead Sea to create electricity by the natural descent of the water. Power stations were also built along the Jordan. The level of the Dead Sea was kept constant by using some of the electricity to pump water out of Lake Tiberias for agricultural purposes.

Altneuland was translated into half a dozen languages, went into many editions, and had much influence, but the future of the Valley was more directly affected by a gathering of world Jewish leaders called by Herzl in Basle, Switzerland, the World Zionist Congress, at which for the first time in almost two thousand years Jews who had been scattered to the four corners of the world spoke about returning to their own ancient land as if they really meant to go back someday in considerable numbers.

At this time permission to buy land or to build had to be obtained from the Ottoman representatives through bribery. Most of the forty-five thousand Jews in Jerusalem and Jaffa depended for their existence on the collection of religious alms from abroad. There were about five thousand Jews living on the land, a few of them in the Valley, the rest scattered through seventeen agricultural settlements, only three or four large enough to be called villages. Some of these pioneers had emigrated late in the nineteenth century from Russia and Poland in what was called the First *Aliyah* ("going up" or "immigration"). They had established four settlements in the Valley. In 1883 at Yesod-Hamaala, in the Lake Huleh region, they founded the first Jewish settlement in modern history; then, seven years later, Mishmar Hayarden, close by; then in 1896 another settlement at Metula, on the present-day frontier between Lebanon and Israel; and two years later, back in the Huleh area, Mahanayim.

The Second Aliyah, sparked by Herzl and the Zionist Congress, brought a great wave of virile, idealistic young men and women from many parts of Europe, bent on self-help and manual labor. Among the many places they chose for their settlements was a spot in the Valley close to where the Jordan flows out of Lake Tiberias. The hills of Galilee were on one side, the mountains of Syria and Transjordan on the other, and in the distance the great white peak of Mount Hermon. They gave it the name Degania, meaning "cornflower." When the men of the Second Aliyah arrived there in midsummer 1909 the air was thick with malarial mosquitoes and the flat valley was like a hot plate, with everything in sight burned brown. The Jordan was a mere trickle. When the rains came conditions grew even worse, for the overflow of the Jordan flooded much of their land. Even after the Jordan subsided, the men of Degania were left with swamps that bred fever and mud that sucked the boots off their feet.

These European intellectuals, who had had no previous experience in farming and who were constantly being attacked by the Bedouins, took the desolate seven hundred and fifty acres of land that had been purchased by a Jewish fund and slowly, by trial and error, evolved agricultural methods that enabled them to convert Degania into a showplace of the Valley, where, after some years, they grew wheat, grapes, vegetables, olives, bananas, dates and apples in abundance, and succeeded in getting as many as eight crops of alfalfa a year from their fields. But the success was not instantaneous. It was bought at the price of immense devotion, and in spite of extreme hardship. The colonists suffered and struggled through two world wars, many Arab attacks, a civil conflict, and years of drought, fever, cattle sickness and miscellaneous discouragement. But finally Degania was held up as proof that the Valley, neglected though it had been for so many centuries, could be brought back into productivity again, and it served as a prototype for hundreds of other Jewish agricultural settlements that sprang up, not only in the Valley but even in places where water had to be piped in, or brought in by truck, and where there was so much salinity that before seeds could be planted the soil literally had to be taken up, bucketful by bucketful, washed of its pollution, and then put back again.

Degania is important in the Jordan story in quite another way. Just as the Essenes so many centuries earlier tried to introduce a new way of life in their monastery on the edge of the Dead Sea, so also did the men of Degania, here in their agricultural settlement sixty-five miles as the crow flies to the north. They had discussed it back in Europe before they left. They talked about it often at Degania after the day's work was done. Joseph Baratz, known as "the father of Degania," once explained:

"We know the land responds to work and to selflessness, but it does not give itself in the same way to greedy hands and rapacious hearts."

To avoid rapaciousness and greed, they organized a cooperative way of life, with emphasis on equality, mutual help, and common responsibility. Baratz was convinced that even as the land of the Jordan had lost its fertility, so had the people who once dwelt there become barren in spirit. He argued that if "we give the land our strength it will give us back our creativeness." So they decided to have neither masters nor paid servants, but to give themselves freely and equally to the soil and to each other's needs. Thus no one would have to be ambitious to acquire money, for money would not exist, and no one would need worry about himself or his family, for the community would care for all. Summing it up, Baratz said:

"Neither lacking nor possessing anything, we hoped that in this way we could manage to live a just, peaceful and productive life."

An agricultural settlement in which this form of communal living is practiced came to be called a *kibbutz* ("a gathering together") and its members were popularly called *kibbutzniks*. Degania was given credit for being "the mother of the kibbutz movement." Fifty years after the founding of this first communal settlement on the Lower Jordan, with an initial population of 273 men, women, and children, there were 230 such cooperative communities, with a total population of almost 80,000, producing thirty percent of Israel's total agricultural output. Once again, on the banks of the Jordan a revolutionary idea had been born.

Early in the twentieth century American advertising, promotion and exploitation methods began to be applied to the sale of religious mementoes from the Valley. One promoter who set up shop close to the baptismal spot advertised that the Jordan water he was selling had been "boiled, blessed and bottled" by monks. Containers of earth were sold to Jews from abroad who apparently had read the words of a Midrash writer:

"I have heard that Palestine dust put on the eyes, on the navel and between the legs of one deceased outside the Holy Land is the equivalent to being buried in Palestine."

But it took a Kentucky colonel to see really sizable commercial possibilities in the wholesale exportation of Jordan water.

In 1906 Colonel Clifford E. Nadaud of Covington, Kentucky, made a trip to the Holy Land and upon his return took back souvenirs of many sorts, including a bottle of Jordan water. When his friends expressed greater interest in the bottle of water than in anything else— even some pieces of exquisite Palestinian needlework—the colonel conceived his great idea. He established the International River Jordan Water Corporation, with a declared capital of five million dollars—a considerable sum in 1906. Then he obtained letters of introduction to Ottoman Empire officials from the Turkish ambassador to the United States and from the secretary of state. In Constantinople, after much talk—and probably the handing out of considerable baksheesh—he obtained from Sultan Abdul Hamid the exclusive right to ship Jordan water to all parts of the world, with the proviso that it be used only for baptisms and other religious purposes.

On the west bank of the river, as close as possible to the spot where the Latin branch of the Church considers the baptism of Christ to have taken place, Colonel Nadaud established his plant. There, in the presence of the American consul to Jerusalem and a few ecclesiastical officials, fifty casks were filled with a total of thirty tons of river water, with the consul and the church officials attesting to the fact that the water in the casks actually was from the holy river.

Back in America, while awaiting the arrival of the casks by slow boat, Colonel Nadaud prepared an intensive publicity and advertising campaign. Some of his slogans read:

THE ROYAL FAMILIES OF EUROPE
USE JORDAN WATER.
Why don't you?

SAVE YOURSELF THE TROUBLE
OF TAKING YOUR BABIES
TO THE JORDAN RIVER
FOR BAPTISM

But the water did not sell fast enough to make the venture worthwhile, so Colonel Nadaud introduced a new idea. His ads in newspapers became models of sentimentality, at the same time giving a hint of his own desperation:

Over the Flower-Strewn Casket of Your Loved One,
Over the Rose-Covered Grave of Your Sainted Dead,
Sprinkle Refreshing Water, Like the Dew of Heaven,
From the Sacred River Jordan.

But there was no noticeable boom in business. Then a commercial tragedy occurred: the stagnant water began to turn a sickly and poisonous-looking green.

Finally the International River Jordan Water Corporation (announced capital five million dollars) went into bankruptcy.

Colonel Nadaud spent his declining years trying to recoup his losses by lecturing on the wonders of the Holy Land and the beauties of the Jordan River. He died an elderly man in 1957. He is buried in Cold Springs Cemetery, Campbell County, Kentucky. No one since his day has attempted the wholesale exportation of Jordan water for religious purposes.

War came again to the Jordan Valley late in 1914. A few weeks after the assassination of the Austrian archduke in Sarajevo, the Ottoman Empire aligned itself with the Central Powers: Germany, Austria and Italy. Then, on November 5, Britain declared war on the sultanate that held in her uncertain grasp not only the Valley but also European Turkey, Anatolia, Syria, Lebanon, Iraq, Yemen, Arabia, a great many islands in the Aegean, and miscellaneous other pieces of geography scattered over a wide area. The world already was calling her "the Sick Man of Europe" but she was not going to succumb to the illness that afflicted her without a struggle.

This was going to be a war such as the Valley—despite all its thousands of years of experience with organized slaughter—had never seen before. Soon airplanes of a rival empire, with its capital far off to the west, were flying over the Great Rift. Until now the Jordan had never witnessed three-dimensional warfare.

For each man in the Valley—and in the rest of the territory of the Ottoman Empire—World War I posed a great problem. Should he remain a loyal subject of the government and respond to conscription and fight on the side of the Turks, or— Each man had to make the personal decision. The Ottoman administration had been relatively easygoing, even though backward and corrupt. Local officials were underpaid and everything was arranged by dispensing baksheesh. Taxation was not punitive, but no services were provided: neither hospitals, schools, roads, nor security. It was a laissez-faire system, with most of the people left to fend for themselves. The country was poor and no one seemed to care. The Jews in the Valley received some help from outside and those who were newcomers had a great deal of natural ambition. The Arabs were the real victims of the situation. For them life was wretched. Stagnation was everywhere. And so it was that the Jews of the Valley, as well as the more enlightened Arabs, decided that hope for all of them lay in an Allied victory.

In Degania, resting up between wars, dwelt Joseph Trumpeldor, who had lost an arm in the Russo-Japanese conflict. One day soon after the start of hostilities he announced he was going to join the British Army. How? He smiled, and a few days later was off, somehow getting through Turkish lines and ending up founder of the Zionist Mule Corps in the British Army.

Degania itself was occupied by Turkish soldiers, who made the colonists move out of their houses and sleep in tents or on the ground. As the Allies advanced in the Middle East, more and more kibbutzniks were suspected of pro-British sympathy and were subjected to arrest and torture. Among the Degania colonists was a slim, elderly man, A. D. Gordon, poet, writer and spokesman for the theory of moral elevation through manual work, who one day heard that the Turks were so suspicious of any Jews who had come from Russia (because Russia was now Turkey's enemy) that they were arresting them and taking them for questioning to Kinneret, a settlement on the west shore of Lake Tiberias. Gordon walked from Degania to Kinneret, found the building in which the prisoners were being interrogated, smuggled himself into the lineup, and when shrieks of pain came from the room in which the suspects were being given third-degree treatment, raised his voice in a Yiddish song that began: "As they draw my blood, I sing a merry tune."

Those in the Valley who hoped for a Turkish defeat rejoiced over each new report that the British were advancing from the south. One way they could tell how things were going was by watching the German planes operating from airfields that had been established at several places in the Valley. Each day fewer returned from their sorties.

It was slightly over three years from the British declaration of war on Turkey to General Allenby's capture of Jerusalem on December 9, 1917. (He entered the city on December 11, but surrender was December 9.) Jericho did not fall for another two months and ten days. When it did the river itself began to play a vital role. For the next seven months the Jordan was being almost continuously crossed and recrossed by troops of various nationalities, among them Jewish Battalions made up of volunteers from Palestine and abroad. In March and again in May, Allenby went over the Jordan and made two raids far east of the river, in the hope of drawing Turkish forces away from the coastal plain. Neither raid was a great military success, but the main purpose was served, because by September, when he finally made his drive up the coastal plain, the Turks had sent all but eight thousand of their troops to the east of the Jordan, while Allenby had a concentration of thirty-five thousand men in the plain.

One of the fiercest battles in the Valley was fought at Tell es Semakh (Tsemah) at the south end of Lake Tiberias. The Fourth Australian Light Horse Brigade captured the village from the Germans in a battle that lasted all of one long night.

Often the Turks and their German allies fled from a village they had occupied before the actual arrival of the British. In the interim, the Bedouins would come sweeping in and steal anything the Germans and the Turks may have overlooked. Australians were the first liberators most villages saw. They came on horses, many of them looking more like farmers than soldiers.

As the Turks fled up the Valley they blew up what few bridges there were, hoping to check the Allied advance. Some of the stones still clog the river, nearly half a century later.

Also it is still possible to find in the bed of the Jordan rusted fragments of German artillery pieces that were abandoned in the flight.

Two Valley cities taken during Allenby's September drive mentioned in all military histories of the campaign are Adam (Damiya) and Beth-Shan (Scythopolis).

The Dead Sea figured in the war in an odd manner. Food was scarce, so the Turks transported overland from Jaffa a considerable number of boats—including at least one motor boat—and used them to transport grain from the east side of the Dead Sea to the west. (These were not the first boats ever seen on the Dead Sea. A few years before World War I, the Greek Patriarch, at great expense, had had a small steamer shipped from Jaffa and launched on the Lower Jordan to take pilgrims on excursions down the Dead Sea. One gala trip was made with the consuls of many nations as guests. Then suddenly orders came from Constantinople that all permission to navigate the Dead Sea was canceled, and the steamer was sent back to Jaffa.)

After the war ended and secrecy was lifted, it was disclosed that the British loss of life in the Jordan Valley from malaria had been greater than all the battle casualties in the entire Middle East during the entire war.

One lasting side effect of World War I for the Valley was that both the Germans and the British mapped the area thoroughly, with the help of air photographs. Thus geographers and fluviomorphologists learned a great deal more than they had ever known about the Jordan.

Thirteen years after the last of the Turks left the Valley, the scion of a distinguished Scottish-Irish family, Lieutenant James Henry Ferguson, R.A., O.B.E., became—so his friends claimed—"the first person who, on his own initiative and by his personal and unaided prowess, succeeded in traveling from the Sea of Tiberias to the Dead Sea by canoe." He was certainly the first explorer of the Jordan to make advance reconnaissance from the air—while flying over the Valley as an R.A.F. pilot. His delightful contribution to the Jordan story is not meteorological, nautical or barometric readings but a story of what he discovered on his second day of travel south from Lake Tiberias. His way was blocked because workmen in charge of a Turkish officer, Mohammed Bey, had erected a dam across a bend of the river. Questioning gradually brought out the story. Several months before the end of World War I, when the remnants of the Turkish Army in Palestine were being hotly pursued up the Valley by Allenby, a transport of Turkish quartermaster's stores left Nablus, in an attempt to escape east over the Jordan, but the transport was trapped in the Valley and obliged to abandon a goodly fortune in food and supplies. Among the goods being transported were twenty-three boxes containing gold. The officer in charge of the transport was Mohammed Bey. He had his men dump the cases of gold into the Jordan at this particular spot, which he carefully noted. Now, thirteen years later, having obtained permission from the Mandatory British Government of Palestine, he was back, to search for the treasure.

Lieutenant Ferguson listened to the story, made a few notes, wished Mohammed Bey well, and went on.

One year later another canoe expedition, this one headed by a British vicar, the Reverend R. J. E. Boggis of Torquay, tried to negotiate the Jordan from one lake to the other. When their canoes reached this same spot, they too found the treasure hunters at work. Two large pumps were in operation day and night, vainly trying to dry up a deep pool directly below a falls. This was the spot at which Mohammed Bey was certain he had had his soldiers dump the cases of gold fourteen years earlier. The Boggis expedition added one detail to the story: the Turkish colonel had blown up a bridge to prevent the British catching up with him. The debris that still littered the river bed made the hunt for the gold more difficult. A short time after this the salvage operation was finally abandoned, so the mystery remains:

Who retrieved those twenty-three cases of gold, or are they still buried in the bed of the Jordan?

As a result of the breakup of the Ottoman Empire after the end of World War I the Jordan River gave its name to a new country. But the Hashemite Kingdom of Jordan was not born either easily or quickly. The east bank of the river had had a strange history. Before the arrival of Moses it had been divided into several small kingdoms. Then two and a half of the Twelve Tribes had settled on part of the land across the Jordan. In the time of David and Solomon their empire included much land east of the Jordan. For many years the Decapolis controlled a great deal of the east bank. Never in history was all the east side of the Jordan in the hands of a single ruler. And there had never been a country called Jordan. After World War I the League of Nations gave Great Britain a mandate over Palestine, including what is now Jordan, and the British, eager to satisfy all the Arab leaders involved in a complicated struggle for power and territory, agreed in 1921 to let Abdullah ibn Hussein, second son of the king in Mecca, come north to Amman and serve as emir or prince (under British direction) over what came to be called Transjordan, being simply that part of Palestine east of the river. Gradually, bit by bit, Abdullah wheedled more and more power and independence from the British, until finally in 1946 Transjordan became completely independent and its National Assembly voted to proclaim Abdullah no longer emir but "His Majesty Abdullah

I, King of the Hashemite Kingdom of Trans-Jordan" (Hashemite being the family name).

While World War I was still in progress the British issued a statement of foreign policy called the Balfour Declaration which caused great celebrating among the Jews living in the Valley, for it declared that "His Majesty's Government views with favour the establishment in Palestine of a national home for the Jewish people . . ." Many assumed that as soon as the Ottoman Empire was crushed and the war ended, a Jewish state would come quickly into existence on both sides of the Jordan. Their first disappointment was over the change in British policy about what would constitute the eastern frontier of Palestine. (Lord Balfour on August 11, 1919, had flatly stated: "Palestine should extend into the lands lying east of the Jordan.") Their greater disappointment was over British failure ever to live up to the promise of the Balfour Declaration—even to the extent, thirty years later, of abstaining from voting on the U.N. Partition Plan that finally brought the Jewish State into existence.

What the Balfour Declaration did do was to raise hope that somehow, eventually, after being dispersed for almost two thousand years, the Jews would finally reassemble in the Valley and in the hills of their ancient land. Even without waiting for diplomats, politicians and soldiers to make it possible, they started returning. Between 1920 and 1938, almost a third of a million Jews immigrated to Palestine, some legally, many illegally; some settling in the Valley, many congregating in the cities, but all of them beginning to give substance to Herzl's dream and beginning to revive life in an area that so short a time ago had rightfully been called as sick a land as ever existed.

This influx led to Arab-Jewish friction: riots, bloodshed, virtual civil war. The Valley came in for its share of it. Farmers worked their fields with guns slung around their shoulders, recalling the days of Nehemiah when "every one with one of his hands wrought in the work, and with the other hand held a weapon . . . Every one had his sword girded by his side, and so builded."

There was excitement of quite a different sort in the Valley in 1925 when someone discovered the remains of a man who had been dead for at least forty thousand years; perhaps a hundred thousand years: the Galilee Man he was called, because his Paleolithic skull—the oldest that had been found in the country up to that time—was discovered in Wadi Amud, a gorge noted for its prehistoric caves, not far from Capernaum, where Christ, who also had been called "the Man of Galilee," had lived for a time in a fisherman's cottage.

The first really important water project on the Jordan—at least in modern times—was the work of a Jewish engineer, Pinhas Rutenberg. In the 1920s he devised a plan for the complete utilization of the power resources of the Jordan, from its headwaters all the way to the Dead Sea. It called for the creation of many artificial lakes for storage, the construction of power and irrigation canals, and the erection of hydroelectric stations. At Naharayim, where the Yarmuk flows into the Jordan, a company organized by Rutenberg built the first of the contemplated power stations, designed to supply most of Palestine with current and assist in the irrigation of the Lower Valley by using water that would be impounded in an immense basin and drawn off as needed. This was the first of many Jewish-planned, Jewish-built, Jewish-financed water schemes that were inaugurated under the British Mandate. (Unfortunately, the Rutenberg plant, as it came to be known, was in Transjordan and in 1948 was destroyed by the Arab Legion.)

World War II, with the killing of six million people in extermination camps, intensified the desire of the Jews for the creation of a state of their own, or at least for some open doors, in order to provide sanctuary for those who were trying to flee Hitler's continent. When the British government not only refused to open the doors a little wider, but even tried to shut them tighter—hoping thus to avoid antagonizing forty million Arabs—the Jews of Palestine continued to volunteer in the British Army to fight against the Nazis, but also engaged in illegal immigration, bringing in tens of thousands of refugees from Europe. Many were landed at night at obscure points on the Mediterranean coast, then were transported as quickly as possible into the Valley, where they were hidden in Jewish villages and cooperative settlements.

The only major war incident in the Valley occurred in 1944 when the Luftwaffe dropped a number of Nazi spies close to the Jordan. Their three objectives were to spy on the British, engage in acts of sabotage, and work with sympathetic Arabs against the Allies. They went into hiding in caves in the Jericho area, but were soon located and appropriately dealt with by the British.

In those days the river separated Palestine, still under British mandate, and Transjordan, which had not yet gained her independence. Both sides of the river were, therefore, virtually part of the British Empire. British uniforms were everywhere and British army engineers constructed many bridges across the river for military purposes.

With the end of the war in 1945, the three underground Jewish armies in Palestine—Haganah, Irgun and the Stern Group—began to sabotage British military installations, especially radar stations being used to track ships bringing in illegal immigrants. Late that year Haganah attacked some hundred and fifty points on the railways, including several places in the Valley near Samach (Samka).

When British Foreign Minister Ernest Bevin in 1946 announced that further Jewish immigration into Palestine would be limited to fifteen hundred per month, the Haganah high command decided to react violently. Three hundred members of Palmach—the Haganah striking force—were divided into twelve groups and began to reconnoiter five key bridges across the Jordan: the Sheikh Hussein bridge opposite Beit-Shean; the Damiah, which carried traffic over the river from Nablus; the Allenby, opposite Jericho, and the Yarmuk and Benat Ya'kob. The scouts made careful note of the times the guards were changed, as well as all avenues of approach and retreat.

Zero hour was supposed to be 11 P.M. on June 16, 1946. Soon after the Palmach unit assigned to blow up the Allenby bridge left Kibbutz Beit Haarava (later destroyed by the Jordanians) they were detected by Arab Legion guards. The battle lasted thirty minutes, after which the Arabs withdrew and the Palmach unit set off their explosives at the west end of the bridge. Most of the span collapsed. The Jewish soldiers then retreated into the desert of Judaea. It took them three days to get back to Jerusalem, after numerous skirmishes with Bedouin tribesmen and British soldiers and police. It took two months to repair the bridge enough for limited use.

The attempts on the Damiah and Sheikh Hussein bridges failed. They were far from the nearest Jewish settlement, and when the Palmach finally reached them, their TNT was of such poor quality that much of it failed to explode. Mines planted near the Damiah bridge killed a British officer as he was trying to dismantle them. The Sheikh Hussein bridge was only cracked. The most successful attempt was on the Yarmuk bridge. A large Palmach unit engaged the Arabs and British in a diversionary operation, while the Palmach demolition squad blew up the bridge. Guards at the Benat Ya'kob bridge were easily overpowered and the span was blown up. The Palmach lost not a single man in these five operations, although that same night—the Night of the Bridges, as it came to be called in Israeli history books—fourteen saboteurs were killed trying to blow up a bridge near the Arab village of Azib, north of Acre.

In these same years the kibbutzim in the Valley were centers for the secret training of Jewish underground soldiers. Some of the largest training centers were at Ein Gev, on the far side of Lake Tiberias, and at Afikim, Beit Hashita, Ein Harod, and Degania.

The settlers in the kibbutzim in the north of the Valley played active roles in helping illegal immigrants literally walk into the country—from Syria and Lebanon. An underground railroad was established much like the one that helped escaping slaves in the United States in the nineteenth century. In this manner thousands of Jews were brought into the Valley and then dispersed round the country.

It was less than two years after the end of World War II—the summer of 1947—when a young Arab herdsman, Muhammad Adh-Dhib, lost a goat from the flock he was supposed to be tending. While searching for it in one of the steep valleys leading up from the Dead Sea he saw a circular hole in the rock. Idle curiosity prompted him to investigate. Picking up a rock, he threw it into the dark abyss. The sound he heard made him flee in terror. The next day he returned with an older companion, and together, braving the terrors of the unknown, they climbed in through the hole and found two lines of tall jars, one of which had been broken by the stone. All were empty except one that contained rolls of what looked like old leather. They stuffed the scrolls inside their jackets and left. In the days that followed they showed their find to many friends. One scroll was seven feet long.

The rest of the story is now an archaeological classic: how the Qumran scrolls finally came into the hands of people who realized their value; how weeks later, on the very day the United Nations was voting on whether or not to partition Palestine, a professor at Hebrew University in Jerusalem, E. L. Sukenik, heard that an antique dealer in Bethlehem had some old Hebrew manuscripts for sale and, despite the tension of the moment, rode an Arab bus to Bethlehem and bought three of the scrolls, bringing them back under his arm wrapped in a newspaper; how when he began studying them he discovered they were approximately two thousand years old and one of the greatest archaeological finds ever made; how his son, Yigael Yadin, later chief of staff of the Israeli Army, bought for a quarter of a million dollars four more of the scrolls in the United States, where they had been taken in search of the highest possible price. Ultimately it was decided that the scrolls probably had formed part of the library of the Essene monastery at Qumran.

After World War II, when the United Nations decided to take a hand in trying to solve some of the problems of the Middle East, it was suggested that Palestine be turned into an independent, bi-national state, with Arabs and Jews in joint control of their own destiny. When this idea met with little enthusiasm, "partition" became the magic word. It was then that many pencils began to make many different lines on maps, trying to divide Palestine so that the bulk of Arabs would be within the frontiers of an Arab state and the bulk of the Jews within the frontiers of a Jewish state, without the necessity of much exchange of population.

The Jordan Valley had a vital interest in all this. At various times in its history the river had served as a frontier between tribes, between countries, between kingdoms—sometimes for its entire length, sometimes for a short distance. Once nine different tribes had had land that came down to the river, on one side or the other. None of the map makers during the partition discussions of the 1940s suggested that either Arabs or Jews be given the entire Jordan Valley. The Partition Plan finally adopted by an overwhelming majority of U.N. votes provided that the new Jewish state should have both banks of the Upper Jordan, all of Lake Huleh, and all of Lake Tiberias. On the Lower Jordan, for about one-third its length, the Israeli border should be the middle of the river. From that point on down to the Dead Sea the land to the east of the river would continue to belong to the already established Hashemite Kingdom of Transjordan, while the west bank would be within a newly created Arab state, which would also control the west shoreline of the Dead Sea down to a point just north of Ein Gedi. The lower half of the Dead Sea would belong to the new Jewish state.

The war that broke out after the British evacuation of Palestine, and after invasion of the newly created State of Israel by armies of neighboring Arab states, made many drastic revisions in the U.N. map. The armistice lines finally established by truce commissions have remained the national frontiers—and will continue to remain the national frontiers until someday a peace conference is held at which revision of these lines will be discussed. Although the many months of severe fighting greatly increased the total area of the Jewish state, it had little effect on the frontiers in the Valley. From Dan down to the southernmost tip of the Dead Sea, Arabs and Jews today have just about the same riparian rights that the U.N. intended each should have.

However, when war erupted in 1948 the Valley became greatly involved. Between May 15 (the day after the State of Israel was officially proclaimed) and May 23, a series of engagements between Syrian and Israeli troops took place at the south end of Lake Tiberias. It became known as "The Battle of the Jordan Valley." The story reads like fiction. The Jewish defenders were in the hundreds, their opponents in the thousands, sometimes tens of thousands. The defenders' equipment might have seemed modern in World War I. But this was 1948—the Atomic Age. What they lacked in numbers and equipment these new-old men of the Valley made up for in bravery and trickery. To convince the Syrians that a great column of reinforcements was arriving, they assembled all the motor vehicles they had, drove them up into the mountains quietly, with no lights showing, turned them around, and then, with headlights full on, came roaring down toward the lake. This was done again and again until the Syrians got the idea that an almost endless column of reinforcements was arriving. At another place in the Valley all available tractors were rounded up and their engines left running at high speed to create a noise similar to that of tanks. Once a fleet of fishing boats was sent out onto Lake Tiberias to open fire on the land-based Syrians, in the hope of completely confusing them.

While all this was going on, children, the sick and the elderly were being evacuated. When the Israelis lost Zemach on the southernmost shore of the lake a wave of despondency swept through the Valley.

On May 19 a delegation from Degania arrived in Tel Aviv to beg for reinforcements and heavy equipment. David Ben-Gurion, who had been elected the new state's first prime minister, gave them this answer:

"There are not enough guns, not enough planes; men are lacking on all fronts. The situation is very severe in the Negev; it is difficult in Jerusalem, in Upper Galilee. The whole country is a front line. We cannot send reinforcements."

Yadin, as chief of operations, told the delegation:

"There is no alternative but to let the Arabs approach to within twenty or thirty meters of the gates of Degania, and then to fight their armor in close combat."

At 4:30 A.M. on May 20 the battle began for Degania and control of the bridge over the Jordan. The Syrians attacked with tanks. The seventy men in the defending force fought with rifles and Molotov cocktails. They knocked out tank after tank until finally the Syrians withdrew. Later that day two Israeli field-artillery pieces arrived in the Valley from Tel Aviv. They came without sights and with gun crews that had only a vague idea how to operate them.

Much of Israel's War of Independence is a Jordan story, but it cannot be told in less than a hundred thousand words—and it has been, by Netanel Lorch, in a book called *The Edge of the Sword*. Enough to report here that the Degania invaders were defeated, many of the attacking tanks were captured, and the settlements of the Lower Jordan were saved.

Meanwhile, the Syrians had established a fuel and ammunition dump close to where the Bridge of the Daughters of Jacob crossed the Jordan, so a suicide squad of Israelis was sent across the river at night, equipped only with light arms and an immense quantity of explosives. The attack was planned as a silent one, without any support. Despite erratic fire by the Syrians, after they became aware of the infiltration, the Israelis detonated their explosives and retreated without a single casualty, but with considerable booty. Lorch says: "The explosions rocked the mountains of Galilee, and the flames and smoke were seen throughout the following day."

A fierce battle was fought for Hazor, where so many historical military actions had taken place. Ein Gev, an isolated Israeli settlement on the east bank of Lake Tiberias, was subject to withering Arab attack. So were many other communities in the Valley. Not until the first truce on June 10, 1948, did all the people of the Valley feel they could relax.

Far to the south, many months later, while armistice negotiations were going on between Israel and Jordan, an anticlimactic Valley episode occurred. An armistice agreement had already been signed between Egypt and Israel, but the Jordanians were still arguing terms. The rule that was being applied was the old axiom that "possession is nine points of the law." Therefore, while the negotiators negotiated, Israeli forces, being careful not to come into armed conflict with Arabs anywhere—in order not to break the truce agreement—carried out what may have been the first amphibious military operation in the entire long history of the Dead Sea. An infantry company and a sappers' platoon, soon after nightfall on March 5, 1949, left Sedom (Sodom), at the south end of the sea. Through the darkness they made their way to the base of the Ein Gedi oasis. There one platoon took up positions on the landing beach, a second occupied the Spring of David, while the third climbed through darkness and rain to the rocks dominating Ein Gedi. When morning came this spot so celebrated in Jewish history, where David once hid in a cave and where Solomon had found inspiration for a poem, was in Israeli hands.

In like manner the Israelis occupied the ancient fortress of Masada, where Herod had once built a palace and the followers of Eleazar ben Yair had committed mass suicide as a final gesture of defiance to the Romans. Because of these actions, when the final agreement was signed with the Jordanians, both Ein Gedi and Masada remained in Israeli hands.

Many different things happened to those parts of Palestine that were supposed to have constituted a new Arab state: during the fighting Northern Galilee was occupied by Israeli soldiers, and the Gaza Strip was taken over by Egypt, while the major area, including the upper part of the Dead Sea and most of the Lower Jordan Valley, was annexed by Transjordan, which then changed its name and became the Hashemite Kingdom of Jordan. Now the river and a country bore exactly the same name.

Jordan, the country, since 1948 has been populated almost exclusively by Arabs, the vast majority also being Muslims. But the intellectual and cultural differences between those who had lived on the west side of the river, in Palestine, and those who had lived in the hills to the east of the river were so great that considerable friction developed. Today when a Palestinian Jordanian speaks of a Bedouin from across the river by saying that he is from the east bank (*"Ad-Difah ash-sharkiyah"* or simply *"sharkiyah"*) he does not mean it as a compliment. Just before or during the 1948 hostilities more than half a million Arabs fled toward the Jordan. Most of these refugees wound up in camps, under United Nations supervision, a majority in the Jericho area, almost within sight of the river. They had been Palestinians. Many had never been across the Jordan in their lives. But by an act of the National Assembly, all were automatically made Jordanian citizens. These refugees (the government of Jordan in 1961 took a census and fixed the total at 630,725) plus 410,000 inhabitants of the newly annexed territory to the west of the river, greatly outnumber the east-bankers, yet the Transjordanians run the country. This has added a new cause for friction along the banks of the ancient river.

The Jewish citizens of Israel are also fractionalized in many ways. Being fierce individualists by nature, they established, in the early days of their new state, close to twenty political parties, most of them with either daily or weekly newspapers. One of these groups—the Herut —has as a major party principle, "territorial integrity of the Land of Israel within its historical boundaries"—meaning, expansion of the present frontiers to include not only that part of the Kingdom of Jordan on the west side of the river, but the eastern bank as well. With the exception of Herut members, however, neither individual Israelis nor any Israeli groups of importance have since the establishment of the state advocated geographical expansionism across the river.

In the years since partition the Jordan Valley has often echoed with the sound of gunfire. Some of the incidents have started with an irresponsible individual on one side of the river firing a single bullet at a man on the other side of the river. Then others begin using firearms;

388

first rifles, then machine guns, and finally artillery pieces. In a few cases even airplanes have gone into action. Neutral truce observers finally arrange a cease-fire and an attempt is made to find out who shot first and why.

Lake Tiberias is completely within the State of Israel, as well as its entire shoreline. Many of the newcomers to the Tiberias area make their living fishing, which is now done at night, by training powerful searchlights into nets in the water. International incidents have often resulted when Syrian gunners in the hills just to the east of the lake have become trigger-happy and aimed their guns at the lights and opened fire. The most serious frontier incidents have been along the Upper Jordan, where the land on either side of the river is a demilitarized zone. Shooting begins when Syrians or Israelis accuse their river-brothers of violating the terms of the demilitarization agreement. And so the Jordan—at least in some places—now serves as a divider of men with different cultures, ideologies and religions. Today in such places if a man on either side attempted to "cross over Jordan" he would set off a burst of gunfire that might send him immediately to his eternal reward.

One of the chief advocates of individualism on the west side of the Jordan in modern times has been the white-haired politician, statesman, journalist, trade union leader, David Ben-Gurion, who became the first prime minister of Israel. One example of his iconoclasm that involved the Jordan was his public statement one day in Tel Aviv that in his opinion Joshua led only "six hundred families" across the Jordan, after their forty years in the desert, instead of some six hundred thousand young males over twenty capable of bearing arms, mentioned in the Book of Numbers, Chapter 26, Verse 51, plus all their women, children and aged. Ben-Gurion's theory was that the Hebrew word used in the biblical quotation, *alif*, means thousand but it also means "family group." He also advanced the theory that a majority of the Hebrews did not leave Canaan when Jacob and his family went to Egypt, but stayed behind to be reinforced later by the returning six hundred "family groups." The controversy that the twinkling-eyed man with the fringe of white hair began that day spread far from the city where he raised the question. Other Bible students all over the world argued the matter. In their book entitled *Joshua*, Thomas B. Costain and Rogers MacVeagh figured out that if half a million nomad warriors, with their families and other impedimenta, marched four abreast they would form a continuous column four hundred miles long. Even if they walked eight abreast, the tail of the column would be back on the Nile River in Egypt, when the first of them were just starting across the Jordan.

Three years after partition, work began on a scheme that was to make a more sudden and dramatic change in the water course of the Jordan than nature had ever made: the drainage of Lake Huleh. It was an idea that had been discussed for decades. In the days of the Ottoman Empire a group of Syrians had obtained a concession for such a project but nothing ever came of it. It had these objectives: to get rid of the malaria that infested that whole section of the Valley; to release an extra fifty million cubic meters of water per year, for the greater benefit of everyone living below this point on the Jordan, Syrians, Jordanians and Israelis alike; to reclaim fifteen thousand acres of swamp, to create a seven-hundred-fifty-acre nature reserve, where all the wild beauty for which Lake Huleh had been celebrated would be preserved; to make it possible to exploit the considerable deposits of peat that nature had manufactured there; to increase the security of the region (the wildness of the almost stagnant lake offered infiltrators a perfect hiding place); and finally to aid in flood control.

Many millennia ago the southern end of the Huleh Valley had been blocked by a sill of basalt rock, as the result of a volcanic eruption. The major task was to blast away this obstruction. Then a temporary artificial barrier was built to hold the water in the lake while giant American dredges cleaned twenty-nine miles of channels through the swamps. The greatest happiness in 1957 over completion of the project was probably on the part of migratory birds. Some had been in the habit of pausing here on their way south from such far places as Russia and the Scandinavian countries. For years, because workmen had invaded the area, they took a different route. After the project was completed and the workmen departed, the news somehow reached the denizens of the wildlife kingdom, and in 1958 the nature reserve became a way station again for migratory birds. They seemed especially pleased with some ponds that had been built for the commercial raising of fish. As many as fifteen thousand pelicans a year pass through, with up to five hundred stopping off at the Huleh nature preserve at a time. One pelican can happily consume six to eight pounds of fish a day. Even as few as a hundred pelicans can clean out a good-sized fish pond in a few hours.

Although much of the papyrus growth was lost, the nature reserve still contains some of the best papyrus in the world. Once a year Jews and Arabs alike are permitted to come in and cut what they please.

A thriving Huleh industry is making floor mats from papyrus. The reclaimed land is so rich that it grows oversized everything. Ears of corn sometimes measure the length of a man's arm.

Since partition, archaeologists have been busy in the Valley. In 1959 at Ubieidiye, not far south of Lake Tiberias, a skull was found that some experts believe may be half a million years old. Two years later Japanese scholars explored the caves in the Wadi Amud, where the Galilee Man had been found, and discovered a complete skeleton of an adult man whose cranium bears all the characteristics of Neanderthal Man. In 1955 at Hazor, nine miles above Lake Tiberias, a team of Israeli archaeologists began a four-year dig which uncovered relics of one city upon another—layer after layer of civilizations. They found charred remains of the Hazor that Joshua destroyed by fire in the thirteenth century B.C., and relics of the city Solomon rebuilt there. Once more archaeology—with Carbon 14 tests and scientific exactness —was being used to prove that the Bible was not a collection of fairy stories but actual history.

Other expeditions found the cave in which the last of Bar Kosiba's followers finally died, while digs at Masada cast new light on the story of Herod and on the tale of the nine hundred and sixty who defied Roman General Flavius Silva and committed themselves to death.

In 1964 James Pritchard of the University of Pennsylvania, at a point in the Valley seven hundred and fifty feet below sea level on the east side of the river in what used to be Gilead but is now part of the Kingdom of Jordan, dug into a hundred-forty-foot mound called Tell es-Sa'idyeh ("the Hill of the Women of the Sa'id Tribe") and found evidence that led him to believe that the Valley had once been the richest and most civilized part of Palestine. Dr. Pritchard surmised that Tell es-Sa'idyeh may have been the Zarethan mentioned in the Bible as the place where the bronze for Solomon's temple was cast—a theory in which Archaeologist Nelson Glueck concurs.

At Tell es-Sa'idyeh, Dr. Pritchard found a mud-walled tomb containing the skeleton of a woman of grand stature, possibly a local queen. Her jewelry had been buried with her: five hundred beads of carnelian and seventy-five of gold, besides silver pins, a silver chain, four ivory boxes, and an ivory spoon on which was carved a human head. Dr. Pritchard figured she had died about the time Joshua was leading the Twelve Tribes across the Jordan.

Jordan came into the news again in 1964 when Queen Elizabeth gave birth to her fourth child and London announced that in accordance with British royal custom for centuries, the child would be baptized with water from the Jordan that was being especially flown over from the Kingdom of Jordan, under supervision of the British ambassador in Amman. This gave the Jordanian government an idea. The Ministry of Information announced that a new department of the government would be inaugurated at once "to provide mothers everywhere with Jordan water for baptizing their newborn children." Henceforth, said the announcement, Jordanian diplomatic missions would be supplied with special bottles of Jordan water for distribution upon request. As souvenirs for those attending the royal christening in London, five hundred such bottles were flown over immediately.

In the almost two decades since partition, many changes have occurred on both sides of the river, from Dan down to the Dead Sea.

Creation of Israel and the ingathering of more than a million Jews since 1948—with thousands upon thousands settling in the Valley— meant a healthy repopulation of a land that had been almost entirely taken over in recent centuries by malarial mosquitoes, wild cactus, the noxious weeds of pestilential swamps, despoiling goats, and thieving nomads. It meant the revitalization of life in an area in which vibrant history was now again being made—and at the cost of a relatively small amount of blood, despite the periodic frontier incidents.

Progress, however, was not confined entirely to the west side of the river. Thanks to substantial financial and technical assistance, first from Great Britain and more recently from the United States and the United Nations, the Kingdom of Jordan in these same years has made measurable strides into the twentieth century. Despite badly eroded soil, dearth of natural resources, lack of any outlet to the Mediterranean, the split between east-bankers and west-bankers, and the centuries-old love of a nomadic life, the people of Jordan have accomplished a certain amount of industrialization, built up a healthy tourist business, and are struggling to avoid being left behind in the whirlwind of change that had swept the region.

Even though there is brittle tension today throughout the Valley, a small gleam of hope for the future can be seen. What happened at Kfar Ruppin proves it.

Kfar Ruppin is a kibbutz twenty miles south of Lake Tiberias—not far from ancient Scythopolis—that has the distinction of being the lowest settlement in the northern part of Israel. Its land runs down to the west bank of the Jordan. In this area the frontier is the middle of the river. The people of Kfar Ruppin boast that the Jordan is forty yards wide at this point, but during much of the year a child can wade across.

That close is the Hashemite Kingdom of Jordan. Just wading distance away.

The kibbutzniks of Kfar Ruppin are hard-working, ambitious people and have prospered. They grow especially good dates. Years ago Arabs from across the river, although knowing that the Jewish farmers carried arms wherever they went, would risk being shot and killed to cross the Jordan and steal dates. Then Kfar Ruppin built ponds for the raising of fish and in order to have a constant flow of water they installed a pump on the west bank of the river that ran day and night, raising water to the fish ponds. Beside the pump were always several large drums of gasoline, for it took sixty gallons a day to keep the pump running. Also, many tools were left there for repairing and adjusting the pump. After the tools and a considerable quantity of gasoline were stolen one night by infiltrators from across the river, Kfar Ruppin decided to post a twenty-four-hour guard over the riverside installation, although they could little afford to use their manpower in this nonproductive manner.

Then, in 1958, across the river within sight of the kibbutz, the Jordanian government, with American technical assistance and financial support, began an agricultural project that doubled, tripled, perhaps even quadrupled the income of all the fellahin living on the other side of the Jordan. This gave the leaders of Kfar Ruppin an idea. They stopped guarding the pump, the tools and the gasoline, on the theory that while a hungry man may risk his life for a few dates, not even a hundred-gallon drum of gasoline is worth the chance, if a man is earning a decent living.

The theory proved to be sound. For the past six years there have been no Israeli guards along the Jordan at this point, and for six years there have been no thefts, no infiltrations, no incidents.

Perhaps, after all, there is hope for peace someday along the Jordan, this river that has seen so little peace in the twenty thousand—or is it eighty thousand?—years of its existence.

13

This has been the life story of the Jordan—its biography, its history, the chronicle of the people who have dwelt along its banks and in the hills lining its Valley, or who have crossed and recrossed the river on errands of mercy or murder. Yet throughout the telling of the story one word has been almost entirely missing: *water*. This final chapter is about the importance of the Jordan as water.

The happiest words in the Middle East are "spring," "stream," "well," "oasis," "water."

Here water makes possible life in the midst of death, green-growing beauty in parched desert places.

Conflicts over water have led to many more deaths by violence in this part of the world than have conflicts over *l'amour* in Latin countries.

Once a million and a half people lived in the Valley. It would be a neat theory to argue that as the water level fell and the Valley's inland seas became smaller, and some of the wadis dried up, and the Jordan carried less and less water on its way to its ultimate destination, so, concomitantly and resultingly, the Valley's richness diminished, its population shrank, its noble cities gradually vanished, and a dust bowl was born. Such a theory would put all the blame on nature. The trouble is that the lowering of the water level occurred in geological times, which are measured by millions of years, while the decline in population and prosperity in the Valley occurred in historical times, which are measured in the hundreds or at most thousands of years.

Then what did cause the decline? What changed the Middle East from a Garden of Eden, a land of milk and honey, into a region that until recently has seemed able to support only a fraction of its former population, and at such a degraded standard of living?

It was the result of no sudden natural disaster, nor even of any slow climatic change. It was man himself who was responsible. The Mongol invaders of the thirteenth century were perhaps more to blame than any others for pillaging the area and ruining the irrigation systems built by wise men who so long ago had learned how to conserve every drop of water that fell from the sky or bubbled up from the earth or raced down the sides of mountains.

The denuding of forests, the neglect of terracing, and the irresponsible practices of nomad tribesmen did the rest. Then add feudalism. Feudalistic exploitation does not necessarily need to be profligate, but in the Middle East it was. Then add goats. These despoiling animals, brought in thirteen hundred years ago in great numbers by Arab tribesmen, did much to change the topography of the Valley as well as its history. They are responsible for two to three feet of topsoil being washed off the hillsides over which they were permitted to roam. Perhaps the ravenousness of the goats was the result of insufficient greenery for them to eat, which in turn may have been the result of insufficient water, and so we are back again to our theme. Whatever you discuss in the Valley generally leads back to water. In France they say *"Cherchez la femme!"* In the Valley it's *"Cherchez de l'eau!"* The lack of water is the root cause of most of the region's troubles.

In times gone by the Valley people well knew the value of water. An old Arab proverb says: "It is the duty of each man in his lifetime to beget a son, plant a tree and dig a well."

There are thousands of references in the Bible to water in one form or another. Warriors go almost crazy with thirst. Chariots are bogged down by a sudden cloudburst and so a battle is lost. Again and again the psalmist sings of springs, waterfalls, brooks, cataracts, bubbling fountains, and places made green-beautiful by water.

("For the Lord thy God bringeth thee into a good land, a land of brooks of water, of fountains . . . " Deuteronomy 8:7)

So important was water in biblical times that when the life story of a king was recounted, the chronicler would mention the wells he had dug. (Uzziah, king of Judah, "digged many wells." And Abraham at Beersheba declared: ". . . these seven ewe lambs . . . may be a witness unto me, that I have digged this well.")

Forts and castles were built to guard water. It was recognized that the quickest way to turn a prosperous country into a frightful wilderness was to destroy its water sources. At one time to stop up a man's well was considered almost as serious a crime as rape or murder. When the Israelites were fighting the Moabites, God helped them win the crucial battle by ordering them to destroy the Moabite wells.

Water is as important to modern man as it was to his ancestors. Today to produce a pint bottle of milk requires one hundred and twenty gallons of water, mostly to grow the necessary fodder for the cow. To produce one pound of oranges takes one hundred gallons of water. If the water used to irrigate an orange grove during the course of a single year stood on the ground long enough to be measured it would be almost three feet deep. The more advanced a civilization becomes, the greater the need for water. It takes much more water to wash an automobile than a bicycle. Three hundred tons of water are required to produce a single ton of steel, one hundred tons to produce a ton of paper.

As for water in the Middle East, it is one of the sad truths of the situation that most of the area's water resources run into some salty sea without being fruitfully utilized.

In this part of the world nothing is ever simple, not even water. The water that bubbles out of the ground or comes down the slopes of Mount Hermon to form the sources of the Jordan is as clear and pure as water can be. But Lake Tiberias is fed by many saline springs, with the result that the lake water contains at least 340 milligrams of chlorine per liter, as compared with twenty in the water of the Upper Jordan. This makes the lake water too saline for certain agricultural uses. But nature—so often compensatory in spirit—corrects this situation by sweetening up the Jordan cocktail. Five miles south of the lake the Yarmuk River, which rises in Syria and for some distance constitutes the boundary between Syria and Jordan, and between Jordan and Israel, tumbles its sweet water into the Jordan, diluting the salinity of the mother river and making it more usable for irrigation and human consumption. The Yarmuk has a normal flow almost as great as that of the Jordan itself, 480 million cubic meters, compared with 510 mcm for the Jordan as it flows out of the lake. (These are pre-diversion figures.)

Lake Tiberias on an average day contains four billion cubic meters of water, equivalent to the outflow from the lake over a period of eight years. The difference between the lake's high and low water marks, which is the way to gauge its reservoir capacity, is one billion cubic meters. Thus it is an ideal warehouse or storage basin.

The total Jordan-Yarmuk system had, before diversions, an estimated annual flow of 1880 million cubic meters, which is a trickle compared with the flow of some of the mighty waterways of other Middle Eastern countries. Also, four countries—Israel, Syria, Lebanon and Jordan—have some sort of riparian rights on either the Jordan, its sources, or its tributaries, giving all four varying degrees of interest in what happens to the water.

Those are a few of the basic facts about water necessary to an understanding of the fluviological, political, diplomatic and military events that have taken place along the Jordan in the past few years.

The story of the present-day Jordan water situation could well begin with a statement made by British Prime Minister David Lloyd George at the Paris Peace Conference in 1919, that his country would not accept a mandate for "a Palestine which should merely include the barren rocks of Judaea, that might at any moment be rendered a desert through the cutting off of the waters flowing through the same . . .

"The waters of Palestine are essential to its existence. Without those waters Palestine would be a wilderness . . ."

But David Lloyd George only partly won his point. The whole of the Jordan was included within the Palestine Mandate territory, but the river's sources and headwaters—the Yarmuk, Banias and Hasbani—were left out. Also the great Litani River was not included in mandated Palestine.

During the days of the Mandate, one of the world's greatest soil and water conservation authorities, Dr. Walter Clay Lowdermilk, former assistant chief of the Soil Conservation Service of the United States government, spent much time in the Middle East and wrote a book, *Palestine, Land of Promise,* in which he proposed a Jordan Valley Authority scheme similar to TVA. By a friendly and joint development of the water resources of the Valley 600,000 acres (perhaps even 750,000 acres) of desert could be made to bloom, a good life could be provided for millions of people, and a billion kwh of electricity could be generated. Lowdermilk said it could be done by diverting the sweet water of the Upper Jordan, the Yarmuk and the Zarqa rivers into canals that would run on both sides of the Jordan Valley and would provide water for irrigation. Alkaline soils would be washed out by this fresh water and made productive. Sea water would be led through tunnels and canals from the Mediterranean across the Vale of Jezreel to the Jordan Valley for the dual purpose of creating electricity by the fall of the water and compensating the Dead Sea for the loss of the diverted fresh water. In brief, his plan called for exchanging salt water for fresh water. Lowdermilk optimistically stated that such a plan could so greatly raise the living standard of both Jews and Arabs that they would wonder why they had ever quarreled. He knew his scheme would sound exceedingly bold to many in the feudal Middle East, so he suggested that it be undertaken step by small step. He said it ought to attract anyone with a sharp eye for a bargain, be he Arab, Jew, or Yankee. Hard-headed bankers pronounced the scheme feasible, declaring that the cost of a quarter of a billion dollars could be amortized over fifty years. In a burst of hope, Lowdermilk quoted Isaiah: ". . . the desert shall rejoice, and blossom as the rose." He said his JVA idea would mean for the Jews the realization of the hopes and aspirations they had kept alive for so many centuries: a fertile, friendly homeland flowing with milk and honey; for the Arabs it would mean an immensely better standard of life, education for their children, political rights for those who had never enjoyed such a luxury before, and a chance to raise the whole level of Arab life. For Great Britain it would mean strong, friendly, alert countries near the mouth of the Suez, ready to defend democracy. To the world it would mean a great stride toward the ideal of tolerance and peace between nations and races. Peering far into the future, Lowdermilk said:

"Once the great undeveloped resources of this region are properly exploited, twenty to thirty million people may live decent and prosperous lives where a few thousand now struggle for a bare existence. Palestine can serve as the lever that will lift the entire Middle East from its present desolate condition to a dignified place in a free world."

Fine words, a sound plan, great idealism, except . . .

The defeat of the Arabs in the war that followed the partition of Palestine left them so bitter that for a time the idea of any collaboration with Israel, even for the common good, was anathema to them. Therefore, Israel, the country with the greatest thirst for water, went ahead on her own, assuming the worst: that the Arab countries would not in the immediate future cooperate in any way.

When the boundaries of the new State of Israel were fixed and statistics compiled, it was discovered what a "poor relation" she was in the matter of water. Apart from two minor water sources—the Yarkon River that flows into the Mediterranean near Tel Aviv, and the Kishon River that enters the sea near Haifa—Israel has only rain, underground wells, and her share of the Jordan water.

Dividing the total annual flow of the rivers in all three Arab countries by the total population, there are three thousand gallons of water available per day for each inhabitant of Syria, Lebanon and Jordan, compared with a mere two hundred and twenty-five gallons available for each inhabitant of Israel.

Israel had a special problem. She was planning some day—for lack of other living space—to send her immigrants to the Negev, the southernmost region of the country where the rainfall averages a mere one inch and a quarter per year, hardly enough to wet a sidewalk, compared with forty inches in the northern areas, where the bulk of her water resources are located. So all her water plans had as their major goal getting a goodly quantity of the life-giving liquid down to the Negev.

As soon as the State of Israel came into existence, all water resources—ground and surface waters, perennial and intermittent springs, drainage water, municipal and industrial waste, all water of whatever sort—were declared public property and put under government control. Even while fighting was going on during 1948, Israel began to study what to do about water. Two years later the first draft of a master plan was ready and before many years two projects involving Israel's minor rivers, the Yarkon and Kishon, had been completed. Then the experts turned to the Jordan.

When work began on draining the forty-four square miles of swamps in the Huleh Valley, Syria objected, stating before the United Nations Security Council that the work was going on in a demilitarized zone. The Security Council ruled that the armistice agreement did not forbid civilian land conservation and that the drainage could continue.

In 1953 work began on the first step in diverting sweet water from the Upper Jordan, near the Bridge of the Daughters of Jacob. At this point the Jordan is only slightly below sea level but is rushing madly downhill at a steep rate of descent. By using this power to operate turbines, more than enough electricity could be generated to send the Jordan water through pipes and canals all the way to Negev. The Israelis were constructing a hydroelectric plant for this purpose when the Syrian government took the issue to the Security Council, contending, again, that armistice terms were being violated because this was a demilitarized zone. The United States, Great Britain and France joined in sponsoring a resolution that would have permitted resumption of the work, but it was defeated when the Soviet Union cast her fifty-seventh veto against it. (Although Russia had voted in 1947 for the U.N. Partition Plan, in more recent years it had taken a pro-Arab, anti-Israeli position on most matters involving the area.)

Meanwhile, the Kingdom of Jordan had been developing its own Jordan water plans. Among those employed was M. G. Ionides, a British irrigation expert who had been director of development for the government of Transjordan for several years and who had conducted the first hydrographic survey of the Jordan Valley. Then a British engineering firm was engaged and prepared what came to be known as the MacDonald Plan. These and other Jordanian schemes called for using water from both the Yarmuk and the Jordan to irrigate Arab lands on both sides of the Valley, and at the same time to generate power. Syria was included because of her interest not in water but in cheap power. In 1953 these two Arab states signed an agreement for the erection of a storage dam on the Yarmuk to serve a hydroelectric station, as well as for diverting the stored waters southward to a canal that would run on the east side of the river almost to the Dead Sea: the East Ghor Canal. Eventually there would be a parallel canal on the other side of the river: the West Ghor Canal.

The United Nations Relief and Works Agency for Palestine Refugees in the Near East—commonly called UNRWA—also became interested, out of a desire to lessen friction and increase prosperity in the area, with the hope of thus speeding up rehabilitation of more than half a million homeless Arab people. UNRWA contracted with TVA, which in turn employed the Boston firm of Charles T. Main, and out of this came a report, "The Unified Development of the Water Resources of the Jordan Valley Region," henceforth known by everyone interested in the Jordan Valley problem as "the Main Report." Part of it read:

"As a problem of engineering, the most economic and the quickest way to get the most use from the waters of the Jordan River system requires better organization of the headwaters of the Hasbani and . . . use of Lake Tiberias as a storage reservoir for the flood flows of the Jordan and Yarmuk rivers. From Lake Tiberias these waters would be made available by gravity flow to irrigate lands on the east and west sides of the Jordan Valley to the south. Gravity flow eliminates expensive pumping facilities . . . Use of the natural reservoir afforded by Lake Tiberias takes advantage of an asset already at hand. There is no known alternative site, at any cost, for a reservoir that would effectively regulate and store the flood flows of the Jordan and . . . the Yarmuk."

If the lake were used as a natural repository it would be possible—reversing the usual procedure—to save on rainy days for sunny days, to store water that otherwise would nearly all go to waste.

Meanwhile the Eisenhower administration had begun a reappraisal of American policy in the Middle East. In 1953 Secretary of State John Foster Dulles and Harold Stassen, Mutual Security Administrator, visited the area. In October of that year President Eisenhower appointed

Eric Johnston, chairman of the International Advisory Board of the Technical Cooperation Agency, as his personal ambassador, with the task of trying to get Israel and the three interested Arab states to agree on a unified water utilization plan. He chose Johnston because, as former president of the United States Chamber of Commerce, and head of the Motion Picture Association of America, he had had years of experience in helping groups with widely divergent ideas work out compromise solutions of their problems.

But Ambassador Johnston went off to the Middle East under no illusions. He was well aware that the Jordan was an engineer's dream but a politician's nightmare; that if there were no frontiers to consider the river might happily be able to irrigate the entire Valley, but there were many frontiers. The partition of Palestine had complicated the situation still further and yet Johnston said:

"Even if the Arabs and the Israelis were living today in neighborly harmony and sweet bliss, there would still be a rumpus over the contested waters of the Jordan. At best it would be difficult to decide who is entitled to how much. Squabbles over riparian rights and water use are as common—and often as violent—as romantic quarrels between suitors.

"In our own country, Kansans and Coloradans have tiffed over the Colorado River—when Arizonians and Californians were not. Being a Westerner I am not unmindful of the disputes in the Snake River country. The quarrels over water rights extend from the Rio Grande to the Helmand in Afghanistan and Iran, and back again . . . It would not take much imagination to envision what would happen in the way of sabotage and even bloodshed if the waters of the Jordan were to remain unregulated indefinitely."

No man ever worked more diligently at an international assignment than Johnston. He made four separate visits to the area during the next two years. He argued, cajoled, begged, pleaded, sometimes even threatened, as he conferred with presidents, prime ministers, kings, technical experts, and here and there an unscrupulous politician. He presented first the proposals of the Main Report. No one was happy with them. The Arab states objected to the use of Lake Tiberias for storing surplus water from the Yarmuk, because it is wholly within Israel, and the stored Yarmuk water, much of it ultimately destined for the use of Arabs on the Lower Jordan, would be at the mercy of the Israelis. Also, they said, Yarmuk water would become much more saline by being mixed with Tiberias water. Also, the rate of evaporation in Lake Tiberias (270 mcm a year) would be much greater than at Maqarin on the Yarmuk in Jordan, where they wanted to build a reservoir of their own to store the Yarmuk water. Lebanon objected that she got no allocation of water under the Main Plan. (Main had no provision in his plan for Lebanon to use Jordan water probably because Lebanon's needs were being fully met by water from other sources.) Israel was disappointed that the Main Plan limited the use of whatever water she would get to the Jordan Valley, whereas it was in the Negev that the water would be needed. Also, Israeli experts said that the allocation to Jordan was so excessive that if the full amount were used it would turn certain parts of Jordan into swampland.

Each interested party was invited to submit its own modifications and proposals. Finally in September 1955 Johnston and his advisers took these individual suggestions and hammered out a new Jordan Valley compromise proposal that they called the Unified Plan. It provided for the expenditure of $200 million, two thirds of which the United States would contribute.

Reduced to simple generalities, the Unified Plan proposed to irrigate vast areas of desert land, prevent millions of tons of water running to waste in flood seasons, raise the living standards of thousands of people living close to the river, and provide power for industrial as well as home use by generating 150 million kwh of electricity—all this to be accomplished by keeping most of the Jordan winter water in storage both in Lake Tiberias and on the Yarmuk River and by building two diversionary canals for the Kingdom of Jordan, the East and West Ghor canals, interconnected by siphons and feeder canals, for the irrigation of the Lower Jordan Valley, and a diversion from the Upper Jordan and Lake Tiberias for Israel.

Israel had been asking for 550 million cubic meters of Jordan water a year. Under the Unified Plan she would get only 400 million. More than sixty percent of the total would go to the Arab countries: 35 mcm to Lebanon, 132 mcm to Syria, and 477 mcm to the Kingdom of Jordan, which would also have 243 from small side streams flowing into the Lower Jordan, bringing its total to 720 mcm.

Despite the cut in her allotment, Israel decided that the long-range political and economic advantages to be gained by winning Arab acceptance of a regional approach justified considerable sacrifice, and so she announced acceptance. A special committee of Arab engineers appointed by the Arab League reported to the League their opinion that the plan was equitable, workable and compatible with Arab interests. Much of the $200 million would be spent in the Arab countries for Arab labor, thus stimulating the local economy. A great new Arab agricultural area would be created. Considerable power for industrial purposes would be made available to the Arab countries. Several hundred thousand Arabs could be settled on the newly irrigated land and be assured of a good life.

Johnston arrived back in the United States in October 1955, a smile on his face. He said there was "not the slightest doubt" but that both Israel and the Arab countries recognized the Unified Plan as "the only logical and equitable approach to developing a river system which belongs, in some part, to all of them," and he expressed confidence that the few remaining minor differences would be easily and quickly reconciled. "I am sure they can be."

The Arabs at this point could note with satisfaction that the development of all their water needs within the Jordan Valley was now assured international support and financial aid. The people of Israel had a right to celebrate too, for a formula had been established by which their national water plans could be developed in peace and harmony with their neighbors, thus easing tensions and possibly paving the way for a general reconciliation and peace. And the Jordan had a right to celebrate, because it was about to perform a new role. In its long history it had had many experiences. Yet seldom, if ever, had it served to unite, to be the catalytic agent in bringing people closer together. Perhaps now it was about to have this adventure.

But late in October 1955 in Cairo the Political Committee of the Arab League held a meeting. Only three of its thirteen members had riparian interests in the Jordan River system, but all thirteen voted. The decision was to "defer decision," on the ground, first, that the plan would involve some degree of cooperation with a state the very existence of which the Arab countries refused to take cognizance, and second, that anything benefiting Israel's economy must be opposed, even if it could be demonstrated that it would be of still greater benefit to Arab economy. It was the old cliché that had been expressed so bluntly on one occasion by an Arab statesman who said: "What is good for Israel is bad for the Arab states."

George Barnes, one of Johnston's advisers, wrote later:

"Rejection of the plan had nothing to do with technical matters. The League's action was motivated wholly by political considerations. It was a clear reflection of the obsessive hatred of Israel that pervades the Arab world. The effect of the League's action was to kill any immediate possibility of going ahead with a major undertaking that offered indisputable benefit to the Arab States themselves."

Ambassador Johnston wound up his comment on the failure of years of heroic effort by saying:

". . . and so every year a billion cubic meters of precious water still roll down the ancient stream, wasted, to the Dead Sea."

Exactly one year after the Arab League's rejection of the Johnston plan—in October 1956—there was another shooting war in the Middle East, following Israel's invasion of the Sinai Peninsula, and the joint British-French attack on Egypt. The Jordan was not in any way involved, although the disappointment of Israel over the Arab attitude toward the attempt to solve the water problem peacefully may have been one of the motivating forces behind Israel's action in Sinai. In turn the hostilities made any collaboration, even for constructive, peaceful reasons—such as water development—more remote than ever.

Late in 1957 President Gamal Abdul Nasser of Egypt formed the United Arab Republic by a consolidation of Syria and Egypt. It was to his advantage to keep the Jordan issue alive and try to convince Syria she faced the likelihood of armed conflict with Israel over water, for this would prove that Egypt's protection was needed. From now on Nasser boldly and baldly used the Jordan River conflict as a device in attempting to assert his personal leadership over the rest of the Arab world. Actually, for the head of the Egyptian state to involve himself in the Jordan controversy was as unwarranted as for the head of the Israeli state to involve himself in some controversy over the Aswan Dam on the Nile.

The two countries most vitally concerned about water—Jordan and Israel—had both been willing to work, each in its own way, to implement the Johnston plan. Now that that was no longer possible, because of the political situation, each began planning unilateral developments.

In 1958 Jordan began work on the East Ghor project, with the United States contributing more than seventy percent of the total cost. The first stage involved a forty-four-mile canal, starting on the Yarmuk six miles back from where it flows into the Jordan. From this point the diverted water flows through a short pipe, then a long tunnel, then into an open canal, and ultimately into Jordanian irrigation ditches. Each year, starting in 1961, a little more of the project was completed and each year a few more thousand acres of desert land were made to bloom, thanks to water that otherwise would have flowed into the Jordan. Thus the Kingdom of Jordan became the first of the riparian powers to divert water from the Jordan River system. By 1966 or 1967 Jordan hoped to finish the second stage of the scheme, the West Ghor Canal, to irrigate Arab land on the west side of the Jordan.

This diversion of Yarmuk water, while benefiting thousands of fellahin whose land could now be productive, had a disastrous effect on the Jordan cocktail, which normally had been sweetened by the addition of the relatively clear Yarmuk water. As more and more Yarmuk water was diverted, the Lower Jordan became more and more saline, seriously affecting its use for either irrigation or human consumption. Both Israelis and Arabs living in the Jordan Valley south of the Yarmuk were affected.

Meanwhile, Israel, blocked by the Soviet veto from continuing work on diverting fresh water from the Upper Jordan, decided that in order to avoid any further political complications she would take the water she needed directly out of Lake Tiberias, no part of which is in a demilitarized zone. This was a bitter decision to have to make. Under the original scheme electricity was going to be generated, some of which could be used to operate pumps to send the water on its way toward the Negev. Under the new plan no power could be created; in fact, a great amount of power would have to be brought in, to operate the many pumps that would be needed to raise the water so many hundreds of feet. Another difference would be the chemical content of Tiberias water compared with Upper Jordan water. But there seemed no choice, now that water had become an international political issue, not only between Israel and President Nasser, but also between Israel and the Soviet Union.

The new Israeli scheme provided for taking water from the northwest corner of the lake. It was realized between 1961 and 1964. The water is lifted by immense pumps into "the National Water Carrier," which conveys it a distance of almost seventy-five miles to Rosh Ha'ayin, just east of Tel Aviv, where it enters two existing pipelines for the balance of its trip to the parched Negev. Because the surface of Lake Tiberias is approximately 689 feet below sea level (the measurement varies according to the time of the year) and because the National Water Carrier sometimes is at an altitude of +120 feet as it crosses the countryside, the water would have to be raised more than eight hundred feet. The main pump was installed inside a mountain close to the edge of the lake, which military experts say is indestructible unless it suffers a direct hit by an atom or hydrogen bomb. There are also many intermediate booster stations along the way. For the first twenty-two miles the water flows mostly through a canal. Then through concrete-lined tunnels in the Galilean and Menashe hills for five miles. Then through forty-eight miles of pipe nine feet in diameter.

The entire project cost $120 million, and the bill was footed by the Israelis themselves, with almost no outside direct help, although some of the money was raised by the sale of Israel Development Bonds in the United States. Machinery had to be brought in from the United States, Switzerland and France, and also—under the Reparations Agreement—from Germany. The Israelis themselves did most of the engineering, using technical experience gained on pilot projects such as the Yarkon River development.

Israeli diplomats repeatedly pointed out that the maximum that would ever be diverted into the National Carrier from Lake Tiberias would be 320 mcm, plus another 80 mcm that would be used for irrigating Israel's land in the Lower Jordan Valley; a total of 400 mcm, which is exactly what she was supposed to get under Ambassador Johnston's Unified Plan. From Lake Tiberias 100 mcm would be permitted to flow downstream in the Jordan for the use of the Jordanians.

However, ever since 1959, Israel's attempt to provide water for the parched Negev had been under attack by Arab politicians, propagandists and diplomats, both at home in the Middle East and abroad.

In Cairo in January 1964 an Arab League summit conference, called principally to deal with the Jordan crisis, brought together for the first time in history the heads of all thirteen Arab states, among them men whose assassination had been urged and even plotted by other members of the select group. The most important decision reached was not to go to war against Israel—as had been threatened—in order to stop her diversion of water from Lake Tiberias, but, instead, to start as quickly as possible on their own diversion of the sources of the Jordan originating in Arab countries. An attempt was made to keep details of the plan secret. The communiqué issued at the end of the four-day conference heaped abuse on Israel, yet was intentionally vague. The Secretary-General of the Arab League said that military, administrative and financial plans had been agreed upon to divert the headwaters of the Jordan and thus increase so greatly the salinity of what water would still be available to Israel that it would be almost useless. Later a few details leaked out. The plan was to keep any water from the Hasbani or the Banias from flowing into the Jordan by building diversion canals down through Syria to the Yarmuk River, where the flow would be impounded by two large dams at Mukheiba and Maqarin.

American engineers who studied topographical maps said the idea was fantastic, for it would mean building canals and tunnels through and around mountains in an effort to make the water run backward and uphill.

"It makes as much sense," said one engineer, "as trying to put water on the moon."

In addition to appropriating $17.5 million so that surveys could be made and blueprints could be drawn immediately, the Arab states agreed to contribute $42 million annually to establish a unified Arab military command and to strengthen the armies of Syria, Lebanon and Jordan so they could resist any Israeli attempt to interfere with the Arab diversionary work. The conference, however, rejected a Syrian demand that military steps be taken at once to force Israel to stop work on her National Carrier.

In an effort to win international support, the Cairo conference agreed on a world-wide campaign to explain the Arab position. King Hussein became the spokesman in the United States, while foreign ministers of many other Arab countries traveled even to such remote places as Argentina, Australia and Communist China advocating their position.

Moscow and Peking competed to see which could give the stronger support to the Arabs. In March 1964 a mass rally was held in the Communist Chinese capital. Speakers accused the United States of "imperialistic aggression and intervention" for encouraging Israel in her plans to irrigate the Negev.

Former Premier Khrushchev then paid a seventeen-day visit to the United Arab Republic and several times denounced the Israeli project as "imperialism" and pledged Russia's support of the Arabs.

Often before the Carrier was completed angry threats were made in some of the Arab capitals that military measures would be taken against Israel the moment water began to flow from the lake into the Carrier. The most explosive statement came from Salah Salem, Nasser's former Minister of National Guidance, who said that if Israel tried to divert any of the Jordan's water it would be considered by the Arabs as a cause for war. Then he added:

"And I don't rule out the possibility that this question might be the prelude to the liquidation of existing affairs between the Arab people and Israel once and for all."

One Israeli answer to the Arab diversion plan (never made officially) was that if by these means the Arabs decreased the Jordan's annual flow into Lake Tiberias by 180 mcm, as planned, Israel would no longer feel obligated to release the 100 mcm now going from the lake into the Lower Jordan.

On May 6, 1964, the first water was seen running uphill in the open portion of the National Carrier. Curious visitors from abroad who asked about it were told:

"We're just testing one section of the Carrier."

On June 5 the first Jordan River water reached the National Carrier's terminus near Tel Aviv. The entire project had taken six years to build.

Israelis have a great fondness for public ceremonies such as the laying of a cornerstone, the dedication of a hospital, the opening of a school, or any other occasion at which speeches can be made, thanks given to God, and praise bestowed upon "those who conceived and executed this noble scheme," and contributed the money. The engineers who planned and built the Carrier therefore became the most frustrated men in the land, when they were told there would be no ceremony; not even a public announcement that the Carrier was in operation.

President Nasser and the other twelve heads of Arab states knew. But Israel decided to permit them to save face. The Carrier is still being "tested," with a constant flow of Jordan water going through the canal and pipeline south to the desert.

Original plans called for taking water from the lake at the rate of 180 mcm per year at the start and gradually increasing this to 320 mcm. But in the spring of 1965 it was discovered that the pumping had to be limited to between 120 and 150 mcm, because of the salinity problem. The pressure of the water level of the lake helps to hold down the flow of water from saline springs on the bed of the lake. If the level of the lake is reduced too much, the flow from the springs increases to the point that water being pumped from the lake into the National Carrier becomes excessively saline.

Israel's prime minister, Levi Eshkol, early in 1964 stated in the Knesset (Parliament) in Jerusalem:

"Israel will draw water from Lake Kinneret (Tiberias) within the limits of the quantities laid down in the Unified Plan. Israel will oppose unilateral and illegal measures by the Arab states and will act to protect its vital rights. We believe that world public opinion will not be misled by malicious misstatements and will reject the campaign of incitements and threats against a legitimate and constructive project of water development. This area needs the benefits that will flow from the waters, not instigation to bloodshed; it needs economic development, not barren strife; cooperation, not envious hostility; the utilization and not waste of its water resources; the advancement of peace and not the fomenting of war."

In June 1964 Prime Minister Eshkol paid a visit to America and conferred with President Johnson. They talked less about the Jordan than they did about schemes and devices to take the salt out of sea water so it can be used for agricultural and human needs—a subject that has as little place in the life story of a river as a tribute to David Ben-Gurion would have in a biography of Gamal A. Nasser. However, President Johnson agreed that a giant nuclear-powered desalinization plant should be set up in Israel as quickly as possible to help the country with its water problem and a joint communiqué was issued putting the United States on record as strongly opposed to the use of force or even a threat to use force in the Middle Eastern water controversy.

Assistant Secretary of State Dutton made it even more specific in a statement in which he said:

"In the event that other Middle Eastern states attempt to frustrate the Israeli plan by other counter-diversion projects, the United States would oppose such projects if it appeared that the Arab riparian states combined were offtaking waters in excess of the combined allocation to the Arab states specified in the 1955 plan."

In September 1964 another conference was called of the thirteen Arab leaders. Meeting at Alexandria, they decided that the first stage of the attempt to deny Jordan water to Israel should be construction of a $28.7 million storage dam at Mukheiba on the Yarmuk. More money was pledged—another $14 million a year for five years—to strengthen the armed forces of Jordan, Syria and Lebanon.

The total cost of the entire project of denying Jordan water to Israel was conservatively estimated at $160 million. A spokesman for the Arab League told a news conference that the various Arab states thus far had contributed only $8.5 million toward the work. Less than a month later, in Amman, Jordan, announcement was made that work had begun on the first stage of constructing the Mukheiba Dam.

Following the Alexandria conference, the Israeli cabinet issued a statement restating Israel's determination "to repel and thwart any aggression." An appeal was made to peace-loving states, to the U.N. and to "enlightened public opinion." A formal note was sent to the president of the U.N. Security Council charging that "the clear purport" of the Alexandria communiqué "is that thirteen member states of the United Nations have set themselves the aim of liquidating another member state" in violation of the U.N. Charter, and that this inflaming of tension in the Middle East constituted a threat to international peace and security.

It was now clear that what the Arab countries had failed to do by either military methods or their attempt at a world-wide economic boycott, they hoped to do by converting the Jordan into a mere trickle of water so salty that it would begin to resemble the fluid that filled the Dead Sea. If Israel was not destroyed in this way, at least the Negev would be kept a wasteland, and further immigration would be made almost impossible.

The Arab scheme had all the earmarks of a spite plan, for Lebanon has so much water that she permits fifty percent of the annual flow of the Litani to go to waste in the Mediterranean, while Syria has both the Orontes and the mighty Euphrates to draw from, and Egypt, the prime mover, has no interest whatsoever—except political—in what happens to Jordan water.

In January 1965 new plans were announced for tapping the waters of the Hasbani River in three places. Lebanon would build a three-mile canal costing two million dollars between the upper reaches of the river to divert the water of the Hasbaya Springs into the Litani River, and then into the Mediterranean. Two other canals would also be built to lead Hasbani water ultimately to a storage dam on the Yarmuk, via Banias.

Israel's answer came from her prime minister, who said:

"The waters of the Jordan are as precious to us as the blood in our veins. We shall act accordingly."

An Israeli Foreign Office expert on Jordanian matters put it differently:

"We hope that we will not have to extinguish by fire what was started by water."

For international lawyers and jurists the controversy raises the question of whether international law or international anarchy is going to rule in the Middle East. Under international law, all states have the right to use the water of rivers flowing through their territory, subject only to the general restriction that they must not cause serious injury to another state. The principle of "equitable apportionment" of benefits among riparian parties has long been recognized in international disputes.

Justice Oliver Wendell Holmes in a case between New York and New Jersey in 1931, put it in these clear words:

"A river is more than an amenity, it is a treasure. It offers a necessity of life that must be rationed among those who have power over it. New York has the physical power to cut off all the water within its jurisdiction. But clearly the exercise of such a power to the destruction of the interest of lower States could not be tolerated. And on the other hand, equally little could New Jersey be permitted to require New York to give up its power altogether in order that the river might come down to it undiminished. Both States have real and substantial interests in the river that must be reconciled as best they may be."

The question that was being asked during 1965 among the diplomats and statesmen in Washington, London and Paris—and probably also in Moscow and Peking—was:

How much are the Arab countries willing to sacrifice in money and national effort to try to strangle Israel, or at least to slow up further immigration because of lack of water?

Engineers all agreed that the headwaters of the Jordan and the tributaries leading into it from the east could—if anyone cared enough—be channeled into the Mediterranean or otherwise diverted to the point that the Jordan would become, even in the springtime, little more than a piddle at the bottom of a deep gulch. But were the Arab states willing to spend the effort and money to do it? Were the Arab countries willing to antagonize enlightened world opinion and risk direct military conflict with Israel? Upon the answer might depend the fate of millions of people—perhaps even the peace of the world, for a full-scale shooting war in the Middle East, with the Great Powers taking sides, might not end short of a world catastrophe.

When President Johnson announced plans for the United States to cooperate with Israel and other countries seeking to develop their water resources he said:

"Water should never divide men; it should unite them. Water should never be a cause of a war; it should always be a force for peace."

Those with a deep-seated interest in peace see hope in several scientific directions. If the time ever comes when atomic energy becomes a cheaper source of power than oil, the entire Middle Eastern situation would be drastically changed, and, similarly, if the price of taking salt out of sea water can be cut in half or a third, the tensions caused by the desperate need for water will at least be eased. When that finally happens, war or peace in the Middle East will no longer depend upon the Jordan, and the river will lose her cataclysmic role in the lives of so many millions of people.

While rival nations construct diversions in the Valley and rival military men prepare for hostilities in case tempers get out of control, the

Jordan still continues to flow in her selfsame bed, wiggling and meandering as much as ever; rushing, pausing, twisting, turning, cascading, doubling back on herself; a strange river; a young river, as rivers go, and yet what sights she has seen, what people she has known, what history she has helped to write, what a life she has led.

INDEX

414

420